- more about religion than civil rts.
6 window onto religion in US life

W.E.B. Du Bois

~

AMERICAN PROPHET

POLITICS AND CULTURE
IN MODERN AMERICA

SERIES EDITORS
Glenda Gilmore, Michael Kazin, Thomas J. Sugrue

Books in the series narrate and analyze political and
social change in the broadest dimensions from 1865
to the present, including ideas about the ways people
have sought and wielded power in the public sphere
and the language and institutions of politics at all
levels–national, regional, and local. The series is
motivated by a desire to reverse the fragmentation
of modern U.S. history and to encourage synthetic
perspectives on social movements and the state;
on gender, race, and labor; on consumption;
and on intellectual history and popular culture.

W.E.B. Du Bois

~

AMERICAN PROPHET

Edward J. Blum

PENN

UNIVERSITY OF PENNSYLVANIA PRESS

PHILADELPHIA

PUBLISHED BY

UNIVERSITY OF PENNSYLVANIA PRESS

PHILADELPHIA, PENNSYLVANIA 19104-4112

Printed in the United States of America on acid-free paper

10 9 8 7 6 5 4 3 2 1

LIBRARY OF CONGRESS CATALOGING-IN-PUBLICATION DATA

Blum, Edward, J.
W. E. B. Du Bois, American prophet / Edward J. Blum.
p. cm. — (Politics and culture in modern America)
Includes bibliographical references and index.
ISBN-13: 978-0-8122-4010-8 (alk. paper)
ISBN-10: 0-8122-4010-3 (alk. paper)
1. Du Bois, W. E. B. (William Edward Burghardt), 1868–1963
— Religion. 2. African Americans—Biography. 3. Civil rights
workers—United States—Biography. 4. African Americans—
Religion. 5. United States—Race relations. 6. Race relations—
Religious aspects—Christianity. I. Title.

E185.97.D73B58 2007
305.896'0730092–DC22
[B}   2006051466

Give us in our day,
O God, to see the fulfillment
of Thy vision of Peace.
May these young people
grow to despise false ideals
of conquest and empire
and all the tinsel of war.
May we strive to replace
force with justice
and armies of murder
with armies of relief.
May we believe in Peace
among all nations
as a present practical creed
and count love for our country
as love and not hate
for our fellow men.
Amen.

W. E. B. Du Bois
CA. 1910

CONTENTS

~

W.E.B. Du Bois

~

AMERICAN PROPHET

INTRODUCTION

~

Rethinking W. E. B. Du Bois,
Rethinking Religion and Race

AT LEAST SIXTY-TWO African Americans were lynched in 1906 and the city of Atlanta experienced one of the worst racial massacres in American history, but this could not quench Hallie Queen's excitement. From her vantage point in February 1907, the nation was changing. One of two African American female students at Cornell University in upstate New York, she had been leading small-group discussions of W. E. B. Du Bois's *The Souls of Black Folk*. The Cornell book clubs were the brainchild of a white student who had heard Du Bois lecture in Philadelphia at the Ethical Culture Society in 1906. As more than thirty young Cornell scholars discussed *Souls*, Queen marveled at how the book touched her white peers. The chapter "Of Our Spiritual Strivings," a poignant discussion of the social and personal struggles of people of color, moved one student to the brink of tears. This undergraduate, Queen wrote in a letter to Du Bois, commented that it "reminded her of the One hundred and thirty seventh Psalm—'By the rivers of Babylon.'" For this student, the Bible not only provided a reference point to comprehend Du Bois's essay; it also served as a lens to view the entire drama of American slavery, segregation, and racial violence.[1]

This reader disclosed a great deal about how she and many others understood *Souls* when she invoked Psalm 137. It is one of the most powerful and disheartening selections in the Hebrew Bible. Driven from their Promised Land and serving in a foreign kingdom, the Jews moaned in despair. They had lost their nation, their sense of community, and perhaps their connection

to God. Adding insult to injury, their captors now demanded that the Israelites intone the hymns of their homeland. As the Psalmist grieved:

> By the rivers of Babylon,
> There we sat down, yea, we wept
> When we remembered Zion.
> We hung our harps
> Upon the willows in the midst of it.
> For there those who carried us away asked of us a song,
> And those who plundered us requested mirth,
> Saying, "Sing us one of the songs of Zion!"

But Babylon was no place for their voices to be lifted in cheer. Certainly, the
Psalmist continued, God would not stand for the oppression of the people.
The evil Babylonians would be punished. The Lord would hear their cries and
save the Israelites.

> How shall we sing the Lord's song
> In a foreign land?
> ...
> O daughter of Babylon, who art to be destroyed,
> Happy the one who repays you as you have served us!
> Happy the one who takes and dashes
> Your little ones against the rock!²

Although Hallie Queen did not elaborate on her peer's association of Psalm
137 with Du Bois's work, it is little wonder that she imagined the two in tandem. Published in 1903, *Souls* was a penetrating analysis of race in the United
States. The parallels between biblical Jews and modern African Americans
were many. Just as the ancient Israelites were a despised people, African
Americans were hated in the United States. Just as the Jews were forced to
labor in a foreign land, people of color had been uprooted violently, held in
bondage, and exploited as beasts of burden. And just as the Israelites longed
for God to supply salvation, African Americans continued to pine for their
promised land. Du Bois's essays appeared to be a new psalm for the modern
age.³

Yet if *Souls* led readers to look backward to the Bible, it also inspired them
to look forward to a brighter future. To Queen, the responses from the book
club demonstrated that the age of racial alienation was coming to an end.

In these discussions, her classmates expressed "all of the pent up sympathy" they had for people of color. If whites could feel the stirrings of black souls, if whites could see the spirit of black culture, and if whites could repent of their wrongdoing and wrong thinking, perhaps the reign of white supremacy could end. Perhaps the joy of universal fellowship could triumph, Queen felt. She wrote to Du Bois with exuberance, invoking his image of "the Veil"—a biblical metaphor he used to describe the social, personal, psychological, economic, and religious fabric that separated blacks and whites. "Surely the 'Veil' is lifting," she penned, "surely the day is not far off. The horizon is broadening here—somewhere the Sun is already high." The reality of racial injustice and violence in the United States could not dissuade Queen from believing that whites could recognize the spiritual angst and contributions of African Americans. In this recognition, she hoped, whites could be transformed and the whole nation reborn. "I am glad to tell you," she exclaimed to Du Bois, that his work led to an amazing "broadening" of "the racial spirit at Cornell, that is, the best kind of racial spirit." Queen refused to let darkness and pain envelop her. Du Bois's *Souls* could be a sacred key to unlock the "pent up sympathies" of the white community. Queen could now imagine and revel in a wonderful world beyond the Veil.[4]

These Cornell undergraduates were not the only readers to reflect on the spiritual elements and the prophetic power of Du Bois's essays, books, and poems. After reading Du Bois's "The Education of the Black Man," an essay on the crisis of southern African American education, an employee of the Freedman's Aid and Southern Education Society remarked in a letter to Du Bois in 1902, "I praise God that you had the courage in several paragraphs to state the bald truth that the South needs to hear. In their blindness they fail to see their own peril." Du Bois stood as a prophet sent from above in the estimation of this writer. Alluding to the Hebrew Bible, particularly the words of Mordecai to the frightened Queen Esther when she wondered whether to challenge Persian violence against the Jews, this Freedman's Aid worker promised to pray that Du Bois's "life may be long spared for the high and noble service for which you are providentially equipped—for surely you have come into the Kingdom for such an hour as this."[5] Similarly, one year later, Reverend Francis J. Grimké, an African American Presbyterian minister, wrote to Du Bois that "God has raised you up at this juncture in our history, as a race, to speak to the intelligence of the country in our behalf."[6]

Throughout the twentieth century, Du Bois's contemporaries continued to link his works with their conceptions of the sacred. Many readers were led to new religious heights by Du Bois and viewed him as the high priest of social

justice and black pride. In "To W. E. B. DuBois — Scholar" (1922), playwright
and poet Georgia Douglas Johnson considered Du Bois a Christ-like figure
who inspired faith and hope for people in a realm of violence and bitterness:

> Grandly isolate as the god of day —
> Blazing an orbit through the dank and gloom
> Of misty morning, far and fair you loom,
> Flooding the dimness with your golden ray, —
> Cheering the mantled on the thorn-set way,
> Teaching of Faith and Hope o'er the tomb,
> Where both, though buried, spring to newer bloom —
> Strengthened and sweet from the mound of decay.[7]

Forty-one years later, in August 1963, as African Americans marched on
Washington at the same moment that Du Bois died in Africa, poet and novelist Langston Hughes reflected on Du Bois's influence on his own life and
the civil rights movement. Hughes underscored how Du Bois's writings and
editorials in the journal of the National Association for the Advancement of
Colored People (NAACP), *The Crisis,* had become part of a religious canon
for African Americans. "My earliest memories of written words are of those
of Du Bois and the Bible," Hughes wrote. "My maternal grandmother in Kansas, the last surviving widow of John Brown's Raid, read to me as a child from
both the Bible and *The Crisis.* And one of the first books I read on my own
was *The Souls of Black Folk.*" For Hughes, Grimké, Queen, and a host of blacks
and whites, Du Bois's words were akin to scripture—or at least considered in
the same intellectual register—for they revealed paths of truth and righteousness in a confusing and terrifying world.[8]

But if Du Bois appeared a saint to some, he was a sinner to others. For
each individual he touched spiritually, there were those who challenged the
legitimacy of religion in his life and writings. An array of Du Bois's peers
viewed him as a grand infidel more interested in injuring faith than inspiring
it. On one occasion, while a professor in the 1890s at Wilberforce University
in Ohio, a small African American college funded by the African Methodist
Episcopal Church, Du Bois wandered into a prayer meeting when "suddenly
and without warning" the leader announced, "Professor Du Bois will lead us
in prayer." Du Bois curtly responded, "No, he won't." For such an offense, he
almost lost his job. No person of faith, several university bishops thought,
would decline an invitation to pray.[9] Several years later, when Du Bois applied
for a position at Atlanta University, faculty members again wondered about

his faith. Du Bois imagined that these professors thought to themselves, "he's studied in Germany—perhaps if you scratch him, you'll find an agnostic."[10] Even the Federal Bureau of Investigation, whose agents tracked Du Bois in the 1940s and 1950s searching for connections he may have had with Communists, was unable to identify Du Bois's religious practices. His dossier in early 1943 recorded that the FBI could not determine if Du Bois had "any church affiliations." But almost a decade later, one Bureau informant did mention that during a lecture in Los Angeles, "Dr. DU BOIS closed his speech with a quotation from Biblical scriptures. He received a tremendous applause."[11]

So, who was Du Bois religiously and what kinds of spiritual influence did he have? What can be learned about religion in the United States from his writings and career? *W. E. B. Du Bois, American Prophet* investigates Du Bois's relationship to faith, belief, religious organizations, and notions of the sacred. It examines the religious life and times of W. E. B. Du Bois to provide new perspectives on this pivotal thinker and to illuminate various aspects of religion in American culture. Taken together, Du Bois's many and varied works—his autobiographies; his historical and sociological studies; his prayers, poems, short stories, and novels; his speeches and lectures; and his personal letters, reflections, and unpublished musings—show that he was one of America's most profound religious thinkers. His perspectives on religion (and not just black religion), his efforts to craft new approaches to the spiritual, and his sacred opposition to racism, materialism, and war offer new windows to witness the power of faith in American society and culture in the nineteenth and twentieth centuries.

W. E. B. Du Bois, American Prophet is also a new analysis of Du Bois's place in American religious history. Attuning to responses to Du Bois and his efforts, from those who read his works and believed they were in the presence of prophecy to those who heard him speak and believed that the divine was present in his words, this book reveals that many of Du Bois's contemporaries approached him as a sacred figure, an American prophet with insight into cosmic realities. To the likes of Langston Hughes and Hallie Queen, Du Bois stood as a spiritual guide, and they repeatedly characterized him as a leader called by God.

This book, moreover, situates Du Bois's works within a variety of social, cultural, literary, and theological contexts to tell a much broader story about religion and race in the United States. His religious sentiments engaged a host of crucial discussions. Du Bois joined other African American authors who used religious idioms to wrestle control of black selfhood away from whites; his works intervened in a century-long theological debate over the

sacred status of racial groups; Du Bois was an exponent of the Social Gospel; his historical and sociological works offered a religious revision of Marxian theory; with fictive renderings of black Christs and dark princesses, Du Bois challenged America's belligerent theology of white supremacy; and he was an unheralded father of both black liberation theology and womanist theology. By the end of his life with the Cold War heating up, Du Bois rejected the hallmarks of America's religious culture—its sanctification of nuclear warheads, unchecked capitalism, and the consumer-based "American Way of Life"— and instead characterized Communism as the social realization of Christian teachings. In this way, Du Bois serves as an entry point to reconsider the power of religion in America. What emerges from Du Bois's imagination is a riveting tale where angels masqueraded as teachers, where demons cloaked themselves as moderates, where economic policies had spiritual outcomes, where prophets postured as professors, and where the seemingly irreligious Du Bois was the nation's holy seer.

   W. E. B. Du Bois, American Prophet defies almost every assumption about religion in Du Bois's life. The FBI investigators who followed him had every reason to be baffled by his religious persuasion, although they were just as easily confounded by simpler questions, such as where Du Bois worked, what courses he taught, and in what discipline he earned his doctoral degree. When it came to matters of faith, Du Bois was purposefully elusive. Coyness was a primary strategy for Du Bois when it came to religion. It allowed him to speak, move, and dwell in a variety of circles without being pigeonholed into a certain camp or controlled by a specific denominational hierarchy. On some occasions, he sounded like an agnostic. Reflecting on his tours of Russia during the second quarter of the twentieth century, for instance, Du Bois applauded the Soviet government for removing religion from civil society. By disempowering the churches, Du Bois maintained, the Soviets had brought their nation into line with enlightened religious sentiments. "Most educated modern men no longer believe in religious dogma," he wrote in his final autobiography in the early 1960s. "Who today actually believes that this world is ruled and directed by a benevolent person of great power who, on humble appeal, will change the course of events at our request? Who believes in miracles?" The implication was clear. As a man of modernity, Du Bois was not one to believe in the faiths of the fathers or grandfathers.[12] But this same Du Bois refashioned traditional Christian creeds with one of his own six decades earlier, and he repeatedly reminded his friends of his personal "Credo": "I believe in God, who made of one blood all nations that on earth do dwell. . . . I believe in the Prince of

Peace.... I believe in Patience ... patience with God!"[13] Which Du Bois should be trusted: the one who criticized faith as a relic of dogmatic and unjust societies or the one who acknowledged belief in a public creed?

Du Bois was even hard to pin down when questioned directly about his faiths. Responding to Cuban priest Father E. Pina Moreno's queries about faith in 1948, Du Bois was consistent with many of his other writings. He said a great deal about religion without indicating what he genuinely believed. Moreno asked Du Bois whether he was "a believer in God" and his "opinion about the Lord Jesus." Du Bois's response simultaneously revealed and concealed his thoughts on God and on Christ. "If by being 'a believer in God,' you mean a belief in a person of vast power who consciously rules the universe for the good of mankind, I answer No," Du Bois wrote. Yet, he continued, if "on the other hand you mean by 'God' a vague Force, which in some uncomprehensible way, dominates all life and change, then I answer, Yes; I recognize such Force, and if you wish to call it God, I do not object." Ultimately, he did not even answer the second question on Jesus. Whether this response pleased Moreno may never be known, but it certainly should not satisfy anyone interested in understanding religion in Du Bois's life.[14]

Although a knotty problem, Du Bois's religion has been characterized as simple by most scholars. This, at first glance, is quite a paradox. Countless scholars from a variety of disciplines, including history, African American studies, sociology, literary theory, and political science, have debated nearly every facet of Du Bois's career. They line up on all sides when discussing Du Bois's approach to education, his views of class, his intellectual heritages, his attitudes toward women, his expressions of manliness, his temperament and personal style, and changes in his opinions. Yet they have formed a consensus on religion in Du Bois's life: that he had little, if any. In chorus, historians assert that Du Bois was not a Christian, that he merely used religious language for rhetorical effect, and that he was just too smart to believe in God or angels or devils. From his initial biographers Francis Broderick and Elliot Rudwick to more recent studies, historians have described Du Bois's life as a somewhat predictable secularization tale—one that in some ways mirrors the supposed secularization of nineteenth- and twentieth-century America. Religion influenced him as a child, scholars have asserted, but trust in science progressively replaced faith in God. This process eventually led Du Bois by the end of his life to embrace atheistic Marxism and Communism.[15]

Even the most thoughtful and articulate of Du Bois's biographers have downplayed religion in their narratives. Literary critic Arnold Rampersad

and historian David Levering Lewis, winner of two Pulitzer Prizes for his biographies of Du Bois, portrayed him as shaped by his boyhood church but
never an individual of faith in the sacred or divine. Their Du Bois was interested in how religious language and organizations could serve his political or
economic purposes. Religion seemingly had only rhetorical and pragmatic
relevance for Du Bois. Rampersad maintained that Du Bois's "belief in science came . . . at the expense of religious faith." David Lewis put it this way:
"Neither the god of Moses nor the redeeming Christ appears to have spoken
deeply to" Du Bois. Concern for the divine, for life after death, and for a reality beyond that of human existence was not a major concern for the Du Bois
of Lewis's and Rampersad's renderings.[16]

Du Bois's alleged irreligiosity has become so commonplace that scholars
rarely feel the need to prove it. Literary theorist Shamoon Zamir needed only
one word to describe Du Bois's stance on matters of faith before disregarding
it: "unreligious." Susan Jacoby, another Pulitzer Prize finalist, felt comfortable
relying on one source (Du Bois's final autobiography) to declare in her *Freethinkers: A History of American Secularism* that Du Bois held "antireligious
views" and that he had "little regard . . . for Christianity."[17]

But Jacoby, Zamir, Rampersad, Lewis, and the others are wrong on this
point.[18] So many facets of Du Bois's life and times are obscured by this scholarly depiction. That he founded the study of African American churches, that
he taught Sunday school classes, that he had favorite hymns and spirituals, that
he repeatedly invoked images of the divine, that he cried out for the "Prince of
Peace" to vanquish the warmongers, that some of his students made religious
decisions based upon what they thought Du Bois believed, and that many of
his contemporaries viewed him as a prophet: all of this makes little sense if
we exclude religion from narratives of Du Bois's life and times. No scholar has
considered in depth the soul of the man who first gained national recognition
for a book on souls, for a book that Cornell students likened to the Psalms,
for a book that still inspires religious introspection. It is the spiritual side, the
soulfulness of his life and the religious power of his prose and personality,
that this book seeks to unveil.

Perhaps most damaging in the approach to Du Bois that neglects his religious contributions is that Du Bois's spiritual insights are kept hidden. By
dismissing religion in his life, scholars cheat American history of one of its
brightest religious stars. Du Bois was not antireligious; he was against faith
used for fraud, belief used to bully, and Christianity when used to control. Du
Bois had much to teach about religious organizations, the power of belief, the

intersections of religion and violence, the necessity of faith for social resistance, and the vitality of spiritual symbolism. In short, we can better understand not only how religion functioned in American society, but also how it informs the human condition if we pay attention to it in Du Bois's career.

Anyone who looks for religion in Du Bois's canon will find it in abundance and will discover a deeply spiritual Du Bois. Take, for instance, his refusal to lead the group in prayer at the Wilberforce meeting. Scholars have read this as evidence of Du Bois's irreligiosity. But as Du Bois remembered the incident later in life, it was the lack of genuine religion at Wilberforce that distanced him from these types of prayer meetings, not his lack of personal faith. "I have seldom been in an institution where there was so much religiousness and so little religion as at Wilberforce," Du Bois penned in an unpublished personal reflection. This "religiousness" had few social or personal outcomes; it failed to improve life for African Americans, and hence was fundamentally irreligious to Du Bois. True faith, Du Bois declared, would show the "eternal connection of Christianity and Latin, of godliness and mathematics, of morality and geography." Du Bois did not want religion to be absent from scholarly or social life. He wanted faith to have a direct and positive impact on what individuals learned and how they lived.[19]

Du Bois was connected to religion in various ways. The reportedly antireligious Du Bois wrote dozens of prayers for his students at Atlanta University. He was a regular conversation partner for ministers and religious leaders on the needs and importance of faith. He crafted poems and short stories that invoked God, Christ, female messiahs, and apocalyptic prophecies. And he spoke with the moral courage and the inspired rhetoric of a prophet.

Even Du Bois's close friend and the literary executor of his estate, Herbert Aptheker, felt the need to protect Du Bois from claims that his unbelief outranked his spirituality. Twenty years after Du Bois's death and following the first round of professional biographies, Aptheker warned in the early 1980s against the dismissal of religion in Du Bois's life. Aptheker maintained that Du Bois "never lost a certain sense of religiosity, of some possible supernatural creative force. In many respects, Du Bois's religious outlook in his last two or three decades might be classified as agnostic, but certainly not atheistic; this remained true even when he chose to join the Communist Party."[20] Alas, Aptheker's plea that the religious side of Du Bois not be lost has gone unheeded. As this book shows, the irreligious Du Bois presented by so many historians, especially David Lewis, is a mythical construction that serves the purposes of the secularized academy far more than elucidates the ideas and

beliefs of Du Bois. The deeply spiritual characteristics of Du Bois's writing and imagination have remained hidden in shadows for too long and the courage of his life work has been too often stripped of its sacred importance.

$\sim$

Approaching religion as an ideological system that explains and orders events, behaviors, and ideas in terms of concepts perceived to be sacred, supernatural, divine, evil, or eternal, *W. E. B. Du Bois, American Prophet* seeks to understand faith in Du Bois's imagination in all its complexity. Judging from Du Bois's words and the assorted ways his contemporaries viewed him, it seems that multiple religious selves existed within Du Bois. One was a religious reformer who called white and black congregations to serve their God and their fellows with truth, dignity, and justice; another was an apostate who disregarded dogmatic teachings. One was a stirring prophet who felt that a higher power had called him to challenge white supremacy and economic exploitation; another was an agnostic who despised the use of religious traditions to coerce individuals or groups. One took up the priest's mantle, authoring prayers and hymns for embattled peoples; the other chastised religious believers for cherishing childish myths. One of these facets of Du Bois led his contemporaries to find spiritual insights; the other became the brunt of attacks that he was too secular, too sacrilegious, and too irreverent. This book refuses to privilege any one aspect of Du Bois at the expense of the others. Du Bois was a complex and multifaceted thinker who was able to maintain faith and reject it, appreciate ritual and despise orthodoxy, and speak to religious issues without being consumed by them. This may have been Du Bois's most profound spiritual lesson and legacy.

Another revelation discerned when including religion in Du Bois's life is his spiritual rage. Beneath the veneer of this genteel, cosmopolitan, German-educated intellectual was a man seething with spiritual anger. When blasting away at white supremacy and economic exploitation, Du Bois routinely invoked concepts of God's righteousness and heavenly retribution. Du Bois often included apocalyptic visions in his novels, and he imagined the Lord chastising whites, destroying western culture, and devastating the defilers of black women and men in his historical works. When religion is accounted for in his life, Du Bois appears in the mold of an Old Testament Isaiah declaring the vengeance of God against a sinful, neglectful, and hateful world of racial and economic disabilities. This spiritual rage touched every element of his career and was one of the defining features of his long and storied life.

Du Bois could never escape religion, and he never seemed interested in doing so. The weight of his persistent and insistent approaches to religion might have crushed the mythological Atlas himself. Time and again, Du Bois addressed the intricate web of religion's role in society, economic relationships, racial imaginations, and national identities. He approached religion in creative and searching ways. Concepts of the sacred, divine, and eternal penetrated every aspect of his writing and theorizing. They permeated Du Bois's sense of self and his place in the world, his sociological and historical conceptions, his understanding of social organization and social constructions, his judgments of white and black society, and his visions for the unification of oppressed peoples.

Religious ideas and rhetoric provided a system of images and reference points for Du Bois to articulate his deepest thoughts and plans. More than any other theorist before him, Du Bois drew attention to the myriad ways religious teachings and beliefs simultaneously upheld and undermined structures of inequality. He recognized how whites connected their racial identity to their conception of the divine. This conflation, he argued, created a spiritual wage of whiteness that legitimated some of the vilest acts in human history. And as an intellectual activist, Du Bois refused to stand for this association. With all of his creative might, he attempted to disentangle white privilege from notions of the sacred. As part of his battle with white supremacy, he posed his own theology that linked oppressed people with God. By suggesting that the poor, the downtrodden, and the exploited were the true children of the Lord, he foreshadowed the theological system that would emerge in the late 1960s known as "black liberation theology." Du Bois was an astute religious theorist who was well ahead of his time. That scholars have failed to address or advance his thoughts on religion not only warps historical understandings of him but also hinders contemporary society from grasping and applying the many religious lessons Du Bois taught.

This is not a religious biography in any conventional sense. Most religious biographers approach their individual of study chronologically. They narrate the life course of the individual to show religious change and development over time. These scholars search for trajectories of faith, tendencies of behavior, and psychological roots of belief or practice. The traditional religious biographer asks, when did the individual convert to a faith? How did the subject transform in theological and spiritual matters? Was the person a

Catholic, a Presbyterian, a Jew, a Buddhist, or a Muslim?[21] Answering these queries, however, would do little to clarify the contours of Du Bois's religious imagination. Labeling certain beliefs or ideas as "Christian," "liberal," "evangelical," "pluralist," "Jewish," "agnostic," or "atheist" can be quite tricky and deceptive. These phrases have meaning in specific contexts and relationships, and they often obscure more than they reveal. To the ears of hyper-religious and hyper-Christian Americans, Du Bois's claim that a god *might* exist may have sounded blasphemous. But this comment could have been considered too spiritual or too religious during his travels to the Soviet Union. What Du Bois believed and when may be even more problematic to establish or define. Mapping routes of belief or unbelief, or ascertaining the subconscious rationales for his statements, may be impossible for any historian. This book does not concern itself with whether Du Bois believed or whether he changed religiously. Instead, it focuses on the varieties of religious contexts Du Bois engaged and the multitude of ways he used religious ideas to respond to black faith traditions, the cultures of white supremacy, the violence of American society, the rise of world capitalism, and the possibility of nuclear devastation.

This religious biography eschews a chronological approach to Du Bois's life, for the contours of his more than nine decades are well known. His childhood in Massachusetts during the 1870s and 1880s, his experiences as an undergraduate at Fisk University and then Harvard University, his graduate studies and travels in Germany, his pioneering work in sociology and history, his foundational role in the NAACP in 1909, his editorship of *The Crisis* from 1910 to 1934, his move to the political left and work for peace in the 1940s and 1950s, his membership in the Communist Party, and his relocation to Ghana in his final years have been presented ably in many historical works, educational videos, and Web sites. Instead, each chapter here highlights one particular genre of Du Bois's work—his autobiographies, *The Souls of Black Folk*, his historical and sociological studies, his creative poems and fiction, and his political turn to Communism—to evaluate what they disclose about him and religion in the nineteenth and twentieth centuries.

This genre-based approach has several advantages. First, it allows Du Bois's ideas to be set within a host of social and cultural frameworks, from the traditions of African American autobiography to theories on the relationships between religion and racial categories. Second, this method provides access to the ways Du Bois considered religion throughout his entire career. Although a chronological structure may more effectively detail how Du Bois's religious views transformed over the decades, it hinders the connection of ideas and

concepts that he reflected on throughout his adult life. Du Bois, for example, continually considered the social, economic, and spiritual roles of the African American church. He lectured and wrote on how black churches could better serve black communities and make social change for better than sixty years. By concentrating on one genre at a time, this book draws together Du Bois's numerous and oftentimes conflicting comments on the black church and other religious issues in order to make some theoretical sense of his considerations. Thus, *W. E. B. Du Bois, American Prophet* focuses less on the subtle theological or spiritual changes Du Bois underwent throughout his life and more on the main religious themes of his work. By interpreting him by genre, the analysis extends well before Du Bois's birth in 1868 and well after his death in 1963.

Many new intellectual vistas are revealed when considering religion as central to Du Bois's efforts. He disclosed new ways to consider religion and race in American history. Du Bois's approach to race in *The Souls of Black Folk* and to whiteness in his scholarly and creative writings demonstrates that historians and race theorists should reconsider the place of religion in racial formation. As Du Bois expressed in *The Souls of Black Folk* and as white supremacist writers claimed in their works, race for nineteenth-century Americans was more than just perceptions of supposed physical differences that were assumed to be immutable and passed from one generation to the next. Racial categories, it was believed, served as spiritual windows into cosmic and eternal realities. White supremacists long insisted that through racial perceptions, one could see the handiwork of God and the devil; one could witness heavenly plans for the world and its future. In *The Souls of Black Folk*, Du Bois responded with a counter cosmic vision. Seeing the religious drama of American and black history through his prophetic eyes, he contended that African Americans had access to the divine and were holy. In short, during the nineteenth century and early twentieth century (if not still today), race revolved around claims to see more than physical differences. It involved the comprehension of the cosmic, the demonic, and the divine. And this, in one sense, is what makes the concept of race so persistent and so devilish itself.

If race in general had religious components, then blackness and whiteness in particular must be understood with relation to how Americans invested them with sacred significance. Du Bois considered religion at the core of the social and cultural construction of whiteness. The white race, he maintained, was created as a category to offer working-class southern and northern whites, including European immigrants, a "psychological wage" that differentiated them from African Americans in their same economic grouping.

But whiteness also had spiritual currency. The association of whiteness and godliness provided whites a sense of eternal value, a value they denied to African Americans, whom whites linked to the demonic, the vile, and the profane. This spiritual wage of whiteness (and the alleged spiritual bankruptcy of blacks) led white Americans to displace the true Christian God with a deity made in their own image—a white god. Much of Du Bois's career, in fact, was dominated by his efforts to expose and destroy this white god and the rituals to honor him.

The spiritual wage of whiteness had dire social implications. To Du Bois, racial segregation in Christian churches was especially abhorrent. It legitimated racial division by strengthening the conflation of whiteness and godliness. To Du Bois, because church services constituted moments when religious believers performed their role as the "people of God," racial segregation allowed whites to imagine their racial group as God's chosen people and to deny African Americans any connection to the Lord. This differentiation of religious spaces and souls, moreover, legitimated racial brutality as many whites conceived of their vicious slaughters of African Americans as rituals of white purity. The linking of whiteness and godliness, in short, explained how murderers could think of themselves as holy and how segregationists could think they were serving God. As whites conflated the jig of Jim Crow with the teachings of Jesus Christ, and as they tightened the noose of Judge Lynch in the name of Jehovah Lord, the spiritual wage of whiteness sanctified the violent white supremacist America from the assassination of Lincoln to the age of Kennedy.

Du Bois's attention to religion as fundamental to racial formation, perception, segregation, and violence indicates that the current state of critical race theory, especially whiteness studies, needs reevaluation. While numerous scholars, including Toni Morrison, George Lipsitz, David Roediger, Alexander Saxton, Matthew Frye Jacobson, and Grace Hale, have investigated the influences of literary works, economic structures, class relationships, legal codes, immigration patterns, and cultural shifts in the making and remaking of whiteness, they have tended to ignore the power of religion. But Du Bois—the sometimes forgotten founder of whiteness studies—situated religious ideas at the center of the construction of white identity. Attention to the ways Du Bois theorized about faith and racial identities may lead to new avenues in study of the social, cultural, and historical fabrication of race in the United States.[22]

Religious historians and theologians also have much to gain from Du Bois. His tales of black Christs living and dying in racist America revealed keen in-

sight into the moral problem of racial evil and violence. Well before the theological revolution of the late 1960s when African American writers created a black liberation theology that reinterpreted Christianity as an ideological system in harmony with the black freedom movement, Du Bois had forged literary associations between images of God and oppressed peoples. Du Bois discussed a black God, a black Christ, a black Madonna, a black Buddha, and even a black female God, all of whom sought to nourish and protect people of color amid the storms of white terror. With his poems, short stories, and novels, Du Bois tried to create a new religious system for an embattled people, one that would transcend the dogmatic and oftentimes parochial practices of African American churches. Du Bois even anticipated the "womanist" revision of black liberation theology that began in the 1980s by suggesting that women of color had a special place in the heart and mind of God. Du Bois, in short, articulated a connection between Christian theology and the experiences of black men and women well before theologians James Cone, Albert Cleage, James Deotis Roberts, Kelly Brown Douglas, Delores Williams, and Alice Walker did so.[23] Examining Du Bois's theological contributions provides further evidence of his deep appreciation for faith and his desire to influence religious belief in others.

By discussing God and Christ in terms of their "blackness," Du Bois identified and defied a hallmark of American culture: the whitening of sacred images. Recently, numerous religious historians have paid much attention to the cultural making of Jesus and other biblical characters in the United States. Historians Stephen Prothero and Richard Wightman Fox, for instance, both published monographs on the image of Jesus in American history. However, they downplayed the racialized aspects of Christ in American culture. Prothero relegated his discussion of race to one chapter in his discussion of the black Christ, concentrating principally on images of Jesus in the imaginations of slaves, Marcus Garvey, and Malcolm X. Fox mentioned Du Bois but referred to his writings on the black Christ as "eminently forgettable." By ignoring Du Bois's attacks on the whiteness of the American Christ and his countercreation of a black Christ, these scholars have missed the racialized war over images of the divine in the United States—perhaps the central aspect of the formation and re-formation of Jesus in America.[24]

All in all, from his attempts to cast down the white God and imagine a black deity in its place to his attacks on capitalism and militarism as anti-Christian, Du Bois had much to say about the religious conditions of his world. His diverse approaches to religion demonstrate keen sensitivity to the power and persuasiveness of faith among individuals and societies. Du Bois

may have been an agnostic (although we can never really know this), but that is no reason to neglect his religious contributions. For in them we find unique religious insight and intriguing spiritual creativity.

⁓

Du Bois's life was one full of religious wonder, questioning, and wrestling. For his twenty-fifth birthday, which Du Bois celebrated as a student in Germany, he conducted his own personal ritual. At midnight on February 23, 1893, he offered a "sacrifice" to "Mercy-God-work." During an elaborate ceremony that day, he sang the hymn "Jesus Lover of My Soul" and dined "with candle, greek wine, oil, and song and prayer." It was a passionate ritual for him, when he "thought of [his] parents," his mother having died five years earlier and his father only a distant memory, then he "sang, cried, etc." He wondered about his self and his mission in the world. "O I wonder what I am—I wonder what the world is—I wonder if Life is worth the striving—I do not know—perhaps I never shall know." But Du Bois pledged to find truth in his pursuits and perhaps even God. "These are my plans," Du Bois concluded, "to make a name in science, to make a name in literature and thus to raise my race. Or perhaps raise a visible empire in Africa thro' England, France or Germany." Du Bois declared that his quest for "the Truth" would never be stopped: "Heaven nor Hell, God nor Devil shall turn me from my purpose till I die." For these ends, Du Bois found moral courage in the words of the Hebrew Bible's Queen Esther. "I wonder what will be the outcome? Who knows? ... I will go unto the king—which is not according to the law and if I perish—I PERISH."[25]

Throughout his life, Du Bois lived out the promises of this ritual. He made a name for himself in science and in literature. He lifted up his race. And he did it all singing hymns and writing prayers oftentimes in the guise of historical monographs, sociological surveys, or autobiographical reflections. In the pursuit, he never lost sight of life's sacred meaning. Almost seventy years after that birthday ritual, Du Bois once again reflected on his life and destiny: this time near the end of his final novel, *Worlds of Color* (1961), published two years before Du Bois's death. The protagonist Manuel Mansart lay on his deathbed in Manhattan. Having lived through the rise of Jim Crow, the lynchings of family and friends, two world wars, the onset of the nuclear age, and the beginnings of the Cold War and the civil rights movement (just as Du Bois had), Manuel's wife asked him: "Have you no hope—I mean—afterward?" Manuel responded with a critique of religion in American life: "If a man faces the facts and says honestly, 'I don't know, and see absolutely no proof that we

will live again'—should such a soul be derided or accused or read out of the Congregation of the Righteous—while hypocrites, liars and fools crowd into that comfortable refuge?" Manuel answered his own question, "Would it not be wiser and better to say, 'I do not know' or 'I do not hope?' No matter what Paul preaches, I know Hope is not Truth. In any case, I will not lie. If others believe in immortality, I respect their right to that belief. But what I fear and hate are the fanatics who would send me to hell for not consenting to lie."[26]

Manuel's advice drives this book. Why has Du Bois been left out of the canon of great religious minds in U.S. history? In a world of dishonesty, Du Bois was honest; in a world of theft and greed, he was giving, long suffering, and friendly. Du Bois was not morally perfect, but that is beside the point. Because of his honesty and in spite of his wonder over the divine or his questioning of the supernatural, he has been barred from the "Congregation of the Righteous," at least among religious historians. But he should have a prominent position there. In the case of Du Bois, whether he believed in God, in Christ, in Buddha, or in Vishnu—and how deeply he believed or did not—is a matter between him and the divinity of choice. This book refuses the audacious assertion that anyone can know such information. An individual's religious pilgrimage is a complicated journey that twists and turns, evolves and revolves. *W. E. B. Du Bois, American Prophet* tries to join Du Bois on his many paths and to write him into the "Congregation of the Righteous." Perhaps then we can be inspired, as Hallie Queen was in 1907, to hope in a world that seems so far away, one beyond the violence, the hate, and the injustice that seems to taint the entire cosmos.

~

The Hero With a Black Face

Autobiography and the Mythology of Self

SHORTLY BEFORE JOINING the Communist Party in 1961 and rejecting the United States in favor of citizenship in Ghana, the ninety-two-year-old W. E. B. Du Bois stepped into the Oral History Research Office at Columbia University in 1960. He was there to share memories from his life with William T. Ingersoll, one of oral history's earliest pioneers. Ingersoll queried Du Bois about his family history, his battles with Booker T. Washington, and his various plans to end racial discrimination and economic inequality. Perhaps because Du Bois had expended so much energy discussing religion throughout his career and perhaps because Du Bois had produced no definitive work on faith, Ingersoll wanted to know more about religion in Du Bois's social evaluations and personal memory. After Du Bois described the African American Methodists in his childhood home of Great Barrington, Massachusetts, for instance, Ingersoll queried, "What was your reaction to the more radical religion of the Methodists?" Later, following Du Bois's mention of attending summer revivals in rural Tennessee as a college student at Fisk University, Ingersoll wondered, "Why did you go to that church, curiosity?" Ingersoll followed by asking Du Bois if he thought religion provided rural blacks with "a reason to knock off and relax a little." In the most direct question about faith in the interview, Ingersoll asked, "What were your own religious experiences at this time?"[1]

In Du Bois's responses, he presented his life as one enmeshed in religious beliefs and organizations. He remembered with fondness his family's religious

heritage and the church of his youth during the 1870s and 1880s. "My grand-parents were Episcopalians, but my mother grew up living near the Congre-gational Church, so she joined the Congregational church and I came up in the Congregational Sunday School," he told Ingersoll. This community of faith left a deep impression, and Du Bois recalled feeling a special love for his church—one that continued throughout much of his life. "All of the activities of the church and Sunday school, I took part in," he reminisced. "I remember when the church was burned down it was a personal calamity to me. I can re-member the text of the sermon when the preacher came to dedicate the new church. Up until a very few years ago, I was in touch with the family of the preacher." Du Bois's adolescent faith was not one of fire and brimstone but of an overarching worldview that made sense of existence, life, and death. "We didn't have much hellfire," he continued, "We took our religion very calmly."[2]

With far less fondness, Du Bois also recounted his numerous battles with black church leaders who taught what he deemed a closed-minded faith and who questioned his religious commitments. Of his experiences as an under-graduate at Fisk in the 1880s, Du Bois recalled feeling particular disdain and ambivalence for church regulations against dancing. "When I went South, I was very much upset," he told Ingersoll, because "a row came about dancing. Now, I'd been dancing all my life. I loved it. It was exercise, and it had no sex provocation—I wouldn't dream of it. . . . But the old deacon in this church down at Fisk wanted to put the members of the church out if they danced, and it caused me a great deal of soul-searching. They brought the old Pauline doctrine out—it may not be bad for you, but it might be for your brother, etc. I had some hard times with myself."[3]

Not all of Du Bois's religious memories from his Fisk years were troubled, however. While church orthodoxy enraged him, authentic expressions of faith were entrancing. When he taught in rural Tennessee during summer breaks, he attended revival services and had a glorious time. The experience shocked him at first, but then it seemed to make him feel part of the community. This was a black community quite unlike his in Massachusetts. "I heard my first Negro spiritual untainted by anything outside" while in Tennessee, he remem-bered. "I was in a church sitting on a bench when suddenly the woman beside me just shot into the air. My God! It frightened me at first. I thought they were going crazy." His fear, however, quickly melted into admiration. "The singing, and the revival, all of the efforts and so forth, the preaching, the minister—it was a ceremonial that took in the whole community. The people brought pic-nic lunches and they sat around outside and gossiped and so forth, and then they went in and were converted. Oh, it was a tremendous experience."[4]

Evaluating the faith of his newfound brothers and sisters, Du Bois suggested that it provided them with necessary explanations for their existence in a racist and exploitative country. Christianity supplied both the conviction that true justice would come one day and the ideals necessary to continue the fight of everyday living in an oppressive land. Religion, he claimed, "enabled them to rationalize life. It didn't make any difference how hard life was, what they had been through. Or how dark the prospects were." Church services and faith in a loving God made pain and strain bearable. "This is a rational world," Christianity taught them, "and while we're suffering here, after all, this is only part of life. In the long run the thing is going to be made right. The people who've got an unjust advantage here are going to get punished, and we who've had an unfair situation are going to be happy. So there's no use giving up and getting discouraged. In the long run, the world's coming out straight."[5]

Du Bois's reminiscences of his religious life at Harvard University, which he attended after Fisk and from which he earned a doctoral degree in history in 1895, were numerous and conflicted. On one occasion, he told Ingersoll, "By the time I went to Harvard, I was not orthodox at all." Du Bois had not abandoned faith in God or Christianity, he explained. Instead, he followed a liberal Christianity that many of his mentors at Fisk abhorred, a Christianity that focused less on the supernatural elements of the Bible, such as the virgin birth or the resurrection, and more on its social ethics, such as injunctions to "love thy neighbor" or to "do unto others as you would have done unto you." "I was by no means radical," Du Bois recalled, "I was rather on the side of the Germans who at that time were beginning to re-interpret and retranslate the Bible." Yet Du Bois had not dumped his overarching religious worldview. "I used to jump on my fellow students who got blasphemous," he claimed. Later in the interview, Du Bois commented of his Harvard years, "I had been pretty orthodox while I was at Harvard. I went to Church every Sunday." To Du Bois, it was no contradiction to say that he was both "not orthodox at all" and "pretty orthodox" at Harvard. His religious self was not one particular identity or another; rather, it was a mix and match of beliefs, styles, and persuasions.[6]

As Du Bois described his adult life, he narrated it in such a way as to indicate that he was often embroiled in religious controversy. Between his Harvard experiences and his professorship at Wilberforce, Du Bois studied at the University of Berlin in Germany. He claimed of these years, "I just forgot religion, practically, and went into economics and sociology." Then at his first professorship at Wilberforce University in the 1890s, he butted heads with church leaders over public prayer. "One of the first things" he experienced at

Wilberforce was strolling "into a prayer meeting. All the students were there, because it was compulsory. Believe me, I shall never forget it." Occupying a seat in the back to "look the thing over," Du Bois was shocked when the group leader announced, "Dr. Du Bois will lead us in prayer." He remembered responding, "No, I won't." He left the meeting and, when compelled later to explain his behavior, Du Bois told the Wilberforce bishops in the 1890s and Ingersoll in the 1960s that "in my home you didn't ask any man to get up and lead in prayer. There were a few deacons that did. But I'm just not interested and I'm not going to."[7]

Du Bois's refusal to lead the prayer and his German education caused these bishops to wonder about his religious faith, and questions of belief dogged Du Bois wherever he went. When he interviewed for a position at Atlanta University in 1897, following his fifteen-month intensive study of African Americans in Philadelphia that resulted in his historical and sociological triumph *The Philadelphia Negro* (1899), he once again had to address the prayer issue. This time, rather than refuse to pray with his students, Du Bois and the university leadership struck a bargain. "The old president said that it was customary for the professors to lead in prayer meetings, and I told him that was a little out of my line," Du Bois commented to Ingersoll. "But finally we compromised and I told him I agreed to read from the prayer book, and I used to improve upon the prayers now and then, reading to the students." As Du Bois explained it, his reasons for not wishing to lead prayer in public did not stem from a lack of faith, but rather from a cultural and denominational background quite distinct from that of his Methodist colleagues. "You see," he told Ingersoll, "in the Congregational Church, the ordinary layman doesn't lead in prayer. He sits and listens and that sort of thing, but I mean, he doesn't take active part in any religious exercises. As I say, I told him at prayer meetings I would read from the Episcopal Prayerbook or from any prayers that I should manufacture myself, so that we got over that."[8]

Du Bois's presentation of his life and experiences to Ingersoll contrasts sharply with the image of Du Bois created by his many biographers. That he remembered his childhood church affectionately, that he defended his position on public prayer as rooted in culture and not disbelief, and that he recalled rebuking his Harvard classmates for blasphemous statements suggest that historical appraisals of Du Bois as both a young man and an old man do not square with how Du Bois imagined himself or at least wanted himself remembered. According to Du Bois's biographers, for instance, Harvard was the time of his "total dismissal of conventional faith" when he fell into a life-

long "serene agnosticism." How could this have been a time when he attended church regularly, embraced liberal Christianity, or felt himself "pretty orthodox" in any way? His old age, again according to his biographers, was supposedly marked by a commitment to Marxist-Communism that precluded any interest in religion, other than as opium for the masses. Historian David Lewis has gone so far as to characterize Du Bois in his adult life as an atheist. "Although he called himself an agnostic," Lewis has written, "it was an agnosticism professing such complete indifference to the hypothesis of an interactive supreme being as to be indistinguishable from atheism." Yet when Du Bois sat with Ingersoll in 1960, he crafted himself not as an opponent of faith but as one deeply influenced by it. And he never referred to himself as an "agnostic" or as an "atheist." Even while he prepared to leave the United States, he had memories filled with religion. He had little difficulty characterizing himself as an individual invested in the life of faith and faith communities. In short, the spiritual side of Du Bois so often dismissed or diminished was one that Du Bois earnestly sought to unveil, one that he chose to highlight before his departure.[9]

~

The contents of Du Bois's oral history disclose several common religious themes that he used when writing his many autobiographies. Religious ideas shaped Du Bois's autobiographical works and stood as constitutive elements of his shifting sense and presentation of self. He recalled a religious childhood. His church and Sunday school imbued him with Christian morals and provided the basis for a belief in communities that transcended racial alienation, where all of God's children felt the pull of kinship and affection. He presented his education and his engagement with social issues as a holy calling, in which higher powers demanded that he speak prophetically. His memories were full of meditations on the African American "sorrow songs" and other religious music. To him, they conveyed deep religious sentiments that allowed him to tap into the heart of the divine and black America. And the adult Du Bois of his autobiographical narratives was a prophet who spoke the truth about the spiritual state of African American communities, white society in the United States, and eventually the political, economic, and moral condition of the entire world. From his memories of childhood joy in New England Sunday Schools to his decision to co-found the NAACP, from his observations of black revivals to his membership in the Communist Party, the Du Bois of his autobiographies refused to forsake religious commitment or commentary. Through his numerous autobiographical acts, Du Bois pro-

duced didactic mythologies of self to reveal the many sides of his soul and to speak sacred truths to the world.

Du Bois's autobiographical narratives did not function merely as "metaphors of self," to borrow literary critic James Olney's phrase, that comprise "monument[s] of the self as it is becoming, a metaphor of the self at the summary moment of composition."[10] More specifically, Du Bois's autobiographical acts served as "mythologies of self," where he drew on a variety of religious allusions and symbolic structures to present his "self" as a hero-priest and a prophet-teacher. His were life journeys bursting with mythical beginnings, demonic forces, holy callings, and prophetic visions. The express intent was to expose inequality and to champion social justice. He used spiritualized language to discuss social concerns and to ruminate on the this-worldly significance of presumably other-worldly teachings.

In many ways, Du Bois's autobiographical narratives followed the trajectory mapped by literary theorist and psychoanalyst Joseph Campbell in his now classic works on myth and mythologies. Linking hundreds of folk tales and myths from the ancient world, Campbell discerned what he called a "monomyth," an all-encompassing meta-narrative at the heart of mythologies that revealed the deep recesses of the human spirit and of cosmic desires. Campbell found a universal "hero with a thousand faces," a man or woman whose adventures and ambivalences, decisions and despairs, and wisdoms and wisecracks unveiled sacred realities about human life. This hero typically emerged from unusual circumstances: birthed in a manger, found among wolves, or the progeny of a human and an animal. At a young age, the hero was "called to adventure" often by an unknown or a distant voice. Obeying the call was an "awakening of the self," and the beginning of what would become a sacred quest. Along the adventure road, the hero encountered a series of trials and tribulations. Followers fall away; dragons or leaders stand against the hero; even nature itself can be a bulwark of opposition. Typically, the hero is entombed underground or swallowed whole by beasts or whales. Each time the hero chooses to follow the arduous path set out by the sacred voice, his or her courage is rewarded with new cosmic insights. By journey's end, the hero becomes a god, if not greater than the gods, and returns to his people with divine knowledge for how to live better in human society.[11]

According to Campbell, whenever folk and mythological hero narratives are interpreted as straight biography or history, the myth is killed and the hidden lessons lost. This has been the case with Du Bois's autobiographical narratives. Historians have most often looked to them for an outline of Du Bois's life, and only recently have scholars approached them as metaphorical

texts or presentations of self and society. Even the most astute biographers have looked to them, not in the tradition of hero narratives but as historical works to find the who, what, and where of Du Bois's life. The narratives mean so much more, however. By casting himself in the model of the hero, Du Bois revealed a spiritualized understanding of his self and also articulated a cosmic understanding of his world. His autobiographical acts, in sum, provided the religious schema by which Du Bois hoped his readers would view him and the world.

Yet the cosmic adventure tales in Du Bois's autobiographical narratives were somewhat distinct from those described by Campbell. Du Bois's works had a racialized twist. He was a hero with a *black* face, not just any face. His call, struggles, challenges, and triumphs were shaped by racial discrimination and racial consciousness. By presenting a black mythology of self, Du Bois participated in and built on a long tradition of African American autobiographizing. These narratives have had a long and venerated tradition for people of color in the United States. They comprise a heroic and subversive tradition, and they speak directly to the spiritual and social strivings of African Americans. While antebellum slave narratives provided African Americans a literary avenue to proclaim their human existence in a society that sought to deny their humanity, postbellum African American autobiographies continued to resist the racism of American society by proclaiming that black people were capable of self improvement and growth. By reading Du Bois's autobiographical narratives in conversation with those of Richard Allen, Frederick Douglass, Sojourner Truth, and Malcolm X, this chapter shows that Du Bois was an important figure in this spiritual tradition. These black autobiographers struggled to create and nourish a religious identity within a larger white supremacist society that tried to deny them spirits and souls. By highlighting the religious hypocrisy of white society and by underscoring the long-suffering patience of African Americans, these writers wrestled for authorial control not only over their own selves but also over the spiritual state of America. For them and Du Bois, religion animated their perspectives on self and society, their conceptions of being and living.[12]

"I Believe": From Birth to the NAACP

Du Bois's first autobiography "The Shadow of Years," was written to commemorate his fiftieth birthday and his leadership in the NAACP. He presented himself as a legendary hero-priest divinely called to battle the demons of a

racist society and to bestow new sacred teachings to the world. "The Shadow of Years" is one chapter in the larger collection of essays *Darkwater: Voices from Within the Veil* (1920). Although never gaining the fame of *The Souls of Black Folk*, *Darkwater* was a tour-de-force. In it, Du Bois used poetry, short stories, fables, sociological essays, and personal tales to vent his rage at white supremacy. The essays indicted white society, envisioned an alliance among all oppressed peoples, and exposed whites to the anger stirring among African Americans. *Darkwater* stung many of its white critics, several of whom derided it as a work of "passion" and not "intelligence," while they attacked its glorification of people of color as a type of reverse racism.[13] But for many African Americans and civil rights activists it was and continues to be an inspiration. Its influence, in fact, has reverberated throughout the twentieth century. Since 1920, it has been reprinted at least six times, and, most recently, has inspired the work of contemporary artist Terry Adkins, whose innovative use of everyday materials to convey meaning about the inner lives of African Americans is well known in New York City and Washington, D.C.[14]

The autobiographical element of *Darkwater* appeared to begin, as so many African American autobiographies had, with the simple, albeit powerful, statement of existence: "I was born." But, in fact, Du Bois prefaced this assertion with two statements of spiritual posturing: his "Postscript" and his "Credo." They positioned Du Bois as a prophet-priest and provided a key to understanding the mythical elements of "The Shadow of Years." The "Postscript," the "Credo," and the autobiographical essay worked together to present Du Bois as a man with divine authority to author a new religious tradition for embattled people of color.[15]

Seemingly mistitled, the "Postscript" was actually the first selection in *Darkwater*. In it, Du Bois unambiguously linked himself to Jesus Christ and other biblical teachers. "I have been in the world, but not of it," Du Bois wrote, using a common trope in Protestant theology that encouraged believers to focus on their status in the kingdom of God, rather than on the kingdom of earth. Although many Protestants considered biblical passages such as John 15:19 where Christ told his apostles that they were "not of the world" to mean that they should disengage from broader society, Du Bois reversed this line of thinking. He suggested instead that his status "in, but not of" the world provided him a prophetic vantage to engage society and politics. It was the point from which he could judge culture and speak truths to it. "I have seen the human drama from a veiled corner," he continued, "where all the outer tragedy and comedy have reproduced themselves in microcosm within. From this inner torment of souls the human scene without has interpreted itself to me in

unusual and illuminating ways." Just as the prophets of old had been chosen by God to stand outside of the community and to see beyond surface appearances, Du Bois had found a niche from which to dispense sacred truths.[16]

Immediately following the "Postscript," Du Bois placed his personal "Credo," a slightly modified version of that which appeared originally in *The Independent* in 1904. It spelled out his social and spiritual beliefs and included points that he would wrap in personal detail in "The Shadow of Years." Du Bois modeled his "Credo" after the Apostles' Creed, a statement of Christian faith that churches and believers have recited since the second century. Extremely succinct, the Apostles' Creed is slightly more than one hundred words. In it the believer makes various personal and communal proclamations about God, Jesus Christ, the Holy Spirit, and the church. "I believe in God, the Father Almighty, the Creator of heaven and earth," the creed begins. The next four sentences focus specifically on "Jesus Christ . . . our Lord." The final sentence contains a litany of beliefs in "the Holy Spirit, the holy catholic church, the communion of saints, the forgiveness of sins, the resurrection of the body, and the life everlasting." While the Apostles' Creed highlights individual faith with its series of "I believe" statements, community aspects of faith—"our Lord," "the holy catholic church," and "the communion of saints"—are subsumed underneath the individual's professions.[17]

Similar to the Apostles' Creed, Du Bois's "Credo" underscored personal faith with a series of "I believe" statements. Unlike the traditional Christian text, however, Du Bois provided a much more extensive list of convictions about social and spiritual issues, including race relations, education, and work. In many ways, Du Bois revised and updated the original creed to speak to the conditions of twentieth-century America. "I believe in God, who made of one blood all nations that on earth do dwell," Du Bois opened. He hammered home his faith in a God that made all races equal, continuing, "I believe that all men, black and brown and white, are brothers, varying through time and opportunity, in form and gift and feature, but differing in no essential particular, and alike in soul and the possibility of infinite development."[18]

By drawing attention to God as the maker "of one blood all nations," Du Bois directly referred to a passage from the Acts of the Apostles (chapter 17, verse 26) and linked religious and racial concerns. The "of one blood" passage was a staple argument used by antebellum abolitionists and other civil rights activists throughout the nineteenth century. In 1907, Samuel Bishop of the Protestant Episcopal Church wrote in a letter to Du Bois that white Americans should recognize the "manhood" of blacks because of "the religious proposition that God made of one blood all nations of man for to dwell

upon the face of the whole earth."[19] Acts was so commonly invoked, in fact, that Thomas Dixon, Jr., the white supremacist author of the quasi-historical romance novels that provided the story line for D. W. Griffith's racist *Birth of a Nation* and helped generate the rebirth of the Ku Klux Klan in the twentieth century, directly attacked it. In *The Clansman: An Historical Romance of the Ku Klux Klan* (1905), Dixon crafted a fictional conversation between radical Republican Congressman Thaddeus Stevens, who staunchly supported civil rights for blacks, and President Abraham Lincoln, whom Dixon used as a mouthpiece for his own colonizationist arguments. After Stevens quoted the "of one blood" passage to justify equal rights for African Americans, Dixon's Lincoln responded, "Yes—but finish the sentence—'and fixed the bounds of their habitation.' God never meant that the negro should leave his habitat or the white man invade his home."[20] Deploying the "of one blood" rhetorical tradition, both Dixon and Du Bois engaged in a social and scriptural battle over the place of African Americans in the United States. For Du Bois, this biblical verse had powerful relevance because whites in the United States refused to honor its implicit suggestion of equality and universal kinship.

In the lines following the opening sentence about God, Du Bois retained the "I believe" format of the Apostles' Creed, yet he abandoned its focal trajectory on Christ, the Holy Spirit, and the church. Instead, Du Bois detailed his beliefs about conditions in the here and now. He waxed romantic about his feelings for people of color. "Especially do I believe in the Negro Race," he wrote, "in the beauty of its genius, the sweetness of its soul, and its strength in that meekness which shall yet inherit this turbulent earth." Du Bois then stressed the importance of "Service—humble reverent service, from the blackening of boots to the whitening of souls." He spiritualized the realm of labor, declaring that "Work is Heaven, Idleness Hell, and Wage is the 'Well done!' of the Master who summoned all them that labor and are heavy laden." Following his paean to work, Du Bois denounced those who sought to thwart racial equality. To the human eye, these individuals may appear as white businessmen, or politicians, or field hands, or teachers. But to Du Bois they were "the Devil and his angels, who wantonly work to narrow the opportunity of struggling human beings, especially if they be black."[21]

In the second half of the "Credo," Du Bois further expanded on his convictions about God and humankind. He highlighted his commitment to peace and his hatred for war, ideas that held new force in *Darkwater* since it was published following the deaths of millions during World War I. Alluding to Christ, Du Bois maintained unequivocally, "I believe in the Prince of Peace. I believe that War is Murder." He then returned to issues of racial discrimi-

nation, fusing religious beliefs with social hopes. "I believe in Liberty for all men," Du Bois proclaimed, "the space to stretch their arms and their souls, the right to breathe and the right to vote, the freedom to choose their friends, enjoy the sunshine, and ride on the railroads, uncursed by color." Finally, Du Bois expressed his faith in patience. "I believe in Patience—patience with the weakness of the Weak and the strength of the Strong, the prejudice of the Ignorant and the ignorance of the Blind; patience with the tardy triumph of Joy and the mad chastening of Sorrow—patience with God."[22]

Du Bois drew on Christian rhetoric in part because American culture was steeped in biblical language and also to indicate that he viewed social concerns as spiritual matters and vice versa. He alluded to Christ's Sermon on the Mount when he claimed that African Americans had the "strength in that meekness which shall yet inherit this turbulent earth." And then when discussing race relations, he attacked whites for not recognizing African Americans as "brothers in Christ." In addition, as Du Bois described his belief in "Service," he identified Christ as Lord and referenced his words in Matthew 11:28. The "Master," Du Bois wrote, had "summoned all them that labor and are heavy laden."[23]

Throughout the early twentieth century, Du Bois's "Credo" was enormously popular. When Reverend Francis Grimké read it, he immediately wrote that he was "delighted with it." To Grimké, the "Credo" was certainly a religious work by a religious man. The "Credo" was a "noble Confession of Faith." In a letter to Du Bois, Grimké maintained, "God has gifted you, in a remarkable degree, with vision and power of statement." The "Credo" "ought to receive the widest circulation," Grimké claimed. "It ought to be hung in all of our homes, and in all of our school houses."[24] And so it was. Countless African American families had it framed and placed on the walls of their homes. Even in England, the Afro-British composer Samuel Coleridge-Taylor placed a copy of the Credo on his wall. It "hangs in a most conspicuous position in our Dining-room," he wrote to a friend, "where everyone can see it."[25] According to Herbert Aptheker, "Next only to *Souls of Black Folk* this one-page essay was more widely read and reprinted than any other single piece of writing by Du Bois."[26] During much of his life, Du Bois treated his creed as shorthand for his most cherished ideals and self-definition. He not only reprinted it in *Darkwater*, but also shared it with Shirley Graham, a young professor at Fisk University and his future spouse, during their first extended period of time together in 1936. In her own "memoir" of life with Du Bois, Graham recalled of that trip that Du Bois handed her a copy of *Darkwater*. "My books do not have wide circulation," she remembered him explaining. "But I want you to

have it, and particularly, I want you to read the first piece. It is—my creed."[27]
First published in 1904, reprinted in *Darkwater* in 1920, handed to Graham in
1936, and remembered vividly by her in 1971, the "Credo" had a long history
in the Du Bois family.

Both the "Credo" and the "Postscript" of *Darkwater* drew upon biblical
passages, Christian motifs, and traditional creeds to prepare readers for the
spiritual and religious elements contained in the rest of *Darkwater* and in the
autobiographical chapter. While the "Credo" provided a key to comprehend-
ing more deeply the autobiography, the creation of a legendary Du Bois in
"The Shadow of Years" validated his status as a hero-priest with the wisdom
and power to pen a sacred creed.

Du Bois opened "The Shadow of Years" by mythologizing his birth in
Great Barrington, Massachusetts. "I was born by a golden river and in the
shadow of two great great hills, five years after the Emancipation Proclamation," he wrote. By providing environmental markers—the "golden river" and
the "great great hills"—rather than the name of the city or the state, Du Bois
universalized and romanticized his birth. But he particularized it when he
connected it to African Americans by supplying the historical reference of
the Emancipation Proclamation, rather than the year of his birth, 1868. Du
Bois further linked himself to people of color and sacralized his birth by placing it in the home of a black mystic, "a South Carolinian, . . . tall, thin, and
black, with golden earrings, and given to religious trances." With these opening statements, Du Bois demonstrated not only his sense of a legendary self
but also his feeling of a deep connection to African Americans in bondage
and freedom.[28]

When further describing his family lineage that included African, Dutch,
and French ancestors—"but, thank God! no 'Anglo-Saxon'"—Du Bois further
mythologized his background by maintaining that he came from a "mighty
family" with a "beautiful-eyed" grandmother and a "strong-voiced" uncle. He
also broadened his relationship to African Americans when he referenced
African social and religious themes as he discussed his grandmother. He remembered her singing, "Do bana coba—gene me, gene me! / Ben d'nuli, ben
d'le," a slave spiritual that Du Bois translated in *The Souls of Black Folk* as "You
may bury me in the East, / You may bury me in the West, / But I'll hear the
trumpet sound in that morning." Framing his early childhood in the context
of his grandmother's sacred song of death, romanticizing his family members, and linking his birth to the Emancipation Proclamation, Du Bois used
the opening paragraphs to carve out a mythical beginning for himself that
cosmically linked him to African and African American cultures.[29]

Of his ancestors, Du Bois expressed the greatest admiration for his pater-
nal grandfather, Alexander Du Bois. Alexander embodied the battle against
hypocritical Christianity that Du Bois himself followed. The son of a French
Huguenot descendant and a slave, Alexander was educated at Cheshire
School in Connecticut, worked in Haiti, and then served as a steward on a
passenger boat that traveled from New York to New Haven. After retiring
to New Bedford, Massachusetts, he battled on behalf of civil rights. In particular, Alexander experienced profound anger over the marginalization of
blacks in churches that were largely controlled by whites. As Du Bois penned,
"When the white Episcopalians of Trinity Parish, New Haven, showed plainly
that they no longer wanted black folks as fellow Christians, he led the revolt
which resulted in St. Luke's Parish, and was for years its senior warden. He
lies dead in the Grove Street Cemetery, beside Jehudi Ashmun." Du Bois held
this grandfather in great esteem for his courage, maintaining, "He was not a
'Negro'; he was a man!"[30]

Focusing on his grandfather's church battle, Du Bois positioned himself
in the line of pioneering African American religious leaders who opposed
inequality in the house of God by forming separate, all-black religious communities. The most famous of these black leaders also authored one of the
first African American spiritual autobiographies, a narrative of which Du
Bois was well aware. Originally published in 1833, *The Life Experience and
Gospel Labors of the Rt. Rev. Richard Allen* narrated the tale of Richard Allen,
founder of the African Methodist Episcopal Church. Unlike Du Bois's "The
Shadow of Years," which structurally and rhetorically resembled mythological narratives, Allen's autobiography read as a Christian conversion narrative,
but with a racialized particularity. While Allen detailed his pre-Christian sinfulness, his conversion to Christ, and the events of his new spiritual life, he
also narrated a parallel description of his physical enslavement, his bodily
emancipation, and his efforts on behalf of African American uplift. Allen's
narrative, in many ways, is a story of physical and spiritual chains broken by
the power of God and the power of man.[31]

Like Du Bois's grandfather, Allen refused to accept mistreatment by white
Christians. He recounted the pivotal moment when abuse at St. George's
Methodist Church of Philadelphia in November 1787 led the black parishioners to seek spiritual community elsewhere. After the congregation had been
instructed to pray on its knees, Allen "heard considerable scuffling and low
talking. I raised my head up and saw one of the trustees, H—— M——, having hold of the Rev. Absalom Jones, pulling him up off his knees, and saying
'You must get up—you must not kneel here.'" Jones, who later formed the

African Methodist Episcopal Zion Church, was in no mood to disrespect the prayer time to obey a racist deacon. "Mr. Jones said, 'Wait until prayer is over, and I will get up and trouble you no more.'" This deacon, however, would not be denied: "He beckoned to one of the other trustees, Mr. L—— S—— to come to his assistance. He came, and went to William White to pull him up. By this time prayer was over, and we all went out of the church in a body, and they were no more plagued with us in the church." This small band of Philadelphia blacks proceeded to establish their own church and eventually two denominations, both of which rose in power and might throughout the nineteenth and twentieth centuries.[32]

To Allen, the hypocrisy of white Christians and the perseverance of the black believers stood as a testament that God was on the side of people of color—a point that Du Bois underscored in his "Credo," his autobiographies, and also in a wide array of his other works. As Allen maintained of the years following their refusal to worship at St. George's and to build a new church, "My dear Lord was with us, and we were filled with fresh vigor to get a house erected to worship God in." Even after local whites attacked the church, Reverend Allen and his compatriots continued to place their trust in God. We "were pursued with threats of being disowned, and read publicly out of meeting if we did continue worship in the place we had hired," Allen wrote, "but we believed the Lord would be our friend."[33] For Du Bois, the religious battles initiated by Richard Allen, Absalom Jones, and Alexander Du Bois were ones that he admired, attached himself to symbolically, and sought to continue.

Returning to the characterizations of his childhood in Massachusetts, Du Bois constructed himself as discerning a great challenge and hearing a divine call.[34] The challenge was racial inequality and the call was the struggle for justice. He described his childhood as idyllic, yet tainted by the absence of a father. Du Bois remembered being "very happy" and that his father "in nature . . . was a dreamer,—a romantic, indolent, kind, unreliable. He had in him the making of a poet, an adventurer, or a Beloved Vagabond." Although Du Bois seemed to cherish his father's poetic and mystical side, he also recognized the anguish that his father's irresponsibility caused his mother. His father had become a preacher, but "mother no longer trusted his dreams, and he soon faded out of our lives into silence."[35]

Du Bois's entry into elementary school provided the occasion for his eyes to open to the terrors of a world built on racial and economic exploitation. Yet it also occasioned his first glimpses of the tools with which he would dismantle this realm. "Here I got acquainted with my world," he penned, "and soon had my criterions for judgment." He signaled a change in the narrative—from

his musings over his mythic beginnings to his recognition of disturbing demons—by returning to the image of the river. As he matured, he learned that
the "river of my birth was golden because of the woolen and paper waste that
soiled it. The gold was theirs, not ours; but the gleam and glint was for all."
He became aware of "the kingdom of snobs," and recognized that the poor,
especially immigrants from Ireland and southern Germany, were despised in
this world.[36]

A new awareness of racial antagonism matched Du Bois's recognition of
class divisions. As a youngster, Du Bois felt a kinship with his white classmates. He was "very much one of them," but "very gradually" the world of racial divisions and classifications manifested itself. "I cannot now distinguish
the steps," Du Bois wrote, "I found myself assuming quite placidly that I was
different from other children." At first, he thought this difference rooted in
intellect, because he was much brighter than his companions. Eventually he
found that some in the community looked down upon his dark skin. "A few,
even several," Du Bois penned, "actually considered my brown skin a misfor-
tune; once or twice I became painfully aware that some human beings even
thought it a crime."[37]

The recognition of racial categories and his status as a member of a marginalized group caused Du Bois much sorrow. "I was not for a moment daunted,"
he maintained, "although, of course, there were some days of secret tears."
Amid the sadness, he heard a cosmic call. When the tears dried, he found
a powerful sense of God's presence and direction. "As time flew I felt not so
much disowned and rejected as rather drawn up into higher spaces and made
part of a mightier mission," he maintained. At this point, Du Bois explicitly
linked his call to that of ancient mythological and biblical narratives, asserting that "at times, I almost pitied my pale companions, who were not of the
Lord's anointed and who saw in their dreams no splendid quests of golden
fleeces." Du Bois, in short, viewed his prophetic calling as part of the larger
anointed status of all black people.[38]

Du Bois's gloom turned to rage when interacting with white girls, especially when young women from out of town or older local girls snubbed him
in public. For him, the white girl seemed to symbolize the devil's "angels who
... believe the worst and work to prove it, hating the image which their Maker
stamped on a brother's soul" that he described in his "Credo." Nevertheless,
these traumatic moments once again led Du Bois to further grasp his sanctified status. When white girls embarrassed him, he was transformed in his
rage into a prophet. "Then I flamed!" he reminisced. "I lifted my chin and
strode off to the mountains, where I viewed the world at my feet and strained

my eyes across the shadow of the hills." As Joseph Campbell has shown, hills, mountains, and rivers often serve as spiritual sites in mythological texts—places of communion between the hero and the cosmic teachers.[39] In Du Bois's mythological construction of himself, racial hatred was channeled into righteous heralding, social disaster into sacred drama.[40]

Recognition of his anointing prepared Du Bois for his sacred journey, literally to Fisk University in Tennessee and figuratively to discover the weapons to vanquish the demons of white supremacy. Before he left, however, Du Bois felt the sting of personal loss. In 1884, his beloved mother was able to attend his high school graduation, at which Du Bois gave a commencement address before a humble crowd of fellow students, parents, and teachers, but "that very year she lay down with a sigh of content and has not yet awakened. I felt a certain gladness to see her, at last, at peace, for she had worried all her life." At no point in "The Shadow of Years" did he use the phrase "dead" or "death" in reference to his mother. Rather, following Jewish and Christian traditions, he suggested that she slept in comfort and could possibly awake at a future date. Moreover, the passing of his mother seemed a rightful conclusion to his childhood in New England. It freed up emotional energy for his new journey. "Of my own loss I had then little realization," he remembered, "That came only with the after-years. Now it was the choking gladness and solemn feel of wings! At last, I was going beyond the hills and into the world that beckoned steadily." The death of his mother was the final element of his call to the world beyond the hills and rivers of Massachusetts. He was now prepared psychologically and spiritually to head on his mythical journey, where the hero Du Bois would grow wiser and stronger as he encountered larger dragons and more diabolical demons.[41]

Du Bois described his years in the South as a period of exile, one where he "was being sent to a far land among strangers who were regarded as (and in truth were) 'mine own people.'" According to Campbell, the first adventure of a hero always involves travel to an unknown region. There, the hero encounters a landscape full of symbolic figures. This is the place where the hero finds his self purified, "cleansed and humbled."[42] At Fisk, Du Bois was united with God's anointed—"the Negro race—the beauty of its genius, the sweetness of its soul"—in the form of black women. Just as white women signified the demonic forces of white supremacy in New England, black women at Fisk stood for a new community of sacred kinship and joy. "Ah! the wonder of that journey, with its faint spice of adventure, as I entered the land of slaves," he wrote, "opposite two of the most beautiful beings God ever revealed to the eyes of seventeen. I promptly lost my appetite, but I was deliriously happy!"[43]

Until recounting his adventures at Fisk, Du Bois rather seamlessly integrated the narrative of his life's events with his mythologized presentations of them in "The Shadow of Years." Yet in the middle of his discussion of his undergraduate years, he broke the flow of the essay and projected a spiritual grid onto the decades of his adulthood. He divided the time from his entry at Fisk to his writing of the autobiography into four distinct parts—"the Age of Miracles; the Days of Disillusion; the Discipline of Work and Play; and the Second Miracle Age." Providing the reader with these organizing rubrics and invoking the concept of miracles twice, Du Bois once again encouraged readers to conceive of his life in spiritual terms.[44]

Du Bois's "Age of Miracles" encompassed the years of his higher education from 1884 to 1896. He loved Fisk and reveled in the supernatural powers of hero-hood. "I was bursting with the joy of living," he recalled, "I seemed to ride in a conquering might. I was captain of my soul and master of my fate! I *willed* to do! It was done. I *wished*! The wish came true." Although he encountered racism on occasion, his time at Fisk stood as a period of mythical tutelage. There, prophets masqueraded as professors and revealed truths about the world. As he put it, "I studied eagerly under teachers who bent in subtle sympathy, feeling themselves some shadow of the Veil and lifting it gently that we darker souls might peer through to other worlds." Read in comparison to his claim in the "Postscript" that he had "seen the human drama from veiled corner," his assertion that his teachers only felt "some shadow of the Veil" seemed to indicate that while he felt indebted to his teachers, he also viewed himself as above them in calling and divine revelation. Their instructions were necessary to develop his prophetic powers, yet he would move beyond them in the years to come.[45]

Upon graduating from Fisk, Du Bois traveled north to attend Harvard, the university of his childhood aspirations. As the hero of his own mythological narrative, Du Bois continued to flex his individual power and might. "I willed and lo! I was walking beneath the elms of Harvard," he maintained. "I needed money; scholarships and prizes fell into my lap." After completing his bachelor's degree, he once again spoke at commencement. Just as his powers and holy calling had expanded since his high school graduation, so had the authority of his audience. As he lectured on how Jefferson Davis embodied the glory and evil of Anglo-Saxon civilization, Du Bois stood "before governor, president, and grave, gowned men." In his commencement speech, Du Bois offered ideas that confounded and amazed his listeners. "I told them certain astonishing truths, waving my arms and breathing fast," he remembered. For Du Bois, it was not the content of his message that mattered (he did not

include any passages from it). It was memorable because it was his first moment to proclaim "truths" to a distinguished white audience. All in all, a sense
of godlikeness and prophetic powers marked Du Bois's "Age of Miracles."[46]

Neglecting in the narrative his first years of graduate work at Harvard, Du
Bois continued by describing how he willed himself funds to study in Germany and by romanticizing the joys of traveling abroad. His experiences outside
of the United States led him to new vistas of human community—ones that
he expressed in his creed as the belief in "God, who made of one blood all nations that on earth do dwell." "On mountain and valley, in home and school,
I met men and women as I had never met them before," he claimed. "Slowly
they became, not white folks, but folks. The unity beneath all life clutched
me." He realized that his struggle was not against the entire world but rather
against the racism and exploitation of the United States. His time in Europe,
he reminisced later, was a magical one, when "I builded great castles in Spain
and lived therein. I dreamed and loved and wandered and sang."[47]

But this "Age of Miracles" could not last forever. It ended with his studies
in Germany, and the "Days of Disillusion" began when he "dropped suddenly
back into 'nigger'-hating America!" During this era, his view of himself and
society fundamentally altered. He lost the feeling of mythical self-power. The
illusion of mastery was proven to be chimera, and racial structures in the
United States led him to wonder about his own strength. "Was I the masterful
captain," he asked himself, "or the pawn of laughing sprites?" Du Bois's self-
doubt led him to question whether destiny had truly called to him: "Who was
I to fight a world of color prejudice?"[48]

For Du Bois, salvation in the "Days of Disillusion" came through hard
work. He embodied the convictions expressed in his "Credo" that "Work
is Heaven" and "Idleness Hell." Looking for a job at a variety of black colleges and universities, he "just got down on my knees and begged for work,
anything and anywhere." Eventually, Wilberforce University, a small African
Methodist college in Ohio, "called" him to teach. Although other job possibilities presented themselves, including a position at Booker T. Washington's
widely heralded Tuskegee Institute, Du Bois refused. He "was so thankful for
that first offer" that he could not turn his back on Wilberforce.[49]

He ventured to Ohio in 1896 with "high ideals" to create a "great university"
in the image of Harvard or the University of Berlin. He taught Latin, Greek,
English, and German, and "began to write books." Yet his efforts were for
naught, for he "found myself against a stone wall." Too many forces hindered
his goals. The campus lacked capable facilities, and Du Bois considered the
students, the faculty, and the administration frustratingly provincial. "Wil-

berforce was a colored church-school," he lamented, not an institution of higher education. It had all of "the problems of poorly-prepared pupils, an in-adequately-equipped plant, the natural politics of bishoprics, and the provin-cial reactions of a country town loaded with traditions." At this point, Du Bois mentioned his defiance of the school's bishops "in the matter of public extem-poraneous prayer," but he did not dwell on it as he would in subsequent auto-biographies and in his oral-history interview with Ingersoll. In "The Shadow of Years," Du Bois showed more interest in pointing out that local African Americans did not shoulder the entire blame for Wilberforce's backwardness. Untrained students, inferior facilities, and parochial leaders were the bitter fruit of the corrupt white supremacist society that circumscribed the lives and imaginations of turn-of-the-century blacks. "The ropes and myths and knots and hindrances; the thundering waves of the white world beyond beat-ing us back" hampered the university. Between his difficulties at Wilberforce and the restrictions imposed on it by the white world, Du Bois "realized that there were limits to my will to do." Du Bois admitted that he "realized that even captains are not omnipotent in uncharted and angry seas."[50]

Du Bois's experiences at Wilberforce led him once again to wonder about his abilities and to question the path he had traveled. These were the years of doubt, when the hero's resolve is tested and if he perseveres, he will rise to new heights and glories. Du Bois described his experiences in terms of spiri-tual life and death, demonstrating his religious approach to his understand-ing and presentation of his life. Musing about his marriage to Nina Gomer, a graduate of Wilberforce to whom he was married from 1896 until her death in 1950, and his acceptance of a job to study African Americans in Philadelphia with the University of Pennsylvania, Du Bois maintained that Nina and the University of Pennsylvania "spelled salvation." For him, "to remain at Wilber-force without doing my ideals meant spiritual death."[51]

He limited his discussion of his years in Philadelphia to one paragraph in order to provide greater detail to the third era of his life, "The Discipline of Work and Play." Twenty-nine years old, Du Bois accepted a new "call" to teach sociology at Atlanta University and to study "the American Negro." He spent his next thirteen years in Atlanta, where he discovered his "real life work." These were also the years, Du Bois remembered, "of great spiritual upturning, of the making and unmaking of ideals, of hard work and hard play." These were the years, Du Bois recounted when "I found myself." From Atlanta, Du Bois published *The Souls of Black Folk* and spearheaded the Atlanta University Studies, which established black sociology as a vibrant academic field. Again, Du Bois described his work and life in Atlanta as part of a sacred journey,

when "I grew more broadly human, made my closest and most holy friendships, and studied human beings."[52]

Moreover, at Atlanta he came into contact with the vicious, blood-lust side
of white racism, unmasked in the lynching of Samuel Wilkes (or "Sam Hose"
as he was wrongly called at the time) in 1899 and the Atlanta Riot of 1906
where white mobs and black militias squared off, resulting in the deaths of
more than twenty blacks. "I saw the race-hatred of the whites as I had never
dreamed of it before,—naked and unashamed!" Du Bois wrote. This racism
was more than an idea or a problem—it was a "great, red monster of cruel
oppression." In response, Du Bois sought a more coherent plan of attack. This
vision of the beast was equaled by the renewed growth of his own power.
"With all this came the strengthening of and hardening of my own character," he maintained. Du Bois "emerged into full manhood, with the ruins of
some ideals about me, but with others planted above the stars; scarred and a
bit grim, but hugging to my soul the divine gift of laughter and withal determined, even unto stubbornness, to fight the good fight." Indeed, the mature
Du Bois—with his laughter, his determination, and his intellect—spent the
years from then until the writing of "The Shadow of Years" waging what he
considered a holy war against oppression and exploitation.[53]

The mythological Du Bois's finding of himself and his spiritual upturning
in Atlanta prepared him for the fourth stage of his life and the concluding section of this autobiography—the "Second Miracle Age." His years in Atlanta
had been fruitful. He had seen the monster and was ready to struggle against
it. Yet he did not know where best to fight. "I faced the great Decision," Du
Bois wrote. "What with all my dreaming, studying, and teaching was I going to *do* in this fierce fight?" The answer came in the "Niagara Movement,"
a series of meetings of civil rights activists that eventually gave birth to the
NAACP. Of the second "Niagara Movement" meeting, which took place at
Harper's Ferry, West Virginia, the location of John Brown's failed abolitionist
raid of 1859, Du Bois claimed that it "arose to the solemnity of a holy crusade."
Leaving Atlanta University to become the editor of the NAACP's journal, *The
Crisis*, and to live in New York City, Du Bois fully entered his "new Age of
Miracles." His new venture was more than a career. It was a sacred enterprise,
and he quoted transcendentalist writer Ralph Waldo Emerson's poem "Sacrifice" to describe his approach to the NAACP: "I came at their call. My salary
for one year was not assured, but it was the 'Voice without reply.'"[54]

This entire hero narrative prepared the reader for Du Bois's response to the
sacred "Voice without reply." The "Age of Miracles," the "Days of Disillusion,"
and the "Discipline of Work and Play" set the stage for the narrative's hero to

enter his "Second Miracle Age." His mythic beginnings, his feelings of omnip-
otence, his frustration with evil, his personal and communal hardships, and
his renewed vision at Atlanta equipped him for this latest effort. The NAACP,
Du Bois seemed to feel at the time, was not only the final piece of his divine
calling, but it was the organization through which the demonic forces of oppression would be vanquished. On a broader level, Du Bois's "The Shadow of
Years" and his "Credo" worked together to portray him as a hero-priest who
had a divine message for American society. Fusing social and sacred concerns
in the "Credo," Du Bois prepared his reader to comprehend the spiritual elements of the autobiography, while the mythic and spiritual journey in the autobiography provided the necessary narrative for the reader to say "I believe"
in unison with the creed.

Sainthood and Plans for a New Heaven and a New Earth

Twenty years passed between Du Bois's first autobiography and his second.
During these two decades, a great deal changed for him. After almost twenty-
five years editing *The Crisis*, Du Bois left the NAACP in 1934 to return to Atlanta University; he published a slew of essays, editorials, and books, including
Black Reconstruction, *The Gift of Black Folk*, and *Black Folk, Then and Now*; he
took an active role in Pan-African Conventions that endeavored to wrench
control of Africa away from European powers and put it in the hands of Africans themselves; he traveled to Africa, throughout Europe several times, and
enjoyed a visit to Russia, where Communism demonstrated to him the possibilities of massive economic planning and racial harmony; his nemesis Booker
T. Washington died in 1915, but a new rival arose with the charismatic Marcus Garvey, who spread his "back to Africa" gospel far and wide.[55] Within the
United States, the roaring twenties gave way to the Great Depression. Segregation still dominated race relations, and racial antagonism took on new force in
the North as millions of African Americans left the South for northern cities
during World War I. Judge Lynch continued to grip American justice by the
throat, as scores of blacks found themselves brutally murdered by white mobs.
The Ku Klux Klan met openly, and New Deal programs did little to alleviate
the economic pains of black communities. On the global scale, Africa continued to be dominated by European powers, and Germany and the Axis Powers
enveloped the world in war and threatened genocide of epic proportions.

As the world spun out of control and as life in the United States became
even more treacherous for people of color, a significant number of African

Americans felt so deeply disenchanted with the nation that they decided to move. Some followed Marcus Garvey's advice and set sail for Africa, while hundreds of thousands of others ventured to the Soviet Union and the promise of economic stability and racial equality.[56] By the end of the 1930s, it appeared to Du Bois and many other African Americans that blacks in the United States needed a new plan, one that integrated the self-help social and economic ideas of Booker T. Washington and the integrationist legal and political convictions of Du Bois and the NAACP.

Du Bois believed himself to be the man to chart such a path, and he crafted a new strategy for African Americans with a new autobiographical narrative. First published in 1940, *Dusk of Dawn: An Essay Toward an Autobiography of a Race Concept* was part autobiography, part historical narrative of national and global events during the late nineteenth and early twentieth centuries, part analysis of white and black society in the United States, and part economic plan for African American empowerment.[57] *Dusk of Dawn* received favorable reviews from white and black readers alike, and its publication occurred at perhaps Du Bois's highest moment of public appreciation. In 1939 and 1940, Du Bois became an incorporating member of the Society of American Historians, was invited to chair a session at the American Historical Association, and was even asked by President Franklin Delano Roosevelt to serve on a committee to establish a home for his presidential library.[58] Throughout *Dusk of Dawn*, Du Bois underscored the development of his intellectual thought—how he observed ideas about race changing throughout his lifetime, how his reading of Sigmund Freud and Karl Marx led him to reevaluate psychological and economic connections between racism and capitalism, and how he abandoned the belief that racism stemmed from ignorance and instead considered racial exploitation and political oppression inextricably linked to economic structures and psychological power. While the Du Bois of "The Shadow of Years" appeared to be a mythical hero, the Du Bois of *Dusk of Dawn* stood as a global analyst and economic planner.

As much as he and society changed, though, the Freudian-influenced and Marxian-inspired Du Bois once again turned to religious symbolism to frame and articulate his sense of self, the nation, and the world in *Dusk of Dawn*. Du Bois had a great deal to say about his disdain for religious dogma and Christian parochialism, and he maintained that white supremacist Christianity stood as one of the major impediments to racial justice and economic reorganization. In attacking the ways whites warped Christian teachings to justify their exploitative system and hate-filled hearts, however, Du Bois drew attention to his own esteem for the biblical Christ's teachings. He character-

ized true Christianity as an honorable belief system that encouraged kindness, compassion, and sacrifice, and he denounced whites for distorting the original teachings of the Bible for their own self-serving purposes. Moreover, although he did not use much of the mythological language that saturated "The Shadow of Years," Du Bois nevertheless attached spiritual significance to social issues and constructed himself in *Dusk of Dawn* as a prophet who had a new economic revelation for the world.

Du Bois's continuing sense of autobiographical prophet-hood was nowhere more apparent than in the thinly veiled personal story that he offered at the commencement exercises of his alma mater Fisk University two years before the publication of *Dusk of Dawn*. His oration, "The Revelation of Saint Orgne, the Damned," was similar to his "Credo."[59] It supplied an interpretive key to read the spiritualized elements of the autobiography and it highlighted the central points for his overarching sense of mission. As Du Bois wrote to the president of Fisk about his impending oration, his "cryptic subject" was a thesis that he had been "developing for some years."[60] In many ways, "The Revelation" was an autobiographical act in the guise of biblical prophecy. The events of "Saint Orgne's"—or "Saint Negro's"—life mapped onto Du Bois's quite nicely. Both Orgne and Du Bois were educated in the North, both traveled abroad for higher education, both worked among rural African Americans in the South, both fell in love with the spirituals, both taught in Ohio, and both traveled to Africa. In the guise of Saint Orgne, Du Bois constructed himself as a prophet to whom God had revealed a new religious and social teaching, one that would handle the twin problems of poverty and racism. All in all, "The Revelation" offered a spiritual guide to the concepts Du Bois developed further in *Dusk of Dawn*.

Du Bois's inspiration for the structure and rhetoric of "The Revelation" came from the biblical Revelation of John. In this New Testament text, the apostle John wrote from the Island of Patmos of his vision of the Lord. Richly complicated and full of symbolism, John's Revelation has baffled, intrigued, and frustrated biblical scholars throughout the centuries. In the vision, the Lord encouraged the early churches to remain strong in the faith, foretold of an Armageddon between the forces of good and evil, and declared the impending triumphant return of Christ. Although the book discussed terrible horrors plaguing the earth, including earthquakes, diseases, and pestilence, John's Revelation was a work of hope. For in the end, Jesus' return heralded the creation of a world without evil, misery, or pain—a "new heaven and a new earth."[61]

Du Bois's "Revelation" and *Dusk of Dawn* were similarly works of hope. The sun would rise. God offered a message to Orgne that was specifically for

people of color. Replete with biblical allusions, references, and metaphors, Du Bois's "Revelation" contained the Lord's indictment of contemporary society and a vision for a new world. The oration opened with Orgne looking at "Life" and wondering about the meaning and relevancy of supposed racial differences. "Can it be true that souls wrapped in black have a destiny different from those swathed in white satin or yellow silk?" he asked. God did not tarry long to answer, and Du Bois likened Orgne to Christ. The narrative that followed, Du Bois maintained, contained "the Revelation and the answer that came to Saint Orgne the Damned . . . as he stood on his Mount of Transfiguration, looking full at life as it is and not as it might be or haply as he would have it." Like Christ, who was revealed to his followers as the heavenly Son of God at the biblical Mount of Transfiguration, Orgne was enabled to see past the illusions of individual perception and social constraint to view the truth about "Life."[62]

Du Bois linked Orgne to the apostle John when he quoted several passages directly from the biblical Revelation. "Blessed is he that reads and they that hear the words of this prophecy for the time is at hand. Grace be unto you and peace, from which was and which is and is to come and from the seven spirits which are before his throne," proclaim both Du Bois's speech and Revelation 1:3–4. Du Bois also quoted Revelation 1:4 and 1:8 when he wrote that Orgne "was in the spirit" when he heard "a great Voice saying, 'I am Alpha and Omega, the first and the last; and what thou seest write.'" Orgne, however, was not only a saint in the biblical model—he was a black man with a special message for African Americans. "I, who also am your brother and companion in tribulation and in the kingdom and the patience, was in the isle that is called America," Orgne maintained of the moment when the Voice came to him. Orgne "saw seven golden candlesticks with one in the midst of the candlesticks; and in his hands seven stars and out of his mouth went a sharp two-edged sword. And when I saw him I fell at his feet as dead and he laid his right hand upon me saying unto me 'Fear not. Write thou the things which thou has seen; the mystery of the seven stars and the seven golden candlesticks.'"[63]

Du Bois used the number seven frequently in the "Revelation." Just as there were seven spirits and seven candlesticks before God's throne, the heavenly Voice spoke to Orgne in seven-year intervals and on seven separate occasions. To view the "Seven Stars of Heaven," Orgne had to climb "the Seven Heights of Hell." As Du Bois and his audience members well knew, the number seven had a powerful meaning in biblical texts. In the Judeo-Christian tradition, seven signified the presence of God. It was the number of completeness, the

number of perfection. In other works, Du Bois characterized African Americans as the world's "seventh sons," clearly alluding to the Jewish belief that children born on the seventh day, month, or year were holy. By invoking it, Du Bois perhaps demonstrated his hopes that the audience would hear his message as a genuinely religious one. At the very least, he harnessed biblical symbolism to his narrative in ways that showed a deeply developed knowledge of Christian and Jewish traditions.[64]

The "Seven Stars of Heaven" that spoke to Orgne contained divine indictments of the contemporary world and teachings for a reformed society. The stars contained messages about "Birth and Family; School and Learning; the University and Wisdom; . . . Work; . . . Right and Wrong; . . . the Freedom of Art and Beauty; and . . . the Democracy of Race." Beyond these "seven heights," Orgne maintained, was heaven—where "there are no vales of Gloom—for the star above is the sun itself and all shadows fall straight before it."[65]

Corresponding with each of the "seven heights," the divine Voice boomed radical lessons to Orgne at moments that paralleled Du Bois's own lifetime experiences. When Orgne was in his childhood, he received the first message on "Birth and Family." On this occasion, "the sun rose slowly above the mountain and with its light spake. Hear ye the Wisdom of the families of black folk." The sun taught that families were the principal agents of forming good individuals. "Gentlemen are bred and not born," the Voice proclaimed, and parenting was more than being a mother or a father, it was a "sacrificial priesthood."[66]

Each time the holy voice spoke to Orgne, it came to him at the moment he encountered or had just encountered the elements of the lesson. The second star of heaven, for instance,—"the wisdom of the elementary school"—appeared to Orgne right before he entered high school. This star inveighed against the United States, particularly the South, for neglecting the proper education of black youth, and it challenged African Americans to expend more energy on elementary schooling. The third star—"the University and Wisdom"—spoke to Orgne while he was in Europe, as Du Bois had been, to study at the University of Berlin. It came as he "sat in a lofty cathedral, glorious in the fretted stone lacework of its proudly vaulted roof. . . . The angels in the choir sang No—Hear Ye! For Wisdom is the principal thing." University learning, Orgne discerned, was necessary for African Americans to eliminate the "widespread ignorance" of their people.[67]

The fourth star, "Work," appeared to Orgne after he had returned from his studies abroad and stood "in the swamp" during "the winter of America." This time, the Voice spoke through African American spirituals. "Suddenly across

the swamp and across the world and up from the cotton fields of Georgia rolled a Negro folk song," Du Bois wrote. The music served as the carrier of the divine. "Orgne saw in music Jehovah and his angels. . . . He saw the Golden Candlestick and heard the revelation of the Star: Hear ye! This is the teaching of the World of Work." This star taught that free-market enterprise was sinful and that people of color should not follow the ways of white capitalists. Too long had African Americans suffered from an unplanned economy and its consequences: unbearable labor, massive poverty, and great disparities of wealth. "There is only one thing for civilized human beings to do when facing such a problem," Orgne heard, "and that is to learn the facts, to reason out their connection and to plan the future." In short, the Voice called African Americans to arrange their economy and to create an all-black socialism that would replace the fluctuations and disruptions endemic to capitalism.[68]

The spirituals' divine indictment of capitalism led Orgne to challenge the masters of property and production. The music touched Du Bois's Orgne deeply and he felt himself embodying their characters and messages. "Always the swinging thunder of song surged above," Orgne remembered of working in the South. He heard the music everywhere: "Jordan rolled; the rocks and the mountains fled away, the Way was crowded." And Orgne followed in the footsteps of the spiritual's heroes. "Moses went down, away down among the cabins in the cotton patch to the crazy church and hysterical crowd of penitents all praying madly to escape debt. Orgne talked to the planter and said 'let my people go,' and worked with the tenants seven long years." For Orgne's labors, his rural compatriots gave him the name "Saint," yet a crooked local minister derailed the plans in the end. He mortgaged the community's land and "ran away with the money."[69]

The actions of this minister exemplified the need for a reformation in black churches, and this was the central message of the fifth heavenly star. It bore the instructions of "the naked crag of Right and Wrong" and appeared to Orgne outside of a chapel in Ohio, as Du Bois had been at Wilberforce. "Saint Orgne the Damned, behold the Vision of the Seven Black Churches of America," the Voice thundered. These churches were responsible for teaching ethics and ethical behavior, but they had failed miserably. "What is this church doing today toward its primary task of teaching men right and wrong, and the duty of doing right?" the Voice asked and replied: "The flat answer is nothing if not less than nothing. . . . Our church has veered off on every conceivable side path, which interferes with and nullifies its chief duty of character-building." Just as the biblical prophets had been called to share God's message of judgment, Orgne was instructed to denounce the churches and cast a vision

for a new way. Du Bois took direct aim at both the biblical literalism of many black believers and the atonement theologies of many Christians that characterized God as demanding the crucifixion of a perfect man in order to satiate his need for blood in return for sin. Black Christians must stop teaching that "the lying and deceitful Jacob was better than the lazy Esau, or that the plan of salvation is anything but the picture of the indecent anger and revenge of a bully."[70]

But the voice did not call Orgne to abandon religion. Rather, Orgne was to build a new church, one based on the "word of life from Jeremiah, Shakespeare and Jesus, Buddha and John Brown." This new church must care for temporal needs as well as ethereal ones. So Orgne "organized a church with a cooperative store in the Sunday-school room; with physician, dentist, nurse and lawyer to help, serve and defend the congregation; with library, nursery school, and a regular succession of paid and trained lecturers and discussion; they had radio and moving pictures and out beyond the city a farm with house and lake." Orgne's new congregation, his institutional church, would provide the structure necessary for the communal economic system the Voice showed him: "They had a credit union, group insurance, and building and loan association. The members paid for this not by contributions but by ten dollars a month each of regular dues and those who would join this church must do more than profess to love God." The church of "fairy tale and dogma," Orgne hoped, would be replaced by a church organization that served the economic and social needs of the black community.[71]

The sixth star appeared to Orgne during his travels to Africa, while he journeyed "on a mission of world brotherhood." Its message was of "the Freedom of Art which is the Beauty of Life." This star answered one of the most important questions of all humankind—what is the meaning of life? "Life is more than meat, even though life without food dies," the Voice declared. "Living is not for earning, earning is for living." The point of life was the freedom of expression and emotion—"the fullest, most complete enjoyment of the possibilities of human existence. It is the development and broadening of feelings and emotions, through sound and color, line and form." Sadly, these freedoms had been largely denied the poor and people of color.[72]

In a historical era of genocide and economic catastrophe, the seventh and final star had a message for Orgne about "Democracy." Although the divine messenger proclaimed the vision of "a new Heaven and a New Earth," Orgne only saw "War and Murder . . . breadlines and starvation, crime and disease." He wondered, "Is not our dream of Democracy gone?" The star presented a different track for African Americans to travel. Rather than seek to be ab-

sorbed into white America as individuals, African Americans must work in unison to bring democracy to the world. "Acting together, voluntarily or by outer compulsion, we can be the units through which universal democracy may be accomplished," the Voice proclaimed. Blacks must vote as a group; they must sell as a group; and they must buy as a group. For this to occur, though, a new plan of racial unity and cooperation must be developed and implemented. "We have no comprehensive plans concerning our unemployment, our economic dependence, the profit economy and the changing technique of industry." It was literally the "dusk of dawn," and African Americans must be prepared for the day. Quoting the biblical prophet Isaiah, Du Bois wrote, "The day of our reckoning is at hand. 'Awake, Awake / put on thy strength, O Zion.'"[73]

Du Bois presented "The Revelation of Saint Orgne, the Damned" to the graduating students of Fisk in the same year that he turned seventy and decided to write a full-length autobiography. "The Revelation" was an important precursor to *Dusk of Dawn*, for it offered a condensed and spiritualized approach to many of the central issues of *Dusk of Dawn*, especially Du Bois's plans for an organized black economy. Orgne was one side of Du Bois, a proud prophet with political teachings, an ethereal priest with an economic plan, a sacred seer with social insight.[74]

Published originally in 1940 and reprinted in 1968 to honor the centennial of Du Bois's birth, which included the text of one of the last major speeches of Martin Luther King, Jr., where he lauded Du Bois for his "divine dissatisfaction with all forms of injustice," *Dusk of Dawn* contained nine chapters.[75] Interspersing personal stories, national and global events, and fictive interactions with a variety of characters, Du Bois sought to explain the development of his own thoughts and plans for racial improvement. To do so, he once again turned to religious rhetoric and convictions. He discussed his own religious development, highlighting the influence of his childhood church and his multiple struggles with black church leaders. He also offered an assessment of the core tenets of Christianity and blasted white society for failing to obey biblical teachings. Furthermore, Du Bois used spiritualized rhetoric to articulate his understanding of key issues such as segregation, democracy, and the economy. Ultimately, the Du Bois of *Dusk of Dawn*, as the one of "The Revelation of Saint Orgne," was a black prophet declaring a sacred vision of a new world.

Du Bois depicted his life in *Dusk of Dawn* as illustrative of broader issues of race in the United States and the world. "My life had its significance and only its deep significance because it was part of a Problem of the future world," he

maintained in the opening "Apology." "The problem of the future world is the charting, by means of intelligent reason, of a path not simply through the resistances of physical forces, but through the vaster and far more intricate jungle of ideas conditioned on unconscious and subconscious reflexes of living things; on blind unreason and often irresistible urges of sensitive matter; of which the concept of race is today one of the most unyielding and threatening." For Du Bois, his life provided the best means to discuss this "problem" and chart a course for its solution. "I seem to see a way of elucidating the inner meaning and significance of that race problem by explaining it in terms of the one human life that I know best."[76]

Although he thought his life history important only because of its example, Du Bois nonetheless construed it in religious terms. He described the time of his life, from 1868 to 1940, as "years of cosmic significance," and, when articulating why he chose to write, Du Bois imported rhetoric from "The Revelation of Saint Orgne." He maintained that his life was important for "its revelation" about ideas of race, and he claimed to have written this new autobiography to "explain, expound and exhort; to see, foresee and prophesy, to the few who could or would listen." Moreover, he asserted that divine tools were necessary for his battle against ideas of race. The war for justice, he asserted, "must fight with the weapons of Truth, with the sword of the intrepid, uncompromising Spirit, with organization in boycott, propaganda and mob frenzy."[77]

In the first chapter, "A New England Boy and Reconstruction," Du Bois situated his early childhood amid a national experiment with democracy, and he used racial and religious issues to set the tone for the entire narrative. He included reflections on his early religious life as part of his discussions of race and class in late nineteenth-century New England and, in so doing, drew attention to the importance of churches in his personal life. "My grandmother was an Episcopalian and my mother, Congregational," he wrote. "I grew up in the Congregational Sunday school." An integral part of Du Bois's memories of his adolescent social life, this Sunday school exemplified his feeling of inclusion in the primarily white community. As he claimed, "In the ordinary social affairs of the village—the Sunday school with its picnics and festivals; the temporary skating rink in the town hall; the coasting in crowds on all the hills—in all these, I took part with no thought of discrimination on the part of my fellows." Church and church leaders were also crucial to his higher education, a point that he neglected in "The Shadow of Years." Du Bois described how "the Reverend C. C. Painter," helped him procure a scholarship to attend Fisk and that "the funds were to be furnished by four Connecticut churches which Mr. Painter had formerly pastored." Ultimately, while Du Bois remem-

bered of his childhood faith that "we were placidly religious," his characterizations of Sunday school and church were useful memories to envision a
community that transcended racial distinctions.[78]

Turning to his education at Fisk, Harvard, and the University of Berlin,
Du Bois discussed how he viewed religion losing much of its social power to
science in turn-of-the-century American and European cultures. "Above all
science was becoming religion," he asserted, "religion went into its heresy trials, in struggle with 'higher criticism,' its discomfort at the 'revised version' of
the New Testament which was published the year I entered college." Du Bois
did not herald the declining significance of religious values as the dawning
of a new and brighter day, however, as did many agnostics and atheists of
the era. Instead, he lamented that greed replaced God. "Wealth was God," he
continued, "Everywhere men sought wealth and especially in America there
was extravagant living; everywhere the poor planned to be rich and the rich
planned to be richer."[79]

Slowly but surely, Du Bois observed that the American system of capitalism, racial discrimination, and the violence of white supremacy worked together to limit the lives of African Americans and the possibilities of reform.
He learned these lessons, furthermore, in tandem with a deeper appreciation
for the spiritual elements of the black community. When teaching in rural
Tennessee during summers, he marveled at what he encountered. "I met new
and intricate and unconscious discrimination," Du Bois penned. He saw both
terrible poverty and beautiful spirits. "All the appointments of my school
were primitive," he reminisced: "a windowless log cabin; . . . almost no books;
long, long distances to walk." There, Du Bois was moved by the music, just as
Orgne had been. He "heard the sorrow songs sung with primitive beauty and
grandeur."[80]

Du Bois also discussed his movement away from traditional Christianity.
His professors were deeply committed to their students maintaining their
faiths. "A very definite attempt was made to see that we did not lose or question our Christian orthodoxy," Du Bois recalled. To the young Du Bois, this
seemed strange "since I had never questioned my religious upbringing." Until
college, Du Bois asserted, his religious beliefs were simple, yet clear: "God
ruled the world. Christ loved it, and men did right, or tried to; otherwise they
were rightly punished." The efforts of his professors had the ironic effect of
distancing Du Bois from orthodoxy. Du Bois remembered becoming "critical
of religion and resentful of its practice." Two particular instances frustrated
Du Bois: a church near Fisk declared dancing a "sin" and the Presbyterian
Church of the United States upheld the heresy verdict of Charles Briggs, an

Old Testament professor at Union Theological Seminary who had criticized notions of biblical inerrancy as "bibliolatry." Du Bois never disclaimed faith in the sacred or the divine in the autobiographical narrative. Rather, he may have pointed to the dancing issue and the Briggs case to underscore what he deemed American Christianity's tendency to nitpick over insignificant individual behaviors or hold onto old-fashioned intellectual approaches, instead of tackling concerns of social justice and equality—an issue he developed forcefully later in *Dusk of Dawn*.[81]

Of the final decade of the nineteenth century and the first of the twentieth century, Du Bois reported that he developed a greater appreciation for the unity of all peoples and became enamored with scientific approaches to studying humanity. Social scientific thinking dominated his imagination while at the University of Berlin, and to Du Bois it led him away from Christian orthodoxy. "In Germany I turned still further from religious dogma," he reminisced, "and began to grasp the idea of a world of human beings whose actions, like those of the physical world, were subject to law." While he desired to bring this scientific approach to the study of humans to Wilberforce, he did not have the opportunity to do so until he went to Atlanta University where he studied African Americans "scientifically." During these years, he became more aware of class conflict in the United States and even felt a greater appreciation for the Populist movement, although its heyday had long since passed.[82]

While discussing his intellectual maturation at Atlanta University and his travails earlier at Wilberforce, Du Bois highlighted conflicts with university leadership over issues of public prayer as another way to present his dissent from church orthodoxy. Again, he made no definitive statement about losing religion or abandoning faith, but instead depicted himself as hindered by religious traditionalists. He related the prayer incident that took place at Wilberforce, and explained, "It took a great deal of explaining to the board of bishops why a professor in Wilberforce should not be able at all times and sundry to address God in extemporaneous prayer." When he moved to Atlanta University and the issue once again came up, this time Du Bois compromised. He agreed "to use the Episcopal prayer book," and wrote several prayers to use. Of his personally crafted prayers, which were collected and published as *Prayers for Dark People* decades after Du Bois's death, he expressed uncertainty about whether God heard them. Yet Du Bois knew they moved his students. "I am not sure that they were orthodox or reached heaven," he maintained in *Dusk of Dawn*, "but they certainly reached my audience."[83]

Although Du Bois rejected much of the church establishment, he contin-

ued to frame his convictions with religious rhetoric. In *Dusk of Dawn*, he proceeded to discuss his controversies with black educator Booker T. Washington, his growing frustration with science's impotence to stop racial violence, and his intense disenchantment with American society. He included the text from the Niagara Movement's manifesto, where he and his fellow civil rights activists impeached the Christianity of whites and characterized racial injustice as a sacred issue. As he wrote for the Niagara Movement, "Stripped of verbiage and subterfuge and in its naked nastiness, the new American creed says: fear to let black men even try to rise lest they become the equals of the white. And this is the land that professes to follow Jesus Christ. The blasphemy of such a course is only matched by its cowardice."[84]

In the middle chapter of *Dusk of Dawn*, "The Concept of Race," Du Bois offered his family's heritage as an example of the massive amounts of sexual mixing among people from a variety of nationalities and backgrounds in the history of North American settlement and inhabitation. Along with his personal lineage, a host of scientific studies and cultural examinations proved a fact that most white Americans were unwilling to admit—that "race lines were not fixed and fast." He once again included the story of his grandfather Alexander and his disdain for racial discrimination within the church, and Du Bois acknowledged a strong cultural connection to Africa. "I felt myself African by 'race,'" he penned, "and by that token was African and an integral member of that group of dark Americans who were called Negroes." Du Bois defined race as a social construction, not a biological reality. Races, he maintained, were composed of individuals who shared common historical and contemporary experiences. In the case of African Americans, their shared oppression made them a "race." Du Bois concluded with sadness that racial oppression, in the form of segregation, had the lasting effect of transforming African Americans into "entombed souls" who "are hindered in their natural movement, expression, and development."[85]

Du Bois directly positioned religion at center stage in his next two chapters, "The White World" and "The Colored World Within." In these chapters, Du Bois presented his reflections on white and black culture, and he repeatedly turned to religious concepts and rhetoric to articulate his thoughts. He characterized ideas of racial supremacy as a form of "spiritual provincialism" and depicted white Europeans and Americans as "villains" who "crucified, enslaved, and oppressed the Negro group." To expose and chastise white Americans for their treatment of people of color, for their paranoid nationalism that resulted in unholy wars, and for their greed for material wealth, he outlined the ways whites failed to live up to what he deemed the core of Christianity.

In the process of situating white religion as a hindrance to racial justice, he expressed great admiration for biblical teachings. In short, these two chapters showed that while Du Bois had little regard for the organized church and even less for whites' Christianity, he nonetheless held Christian beliefs and teachings in high esteem, perhaps even containing the ideals necessary to re-build society in an equitable manner.[86]

"The White World" contained some of Du Bois's most direct statements pertaining to Christianity in theory and in practice. To underscore his deep regard for Christ's teachings and to expose the self-serving ethos of white culture, Du Bois crafted imaginary conversations between himself and two representative white men—"Roger Van Dieman" and "Reverend J. Simp-son Stodges, D.D." Although the contents of this chapter were fictional and seemed to provide little information about Du Bois's life and experiences, they were fundamental to his self identity and understanding of the world. In this chapter, he expressed his feelings toward white society and presented aspects of himself that could not be represented in specific encounters he actually had with whites. By creating fictive dialogues, Du Bois was able to articulate complex elements of his religious and social imagination that may have been missed or misunderstood, particularly contempt for whites' Christianity and a reassessment of authentic faith.[87]

In the first conversation, Du Bois and Van Dieman debated whether there were any truths to notions of racial inferiority and superiority. Van Dieman, whose name signified his status as "the demon" as clearly as Orgne's signified "Negro," approached the world in hierarchical terms and thought himself re-lated to God. Society was composed of "Race superimposed on Race; classes superimposed on classes," Van Dieman believed. The Van Dieman family, moreover, stood at the foundation of society, and under them "is God. God seems to be a cousin, or at least a blood relative, of the Van Diemans."[88]

Du Bois could not have disagreed more with Van Dieman's point of view. Instead of whites as connected to the divine, Du Bois constructed a messianic role for African Americans. He asserted to the dumbfounded Van Dieman, "black folk are the salvation of mankind." To Du Bois, "white and European civilization" was a colossal failure, not the highest expression of humankind's abilities. "As a system of culture it is idiotic, addle-brained, unreasoning, topsy-turvy, without precision," he wrote. "Its genius chiefly runs to marvel-ous contrivances for enslaving the many, and enriching the few, and murder-ing both." To prove to Van Dieman that the status of one's parents bore no relation to one's potential—that "Gentlemen are bred and not born," as the Voice had proclaimed to Orgne in the first star of his "Revelation"—Du Bois

pointed to individual examples of great men, including Jesus, coming from meager beginnings. "Lincoln from Nancy Hanks, Dumas from a black beast of burden, Kant from a saddler, and Jesus Christ from a manger." If such men could come from humble backgrounds, Du Bois declared, then there was no reason to believe that African Americans could not emerge from their poverty and oppression to greatness. For Du Bois, white civilization and its denial of fundamental rights for all people bore a strong relationship to the biblical Romans who opposed Christ, for both groups failed to "exalt the Lynched above the Lyncher, and the Worker above the Owner, and the Crucified above Imperial Rome."[89]

Van Dieman, however, was not to blame for the evils of white society. He merely imitated the lessons he learned elsewhere, primarily from his church pastor. To address the religious leadership of white America, Du Bois turned to his next fictive foil, "Reverend J. Simpson Stodges." The white minister had all of the characteristics of a gentleman in the United States. "He is respectable," wrote Du Bois: "that is, he belongs to the Episcopal Church, the Union League and Harvard Clubs, and the Republican Party. He is educated, in the sense that he can read if he will." When in the pulpit, moreover, Stodges taught what Du Bois considered the fundamental doctrines of Christian faith, a belief system that resonated with the one articulated in Du Bois's "Credo": "Peace on Earth is the message of Christ, the Divine leader of men; that this means Good Will to all human beings; that it means Freedom, Toleration of mistakes, sins and shortcomings of not only your friends but of your enemies." Stodges urged that "the Golden Rule of Christianity is to treat others as you want to be treated and that finally you should be willing to sacrifice your comfort, your convenience, your wealth and even your life for mankind; in other words, that Poverty is better than riches and that the meek shall inherit the earth." This was a gospel with which Du Bois could nod in agreement.[90]

But these were not the values demonstrated in the practices of white society. And Stodges and his fellow ministers did not advocate them when outside of the pulpit. Parishioners like Van Dieman had a difficult time with these messages, and they went to Reverend Stodges during the weekdays to ask, "Could a man live up to all that today?" Stodges, the "companionable fellow" that he was, with his "excellent family, good manners, Oxford accent and Brooks Brothers to-order clothes," assured his buddies that they were not required to live out these convictions. "This Christian business of Peace, Good Will, the Golden Rule, Liberty and Poverty, was, of course, the Ideal," Stodges explained. "But, bless your soul, man, we can't all always attain the heights, much less live in their rarefied atmosphere." It was better to attempt to live as

a "Gentleman" with a capital "G," Stodges instructed. He acknowledged that this was not true Christianity, but practicality was more important than piety. "It is not, of course, the Christianity of the Gospels," he continued, "but it is a good, honest, middle path suited to good, honest, middle-aged men."[91]

The problem for Stodges, Van Dieman, and other white men, Du Bois suggested, was that they neither knew how to be genuine gentlemen, nor had the strength to follow Christ's teachings wholeheartedly. More interested in national defense and economic vitality than in obeying the Bible, they transformed a gospel of grace into a gospel of greed. Bit by bit, Stodges adulterated his pulpit teachings. "In order to defend America and make an efficient, desirable country," he maintained, "we must have authority and discipline." Good Americans must also appreciate hierarchies, no matter what the Bible says about equality. He continued, "There is no use pretending any longer that all men are created equal. We know perfectly well that Negroes, Chinamen, Mexicans and a lot of others who are presuming to exercise authority in this country are not our equals." The desire for national greatness, obsessive concerns for defense, and underlying racist beliefs led whites to embrace the code of the "White Man." This system led to "War, righteous Hate and then Suspicion" and resulted in "Exploitation" and "Empire."[92]

To Du Bois, ministers provided the ideological rationale that allowed white Americans to think of themselves as "Christians" who prized "Peace," "Good Will," "Poverty," and "Liberty," and yet behave as "White Men" who exploited, warred, and cherished imperialism. Stodges's logic led him to develop a new religious system that sanctified values clearly antithetical to the Christianity he taught on Sunday. Du Bois graphically demonstrated the ideological maneuverings of religious leaders like Stodges with two charts. The first revealed the flow from "Christian" to "White Man," while the second exposed the devolution (see facing page). With them, Du Bois showed how a religion of belligerent and jingoistic whiteness replaced the religion of Christianity.

Du Bois concluded that the beliefs of white men destroyed the "the high, ethical dream of" Christ and "twisted that ethic beyond recognition." The bastardization of Christian values, according to Du Bois, allowed whites simultaneously to view themselves as angels and to act as devils.[93]

By drawing attention to the chasm separating the ethics of Christianity and the actions of whites, Du Bois deployed a common discursive strategy in the African American tradition with remarkable clarity. The dissonance between Christian teachings and white Christians' behaviors provided a space for numerous black autobiographers, including Frederick Douglass, Sojourner Truth, and Malcolm X, to assess their own approaches to God, to other hu-

Christian	Gentleman	American	White Man
Peace	Justice	Defense	War
Good Will	Manners	Caste	Hate
Golden Rule	Exclusiveness	Propaganda	Suspicion
Liberty	Police	Patriotism	Exploitation
Poverty	Wealth	Power	Empire

Source: "Christian—Gentleman—American—White Man," in Du Bois, *Dusk of Dawn*, 163.

mans, and to their self presentations. In one way or another, these authors drew attention to the duplicity of white society and ruminated over its consequences and meanings. By judging the faith of whites to be inauthentic and by finding a new strength in their own faiths, these African American autobiographers vied for rhetorical control over the religious state of the nation and endeavored to tear apart the association of whiteness and godliness.[94]

One of Du Bois's lifelong heroes, the nineteenth-century slave-turned-abolitionist Frederick Douglass contrasted the long-suffering patience of the enslaved with the false Christianity of whites on several occasions in his autobiographies. Writing about one of his owners' wives, Douglass asserted that "she *knew* we were nearly half starved; and yet, that mistress, with saintly air, would kneel with her husband, and pray each morning that a merciful God would bless them in basket and in store, and save them, at last, in his king-

Peace	Manners	Propaganda	Exploitation
Good Will	Exclusiveness	Patriotism	Empire
Poverty	Police	Propaganda	Hate
Liberty	Exclusiveness	Caste	War

Source: "Christian—Gentleman—American—White Man," in Du Bois, *Dusk of Dawn*, 165.

dom." Later, after describing the conversion of his owner Thomas Auld at a
revival meeting, Douglass gave him a tongue-lashing for failing to change
his social practices. "His religion," Douglass announced, "neither made him
emancipate his slaves, nor caused him to treat them with greater humanity.
If religion had any effect on his character at all, it made him more cruel and
hateful in all his ways." In addition, Douglass detailed how white churchgoers
thwarted his efforts to lead a Sunday school for other blacks, and even when
narrating his struggles with the belligerent overseer Thomas Covey, Douglass underscored the conflict between Covey's religion and his lifestyle. While
Covey "was said to 'enjoy religion,'" Douglass wrote, he was also "snakish"
with a "semi-lying propensity."[95]

The mistreatment Douglass encountered from his "professedly christian"
masters and overseers led him to a crisis of faith. When approaching a quiet area, Douglass recounted thinking that he should pray: "But how could
I pray? Covey could pray—Capt. Auld could pray—I would fain pray; but
doubts (arising partly from my own neglect of the means of grace, and partly
from the sham religion which everywhere prevailed, cast in my mind a doubt
upon all religion, and led me to the conviction that prayers were unavailing
and delusive) prevented my embracing the opportunity, as a religious one."
What if God were dead or could not hear, Douglass wondered. At the end of
his autobiography, though, Douglass assured his readers that he maintained
faith with an eloquent delineation between what he deemed the true religion
of love and sacrifice and the disdainful practices of slaveholders.

> I love the religion of our blessed Savior. I love that religion that comes
> from above, in the wisdom of God, which is first pure, then peaceable,
> gentle, and easy to be entreated, full of mercy and good fruits, without
> partiality and without hypocrisy. I love that religion that sends its votaries
> to bind up the wounds of him that has fallen among thieves. I love that
> religion that makes it the duty of its disciples to visit the fatherless and
> the widow in their affliction. I love that religion that is based upon the
> glorious principle, of love to God and love to man; which makes its
> followers do unto others as they themselves would be done by. . . . It is
> because I love this religion that I hate the slaveholding, the woman-whip-
> ping, the mind-darkening, the soul-destroying religion that exists in the
> southern states of America. It is because I regard the one as good, and
> pure, and holy, that I cannot but regard the other as bad, corrupt, and
> wicked. Loving the one I must hate the other; holding to the one I must
> reject the other.[96]

One of Douglass's abolitionist contemporaries, Sojourner Truth, also struggled to develop her religious identity amid her racist society, and she too developed a deeper feeling of connection to the divine in her efforts to reconcile the Christianity of the Bible and that of whites. Like Douglass, Truth denounced slavery as anti-Christian and highlighted the fact that American churches supported it. "If there *can* be any thing more diametrically opposed to the religion of Jesus than the working of this soul-killing system—which is as truly sanctioned by the religion of America as are her ministers and churches—we wish to be shown where it can be found," asserted *The Narrative of Sojourner Truth*. For Truth, faith in a just and loving God heartened her even when the antislavery cause seemed to sputter. She made this abundantly clear on one occasion. After hearing Douglass lecture that African Americans must rise up with arms to destroy slavery she "sitting, tall and dark, on the very front seat, facing the platform; and in the hush of deep feeling, she spoke out in her deep, peculiar voice, heard all over the house, / 'Frederick is God dead?'" In fact, her entire narrative was framed as proof that "God was not dead" and that blacks in America, like Jews in Exodus, "have been guided through the dark wilderness of oppression by the 'pillar of cloud and of fire.'"[97]

Attacks on the religious hypocrisy of whites continued to serve African American autobiographers throughout the twentieth century, not only in Du Bois's *Dusk of Dawn* but also in *The Autobiography of Malcolm X*. Written in collaboration between award-winning author Alex Haley and civil rights activist Malcolm X, the autobiography read as a double spiritual conversion narrative where the deviant young adult Malcolm Little first found salvation in the teachings of the Nation of Islam and then achieved a second conversion during his pilgrimage to Mecca. With rhetoric analogous to Truth, Douglass, and Du Bois, Malcolm attacked whites and white culture for their religious hypocrisy. Their religious duplicity served as a foil for his conception of faith. In a Boston prison, Malcolm read books such as Du Bois's *The Souls of Black Folk* and Carter G. Woodson's *Negro History*. They showed Malcolm "how the white man never has gone among the non-white peoples bearing the Cross in the true manner and spirit of Christ's teachings—meek, humble, and Christlike." Then as a Nation of Islam minister, Malcolm considered his sermons on Christianity and the slave trade his "favorite lectures." With them, he assailed whites for their two-facedness. "I know you don't realize the enormity, the horrors, of the so-called *Christian* white man's crime," he told a black audience. "Not even in the *Bible* is there such a crime! God in His wrath struck down with *fire* the perpetrators of *lesser* crimes."[98] All in all, from Frederick

Douglass and Sojourner Truth to Du Bois and Malcolm X, exposing the duplicity of white Christians stood as a way to both indict racial exploitation
and grasp control over religious judgments in American society.

After Du Bois finished pointing out the contradictions and self-serving
rationales of white Christianity in *Dusk of Dawn*'s "The White World," he
turned to his plans to create stronger African American communities in "The
Colored World Within." To him, only as people of color embraced racial segregation and planned a new economic structure for themselves by cooperat-
ing as producers and consumers would they achieve the necessary political
and economic might to bring genuine democracy to the United States. Just
as the Voice had spoken to Orgne, Du Bois called particular attention to the
roles of black churches in this plan. Referring to the reality that the culture of
Jim Crow dominated the church of Jesus Christ as an "eloquent commentary
upon modern Christianity," Du Bois once again admonished white society
and encouraged African Americans to band together more tightly. "So too
in the church," he wrote, "the activities for ethical teaching, character-building, and organized charity and neighborliness, which are largely concentrated
in religious organizations, are segregated racially more completely than any
other human activity." Although church segregation demonstrated vividly
the hypocrisy of white civilization, it provided an amazing opportunity for
African American churchgoers and black intellectuals to work together. The
black church exemplified the type of all-black institution that Du Bois saw as
essential to racial improvement. With the help of African American scholars,
these black churches could aid in the formation of a new black society, one
with health services, information networks, and consumer communes. This
was the plan that Orgne had seen for the new church he was to create.[99]

In the final two chapters of *Dusk of Dawn*, "Propaganda and World War"
and "Revolution," Du Bois returned to his discussion of his own professional
and intellectual development from the 1910s to the late 1930s. He continued to
use religious rhetoric to underscore his spiritualized understanding of social
factors and forces. Du Bois approached Karl Marx as a religious leader. "I
believed and still believe that Karl Marx was one of the greatest men of modern times," Du Bois asserted, "and that he put his finger squarely upon our
difficulties when he said that economic foundations . . . are the determining
factors in the development of civilization, in literature, religion, and the basic
pattern of culture. And this conviction I had to express or spiritually die."
Finally, Du Bois sought to push his fellow African Americans to realize that
"Negroes have no Zion" in the United States or the world. He concluded with
several reflections that again linked supposedly sacred and secular themes.

"I insist," he maintained, "that regardless of income, work worth while which one wants to do as compared with highly paid drudgery is exactly the difference between heaven and hell." His life's tale was one of religious learning and growth. "By means of this I have met life face to face. I have loved a fight and I have realized that Love is God and Work is His prophet; that His ministers are Age and Death."[100]

For Du Bois, *Dusk of Dawn* allowed him to reflect on his intellectual development and to evaluate the world. In so doing, he drew on many of the religious themes highlighted in "The Revelation of Saint Orgne," most emphatically through his overarching self presentation in religious terms. While his "Credo" and "The Shadow of Years" posited Du Bois as a hero-priest with a new body of religious values to teach, the "Revelation" and *Dusk of Dawn* worked together to present him as a prophet-saint able to see divine truths and a sacred plan for justice and uplift. Du Bois toned down the mythological rhetoric of his self-construction in his second autobiography, but he continued to invoke religious themes at every turn. He narrated his personal religious development as heightening frustration with church leaders who focused more on dogma than on doing justice; he used religious language to spiritualize social and intellectual issues; and he indicted whites as religious hypocrites while calling on black churches to join him in his plans for a new African American economy. The Du Bois of "The Revelation" and of *Dusk of Dawn* believed himself to be the saint called to herald the dawning of a new day where social, cultural, and economic planning would foster the creation of "a new heaven and a new earth."

∼

Twenty years after the publication of *Dusk of Dawn*, when Du Bois sauntered into the oral history offices at Columbia University to answer William Ingersoll's questions about his long and adventurous life, Du Bois recalled nine decades full of religious adventures, strivings, and complexity. He was both "orthodox" and "not orthodox at all." He was a church reformer who rarely attended church. He was a priest with no church, a prophet who presented his works as history, sociology, and fiction. But in his "Credo," "The Shadow of Years," "The Vision of Saint Orgne, the Damned," and *Dusk of Dawn*, Du Bois unveiled his sense of himself. In these autobiographical acts, he crafted a mythological life, one whose meaning and substance touched on cosmic truths and values. His rage against white supremacy was a spiritual rage. His critique of black society was a spiritual critique. And his plans for a new world were spiritual plans.

Along with other black autobiographers, including Richard Allen, Frederick Douglass, Sojourner Truth, and Malcolm X, Du Bois attacked white Christianity and society as fundamentally un-Christian and immoral as a means to carve out a space for African American religious, individual, and collective expression. The themes Du Bois articulated in his autobiographical narratives were ones that he would bend, manipulate, and deploy in a variety of other genres. Du Bois developed many of these points in his path-breaking *The Souls of Black Folk*. In no other work of Du Bois's did he better demonstrate his interaction with the culture of white supremacist religion; in no other work did Du Bois more effectively cast himself as a prophet with sacred insight; and in no other work did he shape the religious and racial lives of his readers more.

CHAPTER TWO

~

Race as Cosmic Sight in *The Souls of Black Folk*

AMERICA'S CULTURAL LANDSCAPE was rocked by *The Souls of Black Folk: Essays and Sketches*. First published in April 1903, reprinted numerous times since, and translated into dozens of languages, *Souls* consisted of fourteen essays, an introduction, and a conclusion. Blending history, sociology, autobiography, and fiction to discuss race in the United States, Du Bois created a powerfully moving book. A reviewer for the *Nation* maintained that it was "a profoundly interesting and affecting book, remarkable as a piece of literature." The text's influence knew few bounds, and readers from all sorts of backgrounds declared it a marvel. In 1907, novelist Henry James claimed that *Souls* was "the only 'Southern' book of any distinction published for many a year," while German sociologist Max Weber wrote to Du Bois, "Your splendid work: 'The Souls of Black Folk' ought *to be translated in German*." If Du Bois had no one in mind, Weber even provided the name of a scholar to compose the translation. In another letter to Du Bois, a poor Jewish immigrant from Russia living in New York City maintained that *Souls* left him "a-crying." The book simply "over powered" him. *Souls* continued to influence readers throughout the twentieth century and beyond. In 1956, for instance, poet Langston Hughes mentioned in a letter to Du Bois, "I have just read again your *The Souls of Black Folk*—for perhaps the tenth time—the first time having been some forty years ago when I was a child in Kansas. Its beauty and passion and power are as moving and as meaningful as ever."[1]

When *Souls* first appeared, two reviewers read it explicitly against the works of two vicious and popular white supremacist authors of the era: theologian Charles Carroll and novelist Thomas Dixon, Jr. At the turn of the cen-

tury, few men had done more to stoke the fires of racial antagonism. They tried to sanctify the segregation of African Americans and widespread racial violence by characterizing "Negroes" as soulless beasts. Writing for *The Dial*, W. H. Johnson contrasted Dixon's *The Leopard's Spots: A Romance of the White Man's Burden, 1865–1900*, a tale of post–Civil War America that depicted emancipated African Americans as moral monsters who deserved to be either lynched or expelled from the nation, with Booker T. Washington's *Various Addresses and Papers* and Du Bois's *Souls*. Johnson berated Dixon for his despicable defense of lynching in the guise of a "romance." "It is only the unthinking man that can draw from his baleful picture the final conclusion which the writer desires," Johnson maintained. Moreover, Dixon should read Washington's and Du Bois's works in order to have an accurate understanding of race in the United States. "We commend to Mr. Dixon the intelligent reasoning of Professor Du Bois and Mr. Washington on the subject," Johnson concluded: "He has much to learn from either of them."[2]

John Spencer Bassett, the editor of the *South Atlantic Quarterly*, had a different white supremacist in mind when he read *Souls*. He juxtaposed Du Bois's masterpiece with Charles Carroll's *The Negro: A Beast, or In the Image of God?* In it, Carroll stated unequivocally that the Bible, history, and science proved that "Negroes" were "beasts" who lacked "souls" and were therefore animals. Sure, he claimed, they had minds and bodies; they could speak, plan, and reason. But they lacked the divine spark, the breath of God in the form of a soul. In Bassett's opinion, there was little contest between the two texts. "A more stupid book it is impossible to conceive," he declared of *The Negro: A Beast*, "yet it is worth while to place it and its author side by side with 'The Souls of Black Folk' and its author. Can a 'beast' write a book like the latter?"[3]

Bassett's rhetorical query cut to the heart of some of the most profound questions nineteenth-century America left to the twentieth century—questions that Du Bois, Carroll, Dixon, and a host of other whites and blacks sought to answer: Were blacks connected to the divine? Did "Negroes" have souls? Was access to the sacred determined by race? Did heaven predestine white Europeans and Americans to rule over darker peoples? Were the various races created in the image of God? And had people of color contributed anything of religious value to the world?

When Du Bois published *Souls*, white supremacists and their opponents had been waging a titanic battle over the association of blackness and whiteness with sacred concepts for almost a century. To legitimate the oppression of African Americans—whether in the form of enslavement or in racial seg-

regation—whites crafted a variety of religious and theological rationales for structures of exploitation. At first, white supremacists tended to focus on particular scriptural narratives for evidence that God cursed people of African descent and blessed those of European heritage. Yet, as the century wore on, theologians, ministers, and scientists expanded their religious justification for racial oppression. They began to view the entire Bible as a "white man's book." They advanced creation myths that whites were the only true humans and that people of color were soulless animals or in league with Satan. By 1900, white supremacist theology was firmly rooted in white American mainstream culture. Its arguments and ways of perceiving the world permeated scientific, missionary, and literary discourse in the United States.

Throughout the nineteenth century, a number of African Americans tried their utmost to counter white supremacist theology. They composed religious interpretations that linked people of color with the biblical Israelites, and they highlighted the importance of Africa in the Bible. Yet, before Du Bois, black opponents of white supremacy tended to accept the terrain of the discussion—which meant a focus on biblical exegesis and assessments of Africa. They had great difficulty breaking free of racist interpretive traditions, often replicating many of their key features.

With *The Souls of Black Folk*, Du Bois dove headfirst into the ferocious debate. His penetrating analysis of the United States and of African American religion, music, and culture contradicted the theories of white supremacists at every turn. In the process, he fashioned a new set of conceptual tools for champions of equality and social justice. Read in dialogue with the religious battle over the sacred status of whites and blacks, *Souls* stood as a spectacular intervention, an act of religious defiance and theological creation at the very same moment. Du Bois attacked white supremacists by reversing their spiritual and racialized assessment of the world. With *Souls*, Du Bois tried to tear apart the conflation of whiteness and godliness and, conversely, to connect blackness with the divine. In Du Bois's hands, the story of Africans in America was one that demonstrated that white society, not black society, was morally corrupt and that people of color possessed souls that had much to teach humanity. Focusing on the creativity, endurance, and resourcefulness of black Americans and elevating their political and social aspirations to spiritual realms, he presented American history and culture in new terms. Du Bois, moreover, accomplished much more than defying the tenets of white supremacist theology, which itself was an extraordinary accomplishment based on how deeply white supremacy had pervaded American culture. He

also redrew the lines of debate by shifting away from biblical exegesis and biblical prophecy. Instead, using history, cultural studies, and sociology, Du Bois established new terrain to address questions about race and the soul.

Although religion clearly stood at the center of Du Bois's analysis in *Souls*, it is difficult to assess what, if anything, the text disclosed about his personal spiritual beliefs. He wrote and pieced together *Souls* during the time of his "spiritual upturning" as he described it in "The Shadow of Years." Some of the essays contained autobiographical reflections and accounts, and a great deal of the narrative's rhetoric implied that Du Bois shared the soul life he lauded in the text. Yet while he used religious rhetoric, idioms, and themes throughout the book in ways that contradicted white supremacist theology, it was not necessarily the case that Du Bois articulated any individual belief in the divine or transcendent. It is apparent, however, that he presented himself as a prophet and seemed to hope that readers would approach the book as a religious offering. The book may not have been about the soul of W. E. B. Du Bois, but much of his spiritual life and aspirations shined through its pages.

Souls entered the U.S. cultural landscape as a sacred text. A variety of white and black Americans read it as having spiritual power, and Du Bois was honored time and again as a prophet endowed with sacred insight. Readers found his predictions of racial difficulties and alienation alarmingly accurate and his assessment of the evils of materialism compelling. For many African Americans, *Souls* took a place in their religious canon alongside the Bible, while at least one white supremacist denounced *Souls* as the fanatical utterances of a man in cahoots with the devil. Whether blasting *Souls* or worshipping it, these readers demonstrated that it had the power to reveal and transform—and that Du Bois would be regarded as a spiritual leader for the rest of his career, a position that Du Bois never renounced. With *Souls*, he established himself as an American prophet called by God to shed new light on the souls of white and black folk.

At heart, the reception of *Souls*, the work itself, and the century-long battle over racialized associations of the sacred reveal something entirely new about race in America. Racial conceptions were not just about seeing or perceiving supposed physical differences and considering those differences to be immutable and passed biologically from one generation to the next. More deeply, "race" in the nineteenth and early twentieth centuries served as an alleged window into sacred and cosmic realities. Through skin tone, hair texture, lip size, brow angle, and an assortment of other supposed physical differences, Americans sought to find cosmic meanings—to see God's and Satan's imprints on humankind. White supremacists classified people of Af-

rican descent as racially subordinate—not only to exploit them economically but also to link whiteness to the divine. Du Bois's *Souls* cast a new vision, a new spiritual sight. It offered a new way of seeing race and the spiritual realities behind it.

White Gods and Black Demons in Nineteenth-Century America

When *Souls* burst onto the marketplace of American literature, it ran directly against more than seventy years of white supremacist theology and culture. Throughout the nineteenth century, a host of ministers, theologians, scientists, and authors worked religious ideas into every nook and cranny of racial categories. They strove to sanctify the enslavement of African Americans, the master status of whites, the segregation of emancipated people of color, and the brutal extra-legal lynchings of black men, women, and children. At first, white supremacists focused on a few biblical narratives, especially the story of Noah and his sons. Yet, as the century wore on, white supremacists became more aggressive. They reinterpreted the entire Bible to serve their desires, and, by the turn of the century, the conflation of whiteness and godliness had become so powerful in the white supremacist imagination that every prominent and admirable character in the Bible was declared white, even Jesus himself. "Negroes" were written out of the human family and denounced as soulless beasts.

The use of the Bible to legitimate the enslavement of Africans and their descendants began in earnest in the early nineteenth century. Confronting a rising abolitionist movement in the North that denounced slavery as anti-Christian, and acknowledging the crucial economic role slavery played in the cotton kingdom, proponents of slavery drew on an assortment of scriptural passages that supported master-slave relationships. They looked to Saint Paul's instructions to the church at Ephesus that slaves should "obey their masters." And they highlighted the countless examples of enslavement in the Old Testament. Yet proslavery whites desired more than support for slavery in general. They wanted validation for the particular bondage of Africans and the rule of whites. Proslavery theorists sought biblical evidence that holding Africans and their children in bondage and that mastery for whites was not just supportable, but sacred.[4]

To prove that God desired both the permanent enslavement of Africans and the divine ruler status of whites, proslavery writers turned to the story of Noah and his interactions with his sons after the great flood of the ninth

chapter of the Book of Genesis. This chapter detailed the bizarre events following the deluge, when Noah's children repopulated the postdiluvian world. After Noah, his family, and the animals left the ark and after God had made a covenant with Noah that never again would the entire earth be flooded, Noah planted a vineyard. Drinking too heavily from the fruit he cultivated, however, Noah became inebriated and fell asleep without clothing. His son Ham, the father of Cush, Egypt, Put, and Canaan, found Noah lying naked and proceeded to inform Noah's other two sons, Shem and Japheth. These two covered Noah, and the next morning when Noah awoke, he uttered words that became indispensable to the proslavery cause in the United States:

> Cursed be Canaan;
>   a slave of slaves shall he be to his brothers.
>   ...
> Blessed by the Lord my God be Shem;
>   and let Canaan be his slave.
> God enlarge Japheth,
>   and let him dwell in the tents of Shem;
>   and let Canaan be his slave.[5]

Following Noah's litany of blessings and curses, the Book of Genesis then detailed where the descendants of Ham, Japheth, and Shem proceeded to settle. For thousands of years, biblical interpreters have maintained that these passages disclosed the settlement of Africa by Ham's descendants, Europe by Japheth's, and Asia by Shem's. Genesis 9 was also read to explain differences in skin color among population groups—that either in the womb or because of the curses, Ham's skin was made black and Japheth's white. Although this narrative was riddled with ambiguity, including why Ham's son Canaan received Noah's wrath and not Ham himself or his other sons, white American readers fixated on it as divine sanction for racialized slavery in the United States.[6]

This biblical tale became central to the defense of slavery in antebellum America. Referring to it as the "curse of Canaan," the "curse of Ham," or "Noah's curse," historians have misled readers to think Genesis 9 functioned only to legitimate racial slavery. It did much more than that. The passage was read to contain not only a "curse," but a "blessing" and a "prophecy" as well. With a few creative interpolations, the tale seemed to accomplish all of the cultural work that white supremacists desired. Noah's words were read to suggest that blackness was divinely and permanently cursed and that people of African descent were destined to slavery. The blessing of Japheth, conversely, became

religious justification for white mastery. In 1843, for instance, New Yorker Josiah Priest considered Noah's tale to be evidence that God had ordained white mastery and black slavery. Racial differences and hierarchies, Priest wrote, "pleased the Divine will."[7]

Another white writer rewrote the narrative to suggest that Ham actually begged for the enslavement of himself and his children. This Ham acknowledged his own heathenism and hoped that Japheth would teach his descendants the ways of the Lord. "Take us then and mould us to your will," he begged. "Think for us; guide us; teach us our duty to the God whom we have forgotten and who had made you what you are. Take care of us and our little ones."[8] With biblical renderings like this, slavery and mastery were transformed from economic necessities or traditional social arrangements into sacred trusts. The master-slave society was an obligation to God filled with redemptive relationships: people of color could find salvation only through contact with whites, and whites were serving God by enslaving Africans.

Although it was not a terribly prevalent belief in the antebellum era, some took Noah's curse and blessing to mean that whites had souls, while blacks did not. When approached about teaching Christianity to his slaves, one slave master responded: "You niggers have no souls, you are just like those cattle, when you die there is an end of you, there is [nothing] more for you to think about than living." This view, however, seemed uncommon in the years before the Civil War. Most southern whites seemed to accept that people of color were human and had souls but were just cursed to permanent enslavement.[9]

Racialized readings of Genesis 9 did not satisfy all nineteenth-century white supremacists, however, especially those who valued scientific evidence as well as biblical teachings to determine the origins and differentiation of the races. Other than abolitionists who invoked Acts 17:26 that God had made all peoples "of one blood" and therefore no peoples were predestined for enslavement, the most sustained criticism of this Genesis explanation came from scientists such as Samuel Morton, George Robins Gliddon, Josiah Nott, and Louis Agassiz. Using a variety of data (often manipulated data), such as bones, skulls, and world histories, they maintained that the various races of the world did not originate from a single moment or location but from many. The theory of "polygenesis" asserted that the various races of humanity emerged in different geographical areas at distinct moments in time. Each group, moreover, was endowed with its own particular intellectual and religious abilities.[10]

To these scientists, "Caucasians" were innately blessed with intellectual creativity, abstract thought, and religious genius, while "Negroes" were characterized as subhuman and fundamentally irreligious. Gliddon and Nott wrote,

for instance, that "a man must be blind not to be struck by similitudes between some of the lower races of mankind, viewed as connecting links in the animal kingdom; nor can it be rationally affirmed, that the Orang-Outan and Chimpanzee are more widely separated from certain African and Oceanic Negroes than are the latter from the Teutonic or Pelasgic types." Physical differences, moreover, had their parallel with religious differences. "Many of the African, and all of the Oceanic Negroes," Gliddon and Nott continued, "possess only the crudest and most groveling superstitions."[11] Thus, whites and blacks did not have common ancestors—either biologically or spiritually.

By the middle of the nineteenth century, a clear racialized religious worldview had developed, a worldview that endeavored with theology, biblical criticism, and scientific findings to dissociate blackness and godliness and to link whiteness with the sacred. The Bible, theology, and science became ways not only to explain or create differences among humans, but also to then use those differences to see the spiritual realm. Polygenesists and proslavery theologians alike claimed that their evidence and racial categories provided spiritual sight into souls, the will of God, and the heaven-directed structure of human society.

But whether endorsing polygenesis or racialized readings of Genesis 9, mid-century white supremacists had their share of opponents. White abolitionists, such as Theodore Weld and Angelina Grimké, denounced slavery as inconsistent with biblical teachings and proclaimed proslavery forces to be like demons. Although slavery "seeks refuge in the Bible," they wrote, "it shrinks from the hated light, and howls under the consuming touch, as demons recoiled from the Son of God and shrieked, 'Torment us not.'"[12] Some northern whites even mocked proslavery religion outright. During the Civil War, for example, a popular tune "The New Jim Crow Song, About the Darkies and the War," derided southerners for using the Bible to support slavery and to assert that people of color were soulless.

> If the darkey has no human soul, as we do of'n hear,
> The dev'l may get the master, but the darkey will get clear.
>   ...
> The dixies pick out scripture to prove that slav'ry's right,
> But they do make a bad mistake—that shows they'r not so bright.
> They say because the Bible did once the Jews allow
> To get bondsmen of the heathen, that bondage should be now.
> Why should dixies not be slaves, if their argument is true,
> For who were their ancient fathers? They were heathens too.

Ultimately, this song suggested that southern whites were creating a new religion in the defense of slavery:

> They teach amalgamation and chicken fighting too;
> They soon will teach a Bible new—they find the old won't do.[13]

African Americans in the North and the South also took up the fight against proslavery religion and science with their own religious arguments. As historian Mia Bay has shown, blacks were well aware that white supremacists refused to accept that people of color had souls with the full imprint of God.[14] Two of the most articulate opponents of white supremacist theology were Reverend Alexander Crummell and Reverend Edward Blyden. Although both of these men were adamant spokesmen for African American missionary work to Africa, they did not oppose depictions of modern-day Africans as generally uncivilized. Yet they resented the claims that white Americans were true Christians and that Africans were beyond redemption. They argued that racial categories and perceptions did not provide a window into spiritual realms.

Crummell, whom Du Bois lionized in *The Souls of Black Folk*, based his critique of white supremacy on the conviction that no fundamental differences existed between African Americans and other peoples. "We children of Africa in this land are no way different from any other people," he maintained in a Thanksgiving sermon in 1875. "Many of the differences of race are slight and incidental, and ofttimes become obliterated by circumstances, positions, and religion." Crummell followed this claim by denouncing the notion that people of color were divinely cursed. He stated emphatically, "The Negro race nowhere on this globe, is a doomed race!" In fact, the Bible and human history according to Crummell demonstrated that blacks were "destined" to be "superior" to other races.[15]

In his 1862 speech "The Call of Providence to the Descendants of Africa in America," Blyden acknowledged that Africa was "forlorn" and suffered from a "degraded moral condition." Yet when he considered Genesis 9 and other biblical passages, Blyden found evidence that the condition of Africa would not be poor forever. In Blyden's estimation, history showed that because God's blessing of Japheth had come true (Europeans had conquered much of the globe) then the promises offered to the descendants of Shem and Ham would also be realized. The divine pledges to Asians and Africans, furthermore, were more profound than those given to Japheth, for they were of a spiritual nature, rather than a material one. "The promise to Ethiopia, or Ham, is like

that to Shem, of a spiritual kind," Blyden maintained. "It refers not to physi-cal strength, not to large and extensive domains, not to foreign conquests, not to wide-spread domination, but to the possession of spiritual qualities, to the elevation of the soul heavenward, to spiritual aspirations and divine communication." For Blyden, the biblical passage Psalm 68:31, which stated that "Ethiopia shall stretch forth her hands unto God," stood as the ultimate prophecy that Africa would one day experience a religious renaissance. In another speech, Blyden once again voiced his belief that the sons and daugh-ters of Africa had a spiritual blessing. Blyden went so far as to suggest that, similar to the biblical Jews, people of color were being prepared by God in their oppression to convey a sacred message to the world. "Only one race has furnished the prophets for humanity—the Hebrew race; and before they were qualified to do this they had to go down to the depths of servile degradation. . . . But for the special work of each race the prophets arise among the people themselves." For Blyden, the condition of African Americans, not their al-leged racial features, suggested a link to God and God's people.[16]

Yet for all of their counter-readings of Genesis 9 and their use of other biblical passages to attack white supremacist theology, mid-century African Americans and abolitionists tended to accept the general tripartite division of the human population allegedly outlined in Genesis and the belief that God affiliated with the races in different ways. Benjamin Tucker Tanner expressed this belief even while denouncing whites for their evil ways and calling on God to help people of color in his 1891 poem, "Prayer to Jesu":

> Almighty Jesu, change proud Japheth's heart —
> Make him to know that Thou a Brother art
> To Shem and Ham, the Yellow and the Black.
> From him Thy throne's great face O hold not back.
>
> Almighty Jesu, stay proud Japheth's hand —
> Upraised and dominant in ev'ry land
> He goes—but not for love of Thee and God.
> In pride he scorns to kiss Messiah's rod.
>
> Almighty Jesu, Thou of Shemite blood,
> Remember, O remember Shem, for good;
> Thou Priest, like to Melchizedek, who came
> Of Ham, remember, O remember Ham.[17]

Although Tanner connected African Americans with the divine by associating the Hebrew Bible priest Melchizedek with Ham, and although Tanner denounced whites as uncaring and dictatorial, he remained attached to biblical studies and to the assumption that the Bible conveyed a message that God dealt differently with each race.

While Blyden, Crummell, and a host of others challenged racist biblical interpretations, the Civil War altered how religion functioned in the process of racial formation. The Civil War and emancipation drastically shifted the terrain of racialized associations of the sacred and the profane. Slavery's death detached the legal status of enslavement from African Americans and thus made biblical mandates for slavery socially irrelevant. Black freedom forced white supremacists to develop a new theology, or perhaps to broaden that which they had already established. This new theology was more diabolical than any of its scientific or theological predecessors. To justify racial segregation, disfranchisement, and lynching, white supremacists shifted the weight of their biblical arguments away from defending slavery and toward declaring that African Americans were soulless creatures. In this sacred view, blacks were transformed from heathens into demons, and white men and women became more than masters—they were imagined as demigods themselves.

Rather than suggest that God created the various human races at different locations or that the Lord had created whites and blacks with Noah's children, a body of white supremacist theologians claimed that people of color were not "people" at all. They were the "beasts of the field" created before the molding of the first man and woman, Adam and Eve, who were the only beings made "in God's image" in the Genesis account. The beasts may look and act similar to humans, but they were not humans. These theologians further suggested that the greatest sin was sexuality between (white) humans and (black) beasts. The social implications of this theology were clear—any law, custom, or argument that smacked of social, legal, civic, or religious equality must be opposed, for they would invariably lead to interracial sexuality. By the time *The Souls of Black Folk* was available to the reading public, these new white supremacist teachings had become a staple element of fin-de-siècle American culture.

By re-rendering the Genesis account of creation as one in which whites were the only true humans and people of color were beasts, postwar white supremacist theologians tied whiteness to godliness in unprecedented ways. They maintained that every human character in the Bible was white, that whites were God's highest creations, and that only whites were spiritually redeemable. In *The Negro: What Is His Ethnological Status?* a work of white su-

premacist theology just as interested in the status of whites as of Negroes, one writer claimed, "Noah was also white, with long, straight hair, etc. . . . Adam and Eve were white—with long, straight hair, high foreheads, high noses and thin lips. Our Saviour was also white." Because Adam, Eve, and Christ were white, these writers asserted that the Bible's plan of salvation solely applied to whites. "It was Adam's blood which was in the veins of our Saviour," wrote another theologian. "It was Adam's race that was to be regenerated and redeemed. If there are any other races that fell, and are to be redeemed, God's Word gives no account of them." Having white-washed the Bible through and through, these writers proceeded to claim that whites were God's most cherished creation and had divine qualities. "The Caucasian never was a savage," claimed another supremacist, "The Caucasian was endowed with a high aesthetic faculty, the love of the beautiful." And, finally, "The pure Caucasian stands alone, in his character and his achievement."[18]

While these theologians and ministers deified whiteness, they declared "Negroes" to be members of the animal kingdom who were devoid of souls and perhaps associated with spiritual evil. Lutheran minister G. C. H. Hasskarl described Africa as a place of "every form of human degradation . . . and full of demoniac superstitions" in his *"The Missing Link?" or The Negro's Ethnological Status.* Hasskarl not only maintained that Christians should refrain from missionary work to Africa because soulless Africans could not be redeemed but also that God hated black people. The Bible, he maintained, demonstrated God's "decided disapprobation of the Negro" and "those various attempts to elevate him to social, political and religious equality with the white race." Hasskarl even linked "Negroes" with the kingdom of Satan when he denounced them for their "Sodomite nature and satanic aptitudes." White supremacist theologians such as Hasskarl and Charles Carroll traced the connection between Negroes and evil back to the Garden of Eden, claiming that the "tempter of Eve" was a black "beast of the field" that betrayed Eve's trust.[19]

For white supremacist theologians, their interpretation of the sacred identity of whites and the soulless status of blacks led them to assail any form of racial equality. They especially feared that equality would lead to interracial sexuality, and they spun sex, race, and religion into an intricate web of oppression and control. Some white supremacists blamed the first human sin on a sexual encounter between Eve and a "beast of the field," while others suggested that God punished civilizations for miscegenation between whites and blacks. Attacks on "amalgamation" had the explicit purpose of warning whites in the United States against social equality and interracial sexuality, because they would allegedly lead to the downfall of the white American na-

tion. "In all ages of his history, man has shown a strong disposition to cultivate the most criminal relations with this beast," warned Charles Carroll. "Their indulgence in these shameless crimes not only led God to destroy nation after nation from the face of the earth, but has even led Him to obliterate continents; it frequently occurs that God in His wrath and disgust, decrees that peoples who abandon themselves to these degrading crimes, shall die violent deaths; and that their flesh shall furnish food for this man-eating ape."[20] By declaring whites true humans and blacks subhuman, sexual interaction between whites and blacks was transformed into a sin of bestiality, one that could bring the wrath of God. Thus, the policing of white and black sexuality became a sacred imperative, and white women became symbols and captives of the white holiness they embodied and transmitted to their offspring.

Typically, historians characterize these types of arguments as the province of the cranks and the crazies, the ranting of white supremacist fanatics out of step with the rest of American society. Yet notions of the innate deviltry of people of color and the sacredness of whites abounded in American culture by the early twentieth century. In fact, it seemed to be almost a part of the nation's cultural blood. It is difficult to determine the circulation of books like *The Negro: A Beast* or *"The Missing Link,"* but there is ample proof that they were widely read and culturally influential. The editor of the *South Atlantic Quarterly*, for instance, admitted that Carroll's *The Negro: A Beast* "has had a wide sale and approval among the mass of the white people of the South." During investigative trips through the South, journalist Ray Stannard Baker found Carroll's work gaining notoriety and encouraging the lynchings of black men. Minister and religious writer H. Paul Douglass likewise claimed in 1909 that Carroll's work "has become the Scripture of tens of thousands of poor whites, and its doctrine is maintained with an appalling stubbornness and persistence."[21]

Perhaps more telling than book sales, however, was that white supremacist theological notions about racial differences and hierarchy could be observed working in a number of cultural venues. American supporters of missionary work outside of the United States, for instance, echoed the racial views of Carroll and Hasskarl. One white missionary referred to foreign peoples of color as "children of the forests," and another described the individuals he encountered in the field as "Charles Darwin's missing link."[22] And, of course, white Americans cheered Rudyard Kipling's description of colonized peoples as "half devil and half child" in his poem "The White Man's Burden."[23] Reverend A. T. Pierson, a prominent American minister, probably put it most bluntly and disturbingly when he asserted that "some of the unevangelized

races seem on too low a level to be lifted even by the lever of the gospel. . . . In some not only the image of God, but the image of man, was defaced, if not effaced; they were dumb beasts for shamelessness and wild beasts for brutality and ferocity, not only dehumanized but demonized."[24] Pierson, in short, seemed to believe what Carroll preached—that people of color did not bear the imprint of the divine creator and that one could see these sacred truths through racial perceptions.

Probably the most striking example of white supremacist theology in American literature was Thomas Dixon's *The Leopard's Spots: A Romance of the White Man's Burden, 1865–1900*, a best-selling novel of the era. In it, the former Baptist minister Dixon advanced the main points of the white supremacist theologians by portraying American history from the Civil War to the turn of the century as evidence of the soullessness of people of color and the godliness of whites. Dixon set the tone for the novel with its title and opening inscription based on Jeremiah 12:23—"Can the Ethiopian change his skin or the leopard his spots"—a verse widely invoked by white supremacists in the nineteenth century as biblical proof that God had ordained racial difference and hierarchy. The title and inscription served as a rebuke to whites and blacks who continued to carry hopes that African Americans could find equality and uplift alongside whites in the United States.[25]

From start to finish, Dixon characterized African Americans as beasts in *The Leopard's Spots*. Describing the prevailing mood in the white South following the war, he wrote, "In every one of these soldiers' hearts, and over the earth, hung the shadow of the free Negro, transformed by the exigency of war from a Chattel, to be bought and sold, into a possible Beast to be feared and guarded." On another occasion, a former Confederate soldier recalled seeing African Americans during the war as similar to animals: "their black ape-faces grinnin' and makin' fun of poor whites." Dixon also likened blacks to death and pestilence. To one southern preacher, "the freed Negro" seemed to cast "its shadow over future generations, a veritable Black Death for the land and its people." The character "Dick," whom Dixon described as the "new negro" that emerged after the war, embodied the degeneration, sinfulness, and animality of African Americans. In the novel, Dick had no history, no background. Where he came from, no one knew. But his moral qualities were easy to identify. He was wicked and perhaps demonic. As one white woman commented, "He steals everything he can get his hands on. . . . He's the greatest liar I ever saw." Dick's bestiality was further evidenced by his abduction and rape of a white girl. When Dick was caught, moreover, the leader of the lynch mob minced no words when he declared that Dick was a "black devil."[26]

Dixon contrasted the immorality of African Americans with the godliness of white supremacy's defenders, namely the Ku Klux Klan. Dixon presented a vigorous moral defense of the Klan. In his hands, it was transformed from a vigilante group that bullied and murdered hundreds of whites and blacks in the postwar South into a heroic band of saintly crusaders called by God to redeem Dixie. In the novel, the rape of the young white girl served as "the trumpet of the God of our fathers that will call the sleeping manhood of the Anglo-Saxon race to life again." The Klan's purpose was divine, Dixon maintained, "to bring order out of chaos, protect weak and defenseless, the widows and orphans of brave men who had died for their country, to drive from power the thieves who were robbing the people, redeem the commonwealth from infamy, and reestablish civilization."[27]

Ultimately, with *The Leopard's Spots*, Dixon sought to inculcate the lesson that white Americans were God's chosen people, that different races could not live together in equality, and that people of color were destined to be either ruled or ruined. "Sooner or later we must squarely face the fact that two such races, counting millions in numbers, cannot live together under a Democracy," Dixon spoke through one of his characters. God had demanded that the greater races rule over the weaker ones. As this character continued, "We believe that God has raised up our race, as he ordained Israel of old, in this world-crisis to establish and maintain for weaker races, as a trust for civilisation, the principles of civil and religious Liberty and the forms of Constitutional Government."[28]

By the beginning of the twentieth century, the white supremacist theology of Dixon, Carroll, and others had penetrated deeply into the religious, social, and literary imagination of white Americans. From the portrayals of people of color in novels and missionary literature to religious pamphlets and treatises, this theology worked to sanctify Jim Crow, disfranchisement, violence, and racial hatred. African Americans had responded by rereading the narratives of Genesis 9, by seeking to defend Africa's history and future, and by denouncing whites as wicked evildoers, but they had been largely unable to touch the soul of white America. White supremacists and their opponents were locked in a battle of sacred vision—all seeking to find biblical, scientific, or historical evidence to connect racial categories with the sacred and profane.

It is one of American history's most fascinating ironies that W. E. B. Du Bois disrupted this entire debate as no other individual had. That an African American professor at Atlanta University, who had selected Harvard and the University of Berlin instead of a seminary education and whose religious faith had been questioned time and again, launched such a new assault on white

supremacist theology is one of the great paradoxes of American religious history. It also demonstrates the religious brilliance of W. E. B. Du Bois. He was able not only to see racial and religious constructions in new ways but also to open the spiritual eyes of so many readers.

W. E. B. Du Bois Strikes Back

The Souls of Black Folk confronted white supremacist theology in a dramatic and an extraordinary way. At its most profound level, *Souls* offered its readers a new way to view their selves, their society, their world, and the connections between religion and racial beliefs. Although Du Bois did not name Dixon or Carroll in *Souls*, he acknowledged that the question of African American humanity and spirituality was a pressing one for him and people of color. In one of his essays, he recognized that a belief circulated among whites that "Negroes" were somehow created between man and animal. Southern whites especially seemed to hold "the sincere and passionate belief that somewhere between men and cattle, God created a *tertium quid* [something that defies classification, usually between two groups], and called it a Negro." For African Americans, this white supremacist belief led to questions of black humanity. Blacks wonder, Du Bois asserted, whether "after all, the World is right and we are less than men?"[29]

Rather than turn to biblical passages or to ancient history, Du Bois focused on what he knew best—race relations and the history of people of color in the United States. When looking at the past and present of the lives of black folk in America, he found evidence of precisely the opposite of what white supremacist theologians had maintained. Du Bois discerned the profound immorality of whites and the deep spirituality of African Americans. Steeped in biblical language and prophetic utterances, Du Bois's work inaugurated a new front in the battle against white supremacist theology. He denounced white society as fundamentally sinful, while alternatively underscoring the spirituality of people of color. With its structure, rhetoric, focus, and metaphors, *Souls* inverted the principal arguments of white supremacist theologians and did so with a new set of religious arguments, ones that spiritually dramatized the modern history of race relations in the United States. In this way, Du Bois offered a view of cosmic realities without the clouds of white supremacy.[30]

Du Bois cast his first stone at white supremacist theology with the title of his essay collection. While most scholars have paid attention to Du Bois's use of the word "Folk," revealing Du Bois's interest in notions of racialized nation-

hood circulating in Germany at the time, his specific use of the word "Souls" carried greater significance. This one word set the tone for his assault not only on white supremacist theology but also on the totality of American culture. While others wondered whether blacks had souls, Du Bois had no doubt. Moreover, his book promised to be about those souls. The title also signaled that Du Bois sought to look beyond the physical realities of his subject matter. He wanted to peer deeper, higher, and beyond. He wanted to glimpse and reveal the spiritual realms of life and living. With clarion simplicity, Du Bois's title launched a new attack on white supremacist theology.

Du Bois characterized himself as a modern-day prophet and the book as a sacred revelation with the "forethought." He began *Souls* with his now heralded line that "the problem of the Twentieth Century is the problem of the color-line." This was, in many ways, prophecy. Stated as a direct truth about the future, Du Bois depicted this pivotal statement as prophetic years later. "It was a pert phrase," he recalled in 1925, "which I then liked and which since I have often rehearsed to myself, asking how far was it prophecy and how far speculation?"[31] In *Souls*, Du Bois then proceeded to cast himself as one endowed to reveal the truth about this "problem" to the people. "Leaving, then, the world of the white man, I have stepped within the Veil," he wrote, "raising it that you may view faintly its deeper recesses,—the meaning of its religion, the passion of its human sorrow, and the struggle of its greater souls."[32] The book's purpose, and Du Bois's vocation, was to display the spiritual side of black life, the side that white supremacist theologians denied even existed, the side that could only be viewed by first believing that people of color had souls.

Du Bois linked his work to that of biblical texts in several other ways in the forethought. He set *Souls* in the tradition of a biblical epistle by prefacing his work with a letter to the readers, a common literary trope for early Christians and biblical texts, but not one common in American letters. "I pray you, then, receive my little book in all charity," he wrote, "studying my words with me, forgiving mistake and foible for sake of the faith and passion that is in me, and seeking the grain of truth hidden there." Finally, Du Bois concluded his introduction by connecting himself to black America with rhetoric taken directly from the second chapter of Genesis: "And, finally, need I add that I who speak here am bone of the bone and flesh of the flesh of them that live within the Veil?" Revoicing Adam's words upon first seeing Eve with this rhetorical question, Du Bois aligned himself with a biblical character deemed by white supremacist theologians a "white man." Du Bois reversed this association by using the language to connect himself biologically and spiritually with

African Americans.[33] Working in combination with the book's title and the chapter titles, the forethought instructed readers on new ways of seeing and perceiving: black folk had souls; people of color were spiritually connected in sacred ways; and Du Bois was no mere scholar but a biblical and prophetic writer with the power to reveal the unseen and sacred.

The chapter titles, first announced in the table of contents directly following the forethought, further demonstrated that Du Bois envisioned *Souls* to be read in a religious register. By placing the preposition "of" at the beginning of each chapter title, Du Bois alluded to *The Thirty-Nine Articles of Religion of the Church of England*. First written in 1571 and then revised in the United States in 1801, this Anglican and Episcopal document outlined the cardinal beliefs of the church on such matters as the Trinity, the Bible, the Holy Spirit, and Jesus Christ.[34] With this parallel of the Anglican and Episcopal text, Du Bois signaled that *Souls* was to be taken as a new set of religious articles, a new code of faith for the new century. This book, he directed, carried holy instructions regarding life in a racially divided world. The following list shows similarities between *The Thirty-Nine Articles* and *The Souls of Black Folk*:

The Thirty-Nine Articles	*The Souls of Black Folk*
I. Of Faith in the Holy Trinity	I. Of Our Spiritual Strivings
II. Of the Word or Son of God, which was Made Man	II. Of the Dawn of Freedom
III. Of the going down of Christ into Hell	III. Of Mr. Booker T. Washington and Others
IV. Of the Resurrection of Christ	IV. Of the Meaning of Progress
V. Of the Holy Ghost	V. Of the Wings of Atalanta
VI. Of the Sufficiency of the Holy Scriptures for Salvation	VI. Of the Training of Black Men
VII. Of the Old Testament	VII. Of the Black Belt
VIII. Of the Three Creeds	VIII. Of the Quest of the Golden Fleece
IX. Of Original or Birth-Sin	IX. Of the Sons of Master and Man
X. Of Free-Will	X. Of the Faith of the Fathers
XI. Of the Justification of Man	XI. Of the Passing of the First-Born
XII. Of Good Works	XII. Of Alexander Crummell
XIII. Of Works Before Justification	XIII. Of the Coming of John
XIV. Of Works of Supererogation	XIV. The Sorrow Songs

While the title and the forethought alerted readers to the religious significance of his book, Du Bois set the theoretical and spiritual tone for the essays in the first chapter, "Of Our Spiritual Strivings." He drew on religious
idioms and symbolism to ask and address fundamental questions about what
it meant to be black in America. To him, the question that all whites wanted
to ask but were unwilling to—"How does it feel to be a problem?"—was very
much a religious concern. Considered a problem in the nation, people of col-
or wondered, "Why did God make me an outcast and a stranger in mine own
house?" The sense of being both an American and an African perplexed African Americans. This "two-ness" or "double consciousness" was both a curse
and a blessing. "It is a peculiar sensation, this double-consciousness," he maintained, "this sense of always looking at one's self through the eyes of others, of
measuring one's soul by the tape of a world that looks on in amused contempt
and pity." To Du Bois, double consciousness was an intellectual, spiritual, and
even physical problem: "One ever feels his two-ness,—an American, a Negro;
two souls, two thoughts, two unreconciled strivings; two warring ideals in
one body, whose dogged strength alone keeps it from being torn asunder."[35]

Yet African Americans were neither cursed by God, nor created as soulless
beasts. Rather, Du Bois characterized "Negroes" as God's anointed peoples
with special eyes to see the cosmic realities of everyday living. "The Negro,
is a sort of seventh son, born with a veil, and gifted with second-sight in this
American world," Du Bois declared. Referring to African Americans as "a sort
of seventh son," Du Bois alluded to the sacred status assigned to the number
seven in Jewish and Christian heritages. Because the Book of Genesis held
that God rested on the seventh day of creation, Jews had long honored the
seventh day of the week, the seventh year in a cycle, and the seventh child
born to a family. Given their sacred status, Du Bois insisted, African Americans could not disregard their African-ness or their American-ness. They carried a special revelation. "He would not Africanize America, for America has
much to teach the world and Africa. He would not bleach his Negro soul in
a flood of white Americanism, for he knows that Negro blood has a message
for the world." In short, because of their oppression, African Americans were
a special and unique race. While they bore the brunt of hatred and exploitation, they were endowed with sacred significance. Their "second-sight" was
a gift that allowed them to see beyond the myths and prejudices of modern
America, and their status as a "sort of seventh son" marked them as God's
chosen peoples with "a message for the world."[36]

Further, by invoking the image and metaphor of the "Veil" in the first

chapter and the forethought, Du Bois demonstrated that biblical conceptions deeply influenced his theoretical view of race in the United States and the world. In the biblical Book of Exodus, which detailed the enslavement, liberation, and wanderings of the Israelites, the veil had at least two functions. The Jews placed a veil in their holy temple around the Ark of the Covenant to separate the "the holy place from the most holy" (Exodus 26:33), and Moses used a veil to shield his face from the people after he had spoken with God at Mount Sinai (Exodus 34:33–35). In biblical imagery, the veil divided the holy and the mundane, the sacred and the secular. To Du Bois, a veil of racial separation functioned similarly in America. It not only divided whites and blacks from one another but also from God.[37]

Du Bois routinely drew explicit connections between the Veil and religious ideas. During a lecture in 1897 on race relations in a Virginia town, he discussed how white Americans created a new Christian belief out of the Veil that trumped all other biblical teachings. "The Veil is ever there separating the two peoples," he asserted. "At times you may not see it—it may be too thin to notice, but it is ever there." To Du Bois, the Veil led to a new divine commandment. "And we have added an eleventh commandment to the Decalogue down here; you may have other Gods before me, you may break the kill commandment and waver around the adultery but the eleventh must not be broken; and it reads: Thou shalt not cross the Veil." Years later, Du Bois overtly connected the veil imagery to the divine in *Darkwater*. The top of the veil, he wrote, "nestles close to the throne of God." In all of the cases in which Du Bois referenced the veil, he always had African Americans cloaked behind it, and, in this way, he may have signified that people of color were the "holy of holies" in the United States or the Moses-like characters who must be hidden because of their access to God. Whites did not want to see them for what they truly were, in short, because they shone too brightly.[38]

Following his discussion of double consciousness and the veil in *Souls*, Du Bois then discussed the ways African Americans have sought freedom and self-actualization in the United States. Du Bois implored his readers to see political, social, and economic endeavors as evidence of soul and spiritual life. These were themes he returned to over and again in *Souls*. He used religious language as the primary rhetorical vehicle to discuss the efforts of African Americans. Du Bois followed a long tradition of connecting the experiences of African Americans with the biblical Israelites and also spiritualized the efforts of African Americans in an effort to show that he considered the history and culture to have spiritual relevance. When describing the hopes of enslaved African Americans for liberty, for instance, Du Bois contended, "Few

men ever worshipped Freedom with half such unquestioning faith as did the American Negro for two centuries. . . . Emancipation was the key to a promised land of sweeter beauty than ever stretched before the eyes of wearied Israelites. In song and exhortation swelled one refrain—Liberty; in his tears and curses the God he implored had Freedom in his right hand. At last it came,—suddenly, fearfully, like a dream." Yet the Civil War and the abolition of slavery neither brought African Americans to a land of milk and honey nor redeemed the soul of white America. "The Nation has not yet found peace from its sins; the freedman has not yet found in freedom his promised land," he concluded. By the turn of the century, Du Bois lamented, "The very soul of the toiling, sweating black man is darkened by the shadow of a vast despair." Hope and doubt struggled within people of color and the day when they would feel the freedom to display and stretch their souls in America still seemed distant. African Americans continued to experience "the burning of body and rendering of soul; inspiration strives with doubt, and faith with vain questionings."[39]

Concluding this first chapter and pointing toward the remainder of the book, Du Bois implored his readers to look beyond physical appearances and see the spiritual life of the United States for what it was—a morality play that pitted exploitative whites against largely virtuous blacks. He contrasted the purity of African Americans with the immoral greed of white America, asserting that "there are to-day no truer exponents of the pure human spirit of the Declaration of Independence than the American Negroes, and, all in all, we black men seem the sole oasis of simple faith and reverence in a dusty desert of dollars and smartness." Du Bois instructed his readers that *Souls* was written "with loving emphasis and deeper detail, that men may listen to the striving in the souls of black folk."[40] While the other chapters examined the problem of the color line through history, sociology, autobiography, and fiction, Du Bois hoped his readers would peer with him beyond the surface of the world of African Americans and view the sacred realm they inhabit and the spiritual elements of their lives.

From a variety of angles and vantage points, Du Bois used the rest of *Souls* to highlight the religious themes he announced in the first chapter, the forethought, and the work's title. With biblical idioms and religious rhetoric, Du Bois characterized white America as a godless and sinful nation. In one instance, he turned the poignant question that Sojourner Truth had asked Frederick Douglass during an abolitionist convention—"Is God dead?"—into an affirmative statement and directed it toward whites. The U.S. government, Du Bois contended, behaves "just as though God really were dead." This re-voic-

ing of Truth's classic question also reversed the claim that whites were divinely blessed and painted them as sinful instead. Du Bois went even further in "Of the Sons of Master and Man." He suggested that God would soon chastise the United States for racial inequality: "God seems about to punish this nation." In short, people of color were not the ones cursed by Noah, God, or nature. Rather, the divine would rebuke the white nation for its discrimination, exploitation, and hate of African Americans.[41]

Du Bois expressed specific frustration with white Christians, and he claimed—at times with more ferocity than at others—that they were hypocrites. With his attacks on white believers, however, Du Bois revealed a conviction that authentic Christianity was a religion of freedom and equality. Racial discrimination and prejudice, he wrote in "Of the Sons of Master and Man," forced southern whites to reject their most profound religious and political convictions. "Deeply religious and intensely democratic as are the masses of the whites," Du Bois asserted, "they feel acutely the false position in which the Negro problems place them. Such an essentially honest-hearted and generous people cannot cite the caste-levelling precepts of Christianity, or believe in equality of opportunity for all men, without coming to feel more and more with each generation that the present drawing of the color-line is a flat contradiction to their beliefs and professions." In another essay, Du Bois chastised both white and black Christians for failing to honor biblical teachings, especially those related to murder, theft, and adultery. Referring to the South, he wrote, "She has religion, earnest, bigoted:—religion that on both sides of the Veil often omits the sixth, seventh, and eighth commandments, but substitutes a dozen supplementary ones."[42]

Du Bois did not denounce all whites in the United States, however. He lavished praise on whites who supported people of color, especially northern missionaries to the South following the Civil War. The "crusade of the New England school-ma'am," claimed Du Bois in his chapter on the efforts of the Freedmen's Bureau to aid post–Civil War black women and men, constituted the "Ninth Crusade." Although many of their contemporaries considered their adventure "more quixotic than the quest of St. Louis to his," these teachers were godly matrons. In another essay, Du Bois described them as "saintly souls" who participated in "that finest thing in American history, and one of the few things untainted by sordid greed and cheap vainglory." These white teachers offered what Du Bois so desperately sought for whites and blacks in America, what he thought a world beyond the veil might be like—one that was marked by "the contact of living souls."[43]

One element that contemporary readers will not find in current editions of *Souls*, but that existed in its original, was blatant anti-Semitism. Repeatedly, Du Bois maintained that "the Jew" became the "heir" of the slavebaron, ruling southern plantations and the southern economy. On one occasion, he referred to Jews who moved South after the Civil War as "shrewd and unscrupulous." Fifty years after the original publication of *Souls*, following the atrocities of the Holocaust, Du Bois re-released *Souls* with nine slight alterations. Eight of those changes involved derogatory remarks about Jews. Leading Jewish financier Jacob Schiff complained to Du Bois that these passages "gave an impression of anti-Semitism," but Du Bois stoutly denied it. By 1953, however, Du Bois was ready to change. His original work, he concluded after World War II, "illustrates how easily one slips into unconscious condemnation of a whole group." Even Du Bois, it appears in this case, in 1903 was a captive to his social and religious culture.[44]

While Du Bois imagined and articulated a holy rebuke of whites (and "unconscious" attacks on Jews), he did not envision *Souls* to be a book primarily about oppression. *Souls* was a celebration of black life and spirit, one that contradicted the insights of white supremacist theology with new ways of seeing African Americans and their unique and sacred status. To understand the heart and soul of the southern black community, Du Bois often looked to the church. He considered it the focal point of rural black society. As he wrote in "Of the Meaning of Progress," while the homes of local blacks "were scattered rather aimlessly," the "twin temples of the hamlet, the Methodist, and the Hard-Shell Baptist churches" served as the center of the community. In another essay he claimed, "The Negro church of to-day is the social centre of Negro life in the United States, and the most characteristic expression of African character." Beyond the church, African American religious values expressed the inner lives of people of color. It was "the expression of the inner ethical life of a people."[45]

In opposition to white supremacists who claimed that people of African descent had no discernible or valuable religious history, Du Bois maintained that African Americans had a long religious heritage that extended back to western Africa. The religious life of West Africans, Du Bois instructed, was dominated by "nature worship, with profound belief in invisible surrounding influences, good and bad." The process of enslavement, however, fundamentally altered the faiths of African Americans. The slave ship and the plantation rocked their trust in the power of their ancestors and their home deities. The "Negro church" developed by combining African and Christian rituals and

beliefs. Over time, especially after emancipation, the Negro church became a vast empire, where "considerable sums of money are collected and expended here, employment is found for the idle, strangers are introduced, news is disseminated and charity distributed. . . . The Church often stands as a real conserver of morals, a strengthener of family life, and the final authority on what is Good and Right." And to him, the study of black religion was fundamental to the comprehension of black society. According to Du Bois, examining the history and progression of African American religion provided insight into the most profound elements of existence. "What did slavery mean to the African savage? What was his attitude toward the World and Life? What seemed to him good and evil,—God and devil? Whither went his longings and strivings, and wherefore were his heart-burnings and disappoints?"[46]

Du Bois delved even more deeply into the cultural and social importance of black religion in his analysis of "the Sorrow Songs." To him, the sacred songs created by African slaves and their children were not mere tunes to sing the day away or escape from the world. They were "real poetry" that held deep "meaning beneath conventional theology and unmeaning rhapsody." The songs, such as "Steal Away Home," "March On," and "A Great Camp Meeting in the Promised Land," were the most profound spiritual contribution the United States had given to the world. "The Negro-folk song," Du Bois claimed, "stands to-day not simply as the sole American music, but as the most beautiful expression of human experience born this side of the seas. . . . It still remains as the singular spiritual heritage of the nation and the greatest gift of the Negro people." The spirituals, Du Bois maintained, showed that people of color felt the entire range of human emotions, that they had the divine spark in their souls. The songs demonstrated the "soul-hunger," or the need to be connected with the sacred and with other humans, of African Americans. The songs demonstrated that blacks felt fear and hope and proved that people of color were authentically human and had a special connection to the divine.[47]

Black religion in the United States was also crucial to Du Bois, for it stood against one of the chief sins of white American culture: greed. "In the Black World," Du Bois maintained in yet another essay, "the Preacher and Teacher embodied once the idea of this people,—the strife for another and a juster world, the vague dream of righteousness, the mystery of knowing." Yet in the present day, "the danger is that these ideals, with their simple beauty and weird inspiration, will suddenly sink to a question of cash and a lust for gold." With a series of rhetorical questions, Du Bois juxtaposed the religious idealism of African American culture with the greed of white society to warn African

Americans from turning to riches. "What if the Negro people be wooed from a strife for righteousness, from a love of knowing, to regard dollars as the be-all and end-all of life? What if to the Mammonism of America be added the rising Mammonism of the re-born South, and the Mammonism of this South be re-inforced by the budding Mammonism of the half-awakened black millions?" In place of the "Gospel of Prosperity," Du Bois encouraged people of color to hold fast to the "Gospel of Sacrifice" as the most powerful focus of life.[48]

Du Bois's disdain for materialism was a fundamental element in his attack on Booker T. Washington, perhaps now the most well-known aspect of *Souls*. Du Bois criticized black leaders when he believed that they were leading the community to imitate the ways of materialistic whites. He opposed Washington, in part, on grounds of religious hatred for the acquisition of goods and objects. To Du Bois, Washington advanced a "Gospel of Prosperity." "Mr. Washington's programme naturally takes an economic cast," Du Bois asserted, "becoming a gospel of Work and Money to such an extent as apparently almost completely to overshadow the higher aims of life." On the occasions when Washington encouraged "Thrift, Patience, and Industrial training for the masses," Du Bois maintained that black Americans should act as the biblical Jews. They should "hold up" Washington's "hands and strive with him, rejoicing in his honors and glorying in the strength of this Joshua called of God and of man to lead the headless host." But as firmly as African Americans should support Washington on these occasions, they should battle him when he opposed civil rights and higher education for people of color.[49]

Conversely, Du Bois lauded black leaders who accepted pain and suffering by remaining true to their convictions. With the chapter "Of Alexander Crummell," Du Bois focused on the career of one African American to dramatize the spiritual strivings and frustrations of even well educated people of color. Born in 1819 in New York, Crummell attended an interracial school as a child and then in the mid-1830s decided to join the Episcopal priesthood. Rejected by the General Theological Seminary because he was black, Crummell studied privately and became a minister in 1844. He spent the next forty-four years of his career traveling to England and Liberia as a missionary and fundraiser. He was an outspoken critic of white supremacy, and he was invested in the rehabilitation of Africa. He died in 1898, one year after founding the American Negro Academy. In Du Bois's hands, the tale of Crummell showed that African Americans had bright souls and exquisite religious leaders, but also that white supremacy circumscribed their spiritual lives. Focusing on Crummell's religious struggles (as Du Bois also did in his discussion of his grandfather Alexander in "The Shadow of Years"), Du Bois combated white

supremacist theology at every turn. By highlighting an African American religious personality, he demonstrated that people of color had souls touched by God, informed by God, and with words to lead others to God.[50]

Du Bois linked Crummell with Christ and all of humanity. "This is the story of a human heart," Du Bois intoned with the first sentence. Just as Jesus had been tempted on three occasions by Satan, so too had Crummell experienced three temptations: "the temptation of Hate . . . the temptation of Despair . . . and the temptation of Doubt." Further invoking biblical scripture, this time Psalm 23, Du Bois claimed that Crummell's tale must be heard, for Crummell had braved "the Valley of Humiliation and the Valley of the Shadow of Death."[51]

Du Bois offered a cosmic sketch of Crummell. Referring to his first meeting with Crummell, Du Bois wrote, "Instinctively I bowed before this man, as one bows before the prophets of the world. Some seer he seemed." As literary critic Robert Gooding-Williams has shown, Du Bois modeled his tale of Crummell on traditional Christian pilgrim and martyr stories. Using geographical rhetoric to discuss a spiritual journey, Du Bois followed the example set by John Bunyan in *Pilgrim's Progress* (1678). Du Bois's Crummell and Bunyan's Pilgrim venture from place to place, encountering different temptations. Moreover, Du Bois explicitly referenced *The Whole Duty of Man*, a devotional text first published in the seventeenth century that discusses man's duties to God and to other men, and John Foxe's *Book of Martyrs* (1563), a history of the lives and sufferings of Christian women and men. Crummell as a pilgrim and martyr had a divine call to the priesthood, according to Du Bois. Just as a "Voice" had called Du Bois in "The Shadow of Years," a "voice and a vision called [Crummell] to be a priest, - a seer to lead the uncalled out of the house of bondage." Yet forces of white supremacy stood in his way. First, he was barred from an Episcopal Seminary because of the color of his skin. Then his own people, the African American community, did not heed his wisdom. Through it all, though, Crummell persevered and grew, just as Du Bois hoped for himself and for other people of color. "So he grew, and brought within his wide influence all that was best of those who walk within the Veil. They who live without knew not nor dreamed of that full power within, that mighty inspiration which the dull gauze of caste decreed that most men should not know."[52]

Although Du Bois demonstrated great respect for traditional African American religion and for ministers like Crummell, Du Bois nonetheless critiqued the black church for maintaining what he considered an old-time faith that stood in the way of genuine progress. Du Bois claimed that African Americans who endorsed advanced education for people of color would have

to endure religious scorn from their people, much as Du Bois experienced and expected to encounter in his own life. In "Of the Coming of John," a short story about the life and death of a young African American man from rural Georgia, the main character, John Jones, found himself in direct conflict with traditional black religion because of his educational and social aims. At a town church meeting called to celebrate John's return after years of advanced education, he encouraged the people to develop an ethical system that rose above their particular denominations. He wanted them to focus on ideals of love, beauty, and fraternity. Jones's words may have been what Du Bois wished he had said to those who challenged his own religious faith at Wilberforce and Atlanta University. Interestingly, the complaints sounded quite similar to those of Booker T. Washington during a speech he gave to the Women's New England Club in 1890. "To-day," John echoed Washington, "the world cares little whether a man be Baptist or Methodist, or indeed a churchman at all, so long as he is good and true. What difference does it make whether a man be baptized in river or wash-bowl, or not at all? Let's leave that littleness, and look higher."[53]

The black congregation, however, refused to "look higher" with John. "An old bent man arose" to challenge him. "He was wrinkled and black, with scant gray and tufted hair," Du Bois penned. This elderly man "seized the Bible with his rough, huge hands; twice he raised it inarticulate, and then fairly burst into the words, with rude and awful eloquence." The people were moved by this display and "moaned and wept, wailed and shouted." Although John could not make out the specifics of the reply, he nonetheless realized that he had been "held up to scorn and scathing denunciation for trampling on the true Religion, and he realized with amazement that all unknowingly he had put rough, rude hands on something this little world held sacred." John left the meeting despondent. Later in the tale, he was lynched by a white mob for murdering a man who had sexually accosted John's sister. Spiritually rejected by his own community, John was then crucified by the white one.[54]

While Du Bois admired and shared much with this John and with the Alexander Crummell he created, it is unclear how much *Souls* disclosed of Du Bois's soul. On occasion he included himself in his presentations of black history. For instance, he used the pronoun "our" in his chapter on blacks' "spiritual strivings." On other occasions, however, Du Bois excluded personal pronouns, such as in the case of the chapter "Of the Faith of the Fathers." Du Bois acknowledged that as part of the black community, he attended church each Sunday and sought to detail the religious life of southern blacks for his readers. To church, he claimed in "Of the Meaning of Progress," "my little world

wended its crooked way on Sunday to meet other worlds, and gossip, and wonder, and make the weekly sacrifice with frenzied priest at the altar of the 'old-time religion.' Then the soft melody and mighty cadences of Negro song fluttered and thundered." Du Bois contrasted his experiences at rural church revival with those of his boyhood church life in the North. On a "dark Sunday night," he attended a "Southern Negro revival." "To be sure, we in Berkshire were not perhaps as stiff and formal as they in Suffolk of olden time," Du Bois continued, "yet we were very quiet and subdued. . . . As I approached the village and the little plain church perched aloft, was the air of intense excitement that possessed the mass of black folk." At no point, however, did Du Bois acknowledge praying or not praying, singing or not singing. Whatever communion, if any, occurred between him and the sacred, Du Bois kept it to himself.[55]

Although Du Bois realized that he—like John Jones—would be criticized and challenged by many in the religious establishment, Du Bois nonetheless painted himself as a prophet throughout *Souls*. He used the word "seer" five times in the text, the word "prophecy" twice, and the word "prophet" twice as well. More telling, however, is that when concluding several of his chapters, Du Bois used prophetic rhetoric to drive home his points about whites' immorality, blacks' spirituality, and the religious peril of the nation. At the end of the essay on the Freedmen's Bureau, "Of the Dawn of Freedom," after he had denounced American political leaders for failing to make the Bureau a permanent institution, Du Bois wrote, "I have seen a land right merry with the sun, where children sing, and rolling hills lie like passioned women wanton with harvest. And there in the King's Highway sat and sits a figure veiled and bowed. . . . Three centuries' thought has been the raising and unveiling of that bowed human heart, and now behold a century new for the duty and the deed." In "Of the Training of Black Men," Du Bois concluded by positioning himself prophetically "above the Veil" and used biblical rhetoric to challenge white America for its reasons for holding blacks down. "Are you so afraid lest peering from this high Pisgah, between Philistine and Amalekite, we sight the Promised Land?"[56]

Then, in his essays on African American religion and on the spirituals, Du Bois provided his readers with a prophecy of a new religious ideal and an awakening of righteousness. "Back of this still broods silently the deep religious feeling of the real Negro heart, the stirring, unguided might of powerful human souls who have lost the guiding star of the past and are seeking in the great night a new religious ideal," Du Bois waxed. "Some day the Awakening will come, when the pent-up vigor of ten million souls shall sweep irresist-

ibly toward the Goal, out of the Valley of the Shadow of Death, where all that makes life worth living—Liberty, Justice, and Right—is marked 'For White People Only.'" Then at the end of the final chapter, "The Sorrow Songs," Du Bois declared that if God exists true freedom will come. "If somewhere in this whirl and chaos of things there dwells Eternal Good, pitiful yet masterful, then anon in His good time America shall rend the Veil and the prisoned shall go free. Free, free as the sunshine trickling down the morning into these high windows of mine, free as yonder fresh young voices welling up to me and caverns of brick and mortar below—swelling with song, instinct with life, tremulous treble and darkening bass."[57]

Finally, Du Bois expressed an ambivalent belief in some sort of heaven after death. Du Bois attempted to extend his gaze into the heavenly realms and behold the events therein. Of this heaven, Du Bois claimed uncertainty, but he also asserted that it would be a place where there would be no color line or evil—a place above or beyond "the Veil." In his poignant essay on the death of Du Bois's first child, Burghardt, "Of the Passing of the First Born," Du Bois concluded by hoping that he would someday meet his son. "Perhaps now he knows the All-love, and needs not to be wise. Sleep, then, child,—sleep till I sleep and waken to a baby voice and the ceaseless patter of little feet—above the Veil." Even further, in "Of Alexander Crummell," Du Bois not only hoped that Crummell was glorified in heaven after his death, but he also depicted Jesus Christ as a person of color who associated with the downtrodden. "I wonder where he is to-day?" Du Bois wrote of Crummell. "I wonder if in that dim world beyond, as he came gliding in, there rose on some wan throne a King,—a dark and pierced Jew, who knows the writhings of the earthly damned, saying, as he laid those heart-wrung talents down, 'Well done!' while round the morning stars sat singing."[58] Du Bois, the dark monk, envisioned a dark Christ welcoming his dark priest Crummell.

From start to finish, heaven to hell, *The Souls of Black Folk* was a book deeply informed by religious ideas and idioms. The title alone signified that the work stood against a white supremacist tradition that undermined that notion of black "souls," while the chapter titles signaled that Du Bois intended the text to be read in a religious register. With historical insight, sociological questioning, literary musings, and biblical metaphors, Du Bois cast the saga of American society as a spiritual tale. Unlike white supremacists, he denied the idea that African Americans were soulless monsters with no past, no future, and no link to the divine. Instead, he presented men and women of color as intensely spiritual beings, and *Souls* served as the sacred key to see their spirits. They had profound moral messages for the nation and world.

The "sorrow songs" revealed a side of the human heart and cosmic longings unheard in any other song. The pilgrimages of Alexander Crummell and John Jones testified to the intellectual and religious brilliance of black folk. The sins of segregation and racial violence proved the hypocrisy of white "Christian" America. While it is impossible to know how much of his own soul Du Bois tried to unveil in *Souls*, there is little doubt that spirituality was at the core of the text. And from first readings to the present, countless men and women have found profound spiritual nourishment in Du Bois's *Souls*.

Finding the Soul While Reading *Souls*

Immediately following the publication of *Souls*, a host of white and black readers from across the nation declared Du Bois a spiritual leader and his book a sacred text. To many reviewers and readers, *Souls* proved that African Americans had beautiful souls and that they should oppose materialism as a holy prerogative. Many readers expressed the conviction that *Souls* had opened their eyes to sacred realities from which they had previously been blinded. Throughout the twentieth century, *Souls* has continued to resonate with the spiritual strivings of whites and blacks. More than one hundred years since its publication, *Souls* still stirs readers; it still encourages racial fraternity in a divided world; and it still inspires hope in a world where the problem of the twenty-first century may continue to be the color line.

In several reviews written just after *Souls* was published, writers remarked on the spirituality of the book and how it showed the prophetic power of Du Bois. The reviewer for the *Nation*, for instance, claimed that *Souls* demonstrated "the sensibility, the tenderness, the 'avenues to God hid from men of Northern brain,' which Emerson divined in black people." John Spencer Bassett, editor of the *South Atlantic Quarterly*, recognized that Du Bois's disdain for materialism underpinned his critique of Booker T. Washington. Bassett saw that the book was one of soul and not of spite. Du Bois "does not," Bassett claimed, "believe in the efficacy of the gospel of material wealth. The soul is more than the body. To give up the higher life, which many negroes have longed for, and to seek for riches only would be a backward step. It would be a debasement of the soul." Moreover, Du Bois's book "is the cry of a man who suffers, rather than the reproach of a man who hates. It is a plea for soul opportunity." Bassett harnessed some of Du Bois's own language to suggest that he was a modern day prophet in a segregated world: "Every fair-minded man who reads these words must feel that he who writes them must indeed dwell above the Veil."[59]

A reviewer in Great Britain likewise characterized Du Bois as a seer and focused on the importance of "soul" in the work. "At heart," wrote author and politician C. F. G. Masterman for the London *Daily News*, "Mr. Du Bois is concerned with the soul of his people." Masterman agreed with Du Bois's opposition to the materialism of Washington and seconded the claim that the sorrow songs revealed the emotional and spiritual life of African Americans. "The 'articulate message of the slave to the world,'" Masterman continued, "possesses a dignity, a haunting beauty and tenderness, the voice of the triumph of hope through the centuries over the desperate proclamation of a material bondage which may be of more account in the Kingdom of real values than all the riotous material prosperity and business success of the New America." Masterman believed firmly that Du Bois's work contradicted the white supremacist notion immortalized in Rudyard Kipling's "The White Man's Burden" that people of color were "half devil and half child." Finally, Masterman declared that *Souls* was a sacred revelation. "It is the voice of longing through wandering and hidden ways: a sudden revelation of the soul of a race, otherwise veiled from its conquerors."[60]

Even white reviewers who sided with Booker T. Washington against Du Bois felt compelled to acknowledge and combat the spiritual positions advanced in *Souls*. A writer for the *Outlook*, a popular Christian magazine in the North, suggested that African Americans would be better served by following Washington's emphasis on practical and industrial education. This reviewer counseled blacks against the impatience they read in *Souls*: "Do not push yourself forward. . . . Do not be ambitious for social equality, or industrial equality, or political equality, or any kind of equality." Moreover, the *Outlook* writer suggested that African Americans should not—as Du Bois seemed to suggest—consider their souls. "Do not think about yourselves. Do not think about your woes or your wrongs. Meditate, not on 'the souls of black folk,' but on 'the future of the American negro.' Look out, not in; forward, not backward. Put your thought on your work, not on your soul." Fully aware that Du Bois desired whites and blacks to consider the souls of black folk, this reviewer sought to dissuade people of color from such reflection.[61]

Souls had a marked impact on white proponents of the Social Gospel, the late nineteenth-and early twentieth-century drive to apply Christian teachings to social improvement. Washington Gladden, a white Congregational minister in Columbus, Ohio, who consistently encouraged social welfare in the name of Christianity, encouraged the members of his congregation to read *Souls*, asserting that it held "deeper insight into the real human elements of the race problem than anything that has yet been written." After reading

Souls, the pastor of New York's Grace Episcopal Church, William R. Hunting-don, now believed that "in the name of God" American Christians must insist on "full and equal justice be done to all people."[62]

Several African American readers declared without hesitation that they considered *Souls* the sacred work of a religious leader. In *Alexander's* magazine, John Daniels claimed that readers could not help but be "exalted by the dominating spirituality of the book." Defying reviewers who described *Souls* as a pessimistic book, Daniels instead maintained that its tone "is not hopelessness; far from it; it is full of prophecy of ultimate victory." *Souls* was at heart a spiritual contribution. "Judge his book not as an argument, as an anti-Washingtonian protest," Daniels concluded. Rather, readers should take it "as a poem, a spiritual, not intellectual offering, an appeal not to the head but to the heart."[63]

How many and in what ways everyday women and men were moved by *Souls* is impossible to know fully, but there are some clues to its powerful and spiritual impact. For Gayle Pemberton's working-class maternal grandfather, affectionately referred to as "Papa" in her memoir of growing up black and female in Chicago, Du Bois's *Souls* was an inspirational work. Papa, Clarence Wesley Wigington, owned a seventh edition of *Souls* published in 1907 and had it autographed by Du Bois in November 1909. On the final pages of the work, Wigington added his own poem. In "Beyond the Veil," he expressed his hopes that *Souls* would give courage to black Americans who had to stress and strain to make it in America.

> This day I have stolen in silence and
>   in stealth away
> Yea, Away from the turmoil, the strife
>   the bitter sway,
> From the stifling atmosphere wherein stand
>   hearts all rent
> With poisoned thrust of baleful gaze
>   of willful slander sent
> To conquer struggling souls and
>   blight each star stark dead
> Each burning hope of eager youth, each
>   quavering prayer of silenced head.
>   . . .
> Here midst beetling crag and rugged peak,
>   where wails the eagles hungry brood

I lay me down to die with more
    to sling me with His holy rood
But in the passing came these
    burning lips, these blurring eyes
Freed of their sickness and for the time,
    the breath of pain dropped gently from the skies
Then came my dream first starting like
    the eager prattle of the child
But ending like a soul-starved man
    in search of truth upon the barren wild.

Afar the distant rumbling of might
    hosts with quickening tread
Falls on my ears and serves to
    stir the souls of countless dead:
To call the living to their feet, to
    rub their eyes and peer
To see the lifting of the veil disclosing
    serried ranks of young and old
Like valiant templars triumphant
    bearers of the cross of gold.[64]

A number of whites and blacks wrote to Du Bois after reading *Souls*, and their letters showed that they experienced the book in a religious register. Kittredge Wheeler, a Baptist minister in Chicago, believed that Du Bois's focus on higher education for people of color fit with the teachings of Jesus Christ. "The education of the heart and mind, and soul, the uplifting of a man—that is difficult and long and painstaking," Wheeler maintained. "This means—in a word—the giving of one's self to that man who is to be lifted, or to be helped! This is the way of Calvary! Not an easy road." Wheeler then denounced Washington's educational philosophy as anti-Christian: "The sentiment 'Industrial Education for the Negro' is the shackle—not removed from his hands but in addition, put upon head and heart—upon the whole man—the whole race. Let us fear him, who casts body and soul into hell! Jesus said." Washington's plan, Wheeler concluded, "is a manacle upon the intellectual, moral, spiritual, upon the higher, nature: upon the whole man."[65]

Few blacks or whites went into as much detail in their responses to *Souls* as William Ferris, an African American who studied at Yale and Harvard, worked as a journalist, and was ordained by the African Methodist Episco-

pal Church. In his two-volume tome *The African Abroad*, first published in 1913, Ferris characterized Du Bois as a religious prophet. He had written *Souls* "with his soul on fire with a righteous indignation," and the result was an incredible book. *Souls* changed Ferris's life, he recalled. After reading it and several works by Thomas Carlyle and Ralph Waldo Emerson, Ferris claimed that "these books were epochs and crucial moments in my moral and spiritual life. Henceforth the world was a different world for me. They revealed to me my own spiritual birthright, showed that there was a divine spark in every soul, and that God was manifest in every human soul and breathed his own nature into every human soul." Specifically, *Souls* "proclaimed in thunder tones and in words of magic beauty the worth and sacredness of human personality even when clothed in a black skin." Ferris, in short, read *Souls* as a book that contradicted the white supremacist theology that had come to pervade American culture by the early twentieth century. *Souls* seemed to open the eyes of Ferris's soul to allow him to see the dignity, honor, and divine spark in himself and other people of color.[66]

Ferris also reflected on the religious effect *Souls* had on black communities. He maintained that Du Bois and *Souls* fired the religious and political imaginations of many African Americans. *Souls*, Ferris claimed, "has become the political bible of the Negro race," and Du Bois "is regarded by the colored people as the long-looked-for political Messiah, the Moses that will lead them out of the Egypt of peonage, across the Red Sea of Jim Crow legislation, through the wilderness of disfranchisement and restricted opportunity and equality of rights." In short, Washington was not the "Joshua" called to lead African Americans to their Promised Land. Du Bois was the new spiritual leader for men and women of color.[67]

White supremacists too responded to *Souls* with a great deal of emotion, and at least one characterized it as anti-Christian and Du Bois as diabolical. Thirty-six years after the publication of *Souls*, Thomas Dixon, Jr., denounced Du Bois and his work as fanatical. In *The Flaming Sword* (1939), a bizarre novel in which Dixon rehearsed his white supremacist beliefs amid a story of how African Americans, Communists, and immigrants worked together to overthrow the U.S. government and plunge the nation into chaos, Dixon charged Du Bois as an inflammatory and unholy leader. Dixon assailed *Souls* as a text dedicated to ruining the racial harmony inaugurated by Booker T. Washington. Du Bois, Dixon wrote, hoped to "array race against race in another war of hate" and he had the "deliberate purpose of stirring the worst passions." Dixon claimed that Du Bois's chief goal was interracial marriages and sexuality—the central concern among white supremacist theologians. And, accord-

ing to one of Dixon's characters, Du Bois deserved eternal damnation for his writing. "There can be no hell too deep for the men who are trying to rouse in him hatred of the Southern white man today."[68]

In the immediate years following the publication of *Souls*, countless readers approached it as a religious text. They testified to the power of *Souls* to challenge the myths of white supremacist culture and to the prophetic power of Du Bois. Whether white or black, readers claimed that their reading of *The Souls of Black Folk* irrevocably altered their own souls and that their entire perception of the world had been altered. Years later, white novelist Truman Nelson maintained that Du Bois's "prophetic" powers lay in his ability to reveal hidden truths and deeper realities. Whites, Nelson suggested, had been taught an "ethic of 'not-looking'" at people of color. "Du Bois changes all this," Nelson continued. "After reading him, the black presence invades the whole consciousness."[69]

∼

As Nelson and so many others attested, *Souls* had the power to change one's vision of this world and beyond. Readers' reactions throughout the twentieth century reveal the strength of *Souls* to defy the nineteenth-century link of whiteness with godliness and blackness with deviltry. Writing after Du Bois's death in 1963, for instance, George B. Murphy, Jr., looked to the biblical imagery of a "staff and shield" to articulate his feelings for *Souls*. He claimed that, in tandem with Frederick Douglass's autobiography, "Du Bois' *Souls of Black Folk*, represented for me the staff and shield with which I could do battle in understanding the ghetto world in which I lived." In South Africa, Peter Abrahams claimed in 1948 that *Souls* had "the impact of a revelation . . . a key to the understanding of my world."[70]

Almost fifty years later, while enjoying a church service in Detroit, newspaper columnist Rhonda Sanders mused about the spiritual power of Du Bois and *Souls*. Sanders considered Du Bois her "spiritual father" who "was a gifted messenger and visionary." "I feel renewed each time I re-read favorite passages" from *Souls*, she declared. To her, Du Bois had shown that blacks have as much of a spiritual life as whites, and he "offered balm to a racially sick society and to the wounded souls of black folk."[71]

Most recently, writer and editor Rebecca Carroll acknowledged that Du Bois's fundamental questions and insights about souls remain paramount. Raised by her adoptive white parents in rural New Hampshire in the 1970s, but the progeny of a white mother and black father, Carroll felt a deep sense of racial ambiguity. "Culturally white and cosmetically black," Carroll had a

difficult time discerning where she fit into a culture that tends to think in monolithic terms of white and black. She was left to ponder, "Does my soul matter?" Her salvation came in *Souls*. Her birth mother spoke of its author, W. E. B. Du Bois, and the book repeatedly until Carroll decided to read it for herself. It "was a humbling experience," she recalled, "and also something like stopping at the top of a Ferris wheel and then swinging the bucket seat— dangerous, exciting, while ultimately and essentially, liberating." Throughout her adult life, Carroll read and reread *Souls*. Each time, "passages struck me, shook me." *The Souls of Black Folk* had been so influential in Carroll's life that she decided to interview a host of prominent African American authors, artists, and politicians to see how they have been affected by it. Carroll wanted to know "how contemporary black Americans maintain, uphold, and reconcile (or not) with the words and prophecies Du Bois expressed in *Souls*." She viewed the voices and personalities in each essay as prophetic realizations of Du Bois's lifelong labor, and her collection served as "a collective memoir of souls . . . the souls of black folk."[72]

Carroll's question, "Does my soul matter?" demonstrates that much has changed and much has remained the same since Du Bois first published *Souls*. While she did not doubt that she had a soul, Carroll wondered about its value. In a world that still sees the holy and divine in terms of whiteness, what value could there be in a "black" girl? The white supremacist theology that had permeated American culture in the nineteenth century tried to convince whites and blacks that people of color had no souls, that they were not connected to the divine, and that they could never contribute anything of spiritual value to the world. Thanks in large part to Du Bois and *Souls*, Rebecca Carroll defied these teachings. Still, what was her soul worth in a society that had yet to confront fully its racist past? Historian A'Lelia Bundles provided an answer to this question in the collection of essays, one that was indebted to Du Bois and one with which he would have agreed. To Bundles, her great-grandmother entrepreneur Madame C. J. Walker and Du Bois taught "that we must be taken seriously, that we deserve to be taken seriously, and that we are valuable . . . that we are a brilliant people." From Carroll's questions to Bundles's answers, it is clear that *The Souls of Black Folk* continues to be one of the most powerful religious books in American history.[73]

Read in terms of nineteenth-century discourse on race and religion, *Souls* was a literary act not only of theological and cultural defiance but also of religious creation. With one courageous stroke, Du Bois contested the notion that through racial categories one could see the hand of God in slavery, segregation, and white mastery. Instead, using history, sociology, personal

anecdotes, and fiction to peer beyond everyday realities, Du Bois presented black life as in touch with the heavenly and the sacred. As a prophet of radical reform, Du Bois set out to shred the association of whiteness with godliness and in its place fashion a link between African Americans and the divine. With *Souls*, he provided a new window into cosmic realities, and in the process recast the entire discussion of race as a cosmic sight. In his other historical and sociological works, Du Bois would continue his spiritual striving and extend his vision.

～

A Dark Monk Who Wrote History and Sociology

The Spiritual Wage of Whiteness, the Black Church,

and Mystical Africa

REVEREND WILLIAM L. BULL was deeply concerned. Massive economic, social, and religious forces were transforming the United States at the beginning of the twentieth century, and the church seemed to offer few answers. But with Bull's funds, the Episcopal Church's Philadelphia Divinity School would help. It inaugurated a lectureship in "Christian Sociology" that asked lecturers to apply "Christian principles to the Social, Industrial, and Economic problems of the time." Bull placed only one restriction on the lecture series. The "lecturer . . . shall be a believer in the moral teachings and principles of the Christian Religion." Invited to campus were some of the nation's brightest minds. Reformer and author of *How the Other Half Lives*, Jacob Riis discussed the importance of home life as a social anchor amid the storms of industrialization and urbanization. Statistician, senator, and labor-rights activist Carroll Wright Davidson lamented the state of organized labor and pleaded for sympathy between owner and worker. Preacher and editor Lyman Abbott also discussed the challenges facing an industrializing society. Then, in the wake of the horrific Atlanta race riot of 1906, the Divinity School selected the two most acclaimed African American scholar-activists of the era: Booker T. Washington and W. E. B. Du Bois.[1]

Du Bois certainly pleased the divinity school. He sounded every bit the scholar, the prophet, and the follower of Christ in his two lectures, articu-

lating themes that pervaded his historical and sociological writing. Du Bois approached the past and the present from a religious angle and outlined his theories on the complex relationships among religion, racism, economic exploitation, and social resistance. He crafted a theological distinction between "true Christianity" and "false Christianity" where the former was a belief in equality and justice that led to actions on behalf of the oppressed and the latter was a bastardized faith that justified social hierarchies and abusive traditions. Du Bois pronounced the religious battle between true and false Christianity to be a global phenomenon, one that pitted the hypocritical (and usually white) "haves" against the holy (and usually nonwhite) "have-nots." In his approach to social change, moreover, Du Bois stressed the necessity of a return to genuine faith and Christianity.[2]

Du Bois began his lectures by recognizing that Christianity had a mixed historical record on race relations. On the one hand, "the real Christian church" was embodied in Galatians 3:28, where the Bible taught that "there is neither black nor white, rich nor poor, barbarian, Scythian, bond nor free, but all stand equal before the face of the Master." Du Bois even claimed a spot for himself and his family within the Christian church, specifically the divinity school's Episcopal tradition. "For four generations my family has belonged to this church and I belong to it, not by personal choice, not because I feel myself welcome within its portals, but simply because I refuse to be read outside of the church which is mine by inheritance and the service of my fathers." On the other hand, Christianity had long served as a handmaiden in the exploitation of men and women of color. The financial gain to be had from slavery was just too tempting for so-called "Christian" Europeans and Americans. Rather than turn away from such a lucrative enterprise, whites twisted their faith. "A new adjustment of ethics and religion had to be made to meet" the rise of the antebellum cotton kingdom, Du Bois declared. "In the modification," whites altered their views of African Americans, of humanity, and of God as the creator of the universe. "There was in the first place a denial of human brotherhood," Du Bois concluded. "These black men were not men in the sense that white men were. They were different—different in kind, different in origin; they had different diseases; . . . they had different feelings; . . . so far as this world is concerned, there could be with them neither human nor spiritual brotherhood." The result was a white Christianity marked with hypocrisy from alpha to omega, a religion that "assiduously 'preaches Christ crucified,' . . . and crucifies 'Niggers' in unrelenting daily life."[3]

Yet just as religion served as a tool of oppression, it was also a primary weapon in the long tradition of resistance and uplift. Christianity was essen-

tial to early African American social organizing, Du Bois instructed. Char-ismatic black ministers in the eighteenth and early nineteenth centuries, including Andrew Bryan, Lott Carey, John Chavis, and Henry Evans, demon-strated African Americans' capacities for manhood and improvement. They showed how black men yearned to advance, pressed themselves to improve, and, as Du Bois put it, were "persistently stretching upward."[4]

Religious faith was an animating force of the revolutionary spirit—the courage to lift sword, axe, or musket to win freedom and liberty. Decades before historian Gayraud Wilmore highlighted the importance of religion in black radicalism, Du Bois drew the connection when discussing Denmark Vesey's planned uprising of 1822 and Nat Turner's rebellion of 1831. Unlike white historians who tended to view Vesey and Turner as insane fanatics, Du Bois depicted them as men of God. Vesey and Turner read the Bible sensibly, according to Du Bois, finding within it the moral fortitude to strike against slavery. "It is no wonder that Vesey, as he pored over the Old Testament scrip-tures, found many points of similitude in the history of the Jews and that of the slaves in the United States," Du Bois lectured. "They were both Jehovah's peculiar peoples, one in the past, the other in the present. And it seemed to him that as Jehovah bent His ear, and bared His arm at once in behalf of the one, so would He do the same for the other." Of Nat Turner, Du Bois explained with elegant simplicity: "He was a Christian and a man. He was conscious that he was a Man and not a 'thing.'" Du Bois then likened Turner to two biblical characters: Turner was "like Moses," who "lived in the soliti-tudes of the mountains and brooded over the conditions of his people"; and Turner was also "like John the Baptist," who "when he had delivered his mes-sage, he would retire to the fastness of the mountain or seek the desert, where he could meditate upon his great work." By mixing Turner with Moses and by highlighting Vesey's juxtaposition of biblical Israelites with modern-day African Americans, Du Bois invoked a tradition in black culture that linked disadvantaged blacks with God's chosen people.[5]

Du Bois blasted the United States for rampant church segregation. This was a terrible moral failing, one that had devastating social and spiritual conse-quences. For whites, church segregation ruined their faith. "This utter denial of the very first principles of the ethics of Jesus Christ," Du Bois boomed, "is to-day so deep seated and unquestionable a principle of Southern Christian-ity that its essential heathenism is scarcely thought of, and every revival of re-ligion in this section banks its spiritual riches solidly and unmovedly against the color line, without conscious question." For blacks, Jim Crow's lordship in the house of Jesus Christ distanced them from much-needed guidance

and brotherhood. "Among the Negroes," Du Bois continued, "the results are equally unhappy. They needed ethical leadership, spiritual guidance, and religious instruction." Yet whites were unwilling to offer genuine friendship and aid. Invoking a theme popularized by William T. Stead's exposé *If Christ Came to Chicago* (1894) and Charles Sheldon's best-selling novel *In His Steps* (1896), Du Bois wondered aloud, what would Jesus do if he went South. To Du Bois, the answer was simple. White Americans would crucify their alleged savior for standing against racial etiquette and white supremacist religion. "Who can doubt that if Christ came to Georgia to-day one of His first deeds would be to sit down and take supper with black men, and who can doubt the outcome if He did?"[6]

Concluding his lectures, Du Bois called for a renewal of what he considered the original teachings of Christ. For race relations to improve, for economic discrimination to end, and for genuine fraternity to sweep across the land, the United States must experience a change of spirit. The question for the nation was clear, "Is the civilization of the United States Christian?" As Du Bois saw it, the answer was equally apparent. "The precepts of Jesus Christ cannot but mean that Christianity consists of an attitude of humility, of a desire for peace, of a disposition to treat our brothers as we would have our brothers treat us, of mercy and charity toward our fellow men, of willingness to suffer persecution for right ideals and in general for love not only toward our friends but even toward our enemies." Based on this standard, "it is absurd to call the practical religion of this nation Christian." Only a return to true Christianity could save the people. "The problem that lies before Christians is tremendous," Du Bois asserted, "and the answer must begin not by slurring over the problems where these different tests of Christianity are most flagrantly disregarded, but it must begin by a girding of ourselves and a determination to see that justice is done in this country to the humblest and blackest as well as to the greatest and whitest of our citizens." The road to justice may be treacherous, but it must be followed. "It may be that the price of the black man's survival in America and in the modern world, will be a long and shameful night of subjection to caste and segregation," Du Bois cautioned, but if "so, he will pay it, doggedly, silently, unfalteringly, for the sake of human liberty and the souls of his children's children." The stakes went beyond economics, politics, and culture. They struck to the core, the soul of each person and the nation.[7]

Du Bois's lectures at the Philadelphia Divinity School—his attention to the power of religion and Christianity for good and for ill—provide a fresh perspective on his historical and sociological works. Most historians point out that in his early years, Du Bois was most influenced by Harvard professors

Albert Bushnell Hart, whose "scientific" approach to history drove Du Bois
to privilege evidence over sentiment, and William James, whose philosophi-
cal pragmatism led Du Bois to strive to reconcile ideas with realities. Then at
the University of Berlin in the early 1890s, Adolph Wagner and Gustav von
Schmoller showed Du Bois the importance of economic factors in history
and society. In the twentieth century, though, as Du Bois failed to make social change via sound, passionless scholarship, he sought new intellectual approaches. During the 1920s and especially in the 1930s, he gravitated to the
writings of Karl Marx, Sigmund Freud, and their followers. Marx and Freud,
scholars of Du Bois maintain, led him to reconsider race, society, the economy, and human actions writ large. At the same time, Du Bois became more
global in his historical and sociological mind, particularly in his concern for
African history and traditions. The intellectual trail of Du Bois, as mapped
out by biographers and historians, is one that takes Du Bois's scholarly activities from patience to propaganda, from pragmatism to Marxism.[8]

This narrative of Du Bois's intellectual trajectory neglects a great deal. It
refuses to take seriously his consistent use of religious rhetoric; it silences his
hopes that true religion would someday transform the world; it shrugs off his
cosmic understanding of Africa; and, perhaps most tragically, it fails to account for the moral passion and the spiritual rage that pulsated through his
historical and sociological works. One facet of Du Bois's intellectual life that
seemed steadfast—from his tutelage under Hart to his devotion to Marx—
was his commitment to religious ethics and ideals. Du Bois consistently used
religious language to frame his topics and animate his points, not only in his
early works such as *The Suppression of the Slave Trade* (1896), *The Philadelphia
Negro* (1899), and *John Brown* (1909), but also in his later studies of American and African history that included *Darkwater* (1920), *Black Reconstruction
in America* (1935), *Color and Democracy: Colonies and Peace* (1945), and *The
World and Africa* (1946). Du Bois viewed religion as both a tool of oppression
and a weapon of the weak, a diabolical driver of human suffering and a heavenly key to human advancement.

Du Bois's contributions to the study of religion were legion, and many of
his insights have yet to be explored fully. He discussed a spiritual wage of
whiteness as a constitutive part of racial imaginations, a racial and religious
belief that whites were close to God and therefore innately and cosmically
superior to other races. He assailed the whitening of Christ and the segregation of the church as sociological and ethical travesties. Du Bois also showed
an intense respect for faith in the lives of individuals and groups he studied,
pioneering the study of the black church. Finally, Du Bois rooted his pan-Af-

ricanism—his hopes that the peoples of Africa could rise up against their oppressors—in notions of the sacred. He assailed western imperialism as a great
sin and looked to Africa with messianic hopes that one day it and its people
would renew the world.

Du Bois was a moral historian and a sociological prophet who never shied
away from tough or perplexing ethical problems. In fact, these were the issues he relished for there the mythologies and mysteries of American society
and history could be unmasked and true faith taught in their place. Including
religion in the discussion of his intellectual matrix reveals that Du Bois may
be best understood as a "dark monk," as he would refer to Martin Luther, who
strove for a global revolution in ethics, morals, and religion.

Ungodly America and the Spiritual Wage of Whiteness

In his historical and sociological monographs, along with his many essays
and articles, Du Bois demonstrated that he viewed Christianity as a religion
that taught the most exquisite moral values the world had ever known. Sadly, Christ's alleged followers, especially his white ones, rarely adhered to his
instructions. Christianity had been undermined by women and men who
warped the spirit of Christ for their own economic and psychological gain.
That whites patrolled their churches and enforced a strict policy of racial segregation struck Du Bois as one of the most heinous examples of the belief
that the white race was connected to God in ways that other peoples were
not. This spiritual wage of whiteness not only legitimated the exploitation of
people of color, but it sanctified the oppression as divine. By exposing this assumption, Du Bois tried to undo it, and by critiquing the so-called Christian
nationalism of the United States, he offered a blistering attack on one of the
most persistent myths in American culture.

Du Bois considered Christianity a practical religious system that encouraged individual morality, social equity, and universal brotherhood. Speaking
to a convention of black leaders in Boston in 1891 when still an undergraduate
at Harvard, Du Bois stressed the importance of religion in ethical training. He
encouraged them to instruct the community in "Practical Christian Work"
and asserted that "the Christianity which Jesus of Nazareth taught the world
means manliness, courage and self-sacrifice or it means nothing."[9] Christianity contained for Du Bois the essential elements for how a just society should
function, and he made this point in his written works and in his classroom
teaching. In the prayers he composed for his history and sociology students

at Atlanta University in 1909 and 1910—prayers written to alleviate university fears about his faith—Du Bois expressed an extensive list of social gospel concerns. He looked to God to inspire the social action necessary to end war, poverty, and sickness. Du Bois enlisted the Lord's aid for orphans, cripples, miners, trade unions, and women's rights activists. "Mighty causes are calling us," he prayed with his young scholars, "the freeing of women, the training of children, the putting down of hate and murder and poverty—all these and more."[10] The true follower of Christ would seek not only to transform individuals but to change social institutions and structures as well.

Biblical narratives of the life and words of Jesus of Nazareth stood at the center of Du Bois's conception of Christianity. He regularly listed Christ as one of the world's greatest moral teachers. He told the National Colored League of Boston in 1891 that if African Americans wanted to enjoy full lives, they "must know what Aristotle thought, what Phidias carved, what Da Vinci painted, what Bacon knew, what Leibnitz created, what Kant criticized, and how Jesus Christ loved—this is education, this is life."[11] To Du Bois, the Christ of Christianity was a poor man who defied materialism, who hated war, and who loved all. White Americans seldom imagined an impoverished Christ, Du Bois charged, and instead replaced the gospel of the carpenter Jesus with that of the banker J. P. Morgan. This enraged Du Bois. The power of big business appalled him, especially since the United States claimed to be a Christian nation. "What church of the lowly Jesus, who railed against the rich, would for a moment" accept the commercialization of society, he asked rhetorically in the early 1950s as he defended himself against Red Scare accusations that he was working for Russian Communists.[12] Religion in the United States had become dominated by a "cynical practical religion of success," he lamented during a lecture fifty years earlier: "The glory of God's sunsets are worth nothing to it for sunsets pay no dividends." It was not the rich that were virtuous to Du Bois but the poor. They, including Christ, embodied the glory of all peoples and nations. "Look at the history of human life," Du Bois proclaimed, "who are the men before whom the world with one accord has bowed: Socrates, Seneca, Luther and Horace Mann, John Brown and Jesus Christ—poor men, paupers if you will, but *men*."[13]

Du Bois routinely identified slavery, segregation, and materialism as religious and spiritual concerns. Speaking before the American Historical Association in 1891, for instance, Du Bois referred to slavery as a "political and moral crisis."[14] Concluding *The Philadelphia Negro* (1899), Du Bois further declared that the situation he described—the poverty and the pain, the brokenness and the betrayal—for African Americans was "a disgrace to the city—a disgrace to its Christianity, to its spirit of justice, to its common sense."[15] Then

years later, speaking on behalf of the NAACP in a lecture on "Violations of Property Rights," Du Bois claimed, "All through this history of subterfuge and evasion has run the great and dominating fact of a race prejudice which denies the application of the ethics of Jesus Christ in the relations of men if these men happen to be of a different race."[16]

Throughout his career, Du Bois drew special attention to the segregation of communities of faith. In one unpublished scrap in his personal papers, perhaps the basis for a *Crisis* story that was never finished, Du Bois contrasted the rhetoric of Christianity with the reality of segregation. In one "prominent Baptist church in Memphis," he wrote, "there was published a large notice: 'Come in, rest and pray.' Under this notice was a drinking fountain and on that in small letters: 'For white folks only.'"[17] Then in a realized *Crisis* article in 1929, he complained, "The American Church of Christ is Jim Crowed from top to bottom. No other institution in America is built so thoroughly or more absolutely on the color line. Everybody knows this." Jim Crow's rule in the house of Jesus Christ held particular importance because churches were more than just social clubs. "The church does not usually profess to be a group of ordinary human beings," Du Bois further intoned in 1929. "It claims Divine Sanction, It professes to talk with God and to receive directly His Commandments." Hence, if the church deemed racial separation acceptable, it deemed it divine. Jim Crow was more than a law of man; it became a law of God because the church performed it. In the process of proclaiming "directly His Commandments," church segregation shored up a spiritual association of racial categories with sacred elements.[18]

The shame of modern civilization was that so-called white Christians rarely, if ever, followed the example of the true Christ. Whites subverted Christian ideas for their own selfish aims, and Du Bois refused to accept that this Christianity was authentic. Du Bois denounced white Christians as blasphemers who stooped to any depth to retain their own status and privilege—even to the point of soiling the beautiful teachings of the God they claimed to hold dear. In one section of *The Philadelphia Negro*, his pioneering work of African American and urban sociology which resulted from fifteen months of intensive interviewing and observing blacks, Du Bois drew attention to the ways churches and church segregation shored up white supremacy in the city. One large church had erected a new building for offices, but a black minister had overheard that no African Americans would be employed there. Refusing to believe this was true, mainly because several well-established African Americans were members of that church, the minister sought out the building manager and the church board. Much to his chagrin, this minister discovered that

the church indeed refused to hire any person of color. When pressed on the obvious hypocrisy of this decision, one of the board members exclaimed, "That building is called the —— Church House, but it is more than that, it is a business enterprise, to be run on business principles. We hired a man to run it so as to get the most out of it. We found such a man in the present manager, and put all power in his hands. . . . The question of hiring Negroes had come up and it was left solely to the manager's decision. The manager thought most Negroes were dishonest and untrustworthy." Therefore, the manager would not hire them. "And thus," Du Bois concluded, "the Christian church joins hands with trades unions and a larger public opinion to force Negroes into idleness and crime."[19]

To Du Bois, American racism, discrimination, and emphasis on material wealth demonstrated that the United States was anything but a "Christian nation." From the first British settlers in the New World to the present day, ministers, opportunists, reformers, historians, politicians, and an assortment of others have constructed the United States as a "Christian nation." The nation was destined to further the kingdom of God in the realm of humanity. For some, this alleged sacred status meant that the United States could do no wrong, that its actions were akin to God's, and that its foes were evil.[20] Du Bois challenged this as a dangerous, perhaps even unforgivable, sin. Speaking at a convention in Des Moines, Iowa, in 1904, Du Bois asked and answered, "What today, then, is the character of our national immorality? It is without doubt stealing. The way in which the Sinai thundered command, 'Thou shalt not steal,' is broken in this land is enough to make every honest American hide his head in very shame."[21] Two years later, after detailing the many wrongs committed against African Americans throughout American history in the resolutions of the Niagara Movement, for instance, he concluded, "And this in the land that professes to follow Jesus Christ. The blasphemy of such a course is only matched by its cowardice."[22] This line, moreover, stuck with Du Bois throughout his career, and he quoted it verbatim all the way into the 1950s.[23]

Du Bois grasped the language of Christian nationalism and wielded it as a rhetorical weapon in his calls for racial justice. "We do expect in a Christian, civilized land, to live under a system of law and order," he declared at the first Georgia Equal Rights Convention in 1906, "Brethren of the white race, living together as we do, let us be friends and not enemies. Let us not stir up the darker, fiercer passions. Let us strive together, not as master and slave, but as man and man, equal in the sight of God and in the eyes of the law, eager to make this historic state a land of peace, a place of plenty, and an abode of Jesus Christ."[24] The "race issue" was Du Bois's litmus test for the authenticity

of whites' Christian faith. And, in most cases, the treatment of black men and women proved the profound un-Christianness of this Christian nation.[25]

Exploitative economic conditions made it so that the tenets of "true Christianity" were rarely followed. In an argument that squared nicely with Marxian theory, Du Bois suggested that unequal material conditions led religious believers to alter their egalitarian religious faith, which in turn then offered religious justification for those exploitative conditions. In the American context, slavery led white Christians to repudiate the leveling principles of true Christianity and their new version of the faith merely upheld the racial status quo. Du Bois's first book, *The Suppression of the Slave-Trade to the United States of America, 1638-1870*, hammered home this point. *Suppression* merged a particular historical narrative (the failure of the United States to abolish the slave trade) with sociological theory (how economic and ideological forces interact). In it, he discussed how slavery (an economic priority) triumphed over freedom (a religious and ethical value) and in turn legitimated a pro-slavery, otherworldly Christianity (a new set of morals to sanctify the reigning social order). Even in colonial New England, where slaves were of little economic benefit locally, financial interests defeated moral prerogatives. "Here, too, a feeble moral opposition was early aroused," Du Bois penned, "but it was swept away by the immense economic advantages of the slave traffic to a thrifty seafaring community of trades. This trade no moral suasion, not even the strong 'Liberty' cry of the Revolution, was able wholly to suppress." According to Du Bois, "Only the moral sense of a community can keep helpless labor from sinking" to the level where an owner can work a slave to death. "And when a community has once been debauched by slavery, its moral sense offers little resistance to economic demand."[26]

In his final chapter of *Suppression*, where Du Bois sought to make theoretical sense of his historical findings, he pointed to the religious importance of his study. When "the moral standard of a people is lowered for the sake of a material advantage," he wrote, moral sensibility is lost and "moral apathy" ensues. The lesson from the past was that the nation must be willing to act on its moral convictions, and not the bottom dollar. "No American can study the connection of slavery with United States history, and not devoutly pray that his country may never have a similar social problem to solve, until it shows more capacity for such work than it has shown in the past. . . . One cannot, to be sure, demand of whole nations exceptional moral foresight and heroism; but a certain hard common-sense in facing the complicated phenomena of political life must be expected in every progressive people. In some respects we as a nation seem to lack this."[27]

The ways whites manipulated the teachings of Christ offered proof to Du Bois that white society was morally bankrupt. "Religion became organized in social clubs where well-bred people met in luxurious churches and gave alms to the poor," he maintained in 1946 in his *The World and Africa*. "On Sunday they listened to sermons—'Blessed are the meek'; 'Do unto others even as you would that others do unto you'; 'If thine enemy smite thee, turn the other cheek'; 'It is more blessed to give than to receive'—listened and acted as though they had read, as in very truth they ought to have read—'Might is right'; 'Do others before they do you'; 'Kill your enemies or be killed'; 'Make profits by any methods and at any cost so long as you can escape the lenient law.'"[28] In short, white Euro-Americans distorted Christianity to make it conform to their lust for power and money.

To Du Bois, the injustices and evils of false Christianity emerged from and then solidified a spiritual wage of whiteness. This spiritual wage justified oppression and served as a fundamental element in racial and class constructions. While a good deal of race theorizing since the 1980s has focused on the historical and cultural making of whiteness, little of it has paid attention to religious ideas.[29] Yet in American society, as Du Bois well recognized, notions of the sacred, of the eternal, of the demonic, and of the angelic have shaped profoundly the making and re-making of racial categories and identities. As he did with *The Souls of Black Folk*, Du Bois railed against the various connections between whiteness and goodness on the one hand and blackness and badness on the other. In *The World and Africa*, he wrote, "The white race was pictured as 'pure' and superior; the black race as dirty, stupid, and inevitably inferior."[30] Du Bois assailed this association as a religious problem. On another occasion, Du Bois referred to white supremacy as an "eleventh commandment," one that was far more important than the original ten. Whites, he claimed in 1904, "have an eleventh commandment, and it reads 'Thou Shalt not Cross the Line.' Men may at times break the sixth commandment and the seventh, and it makes but little stir. But when the eleventh is broken, *the world heaves*."[31]

In "The Souls of White Folk," one of his most trenchant essays, published originally in 1910 and then again in *Darkwater* in 1920, Du Bois portrayed himself as a spiritual prophet with insight into the white psyche. "I know many souls that toss and whirl and pass, but none there are that intrigue me more than the Souls of White Folk," he began. "Of them I am singularly clairvoyant. I see in them and through them. I view them from unusual points of vantage. . . . I see these souls undressed and from the back and side. I see the working of their entrails. I know their thoughts and they know that I know."

According to Du Bois, whiteness as a personal and social identity was "a very modern thing," created in the nineteenth and twentieth centuries. He drew particular attention to its spiritual component: "The paleness of their bodily skins is fraught with tremendous and eternal significance." "This assumption of all the hues of God whiteness alone is inherently and obviously better than the brownness and tan leads to curious acts," he continued. It leads even "the sweeter souls of the dominant world" to think when they met men like Du Bois, "My poor, unwhite thing! Weep not nor rage. I know, too well, that the curse of God lies heavy on you. Why? That is not for me to say, but be brave! Do your work in your lowly sphere, praying the good Lord that into heaven above, where all is love, you may, one day, be born—white!" To whites, Du Bois continued, whiteness stood as a divine privilege—that "whiteness is the ownership of the earth forever and ever, Amen!" Whiteness, moreover, was at the core of American ethics. He asked rhetorically, "Are we not coming more and more, day by day, to making the statement 'I am white,' the one fundamental tenet of our practical morality?" In short, the making of a white race was more than an economic or psychological reality; it constituted a new religious faith.[32]

Yet all was not as it seemed. Whiteness led not to heaven but to hell. The road was not paved with good intentions but with racism cloaking itself as godliness. After establishing and believing in whiteness, Du Bois asserted, "the descent to Hell is easy. On the pale, white faces which the great billows whirl upward to my tower I see again and again, often and still more often, a writing of human hatred, a deep and passionate hatred, vast by the very vagueness of its expressions." Whiteness corrupted Christianity, Du Bois declared. "I fear the atrophy of soul which this teaching must bring. Both mentally and morally white folk today are suffering from this attempt to transmute a physical accident into a moral deed—to draw unreal distinctions among human souls."[33]

Du Bois later alluded to this notion of a spiritual wage of whiteness in American history in his *Black Reconstruction in America*. He titled one of his chapters "The Transubstantiation of a Poor White." On the surface, this portion of *Black Reconstruction* was about the disastrous presidency of Andrew Johnson. It recounted his antebellum support for common folk and workers, his blustering and self-aggrandizing speeches following Abraham Lincoln's assassination, his postbellum betrayal of black and white farmers, his destruction of radical Reconstruction, and his courting of wealthy white southerners. But the rhetorical use of "Transubstantiation" was telling. A theological doctrine that the wafers and wine used during Christian communion services become the physical flesh and blood of Jesus Christ, transubstantiation in-

dicated that the narrative had a deeper meaning, that some spiritual process beyond the human history imbued it with sacred significance. By turning his back on common folk, Johnson and his spirit were irrevocably "transformed." Du Bois put it this way: "The transubstantiation of Andrew Johnson was complete. He had begun as the champion of the poor laborer." But then, "thrust into the Presidency, he had retreated. . . . Because he could not conceive of Negroes as men, he refused to advocate universal democracy . . . and made strong alliance with those who would restore slavery under another name." The transubstantiation and tragedy were bigger than Johnson, though. They represented the broader "tragedy of American prejudice made flesh."[34]

Andrew Johnson's rise to the presidency—his "transubstantiation" from a common poor white—represented for Du Bois the spiritual side and history of white America. The supposedly sacred transubstantiation of the white race, where whites became gods, was in fact chimera. Whiteness was not ordained in heaven but was a plot of hell. Despite having access to the lessons of Christ, white Americans chose instead demagoguery, racial exploitation, material wealth, national chauvinism, church segregation, unmitigated violence, and a belief that they were linked to a heavenly deity in ways that others were not. Throughout his decades of writing and teaching history and sociology, Du Bois repeatedly highlighted the un-Christianity of the United States, the moral bankruptcy of white culture, and the dastardly spiritual wage of whiteness made to sanctify the unsanctifiable. To locate true Christianity and authentic spirituality, Du Bois turned to those assumed by American culture to be soulless—the oppressed of the nation and the earth. There, and in a handful of whites, Du Bois identified a cosmic power and social reality that had the strength to change the world, if only it could be guided appropriately.

"God Had Come to America"

Although Du Bois attacked Christian churches and people for endorsing inequality and injustice, he did not reject the power of religion to make positive social change. He encouraged his readers to look back to individuals who challenged and changed society by living a "true" Christian life. He also applauded the "Negro church" as the fundamental core of African American society, although he had criticisms of it. Moreover, he expressed routinely the conviction that only religious faith and institutions had the influence to right the social wrongs of America and the world. Through a return to the tenets of "true Christianity," he maintained, society could be altered fundamentally.

At first glance, Du Bois's assertion that religious leaders and ideas helped rationalize and legitimate capitalistic exploitation seems to show that he was using a fairly simple Marxian approach. But looking at a variety of Du Bois's other texts suggests that he broke with the Marxian base-superstructure analysis by claiming that an ideological value, "true Christianity," could make social change; if a renewal of true Christianity struck society and masses of people subscribed to the radical teachings of Christ, a new economic base could result, one of economic justice and brotherhood. By focusing on racism and religion as powerful social forces, Du Bois offered a sophisticated revision of Marxian theory. In Du Bois's scholarly writing, a religious renewal could have the power to change economic structures, a position that would have been anathema to any strict Marxist.

Du Bois encouraged his readers and listeners to emulate Christian leaders of the past and present who endorsed universal human brotherhood and uplift. In several articles on the history of slavery from the beginning of civilization to the nineteenth century, for instance, he characterized early Christianity and "its strange, new doctrine of Human Brotherhood" as the first ideological system to challenge human bondage. True followers of Christ, he maintained over and again, stood against any racism, caste, and greed. "The eternal Voice rises and sings in this Wilderness," he wrote in 1924, "The present travesty cannot endure. It is a denial of the fundamental tenets of Christianity."[35]

In this light, Du Bois heaped praise on white, or European, Christians who had embraced poverty or the disadvantaged, such as Saint Francis of Assisi and the abolitionist John Brown. When giving a commencement address for the graduating classes of black high schools in Washington, D.C., in 1906, Du Bois encouraged the students to follow in the footsteps of Saint Francis, a twelfth- and thirteenth-century Catholic mystic who founded the Franciscan Order. A boy showered with wealth and privilege, Francis realized what Socrates and Jesus had also realized—that the world was rife with inequality and that people had responsibilities to help. Rather than choose military glory or wealth, Francis chose to follow God and so should the African American graduates in Du Bois's audience. "Quaintly and cheerfully he began his life work," Du Bois maintained of Francis, who accepted poverty as his bride and "became the little brother of the poor, a beggar and an outcast among men, a listener to birds and little children." Saint Francis's life taught that souls matter, not money, and that to be "more unselfish" means to be "more broadly *human*." For disadvantaged blacks in America, Saint Francis beamed with a righteousness that never yielded in times of adversity. "Face

defeat as cheerfully as triumph," Du Bois exhorted, "Face success as coolly as defeat. Face anything that comes and then *not only here tonight* but there in the mists of God's great morning, when his darker children bring their hard-won triumphs up from the Gates of Despair and the Valley of the Shadow of death, lay your laurels not on your own heads but at the feet of those mothers and fathers who have nurtured you and toiled for you and smoothed the way of your life with their own grey hairs and tears—with their own life-blood."[36]

Even more than Saint Francis, Du Bois looked to abolitionist John Brown—his life and faith—for religious and political inspiration. Best known for leading the failed raid on the federal arsenal at Harpers Ferry, Virginia, in 1859 to arm slaves and bring down the entire slave system, Brown was eventually executed for treason by the U.S. government. In a biography of Brown, Du Bois crafted Brown as a man for whites to emulate. Du Bois's biography was surely not his best work. It was hastily written and relied on secondary sources, often quoting them extensively. But for decades, Du Bois "regarded [it] as one of the best things that I had done."[37] With the biography and a series of wildly popular lectures at African Methodist Episcopal Church congregations on Brown, Du Bois hoped to resurrect the image of Brown. In the late nineteenth century, historians and other writers depicted the abolitionist as a fanatical "mischief-maker" who helped precipitate a senseless war.[38]

Du Bois's biography, as he put it, "is at once a record of and tribute to the man who of all Americans has perhaps come nearest to touching the real souls of black folk." Du Bois characterized Brown as a biblical sage, a man of God in a godless land. Using scriptural passages as epigraphs for each chapter, Du Bois framed Brown's life with sacred metaphors. Brown carried the spirits of Jesus, John the Baptist, and God himself in the United States. For the chapter on Brown's birth, for instance, Du Bois drew on John 1:6, which discussed John the Baptist: "There was a man called of God and his name was John." Then, when discussing Brown's labor as a shepherd in the Allegheny Mountains, Du Bois likened Brown to the shepherds visited by angels before Christ's birth. Later, when detailing Brown's plans to attack slavery, Du Bois used the words of the prophet Isaiah that Jesus later read in the temple and declared to be about himself: "The Spirit of the Lord God is upon me; because the Lord hath anointed me to preach good tidings unto the meek; He hath sent me to bind up the broken-hearted, to proclaim liberty to the captives, and the opening of the prison to them that are bound."[39]

Throughout the biography, Du Bois expressed reverence for Brown's religious values. Regarding Brown's sacred sensibilities, Du Bois maintained that his "nature was in its very essence religious, even mystical, but never su-

perstitious nor blindly trusting in half-known creeds and formulas." Du Bois even offered a providential reading of Brown and his life, suggesting that God worked in the world through Brown and his compatriots. "To the unraveling of human tangles we would gladly believe that God sends especial men—chosen vessels which come to the world's deliverance," Du Bois asserted. And with John Brown, "so it was."[40] Du Bois undercut the depiction of Brown as a crazed fanatic and offered a countertheological view that sanctified white support for black folk. Of the many lessons taught by Brown's life—from the importance of striking against injustice to the honor of standing up for the right in the face of the majority—the moral meaning seemed most essential. "Was John Brown simply an episode, or was he an eternal truth?" Du Bois asked and then offered his own assessment, reiterating his consideration of Brown as an embodiment of true Christianity. There was a cosmic meaning behind the history of Brown; he was Christian ethics in action: "John Brown loved his neighbor as himself. He could not endure therefore to see his neighbor, poor, unfortunate or oppressed. This natural sympathy was strengthened by a saturation in Hebrew religion which stressed the personal responsibility of every human soul to a just God."[41]

While Du Bois underscored the efforts of noble whites, he expended far more scholarly energy cheering and critiquing black religion. To Du Bois, African American religious beliefs, leaders, and institutions were vital to the past, the present, and the future. Black religion carried the seeds of true Christianity and, if properly fertilized and watered, the roots of the black uplift movement. In two of Du Bois's early sociological studies, *The Philadelphia Negro* (1899) and *The Negro Church* (1903), as well as in editorials for *The Crisis*, he was highly critical of some black ministers and churches. "Everybody knows that the Negro church has a large number of disreputable scoundrels in its ministry," he wrote in 1914 for *The Crisis*, but against "these venal, immoral men . . . the forces of honesty and uplift in the church are fighting and making gradual headway. But they have not won."[42] His criticisms did not indicate disdain for black religion. Rather, they were calls to reform the church so that it would be more useful in the freedom struggle. In many ways, Du Bois used his historical and sociological studies as he did his autobiography *Dusk of Dawn*—to function as prophetic critiques of black churches as a means to call them to transformation, to make them into spiritual, economic, and political powerhouses.

Du Bois recognized that the African American church stood at the center of the black community and provided the spiritual power to resist white supremacy. He lauded these churches in *The Philadelphia Negro* for being the

"birthplaces of Negro schools and of all agencies which seek to promote the intelligence of the masses," and he described the typical local minister as a man "of executive ability, a leader of men, a shrewd and affable president of a large and intricate corporation, . . . and usually is, a striking elocutionist."[43] In *The Negro Church*, Du Bois further intoned, "The African church is the oldest Negro Organization . . . and here Negroes have had the most liberty and experience."[44]

The function of churches and religious leaders was clear to Du Bois: to inculcate beliefs in justice, liberty, and morality into their parishioners and to create a truly Christian society. This responsibility was especially crucial for African American ministers. Du Bois viewed them as essential to the uplift of the race because they had the power to install the moral fiber necessary to disprove and combat white supremacists. Ministers were crucial, in Du Bois's opinion, because he conceived of the war against white supremacist culture and theology as a religious war. Much of *The Negro Church*, for example, evaluates the morality and behaviors of African American ministers in order to assess and improve the quality of religious leadership for people of color in the United States.[45]

Organized, arranged, and edited by Du Bois, educator Mary Church Terrell, and professor Kelly Miller, *The Negro Church* constituted the eighth volume in the twenty-volume "Atlanta University Conference for the Study of the Negro Problems." *The Negro Church* was the first sociological study of a religious body or organization to be based on empirical evidence, and it stood as an innovative and engaging analysis of African American religious life.[46] It showcased a wide variety of voices, oftentimes contradictory ones, from African American ministers calling for social change to white moderates instructing black leaders to "keep politics out of the pulpit" and "quit trying to reform white folks."[47] *The Negro Church* highlighted the religious beliefs of adolescent African Americans as well as the elderly; and it endeavored to compare the ministerial training of black students with that of white students.

Perhaps one of the most interesting elements of *The Negro Church* was its assessment of religion among young African Americans. Du Bois and his coterie interviewed and surveyed more than one thousand young blacks. Some of their responses were fascinating, and the ones Du Bois focused upon may have revealed a great deal about his own approach to religion. One child, the editors claimed, seemed to be a nascent Christian socialist and liberationist—identifying "a Christian as 'a poor man!'" Ultimately, according to Du Bois, these children maintained a powerful, albeit flawed, understanding of Christianity:

The children of twelve and under had the clearer and simpler idea of the direct connection of goodness and Christianity. The older children tended more toward phrases which sought to express the fact that religion had reference to some higher will. Indeed this was the more popular idea, and 70 per cent. of the children spoke of Christianity as "Love for God," "Belief in Christ," or some such phrase. Clear as such phrases may be to some minds, they undoubtedly point to a lack of moral training of Negro children. They evidently are not impressed to a sufficiently large extent with the fact that moral goodness is the first requirement of a Christian life.

By underscoring, yet nonetheless critiquing, the faiths of these children, Du Bois once again demonstrated his respect for black religion and also his belief that a true Christianity existed, that he knew what it was, and that his work was part of an effort to see it nourished.[48]

The Negro Church presented African American church and religious life as vibrant and multifaceted, as part of the social and cultural essence of the black community. At the end of the work, Terrell, Miller, and Du Bois pleaded for a renewal of true Christianity to usher in a new era of racial friendship and uplift. African Americans needed faith, they claimed, because "the great engine of moral uplift is the Christian church." Whites needed true Christianity, moreover, because it would divest them of their racism and lead them to equitable treatment of disadvantaged groups. "Religious precepts would rob the white man of his prejudices and cause him to recognize the Fatherhood of God and the brotherhood of man," they asserted. "Christianity is contrary to the spirit of caste—spiritual kinship transcends all other relations." Without reservation, they concluded, "The race problem will be solved when Christianity gains control of the innate wickedness of the human heart, and men learn to apply in dealing with their fellows the simple principles of the Golden Rule and the Sermon on the Mount." Indeed, the supposedly irreligious Du Bois seemed to have more faith in the social power of Christianity than many of its proclaimed believers.[49]

Although some scholars have suggested that Du Bois's critiques of black ministers indicated his distance from black religion and religion in general, they have neglected that many black ministers looked to Du Bois for aid with church life and that many leading African Americans of the day were critical of black pastors. In 1916, Reverdy Ransom, the editor of the African Methodist Episcopal *Church Review*, asked Du Bois to write an article for the journal on black ministers and congregations.[50] Booker T. Washington,

in his autobiography *Up from Slavery*, denounced the "wholly ignorant men who preached" in many black churches and called for an educated clergy.[51] The pioneering black filmmaker Oscar Micheaux used one of his first feature films, *Body and Soul* (1925), to underscore the danger of putting too much power and authority in the hands of African American ministers. Reverend Jenkins of the film, played brilliantly by Paul Robeson, was a hustler, an alcoholic, and a rapist. His assault on the young Isabel and his theft of the family savings, while members of the community put almost unquestioning faith in him, highlighted the dangers of an immoral ministry.[52] Followers of Marcus Garvey, moreover, routinely assailed black ministers who did not support the Garvey cause as "weak-kneed" and lacking "backbones."[53] These critiques, including Du Bois's, did not reveal a rejection of black faith. If they had, there would have been no reason for Ransom and others to contact Du Bois. Rather, the point was to reform black Christianity.

There may be no greater proof of Du Bois's esteem for black churches and his hopes for them than in his adoration for men of the cloth. In *Souls of Black Folk*, he virtually worshipped Alexander Crummell; in Du Bois's autobiographical "The Shadow of Years," he heaped praise upon his grandfather Alexander and his ministry. And in a eulogy to Henry McNeil Turner, a bishop and leader in the African Methodist Episcopal Church, Du Bois described him as "a man of tremendous force and indomitable courage." "In a sense," Du Bois continued, "Turner was the last of his clan: mighty men, physically and mentally, men who started at the bottom and hammered their way to the top by sheer brute strength; they were the spiritual progeny of ancient African chieftains and they built the African Church in America."[54]

With *The Negro Church*, *The Philadelphia Negro*, *The Souls of Black Folk*, and numerous other works, Du Bois established the groundwork for African American religious history. His influence, moreover, seems to increase with each passing generation of religious scholarship. After Du Bois, black scholars Carter Woodson, Benjamin E. Mays, Joseph W. Nicholson, and E. Franklin Frazier took new looks at black religion. Invariably, they all followed Du Bois's lead. As a graduate student at the University of Chicago, Carter Woodson wrote to Du Bois in 1908 asking for help on his study of the black church and, after receiving a copy of Du Bois's *The Negro Church*, published his own *History of the Negro Church*.[55] Even E. Franklin Frazier, who dissented from Du Bois regarding the African origins of African American Christianity, nonetheless cited Du Bois's works and agreed with him on many points. On the economic life of African Americans, for example, Frazier acknowledged, "As Du Bois pointed out more than fifty years ago, 'a study of economic co-

operation among Negroes must begin with the Church group.'" Frazier, Mays, and Nicholson did move beyond Du Bois by examining the transformations of black religion wrought by the Great Migration and urbanization, which included the rise of "Negro Cults" like Father Divine's Peace Mission Movement or the Moorish Science Temple of America.[56] Historian and theologian Gayraud Wilmore, though, put it best when he wrote that Du Bois's "understanding of the origin and nature of black religion is incomparable."[57]

In the last two decades of the twentieth century, scholars of African American religious history pushed in more diverse directions, but they continued to draw insight and imagination from Du Bois. Anthony Pinn and Michael Eric Dyson have located black religious and theological sensibilities outside of the "Negro church" mainstream in everything from black literary expression to gangsta rap, and both of them have credited Du Bois as influential in their new formulations.[58] Perhaps the most profound critiques of Du Bois's approach to black religion and the black church may have come from women's historians. While Du Bois acknowledged black women in African American congregational life, he never centered his analysis on their efforts or activities. Sociologist Cheryl Gilkes and historian Evelyn Brooks Higginbotham, however, have shown that black women were in many ways the backbone of African American churches. Analyzing the influence of women in congregational and community activism, in organizing church functions, and on the ideas of black women in holiness churches, Gilkes has revealed that "if it wasn't for the women," there would be no "black church." Higginbotham has shown how African American churches served as crucial sites for black women to articulate frustration with racism and misogyny. The black church was not just a place for racial uplift but for gender uplift as well. Yet even when critiquing Du Bois, both Gilkes and Higginbotham pay homage to him as the founder of black religious history. Gilkes linked Du Bois with Emile Durkheim as the two most important founders of sociology, while Higginbotham has applauded Du Bois for being the first to "identify the black church as a multiple site—at once being a place of worship, theater, publishing house, school, and lodge."[59]

According to historian David Lewis, Du Bois's early belief that the black church could be a useful tool in the struggle for civil rights gave way to a disregard for the church. The mature Du Bois, Lewis insisted, saw black churches as an arcane and useless institution. Du Bois of the 1930s and 1940s, so Lewis wrote, conceived of "virtually no modern role assigned to the Negro church" for the betterment of the world or the race. Yet a host of evidence contradicts this assessment. As late as 1950, Du Bois continued to reiterate his key points about the "Negro Church." In an article for the *Pittsburgh Courier*, Du Bois

asserted, "The Negro church during the Twentieth Century has lost ground."
"It is no longer the dominating influence that it used to be, the center of social activity and of economic experiment." The church, though, remained a
vital institution. "Nevertheless, it is still a powerful institution in the lives of
numerical majority of American Negroes if not upon the dominant intellectual classes. There has been a considerable increase in organized work for
social progress through the church, but there has also been a large increase
of expenditure for buildings, furnishings, and salaries; and it is not easy to
find any increase in moral stamina or conscientious discrimination within
church circles." Then, in 1958, as the modern civil rights movement was in full
force, Du Bois recognized that black churches played a foundational role and
encouraged it to keep pressing. "The Negro church," he asserted, "which stops
discrimination against bus riders must next see how those riders can earn a
decent living and not remain helplessly exploited by those who own busses
and make jim-crow laws."[60]

In a variety of other historical works, Du Bois rhetorically juxtaposed the
religious beliefs of blacks and whites in an effort to further demonstrate the
genuineness of black society and the hypocrisy of white society. He used this
tactic most effectively in *Black Reconstruction*, his stunning revision of Reconstruction historiography and attack upon racism in the American historical
profession. The work, which showcased Du Bois's use of Marxian and Freud-
ian theories, was not devoid of religious reflection. At the end of one chapter
on the ways African Americans experienced freedom, aptly titled "The Coming of the Lord," Du Bois posed a series of singular questions. The intent was
to stymie and confuse the reader, but in the end cut to the heart of his social
and religious critique of the nation. "Suppose on some gray day, as you plod
down Wall Street, you should see God sitting on the Treasury steps, in His
Glory, with the thunders curved about him? Suppose on Michigan Avenue,
between the lakes and hills of stone, and in the midst of hastening automo-
biles and jostling crowds, suddenly you see living and walking toward you,
the Christ, with sorrow and sunshine in his face?" Du Bois assumed that his
readers would find the entire scenario idiotic. "Foolish talk, all of this, you
say, . . . because no American now believes in his religion."[61]

But not so for African Americans. To those who had just won their freedom in the Civil War, "God was real" and the divine hand had moved in human history. African Americans knew God, "They had met him personally in
many a wild orgy of religious frenzy, or in the black stillness of the night. His
plan for them was clear; they were to suffer and be degraded, and then after-
wards by Divine edict, raise to manhood and power; and so on January 1, 1863,

He made them free." It was a tremendous and sacred moment. "There was joy in the South. It rose like perfume—like a prayer. Men stood quivering. Slim dark girls, wild and beautiful with wrinkled hair, wept silently; . . . and old and broken mothers, black and gray, raised great voices and shouted to God across the fields, and up to the rocks and the mountains." A new hymn, "the loveliest thing born this side the seas," went up. And although whites abused the song by demeaning black souls and attacking black bodies, they could not hold back the burst of melody. "It lived and grew; always it grew and swelled, and lived, and it sits today at the right hand of God."

Then concluding this chapter, Du Bois once again portrayed the history of the United States in terms of sin and redemption as he had in *The Souls of Black Folk*. "The nation was to be purged of continual sin not indeed all of its own doing," he penned, "due partly to its inheritance; and yet a sin, a negation that gave the world the right to sneer at the pretensions of this republic. At last there could really be a free commonwealth of freemen." God had worked in emancipation to save not only African Americans but the entire soul of the nation. "Suddenly the world knew why this blundering horror of civil war had to be," Du Bois summed, "God had come to America, and the land, fire-drunk, howled the hymn of joy."[62]

Even though critical of some elements of black religion, Du Bois maintained without reservation that African Americans were the truest Christians in the United States. In an essay entitled "The Negro as a National Asset," published in *Homiletic Review* in 1927, he wrote,

If one should ask you how many persons in the United States are seriously trying to practise the ethics of Jesus of Nazareth—the number would not be large. There can be no doubt as to the worth and organization of our churches, but there is tremendous doubt as to their practical effort to practise the Golden Rule and realize human brotherhood. In these matters the American black man occupies a singular place. First of all, he himself as a group exemplifies Christian ethics to an astonishing degree; he represents the meek and the lowly; he has been "slow to wrath and plenteous in mercy." He has attempted, on a scale seldom equaled before in a civilized community, to forgive his enemies and turn the other cheek.

As Du Bois saw it, "black men have the right to say that they founded here the only real Christian church open to all men and willing to serve all men. And however imperfect the organization may be, it certainly points a tremendous moral."[63]

African Americans, furthermore, exemplified the teachings of Christ in their day-to-day lives. Because they encountered hatred as individuals and as a group, African Americans offered "love and sympathy, even for their enemies, for those who despised them and hurt them and did them nameless ill. . . . They have given friendship to the friendless, they have shared the pittance of their poverty with the outcast and nameless; they have been good and true and pitiful to the bad and false and pitiless and in this lies the real grandeur of their simple religion."[64]

Du Bois incorporated religious ideas and convictions in countless other ways in his historical and sociological writing. He depicted the home as a spiritual place, a location where mothers mold "mind and soul" of little ones.[65] Time and again, he described work as a gift from God. "The father may give him wealth and the mother love," Du Bois asserted in an essay for the *Church Review* of the African Methodist Episcopal Church, "but the gift of God is work."[66] He even presented the Protestant Reformation leader Martin Luther as a role model for African Americans like himself. Luther was "the dark monk [who] faced the emperor of all the world, daring to be honest rather than orthodox."[67] And on the Christian socialism of Russian author Leo Tolstoy, a modern-day Saint Francis in many regards, Du Bois wrote, "It is easy today to show with some clearness that his conception of the religion of Jesus Christ was unworkable, either in Russia of his day or in the United States of ours. . . . but the great thing for us to remember now, one hundred years after his birth, is that here is a man that dared try; who had before him a vision of simplicity, poverty, unselfishness and peace, such as would transform the world and make it anew, if a sufficient number of people would follow his footsteps. Very few men have dared this straight and narrow path. Very few men will dare. But it remains before the eyes of all seers and prophets, a Path."[68]

The "Path" did remain in front of Du Bois, the historical and sociological prophet. He wished to follow the road trod by the "dark" Martin Luther and face the emperors of the world with honesty rather than orthodoxy. He wanted African Americans and whites to follow the paths set out by Tolstoy, by Luther, by John Brown, by Saint Francis, and by the millions of men and women of color who had gone to their churches searching for a God and a future that would love the socially despised, hold the hurting, and make a new and better world. With his sociological and historical writing, Du Bois assailed white Christianity in practice and critiqued black ministers, but he lauded Christian ethics in theory and their expression among some whites and blacks. Through it all, Du Bois held fast to a notion of a "true Christian-

ity," one that could one day defeat the false Christianity of economic exploitation, white supremacy, and imperialistic war.

Always Something New from Africa

As Du Bois attacked white American society for its religious duplicity and applauded African Americans for keeping faith amid such devastation, he turned his religious scope to the history of modern imperialism and Africa. During the late nineteenth and early twentieth centuries, Africa gained a prominent place in African American imaginations. With the collapse of Reconstruction in the South, hundreds of southern blacks entertained notions of emigrating to Liberia. Then with the missionary and newspaper narratives of the intrepid adventurer David Livingstone into the heart of Africa, the Berlin Conference of 1884–1885 (in which European powers carved up Africa for colonialism), the War of 1898 (in which the United States engaged in military conflict throughout the world), and the Boer Wars of 1899 to 1902 (in which the British and Dutch battled for supremacy in South Africa), Americans white and black tuned in to Africa and global events with new vigor.[69]

Surrounding these tumultuous years, Du Bois became a founding leader of the "pan-African movement." Through a series of conferences, pan-Africanists such as Du Bois pushed for a slow withdrawal of European powers from Africa and for the empowerment of local Africans. Unlike Marcus Garvey and other "back to Africa" leaders, Du Bois never advanced the idea that all peoples of African descent should return to the continent. Rather, he hoped for a global alliance of all "colored" and oppressed people. This alliance, he believed, would have the strength to cast off the yoke of imperialism. As historian Ibrahim Sundiata has shown, Du Bois so mythologized Africa and Africans that he was unable to see the harsh realities of the dismal state of the continent, particularly those in Liberia. Other historians, namely Molefi Kete Asante, have depicted Du Bois as one of the nation's first exponents of "Afrocentricity," an academic and political stance that calls into question the notion that Europe was the only seedbed of the modern world and that positions Africa as vital to global history and development. As another weapon in his historical and sociological crusade, Du Bois's writings on Africa contributed to his attack on white supremacy. Africa became a central sacred symbol in his rewriting of human history and social relations, a place whose history he could use to denounce the hypocrisy of white supremacy and prophesy of a world reborn through black spirituality.[70]

    Religion played an especially important role in Du Bois's writings on Africa.
Specifically in three works, *The Negro* (1915), "The Hands of Ethiopia" (1920),
and *The World and Africa* (1946), Du Bois mapped a Christian metanarrative
onto Africa as the loci of past creation, of present suffering, and of future redemption. In many ways, Africa became a Christ figure for Du Bois—there at
the beginning, suffering for humankind, and eventually redeeming the world.
When approaching Africa, Du Bois paid great attention to its importance in
the histories of world religions. He depicted western imperialism as sinful
and diabolical, and he contrasted the hypocrisy of missionaries with the sacred brilliance of everyday Africans and African culture. Du Bois attempted
to link African history to the traditions of the world's major religions, and he
pushed for Africanized symbols of faith and belief. All in all, his approach to
Africa signaled a deep interest in the resurrection of the continent's reputation and the redemption of blackness itself.

    Tearing apart the conflation of whiteness with godliness stood as the key
endeavor of Du Bois's critique of the European imperial project. The slave
trade, the expropriation of lands from Native Americans, and the partition
and exploitation of Africa proved that western societies were tainted with sin.
Any claims made by western civilization to following the edicts of Christianity were false and hypocritical. The exploitation of the Congo, Du Bois asserted in 1915, "will long stand a monument of shame to Christianity and European civilization." Religious hypocrisy, in fact, was the dominant theme of
western society. "The white followers of the meek and lowly Jesus stole fifteen
million men, women and children from Africa from 1400 to 1900 A.D. and
made them working cattle in America," he grieved. On another occasion Du
Bois linked the sins of the white Christian world with those of Adolf Hilter's
Nazi Germany. "There was no Nazi atrocity," claimed Du Bois, "which the
Christian civilization of Europe had not long been practicing against colored
folk in all parts of the world."[71]

    On several occasions, Du Bois unleashed a torrent of criticisms on white
missionaries and the evils of imperialism. At the first Pan-African Congress,
held in 1900 in London, Du Bois railed against Christian hypocrisy. "Let not
the cloak of Christian missionary enterprise be allowed in the future," he
boomed, "as so often in the past, to hide the ruthless economic exploitation
and political downfall of less developed nations, whose chief fault has been
reliance on the plighted faith of the Christian church."[72] Just as the treatment
of African Americans in the United States had ruined white American Christianity, so had the treatment of Africans by European powers soiled western
faith. The greed and belligerence that fueled World War I, Du Bois noted,

was only possible because of an alteration to Christianity, one that was necessary to legitimate the exploitation of Africa. "To the furtherance of this highly profitable economic dictum has been brought every available resource of science and religion," Du Bois declared in "The Hands of Ethiopia." "Thus arises the astonishing doctrine of the natural inferiority of most men to the few, and the interpretation of 'Christian brotherhood' as meaning anything that one of the 'brothers' may at any time want it to mean."[73] On another occasion, Du Bois penned, "There is the modern paradox of Sin before which the Puritan stands open-mouthed and mute. A group, a nation, or a race commits murder and rape, steals and destroys, yet no individual is guilty, no one is to blame, no one can be punished."[74] In fact, Du Bois felt so much rage for imperialism and diabolical missionaries that at least on one occasion he wished that God had wiped whites from the earth. "Who can help forming an indignant wish that the hand of Heaven, by some miraculous interposition, had swept these European tyrants from the face of the earth"?[75]

Global white supremacy and its religious outcomes frustrated Du Bois as well because he believed the imperial project and the racism that emerged from it mocked the faiths of Africans and demoralized people of color throughout the globe. In *The World and Africa*, he claimed that the repeated elevation of whites' religious faiths and the simultaneous denigration of tribal African beliefs bred an inferiority complex among Africans—a topic psychologist Frantz Fanon so eloquently discussed in *Black Skin, White Masks* (1967). "The old religion was held up to ridicule, the old culture and ethical standards were degraded or disappeared," Du Bois maintained, "and gradually all over Africa spread the inferiority complex, the fear of color, the worship of white skin, the imitation of white ways of doing and thinking, whether good, bad, or indifferent." He also contended that religious separation and the conflation of whiteness with godliness crippled the souls of people of color. In one of his short stories published in *Darkwater*, after a white church turned away a black character, shouting, "We don't admit niggers!" he began to worry about the state of his soul and that of his brethren. "The fear beside which other fears are vain imaginings" struck him, claimed Du Bois. "The fear lest right there and then you are losing your own soul; that you are losing your own soul and the soul of a people; that millions of unborn children, black and gold and mauve, are being there and then despoiled by you because you are a coward and dare not fight!"[76]

Yet not all white missionaries were tools of capitalism and oppression. Du Bois never seemed to hold the notion that all white folk were unredeemable or unable to act with compassion. As he wrote in "The Hands of Ethiopia,"

"Missionaries and commerce have left some good with all their evil."[77] Du Bois lauded missionaries like Albert Schweitzer, a German and French theologian who decided to venture to Africa as a medical doctor, rather than as a preacher. For his many humanitarian efforts, Schweitzer received the Nobel Peace Prize in 1952. According to Du Bois, Schweitzer was "a missionary and a scientist . . . an artist. He believed in the Christian Church but not blindly in the Christian dogma." Du Bois cheered Schweitzer for being "interested in the historical Jesus" and for writing a dissertation on "the religious philosophy of Kant." But, most important, Schweitzer was a true friend of people of color. "The little handful of people whom he helped saw in him a vision and a promise; a white man who was interested in them as human beings; who assuaged their bitter pain, who healed their wounds."[78]

Missionaries such as Schweitzer and the religious faiths of good Europeans, even Germans, were crucial to making a new and better world. As Du Bois wrote in *Color and Democracy* (1945), his exposé of the connections among racism, economic exploitation, colonialism, and world wars, "Democracy has failed because so many fear it. . . . So the world stews in blood, hunger, and shame. The fear is false, yet naught can face it but Faith. Once two great Germans [Ludwig van Beethoven and Karl Bohm] appealed to this faith in brotherhood. With high art in word and melody, they called all men to the magic of life; they summoned them, fire-drunk and reeling through stars of God into the sanctuary of Joy, daughter of Elysium."[79] On a more pragmatic note, Du Bois recognized that religious beliefs were needed for uplift. "It is all too clear today that if we are to have a sufficient motive for the uplift of backward peoples, for the redemption and progress of colonials, such a motive can be found only in the faith and ideals of organized religion; and the great task that is before us is to join this belief and the consequent action with the scientific knowledge and efficient techniques of economic reform."[80]

To defy western and missionary depictions of "heathen Africa" and "the Dark Continent," Du Bois approached Africa as a land of spiritual and mystic wonder. When visiting Monrovia, Liberia, in 1924, for example, he described a Christmas celebration by linking black people with the sacred. "There were young women and men of the color of warm ripe horse chestnuts, clothed, in white robes and turbaned. They played the Christ story with sincerity, naivete and verve. Conceive 'Silent Night' sung in Kru by this dark white procession with flaming candles; the little black mother of Christ crossing with her baby, figured in blue, with Joseph in Mandigan fex and multi-colored cloak and beside them on her worshiping knees the white wreathed figure of a solemn dark angel. The shepherds watched their flocks by night, the angels sang; and

Simeon, raising the baby high in his black arms, saying . . . Kru-wise, 'Lord now lettest thou thy servant depart in peace for mine eyes have seen thy salvation!" For Du Bois, this travel narrative subverted white supremacist notions in a variety of ways: it figured biblical characters as black; it showed Africans performing a religious ritual that whites in Europe and America did as well; and it showed Africans behaving with dignity, community respect, and sacred sensibilities.[81]

Du Bois turned basic assumptions of western culture on their head by characterizing Africans as godly and Europeans as ungodly. To articulate the differences between Europeans, Africans, and Asians, Du Bois claimed, "Africa saw the stars of God; Asia saw the soul of man; Europe saw and sees only man's body, which it feeds and polishes until it is fat, gross, and cruel." Europeans were not religious, they were carnal and greedy. Africans were not heathens; they were the folk who had seen God in the sky. West African culture, Du Bois declared, was not heathenish. It was religious at its core. "West Africa was developed around the Africans' ideas of religion: the worship of souls of trees and plants of animals; the use of the fetish; the belief in fairies and monsters."[82]

Du Bois's insistence that people of African descent were intensely religious and spiritual was but one of the ways he constructed a countertheology to white supremacy with his historical and sociological writing. He also tried to show the importance of Africa in the rise and evolution of Judaism, Christianity, and Islam in the modern world. Writing Africa into the historical narratives of the world's major religions was part of Du Bois's attempt to annihilate philosopher Georg Hegel's "ancient lie" of 1833 that "alone of all the continents, the African has no history." This was a lie that countless white Americans and Europeans had accepted, for it was a functional fib. It justified enslavement; it legitimated exploitation; and it sanctified the destruction of body, heart, and soul. In direct opposition to Hegel, Du Bois suggested that from the beginning of humankind until the twentieth century, Africa and Africans played a foundational role in the development of society and culture. This was nowhere more apparent than in the history of prominent world religions, a history that western culture wanted to neglect if not outright obliterate.[83]

Du Bois attacked whitewashed histories of Judaism, Islam, and Christianity. He quoted dozens of biblical passages that included direct connections between the people of Israel and Africa, especially the land of Ethiopia: Moses, for instance, married an Ethiopian woman; a minister from Ethiopia, Ebedmelech, rescued the prophet Jeremiah when he was imprisoned; and Jew-

ish writers like Daniel expressed a great deal of envy for the resources of the Ethiopians. Similarly, regarding the rise of Islam, Du Bois drew attention to the roles of Bilal of Ethiopia and Tarik-bin-Ziad in the historical foundations of the faith of Muslims. Bilal of Ethiopia was Muhammed's liberated slave and became one of his closest friends and allies. Tarik-bin-Ziad, another enslaved follower of Muhammad, led the Moorish Army against Spain and became a hero in Turkish Islam. Another African, Zayd bin Harith, was Muhammed's third convert and ascended to a position of military leadership in the early Muslim community.[84]

In *The World and Africa*, Du Bois even challenged the whiteness of western culture's most powerful sacred symbol: the white Christ. Roughly two millennia ago, Du Bois observed, "there was born in the Egypto-Syrian area, with its Mongoloid and Negroid elements, a social reformer called Jesus Christ." Hypocritical white Europeans and Americans refused to acknowledge that he was anything but white. As Du Bois maintained, "Nordics who have never accepted his doctrine of submission to evil, repudiation of riches, and love for mankind, have usually limned him as Caucasoid." Of course, the biblical Jesus was not white. He was a "Syrian Jew," one whom Du Bois described as perhaps bearing a "hooked nose and curled hair." Christ may have "even inherited Ethiopian blood."[85]

Following hard on the heels of the Holocaust, Du Bois's association of Africans and Jews in the form of Jesus was intended to move the reader. This Jesus, Du Bois continued, probably looked similar to the "Jew at whom Hitler stared in Vienna" and then began his bellicose career as an anti-Semite. As Hitler wrote in *Mein Kampf*, "One day when I was walking through the inner city, I suddenly came upon a being clad in a long caftan, with black curls." "From that day," Du Bois maintained, "dates his active anti-Semitism." Hated blacks and Jews, though, were like the biblical Christ in appearance and attitude. "Jesus tried to make men better, simpler, truer," Du Bois intoned, but "he did not succeed." "He was charged with blasphemy and treason, and hanged on nails until he was dead." Just as Africans had been enslaved, as African Americans had been lynched, and as eastern European Jews had been gassed, so too had Jesus been wrongly murdered. By juxtaposing the historical poor and oppressed Jesus against modern-day conceptions of Christ as Anglo-Saxon, and by connecting the violence committed against Jesus with that against other minority groups, Du Bois provided yet another example of his challenge to the spiritual wage of whiteness and his efforts to redeem men and women of color.

The history of Christianity and Christian kingdoms, moreover, was not intelligible without an appreciation for Africa. Du Bois highlighted the fact that Africans and people of color had been displayed prominently in Christian iconography and art well into the Middle Ages. From sculptures and paintings of black Virgin Marys to Italian artists depicting one of the three "Magi" who visited Christ at his birth as "a black Negroid," people of dark skin were present in early Christianity. Du Bois also considered Christians in Africa responsible for restraining Muslim Arabs from pouring into and dominating Western Europe. Finally, akin to his appreciation for the Christmas celebration in Monrovia, Du Bois applauded contemporary literary works that set Christian tales in Africa and included African characters. Writing a foreword for Lorenz Graham's *How God Fix Jonah*, a tale in which the "stories of the Christ child, of Jonah, Ruth, Job, Solomon and other Biblical characters are told here in the words and thought patterns of a modern African boy," Du Bois lavished it with praise. "This is the stuff of which literature is made; and in the lore of the world, the literature of Africa has its place although this is often forgotten."[86]

Through his travel writings, his historical works, and his sociological prose, Du Bois stood as a dark monk of pan-Africanism. He even mapped a Christian typology onto Africa. It was the location of human creation, human suffering, and human redemption. In *Darkwater*, Du Bois traced all life back to Africa, "the primal black All-Mother of men."[87] It was the "cradle of the human race," he further declared in *The World and Africa*, the location where humankind first achieved cultured civilization in Egypt, and where the first religions and mythologies emerged.[88] Africa was also the place of slavery, the middle passage, and unmitigated exploitation. During this "rape of Africa," Du Bois suggested, the forces of good and evil faced one another. "It was a bitter struggle between Good and Evil—between fine and noble souls and conscienceless desire for luxury, power, and indulgence. The forces of Evil were continually reinforced by the vast power which slavery and the exploitation of men put into the hands of the betrayers of labor, making them the envied of the earth, until nations became willing to destroy the earth in order to gain it. Suppose that at any point in this Descent to Hell, Right had received help and reinforcement?"[89]

In the future, though, Africa would renew the world. In "The Hands of Ethiopia," Du Bois tried to explain the biblical passage of his title as hope for the future, hope that Africa would one day even save God: "The hands which Ethiopia shall soon stretch out unto God are not mere hands of helplessness and supplication, but rather are the hands of pain and promise; hard, gnarled,

and muscled for the world's real work; they are hands of fellowship for the half-submerged masses of a distempered world; they are hands of helpfulness for an agonized God." Only from Africa, Du Bois continued, will the world be saved from "war and wealth, murder and luxury." From Africa, men and women will learn "a new peace and a new democracy of all races,—a great humanity of equal men."[90] "Despite the crude and cruel motives behind her shame and exposure," Du Bois later maintained in *The World and Africa*, "her degradation and enchaining, the fire and freedom of black Africa, with the uncurbed might of her consort Asia, are indispensable to the fertilizing of the universal soil of man." Indeed, as Du Bois quoted Raphael Armattoe, a Ghanaian poet and doctor, he believed that Africa was necessary "to restore ethical principles to world civilization."[91]

In the decades following Du Bois's work on Africa, a flood of scholarship has looked in general into Africa's contributions to the rise of western civilization and in particular into the continent's influence on Christianity, Islam, and Judaism. During the 1980s and 1990s, Martin Bernal rocked ancient scholarship with his "Black Athena" thesis, an argument that borrowed heavily from Du Bois. Bernal maintained that ancient Greek civilization, which is almost uniformly viewed as the basis for western civilization, borrowed significantly from Egyptian and Middle Eastern cultures and that this history was suppressed during the late eighteenth and nineteenth centuries to legitimate white supremacy. Bernal's critics have been vociferous in their denunciations. At the lead has been Mary Lefkowitz, who has declared the Afrocentrism of Bernal and others as mere "propaganda" and even a "racist approach" to history.[92]

Yet if the African-to-Greek connections are contested, religious historians have shown innumerable and undeniable links between Africa and ancient Judaism, Islam, and early Christianity. David Goldenberg and others have examined the relationships among Africa, blacks, and slavery in Jewish, Christian, and Muslim societies, and have demonstrated precisely what Du Bois maintained decades ago—that Africa and Africans played a crucial, albeit historically minimized, role in the origins and shape of modern world religions. Current scholarship does not even debate whether northern Africa was an element in ancient Judaism and Christianity. Rather scholars debate what constituted "Africa" and "black" in the Ancient world. What Du Bois set out to reveal to a broad audience has become an accepted academic truism. The academic jury has made no final decision regarding the place of Africa in the history of western civilization, but it is clear that Hegel's "ancient lie" is now ancient itself.[93]

At the level of popular ministry and culture, African influences on Christian history have now achieved a level of respect, at least among people of color. There are now "study bibles" that include special annotations "relative to the African/Edenic perspective." There are now board games and posters "celebrating God's hand in black history," which include studies of black heroes in the Bible, skits, songs, crossword puzzles, and craft ideas.[94] There are sermons devoted to "the beauty of blackness in the Bible," and there are videos for churches to use from prominent scholars, such as Cain Hope Felder, on "the presence of the Black in Biblical antiquity."[95] Even in popular novels by African Americans, the Africanness of world religions has found a place of honor. In Marita Golden's *The Edge of Heaven* (1992), a story about three middle-class African American women in Washington, D.C., and their attempts to make sense of themselves, one character describes her travels in Europe as a time of spiritual growth, one that could have been taken directly from Du Bois's works: "I discovered an African aspect to European history we never hear about here, the Moors, the Black Madonna. I wasn't a stranger there. They'd seen me before." On other occasions throughout the novel, the characters decorate Christmas trees with "Black angels with papier-mâché wings and Afros and kente-cloth scarves around their necks."[96]

Certainly Du Bois was not solely responsible for the attention to Africa in religious history. Other scholars of Du Bois's era, including Melville Herskovits, Chapman Cohen, and Reginald Coupland, drew attention to the importance of Africa in Christian history. Theologians and ministers in the years following Du Bois, such as Albert Cleage and James Cone, moreover, have drawn direct attention to the importance of black figures in African American religion, while black artists and literary figures, including James Weldon Johnson, Romare Bearden, and Archibald Motley, Jr., explored ways of linking biblical characters with Africans and African Americans. Perhaps most crucially, the civil rights and the Black Power movements both encouraged a sense of African cultural nationalism that promoted the identification of people of color with Africa and black symbolic figures. Just as "white dolls" were believed to denigrate the race, "white Christs" and "white saints" were believed to spiritually undermine people of color. Hence, by the 1950s and 1960s, much greater attention among African Americans was focused on the racialization of sacred symbols.[97]

Yet, while Du Bois was not the only force in this revolution in sacred symbolism and religious history, it is a tragedy of history that Du Bois is not more often discussed in these transformations. Du Bois was a key player in the resurrection of Africa in the religious imagination of African Americans, and he

never shied away from characterizing himself a prophet of pan-Africanism. This presentation of self, moreover, was reinforced by his contemporaries. While a professor at Atlanta University in the early twentieth century, for example, Du Bois often led his students in prayers that encouraged global awareness and solidarity. He sought to connect his students and oppressed peoples throughout the world into one spiritual community. "Remember, O God, thru'out the world this night those who struggle for better government and freer institutions," he prayed. Then later, he intoned, "Help us to realize that our brothers are not simply those of our own blood and nation, but far more are they those who think as we do and strive toward the same ideals. So tonight in Persia and China, in Russia and Turkey, in Africa and all America, let us bow with our brothers and sisters and pray as they pray for a world, well-governed—void of war and caste, and free to each asking soul. Amen." Before another class session, he looked to the Lord to "remember with us to-night, O God, our kindred beyond the seas; they that sit in darkness without the shining of the mighty light that beats upon these leading lands. Forget them not, O God, for they are Thine and ours."[98]

On other occasions, Du Bois explicitly spoke as a prophet of pan-African-ism. Du Bois ended *The World and Africa* as he did many of his other works, with a cosmic call to the reader. It entailed a vision for the future, one that matched well with his "Credo" of forty years earlier. "I dream of a world of infinite and invaluable variety; not in the laws of gravity or atomic weights, but in a human variety in height and weight, color and skin, hair and nose and lip. . . . all possible manner of difference, topped with freedom of soul to do and be." Although shorn of its explicit biblical rhetoric, this message once again demonstrated Du Bois's presentation of self as a prophet and empow-ered him to cast a vision for a renewed world.[99] Or, as he wrote with clearer religious symbolism in *Color and Democracy*, published one year before *The World and Africa*, "The day has dawned when above a wounded, tired earth unselfish sacrifice, without sin and hell, may join through technique, shorn of ruthless greed, and make a new religion, one with new knowledge, to shout from old hills of heaven 'Go down, Moses!'" Linking the spiritual of God's anointed "Go Down, Moses," to a new religion that mixed the best of religion and science, Du Bois by midcentury hoped for a new faith, a new church, and a new power to redeem the earth that had convulsed under so much carnage and mayhem.[100]

The effect of Du Bois's work on Africa was impressive. Several reviewers seemed to approach him as a religious leader, one whose work was a "revela-

tion." According to W. M. Brewer, a professor of history at Miner Teachers College in Washington, D.C., "His vision easily transcends that of any colored leader that has yet appeared. Here is a voice that appealed through the darkness of prejudice and inhumanity to man with a tardy triumph in spite of concerted efforts to suppress stinging truths always anathema to the white world." "His sacrifices and devotion for colored people," Brewer continued, "speak mightily through the respect which he enjoys as a leader that has risen irresistibly from the choice of his people as every real leader does." Brewer concluded that no "one who is interested in world reconstruction on a saner basis can afford to miss the revelation of the role of Africa in world history or the place of its myriad peoples and cultures in the drama of all mankind." Eric Williams, the brilliant historian of capitalism and slavery, commented that Du Bois's work "will come as a revelation to the ordinary citizen as well as to the average student." Another reviewer, Myrtle M. Bowers, compared Du Bois with John the Baptist. "For the larger portion" of Du Bois's career, he has been "a voice in the wilderness crying out for equality for his people."[101]

Du Bois was not the only voice of his era speaking on religion, church reform, race, imperialism, war, materialism, and social uplift. But he was certainly the most articulate and the most comprehensive. From the Christian typologies he mapped onto Africa to his insistence that imperialism was a sin in the eyes of God, from his portrayal of the "Negro church" as the fundamental social institution of black life to his denunciations of the spiritual wage of whiteness, Du Bois repeatedly used religious idioms and concepts in his approach to history and sociology. He conceived of himself as a dark monk in the lineage of Martin Luther, a man who by will, erudition, and faith would lead a religious revolution with his pen.

∽

In the early 1970s, a young African American sociologist set out to learn more about the legendary Du Bois. Dorothy Yancey, a professor at Georgia Institute of Technology in Atlanta and later the president of Johnson C. Smith University in Charlotte, North Carolina, wanted to know what Du Bois's students and colleagues thought of him. On locating ten of his former Atlanta University students and colleagues, she found a number of surprising, and not so surprising, facts. Du Bois would bring coffee and cookies to his graduate seminars; he was never without his cane; he rarely remembered a student's name, even well into the semester. When interviewing Samuel Usher, Yancey received perhaps her most shocking reflection. Usher reminisced that as a

college student, he was convinced that his history and sociology professor was an Episcopalian. And, if this faith was good enough for Professor Du Bois, then it was good enough for young man Usher. Upon graduation, Usher attended an Episcopalian seminary and became Reverend Samuel Usher. He spent his entire career in the church, in part, because of Du Bois.[102]

What moved Samuel Usher to become a minister? Perhaps it was the prayers that Du Bois shared with his classes, prayers that invoked a social gospel and called for an alliance of all oppressed peoples. Perhaps Usher was drawn to the content of Du Bois's historical analyses, where he often discussed personal, national, and global religious history, identifying himself and his family as Episcopalian but calling for a reformation of all religion. Perhaps it was Du Bois's sociological work that situated the "Negro church" at the center of African American society. Or, perhaps it was Du Bois's claim that future improvement of the world and of the race would necessarily come from religious folk and organizations. Whatever it was, some aspect of Du Bois's teaching, his persona, his presentation, or his reputation led this young man to find a religious mission. Perhaps there was no greater testament to the religious power of Du Bois than his influence on Usher.

Du Bois's affect was apparent with Samuel Usher as it was in so many other areas. Du Bois approached his scholarship as a moral intellectual, one whose research spoke to ethical and religious problems in the United States and the world. Like Martin Luther, Du Bois was a "dark monk" who saw the power of religion, felt frustrated by its dogmas, and tried to reform it. What Du Bois wanted was a new reformation, a return to the original teachings of Christ, not to help people make it to an otherworldly heaven but to create heaven on earth. In the fusing of scholarship and belief, Du Bois hoped to create a new path for the United States and for the world. He hoped to make a stronger race of black ministers, men who would preach not only Christ crucified but also against the crucifixion of black men and women. He hoped to chastise white ministers for failing to live up to the likes of John Brown or Saint Francis of Assisi. In the process, he reconfigured Africa, the racialized structure of American history and society, and even the image of Christ.

It was in his poetry, prose, and historical novels that Du Bois would bring this reimagining of Christ to a new plane. By linking Christ's life and death with those of embattled African Americans, Du Bois joined a chorus of men and women of color seeking to make religious sense of the racial brutality they experienced in the United States. While racial violence for whites became an important part of their social cohesion, black Americans had to

wrestle with the question, how could a supposedly all-loving, all-powerful god allow such bloodshed and tears? With new renditions of biblical stories and a host of fictive prophets, priestesses, and messiahs, Du Bois looked for dramas of redemption in places that others refused to look. From the hanging bodies of black men and the anguished cries of black women, Du Bois saw and heard the calls of salvation.

∽

Black Messiahs and Murderous Whites

Violence and Faith in Literary Expression

AWAITING EXECUTION, Bigger Thomas sat brooding in his prison cell. The fictional lead of Richard Wright's gripping novel *Native Son* (1940) now had to endure the visit of an African American minister from his mother's church. The pastor begged Bigger to accept the love of God. "Fergit yuh's black," Reverend Hammond implored, "Gawd looks past yo' skin 'n inter yo' soul, son. He's lookin' at the only parta yuh tha's *His*. He wants yuh 'n' He loves yuh." Bigger wanted to be left alone. The judge wasn't going to forget Bigger's blackness; neither would the jury. To pacify Reverend Hammond, Bigger accepted a small cross and wore it on a necklace. Shortly after the minister left Bigger, white policemen escorted him to the crime scene—the large home of the Daltons where he had murdered their white daughter. When he approached the house, Bigger noticed in the distance a white mob and "a flaming cross." The image confused and dismayed Bigger. "But why should they burn a cross?" he wondered. The blazing wood reminded him of how Reverend Hammond spoke "intensely and solemnly of Jesus, of there being a cross for him, a cross for everyone, and of how the lowly Jesus had carried the cross, paving the way, showing how to die, how to love and live the life eternal." Perhaps, Bigger conjectured, the white mob "want[ed] him to love Jesus, too?"[1]

Bigger realized quickly, however, that this burning cross was different. "No! That was not right; they ought not burn a cross," Bigger thought. The two different crosses left him with two distinct emotional reactions. "The cross the preacher had told him about was bloody, not flaming; meek, not militant. It

made him feel awe and wonder, not fear and panic. It made him want to kneel and cry, but this cross made him want to curse and kill." Then it dawned on Bigger: This flaming cross was of the Ku Klux Klan. With it, they sought "to tell him they hated him!" The cross of anger and vengeance transformed his feelings for the cross around his neck. Emotion surged through Bigger. "He wanted to tear the cross from his throat and throw it away. He was feeling the cross that touched his chest, like a knife and pointed at his heart. His fingers ached to rip it off; it was an evil and black charm which would surely bring him death now." When Bigger returned to his cell hours later, he got his wish. Twice, he cast the cross to the ground. The second time, he threw it "through the bars of the cell. It hit the wall beyond with a lonely clatter." Bigger had rejected the cross and all of its symbolic power and confusion.[2]

W. E. B. Du Bois was no Bigger Thomas, although the two appear similar in terms of religion if one listens to Du Bois's biographers. Violent white hypocrisy and the irrelevant religious platitudes of blacks, it seems, led the fictive Bigger and the real Du Bois to cast away the cross. Du Bois may not have rejected it in a prison cell, but he allegedly did so in his university office, in his mind, and in his heart. Yet more than ten years before Wright's *Native Son*, Du Bois offered a striking counterliterary approach to race and the cross. In "The Son of God," published in *The Crisis* in 1933, Du Bois depicted a black Christ living, healing, teaching, and dying in Great Depression America. The tale began with "Joe" striking his fiancée "Mary." Unwilling to believe that the baby growing in her womb was "the Son of God," as Mary kept repeating, Joe determined to find out whom the father was. He never did. Mary's son "Joshua" (the correct translation of Jesus' Hebrew name) baffled Joe even more in life. As a young man, Joshua spent a great deal of time "hanging around with a lot of Communists and talking on street corners, and saying things about property that white folks ain't going to stand for." Joshua even befriended white prostitutes and other undesirable figures. The connection between the modern Joshua and the biblical Christ was unmistakable; at one point, Du Bois had Joshua raise his friend "Laz" (Lazarus) from the dead.[3]

With a growing public presence, Joshua addressed a crowd outside of a courthouse and gave a riveting speech. With a beautiful revoicing of Christ's Sermon on the Mount, Joshua proclaimed a new vision for heaven and earth, one that resonated with the concerns of many poor, disfranchised, and brutalized blacks and whites during the Great Depression. "Heaven is going to be filled with people who are down-hearted and you that are mourning will get a lot of comfort some day," Joshua declared. "It's meek folk who are lucky, and going to get everything; and you that are hungry, too. Poor people are bet-

ter than rich people because they work for what they wear and eat." He then made a bold proclamation about the hereafter: "There won't be any rich people in Heaven." Joshua implored his audience to be kind in an unkind world, to find joy in a joyless journey, and to take the moral high road in a world of low roads: "You got to be easy on guys when they do wrong. Then they'll be easy on you, when you get in bad. God's sons are those that won't quarrel. You must treat other people just like you want to be treated. Let'm call you names. Listen! They have called some of the biggest folks that ever lived, dirty names. What's the difference? Which ones do we remember? Don't work all the time. Sit down and rest and sing sometimes. Everything's all right." "Give God time," Joshua concluded, echoing Du Bois's "Credo" where he announced his belief in "patience with God."[4]

Neither Joe nor the rich white folk in the audience wanted to hear such words. Joe rejected his son, claiming that Joshua's teachings were "damned nonsense." Joe knew what became of black men who congregated with white women, who pushed too hard and too fast for economic change, and who gained notoriety. And Joe was right; Joshua's teachings incensed the white community. At the age of thirty, he was "seized by a mob and they had hanged him at sunset." No one knew exactly why they killed Joshua. As Du Bois narrated, "The charge against him wasn't clear: 'Worshiping a new God.' 'Living with white women!' 'Getting up a revolution.' 'Stealing or blasphemy,' the neighbors muttered." Yet it seemed apparent that Joshua had violated the most deeply held feelings of American society. And he died for it.[5]

Unlike Joe, Mary never wavered in her faith. She continually described Joshua as a neo-Christ, drawing on biblical passages to reassure herself. She referred to Joshua as "despised and rejected of men" (Isaiah 53:3) and claimed that his "name shall be called Wonderful, Councillor, the Mighty God, the Ever-Lasting Father and the Prince of Peace" (Isaiah 9:6). Even after the lynching, Mary held firm. "Behold the Sign of Salvation–a noosed rope," she declared. In her mind and faith, Mary transformed the noosed rope into a sacred symbol. That which snapped her son's neck was now that which would save her son's people.[6]

Interestingly, Du Bois concluded this modern version of the death of Jesus Christ with the image of Joe weeping, not with a divine resurrection of Joshua. After Joshua's death, Joe "crawled out to the barn and leaned against it; gripping its planks with bleeding hands." He witnessed the shadow of the noose spreading across the entire globe and heard Mary's voice once more proclaim, "He is the Son of God." Joe then "buried his head in the dirt and sobbed." The story was finished, but so many questions remained. Was Joe hiding or pray-

ing? Did he call out to his son for help? Or, did he cry from a sense of futility? Du Bois gave no indication. Perhaps more profound questions emerge from Du Bois's neglect of the resurrection. If the black community could not rely on a risen savior, then where should they turn? What actions should they take, given the ethical teachings of this black Christ and his example?

As demonstrated in "The Son of God," biblical narratives of Christ and his execution provided a vivid set of images for Du Bois to delve into the inner workings of faith, race, and violence in American society. Contained within the passion narrative, Du Bois presented an assortment of possible responses to American society: the messianic prophet, the resolute believer, and the realistic skeptic. The Christ-like prophet Joshua defied the defining features of dominant culture in the 1930s United States: free-market capitalism, racial hatred, misogyny, and anti-Communism. Through Joshua's words, Du Bois gave voice to the profound dissonance between the Christianity of Christ and the racialized and capitalist structure of the United States. Joshua's mother represented the African American believer. She may have been brutalized by her husband; she may have been confused by her son's actions; she may have had moments of disbelief or despair. But Mary always returned to faith in her son, her God, and her race. Her black boy was a child of God, irrespective of the conditions of his birth; he had knowledge of the divine, irrespective of the composition of his comrades; and he was a savior, irrespective of the mob's hatred. With her faith, Mary overpowered the madness of the mob and transformed the horrific execution into the holy workings of God. Joe, alternatively, stood as a predecessor to Bigger Thomas as the skeptical unbeliever. He knew America's racial and economic realities and wanted to steer clear of anything that would get him killed. The price, of course, was rejecting his son, refusing to believe in his marvelous teachings, and finding only despair.

Playing with images of the cross and Christ, Du Bois and Wright joined a long tradition of African American uses of biblical symbolism to speak to racial violence. For hundreds of years, the African American experience has been marked by intense faith, intense brutality, and an intense drive to reconcile the two. As an object of redemption and execution, the cross has been invested with symbolic and elastic meaning among women and men of color. Of course, most African Americans did not reject Christianity as Bigger did. But Joe and Bigger spoke for the awareness of African Americans to the social and religious situations they faced. How could they believe in a loving, omnipotent God, and yet live under an avalanche of persecution? How could they worship the same God as those who oppressed them? And how could they reside in a "Christian nation" and yet fear cruelty every single day?[7]

Nowhere was the paradox of faith and bloodshed more apparent than in the practice of lynching, the fate of the fictive Joshua and thousands of real African Americans. This brutal, extralegal practice marred the American landscape, especially during the late nineteenth and early twentieth centuries. Judge Lynch terrorized African Americans in body, mind, and soul. But mass violence also inspired women and men of color to new heights of intellectual and religious creativity. Although Bigger Thomas was unable to reconcile the cross on his neck and the cross of the Klan, artists like Du Bois developed ways to reclaim and redeem these Christian symbols. Many African American writers, artists, and leaders created religious meaning amid the brutality of their world by depicting lynchings as crucifixions and Christ as a contemporary black man. Mapping biblical symbols onto racial violence was a brilliant maneuver. It reversed the cosmic order asserted and upheld by the lynch mob, one that linked whiteness with godliness and blackness with sinfulness. By associating black victims with the biblical Christ, black writers turned this white supremacist cosmology on its head. They sought to reveal lynchings for what they really were—evil mob murders committed against innocent African Americans by bloodthirsty and unchristian whites.[8]

Du Bois is the most underappreciated figure in this already underacknowledged sacred revision, but he may have been the most exceptional. Many students of African American life and culture would be shocked to learn that the allegedly agnostic W. E. B. Du Bois expended a great deal of literary energy imagining the manifestation of a black Christ in the United States, of translating Jesus' teachings into the American scene, of populating his tales with apocalyptic visions, and of singing dramas of redemption. His poems and short stories in *Darkwater*, his passion narratives in *The Crisis*, his dramas, his novels *The Quest of the Silver Fleece, Dark Princess: A Romance*, and the Black Flame trilogy provide another vision of the depth of his religious imagination. Du Bois linked Christ's crucifixion with the lynching of African American men and drew on a variety of religious concepts to reveal the demonic spirit of white America and to reassure the black community of its access to the sacred and divine. These tales played an integral role in his challenge to racial and economic discrimination, and they revealed a religious ingenuity rarely recognized. If these tales offer insight into Du Bois's inner beliefs, they reveal a keen appreciation for the sacred, a belief that the actions of men and women on earth have cosmic significance, and a hope that God's righteousness would invade humanity through a select number of modern prophets, priests, and messiahs such as himself.

As broad and deep as Du Bois's religious imagination was, he most often

returned to the image of Christ in his creative work. The teachings of Christ, Du Bois maintained, provided evidence for all that was wrong with American capitalism and racism and all that was right with African American culture. As several other African American artists and writers did in the twentieth century, Du Bois wondered what Christ would look like and how he would live in the contemporary United States. What would Jesus do in the American South during the early twentieth century? Who would follow him? Who were the neo-Pharisees? Du Bois concluded that Christ would sympathize with black people in their oppressed condition, that he would chastise whites, and that God would need the help of brave black women and men. In his poetry and prose, Du Bois's black Christ not only embodied virtue in a nation mad with sin and malevolence but also heralded a call to rise up and strike against the caste and race systems.

By suggesting that Christ's teachings, example, and affiliation positioned him on the side of oppressed African Americans, Du Bois presaged the black liberation theological revolution of the late 1960s. As champions of civil rights and black power assaulted the citadels of white supremacy during the second half of the twentieth century, images of a blonde-haired, blue-eyed, "honky Christ" came under fire. Many African American preachers, theologians, and churchgoers had tired of a Jesus that looked so similar to their oppressors. One African American woman voiced this feeling when she commented that it was clear to her that "no white man would ever die on a cross for me." In defiance of the whitened gospel, African Americans proceeded to "blacken" the faith. They repainted statues of white Christs with black paint, and a host of black Madonnas appeared. *Ebony* not only carried a story on the "Quest for a Black Christ" in March 1969 but also printed an image of a black, kinky-haired Jesus on its cover.[9]

As part of the assault on the white Christ and white Christianity, theologians James Cone, Albert Cleage, Jr., J. Deotis Roberts, and William Jones crafted a "black liberation theology" that centered on the blackness of Christ and God.[10] The principal theological and social project of black theology was "to analyze the nature of the gospel of Jesus Christ in the light of oppressed black people so that they will see the gospel as inseparable from their humiliated condition, bestowing on them the necessary power to break the chains of oppression."[11] Collectively, these scholars maintained that God was not white, that Christ was not white, that he was not a middle-class businessman hawking a gospel of moderation, and that true Christianity supported the black freedom struggle. As Cleage prayed to God during a service at his Shrine of the Black Madonna in Detroit, "Certainly thou must understand that as black

people, it would be impossible for us to kneel before thee, believing thee to be a white God."[12]

The central features of black liberation theology existed in spirit, if not in name, well before the 1960s. They were present in Du Bois's literary works. Du Bois, moreover, even foreshadowed the womanist revision of liberation theology, which challenged the misogyny of white and black Christianity by affiliating Christ with disadvantaged women of color. Du Bois offered messianic roles for some of his fictional female characters as well, and in several of his poems, stories, and novels, Du Bois not only presented a black Christ and a black God with special relationships with African American women but also even spoke of God as a black woman.

Beyond his early formation of a black liberation theology, Du Bois offered a revolutionary way for scholars to consider links between religion and violence.[13] The passion narratives of Du Bois and other black artists suggest that they were attuned to the ways Christian narratives had the power to undermine religious justifications for violence. They recognized that lynchings and white supremacy were woven into the fabric of religion in the United States. Through murdering African Americans, witnessing the events, and chronicling the destruction in stories and pictures, whites created a series of what religious scholar René Girard has termed "persecution texts." Narratives from the perspective of the persecutor that sanctify their oppressive actions, persecution tales invest the violence committed against minority peoples with sacred meaning. Throughout history and especially at moments of social crisis, Girard maintained, societies have formed and re-formed themselves by rallying against a "present outsider," destroying that outsider, and then crafting persecution texts to commemorate the process. In the medieval period, for instance, Christians in Europe tended to blame Jews for large social problems and find communal solace only through murdering or expulsing them. Then, with written accounts of the purges, these Christian European communities proclaimed and shored up their sense of self-righteousness.[14]

Although "Christians" committed many of these atrocities and authored many of these persecution texts, Girard suggests that if read properly the Christian Bible supplies the antidote for the persecution narrative. The biblical gospels are tales of a scapegoated victim—Jesus Christ—told from the perspective of the victim (rather than the oppressor). And in the gospel narratives, Jesus was not an evil "present outsider" whose death is necessary for the social good of the community. Rather, he was an innocent victim murdered for no discernible reason. By approaching violence from the standpoint of the victim, rather than the victimizer, the biblical passion narratives decode and

unmask the myths supporting collective violence throughout human history. The murdered is not to blame for society's ills but is a victimized scapegoat used by the dominant culture to solidify itself. In the gospels, the oppressed is shown for what it truly is, an innocent casualty assaulted by a society building itself on violence. Only by reversing persecution narratives can their power be stolen and redemption won.[15]

African American writers like Du Bois tapped into this understanding of the Christian gospels. In the American context, the battle between persecution narratives and antipersecution narratives found a niche in commentaries on lynching and other racialized violence. In whites' representations of lynchings, African Americans constituted evildoers whose punishment would save the community. In turn, African American authors such as Du Bois followed the trajectory of the Christian gospels by conflating the experiences of the scapegoated Christ with that of American blacks to strip the brutality of its sacred connotations. Simultaneously, by charging the lynch victim with divine status, Du Bois and others offered a new deity to replace the god of whiteness, and they cast a vision of a new world beyond racism and economic exploitation. They offered instead a merciful deity who encouraged patience and kindness, brotherhood and justice, sacrifice and integrity, and who crossed racial, national, and gender lines.

All in all, Du Bois's literary creations display dynamic religious creativity and ingenuity. He filled his literary works with black messiahs and gods, with prophets and priests of various hues, with apocalyptic vision and baptisms of blood, with dramas of redemption and comedies of sin. Du Bois clothed the mundane in cosmic garb, endeavoring to reveal hidden and deep realities of life. In this world of angels and demons, prophets and princesses, black Christs and white sinners, Du Bois proved himself one of America's most thoughtful religious writers. He was no Bigger Thomas. He refused to cast down the cross and let whites maintain their grip on it. Instead, he seized it from American culture, refashioned it time and again, and wielded its power in opposition to the persecution texts of white mastery and black inhumanity.

American Persecution Narratives and the God of Whiteness

The history of Africans in America is one of extreme and routine brutality. The process of enslavement was vicious. The "Middle Passage" constituted a horrid affair. Millions of Africans perished, and those who survived carried emotional scars for the rest of their lives. When in the United States, the

Caribbean, and Central and South America, moreover, the physical, psychic, and emotional violence continued. Slave auctions served as instruments of dehumanization as white buyers, sellers, and onlookers sought to divorce the person of color from his or her personhood. Whippings, beatings, and murders plagued plantations, and threats of physical damage were every-where. Whether owners had the "legal right" to abuse their slaves was a moot point—for the enslaved had little access to courts, attorneys, or the police, unless of course they were suspected of running away. Black women encoun-tered much of the brutality in the form of rape—a history that many whites still refuse to acknowledge.[16]

Emancipation in the United States brought no end to the brutality. White vigilante gangs, such as the Ku Klux Klan and the White Caps, terrorized African Americans and their supporters. Systems of convict labor decimat-ed black populations. Widespread debt peonage arrangements developed throughout the South. No example of racial violence was as gripping as lynch-ings. Antilynching crusader Ida B. Wells believed that white mobs lynched more than ten thousand African Americans between 1865 and 1900. Most historical assessments place the number of lynchings lower, but even conser-vative estimates reveal mob violence to be widespread especially from 1880 to 1920. Between 1889 and 1899, for instance, whites lynched at least one thou-sand African Americans–or about one every three days for the entire decade. The lynchings were practiced, remembered, commemorated, and celebrated thousands of times more than that through newspaper stories, photographs, postcards, souvenirs, and stories told at the fireside.[17]

The late nineteenth century constituted a social crisis in the South as it faced economic, social, and religious modernization; the Populist rebellion; increas-ing class tensions; women seeking to enter politics; and the rise of the "New Negro." In the face of such social disorientation, a variety of whites sought a way to reconsolidate white society. African Americans became the "present outsider" and "scapegoats" by which poor, middle-class, and elite whites reso-lidified their society. By targeting and then murdering black men, whites of all distinctions rallied together amid their social confusion and upheaval.[18]

Death at the hands of the lynch mob was gruesome. People of color, gen-erally men, were beaten, tortured, burned alive, and dismembered. Some of the victims had their genitals mutilated, while others were decapitated. In the late 1880s, many of these events became public spectacles as whites joined to watch, photograph, and revel in the killings. With staged photographs and postcards of the murders, newspaper reports lionizing the mob, and souve-nirs taken from the bodies of the deceased, southern whites created their own

set of "persecution narratives" whereby they commemorated their newfound social cohesion. The thousands of lynching photographs of white audiences served as testaments to the reconsolidation of whiteness and as threats to the black community.[19]

The only way such "God fearing" white Americans could practice and commemorate such vicious behavior was through the sanctifying of their actions. In both practice and imagination, the lynchings of thousands of African Americans had serious and apparent connections to religious rituals and beliefs. As Orlando Patterson, Ralph Ellison, Donald Mathews, and W. Scott Poole have maintained, lynchings had all of the trappings of a religious blood ritual. Steeped in biblical theologies predicated on violence (most notably concepts of retributive justice and atoning sacrifices) and living in a society in which religious leaders condoned and sanctified racial segregation, southern whites throughout American history fused and confused their faith in white supremacy with their faith in Christianity. As twentieth-century white author Lillian Smith remembered of her youth, she and other whites learned "to love God, to love our white skin and to believe in the sanctity of both."

The connections between lynchings and southern religion were profound and varied. On some occasions, whites followed Sunday church services with vigilante murders, and white ministers were notorious for either condoning the mayhem or participating in it. Some even offered opening prayers at lynchings. During the lynching, some participants discussed feeling a sense of sacred "awe," especially when a hush of silence fell over the crowd. This was a calm before the storm, for after the silence the crowd would become frenzied and sometimes tear the victim limb from limb. At least one observer noted that the energy of the lynch mob seemed similar to that of a revival congregation, and the connection to an atoning blood ritual or a rite of exorcism seemed pervasive in the event. In fact, when writing a letter to his sister in Atlanta about a lynching in the area, seminary student Earnest Cox actually crossed out the word "killed" in reference to the African American men and replaced it with "sacrificed."[20]

The language of demonology was ubiquitous in newspaper reports of the events. Time and again, southern whites referred to black men accused of crimes as "demons," "devils," and "imps from hell." Most often, these terms came as the result of alleged rapes of white women or murders of white families. In Statesboro, Georgia, in 1904, for instance, Will Cato and Paul Reed stood accused of murdering a white family. Local and regional newspapers denounced them as subhuman devils. The *Atlanta Journal* claimed, "human beings with immortal souls, possessed of ordinary sanity, are not equal to it. It

requires the lowest order of brute; the devilish ingenuity of a fiend, to concoct and commit such a crime." The actions of lynch mobs, moreover, were sanctified in the press. A mob in Indiana in 1901 "did God worshipful service" by killing a black man, claimed one southern paper. "It is the unwritten law of the glorious South, and in spite of cravens and Pharisees it will continue to be unrepealed . . . while manhood of the civilization of the South endure. . . . It is part of the religion of our people."[21]

Popular literature and film linked racial violence and notions of God as well, creating a deep-seated psychic link between violence against black bodies and the sanctity of white society. Literary critic Trudier Harris has shown how lynch acts served as "rites of exorcism" whereby white Americans sought to eradicate "the black beast" from their midst. The boldest white supremacist authors had no problem associating the violence committed against people of color with the sacred. In the literary imagination of Thomas Dixon, Jr., for instance, the Ku Klux Klan and white lynch mobs were God's hands and feet in the United States. Likening the Klan to Oliver Cromwell's Puritan forces in England, Dixon claimed that the Klan fought for "their God, their native land, and the womanhood of the South." It is little wonder, then, that when D. W. Griffith transformed Dixon's white supremacist, Klan-glorifying novels onto the silver screen in *Birth of a Nation*, Griffith made sure to use an image of Christ. At the end of the film, after the Klan had "redeemed" the white South from the clutches of "Negro rule," a white Jesus rises above the entire scene to provide a divine blessing on the new South and the new nation.[22]

African American journalist George Schuyler observed this meshing of sacred and profane with great insight and sardonic wit in his now-classic *Black No More* (1931). In this tale, a new scientific process that whitened blacks wrought social havoc in the United States. With no way to tell who was authentically "white" and who was not, panic reached epic proportions. Near the end of the novel, rural whites became so frustrated that they turned to a new faith. Reverend Alex McPhule (perhaps pronounced McFool or McFuel) spearheaded this new belief and the new church that went with it. McPhule needed a sign from heaven of his prophetic position and he knew just what to look for—some black men to lynch. "If the Lord would only send him a nigger for his congregation to lynch! That would, indeed, be marked evidence of the power of Rev. Alex McPhule," Schuyler penned. Then McPhule got his wish. A black bat flew though one of his services, and the congregants took it as a sign—they would lynch the next blacks they found. God did not disappoint. Two white leaders of the Anglo-Saxon Association showed up in town

dressed as black men so that no one would recognize them, and the congregation jumped to action. "The Sign! Look! Niggers! Praise God! The Sign! Lynch 'em!" the crowd roared. Praising God as they went, the white mob assailed the black-faced men. The "two men . . . were stripped naked . . . their ears and genitals cut off with jack knives. . . . Their ears [were sewed] to their backs and they were released and told to run. . . . A half-dozen revolvers cracked and the two Virginians pitched forward into the dust amid the uproarious laughter of the congregation."[23]

Hovering over and sanctifying the religious violence stood the image of a white Jesus and white God, characterizations that by the early twentieth century seemed to invade all elements of American culture. Beginning in the early nineteenth century with illustrated and picture book Bibles, American consumers drank in images of whitened Christs and other biblical characters. The biblical characters represented in such works as Harper's *Illuminated Bible* (1846), which contained more than fifteen hundred images, represented such biblical characters as Abraham, Moses, Jeremiah, and Jesus, with physical features that connoted whiteness: straight hair, narrow lips, pale skin, and high foreheads. Then, in the late nineteenth century, French artist James Jacques Joseph Tissot's watercolor exhibition *The Life of Our Saviour Jesus Christ* captivated thousands of Americans. It presented Christ as a virtuous Victorian, and his light skin and Anglo look contrasted with the sinister hook-nosed Jewish characters who challenge him. Tissot's contemporaries praised his images of Christ for being "luminous," for showing an "incandescence," and for having a "certain awfulness of light and whiteness." Tissot's Anglo-Saxon Christ figures made their way into American prints and the early film industry, and the image of a white Christ was everywhere by the early twentieth century.[24]

Images of a white Christ, the rituals of the lynch mob, and the theologies of white supremacists all worked together in the late nineteenth and early twentieth centuries to sanctify the racial violence that was exploding all over the nation. Rather than act in secret or express any guilt for mob lynchings, whites across the nation cast themselves as heroic Christian men vanquishing the devils from their sight. Rather than devilish murderers, they conceived of themselves as divine missionaries. Lynchings became the ultimate persecution narratives by which white American society refashioned itself and proclaimed itself God's gift to humankind. In this way, lynchings became acts of Christian service, black men became devils incarnate, and white women became angels.

"That's a Damned Lie! Jesus Was Black!"

African American men and women could not help but have religious and spiritual questions in the face of this long tradition of ferocity. If God were loving, good, and powerful–as Christianity seemed to suggest–why did black folk encounter so much horror, and so much more than other groups? Why were they so hated and brutalized? Eighteenth-century poet and African American writer Jupiter Hammond acknowledged his profound confusion over such questions when addressing a group of African Americans in New York: "While I have been thinking on this subject, I have frequently had great struggles in my own mind, and have been at a loss to know what to do." In the South, enslaved men and women sang the religious problem of oppression with profound insight in the spiritual "Didn't my Lord deliver Daniel":

> Didn't my Lord deliver Daniel, deliver Daniel, deliver Daniel?
> Didn't my Lord deliver Daniel, and why not everyone?

Decades later, confronted by the rise of lynchings in the twentieth century, Mary Church Terrell, one of the founders of the NAACP and the National Association of Colored Women, voiced a similar religious conundrum. "For a time [lynchings] came near upsetting my faith in the Christian religion," she asserted in her autobiography. "I could not see how a crime like that could be perpetrated in a Christian country, while thousands of Christians sinfully winked at it by making no protest loud enough to be heard or exerting any earnest effort to redress this terrible wrong."[25]

According to religious theorist Anthony Pinn, while African Americans have responded to the moral evil of racism in a variety of ways, most have found solace in a theory of "redemptive suffering." Put simply, a large number of blacks from the eighteenth century to the present have interpreted evil and suffering as a means by which God sought to teach and purify them. Yet explaining the origins of this evil (whether it was redemptive or not) was only the beginning of the dilemma. African Americans had to confront the actual violence; to address the existential angst it produced; and to overcome the brutal acts, the persecutors, and the persecution narratives that sanctified these events.[26]

In response to mass violence and to whites' persecution narratives, African American authors tried to redeem the lynch victim and, in so doing, the entire race. They had to take on the white God, the white Christ, the persecution

texts, and the persecution itself. While some African Americans responded by denouncing Christianity and establishing new religious traditions, Du Bois and a host of African American authors and artists chose instead to associate the black victim with the biblical Christ. With this link, they tried to divest white violence of its sacred status by destabilizing the myths of white civility and black brutality. A number of African Americans joined Du Bois in this work, including Langston Hughes, poet Countee Cullen, playwright Georgia Douglas Johnson, and painters Henry Ossawa Tanner and Aaron Douglass. In one way or another, all sought to convert the lynched African American from an object of disdain into a paragon of virtue. Yet the alleged black sinner became more than a saint in this literary and artistic tradition. He became a potential savior not only for the oppressed community but also for the persecutors, the whites. In the conflation of violated blackness and the divine–generally through the creation of a black Christ–African American artists, poets, playwrights, and painters did not seek to answer the problem of evil as it related to people of color. They accepted the reality of their historical situation, but with theological and literary skill endeavored to recast it as a cosmic tale.[27]

From the beginning of the nineteenth century to its end, a growing number of African Americans problematized the whitening of Jesus, God, and other messianic characters by imagining nonwhite sacred figures. In 1829, Robert Alexander Young, a northern black, looked forward to a messiah of ambiguous racial classification in his *The Ethiopian Manifesto, Issued in Defense of the Blackman's Rights, in the Scale of Universal Freedom* (1829). He quoted the biblical God as saying, "surely hath the cries of the black, a most persecuted people, ascended to my throne and craved my mercy; now, behold! I will stretch forth my hand and gather them to the palm, that they become unto me a people, and I unto them their God." And God had already sent a deliverer, Young insisted. The new savior was in the form of a mixed-race messiah, "in him will be seen, in appearance, a white man, although having been born of a black woman."[28]

Published the same year as Young's *Ethiopian Manifesto*, David Walker's *Appeal to the Coloured Citizens of the World* was a stirring indictment of white Christianity in the name of a militant black faith. Running a clothing store in the 1820s in Boston, Walker was active among the abolitionists in the city and he had no objections to militant resistance. His "Appeal" was really a righteous diatribe calling for the forceful dismantling of slavery. Appearing just before Nat Turner's slave revolt in Virginia, Walker's text frightened southern slaveholders, especially when copies were found sewn in the clothing of

sailors. Walker mocked the hypocrisy of "the white Christians of America, who hold us in slavery . . . [and] treat us more cruel and barbarous than any Heathen nation did any people whom it had subjected." Walker called these whites "pretenders to Christianity" who were an "unjust, jealous, unmerciful, avaricious and blood-thirsty set of beings, always seeking after power and authority." In the United States and the world, Walker maintained, blacks were the only hope for true Christianity. "It is my solemn belief, that if ever the world becomes Christianized . . . it will be through the means, under God of the *Blacks.*" The Lord will help black Americans, he continued, "God will indeed, deliver you through him from your deplorable and wretched condition under the Christians of America." And if whites did not repent, the result would be a holy bloodbath where men and women of color would strike against their oppressors.[29]

By the late nineteenth and early twentieth centuries, a growing number of African Americans may not have expressed as much clear rage as Walker, but they nonetheless continued to deny any connection between Christ and whiteness. In the art world, Henry Ossawa Tanner, the son of African Methodist Episcopal Church bishop Benjamin Tanner, offered darkened depictions of Christ and other biblical characters. In his *The Resurrection of Lazarus* (1897) and *Nicodemus Visiting Jesus* (1899), the French-residing, award-winning artist painted Christ with dark skin, a black beard, a moustache, and dark eyes. Tanner's Christ figures looked distinctly Mediterranean and, because Tanner had toured through Palestine, it made sense that he painted biblical characters to look like contemporary Middle Easterners.[30]

Most prominently, minister Henry McNeal Turner assailed the association of whiteness and godliness in a series of lectures in the 1890s. "In this country," he declared, "white represents God, and black the devil, but little thought is given to the Black man's future." Turner worried that African Americans had internalized this racialized belief system and could never achieve their true destiny without breaking away from it. He made no mistake that African Americans should imagine Jesus as a black man. "We have as much right biblically and otherwise to believe that God is a Negro, as you buckra and white people have to believe that God is a fine looking, symmetrical and ornamented white man. For the bulk of you and all the fool Negroes of the country believe that God is white-skinned, blue-eyed, straight-haired, projecting nosed, compressed lipped and finely robed white gentleman, sitting upon a throne somewhere in the heavens." Turner wondered aloud why whites could imagine Jesus as white, but blacks could not imagine Jesus as black: "as long as we remain among the whites the Negro will believe that the devil is black and

that he (the Negro) favors the devil, and that God is white and that he (the Negro) bears no resemblance to Him, and the effect of such a sentiment is contemptuous and degrading, and one-half of the Negro race will be trying to get white and the other half will spend their days in trying to be white men's scullions in order to please the whites."[31]

A segment of black Pentecostals in the early twentieth century followed Turner's lead. In Wrightsville, Arkansas, William Christian of the Church of the Living God created a catechism that tied biblical characters to black America. His question-and-answer approach to teaching religion contrasted markedly with the antebellum *Catechism of Colored Persons* developed by white missionaries on slave plantations. Before the Civil War, these missionaries taught enslaved black women and men a bastardized version of Christianity that claimed that God made black people to work and to obey white people. William Christian's catechism followed quite a different track, tying blackness to the Bible. In many ways, Christian's discussion of blackness in the Bible squared with Du Bois's in *The World and Africa* and *The Negro*:

> Q: What color was Job?
> A: He was black. (Job 30:30)
> Q: Who was Moses' wife?
> A: An Ethiopian (or black) woman. (Numbers 12:1)
> Q: What color was Jeremiah?
> A: He said he was black. (Jeremiah 8:21)

And perhaps the most radical question

> Q: Was Jesus a member of the black race?
> A: Yes. (Matthew 1)[32]

Another turn-of-the-century black leader, F. S. Cherry, declared, "Jesus was a black man and I'm offering fifteen hundred dollars cash to anyone who can produce an authentic likeness of Jesus Christ and show I'm wrong!" When a member of the crowd flashed a picture of a white Jesus, Cherry lashed out in response, "Who the hell is this? Nobody knows! They say it's Jesus! That's a damned lie! Jesus was black!"[33]

For many blacks, a host of forces collided in the early twentieth century to lead them to reject the Christianity of their mothers and fathers, or at least to alter it substantially. The hypocrisy of white Christians had long frustrated men and women of color, and images of the biblical Christ that looked ee-

rily similar to the same men who were killing black men only compounded the problem. Moreover, the movement of hundreds of thousands of African Americans from the rural South to the urban North in the Great Migration created a new population with new religious needs. In northern cities, leaders like Father Divine, Marcus Garvey, W. D. Fard, Elijah Muhammad, Timothy Drew, Elder Lightfoot Solomon Michaux, and "Daddy" Grace offered a wide variety of religious alternatives. Father Divine presented himself as God in the flesh with a cooperative economic plan to help all Americans in hard times. Drew's Moorish Science Temple of America claimed that African Americans were the "true Jews." Although not a rejection of Christianity outright, Marcus Garvey and his organization pushed for a new, universal black faith in their efforts to link all people of African descent. Universal Negro Improvement Association (UNIA) meetings felt like religious services, including hymns, prayers, and sermons, while UNIA leaders drew up a "Negro Catechism" and declared Christ to be the "Black Man of Sorrows." In Detroit, W. D. Fard and then his devotee Elijah Muhammad railed against the Bible and Christianity to form a new black-centered faith. They claimed that the first humans were black, that white Christians were "devils," and that black Christians were dupes in need of "mental resurrection."[34]

Malcolm X, a long-time follower of Elijah Muhammad's teachings and the son of a Garveyite, routinely incorporated an attack on the "white Christ" into his ministry. Recounting his years in a New England prison, for instance, Malcolm described an encounter with a "blond, blue-eyed" seminary student from Harvard—a "perfect 'devil,'" as Malcolm described him—over race and religion. Malcolm acknowledged that this "devil" had tremendous knowledge of the Bible, but Malcolm sought to best him. "I puzzled and puzzled for a way to upset him, and to give those Negroes present something to think and talk about and circulate." Eventually, Malcolm "stood up and asked, 'What color was Paul?' And I kept talking, with pauses, 'He had to be black . . . because he was a Hebrew . . . and the original Hebrews were black . . . weren't they?'" The seminary student became flustered, and "started flushing red. You know the way white people do. He said 'Yes.'" But Malcolm was not done. "'What color was Jesus . . . He was Hebrew, too . . . wasn't he?'" This question grabbed the attention of the inmates. "Both the Negro and the white convicts had sat bolt upright. I don't care how tough the convict, be he brainwashed black Christian, or a 'devil' white Christian, neither of them is ready to hear anybody saying Jesus wasn't white. The instructor walked around. He shouldn't have felt bad. In all of the years since, I never had met any intelligent white man who

would try to insist that Jesus was white. How could they? He said, 'Jesus was brown.' I let him get away with that compromise."[35]

There were ways to reject the hypocrisy of white Christianity, though, without rejecting Christianity completely. One method was to apply the symbols and ethics of the Bible to modern society, and many authors and artists did just that. Aaron Douglass and Zell Ingram, for instance, created figurative bonds between people of color and Jesus by depicting Christ as a poor African American in several paintings during the 1920s. Sometimes, this black Christ was a weary traveler in the South. Other times, he was a member of the "Scottsboro Nine," the group of young African American boys wrongly accused and held in prison for the alleged rape of two white women. Playwright Georgia Douglas Johnson in her "Sunday Morning in the South" pitted her audiences' physical senses against one another. While their eyes witnessed a white mob lynching an innocent black man, the audiences' ears heard hymns from a black church. The music of "Amazing Grace" and "Alas and Did My Saviour Bleed?" matched the groans of the victim. Johnson seemed to ask the onlookers whether these messages were discordant or in agreement. In either case, the juxtaposition had an unnerving effect. Johnson compelled the audience to confront the racialized violence that offered religious legitimacy to lynchings.[36]

In the realm of poetry, Claude McKay, Countee Cullen, and Langston Hughes made creative associations between the lynch victim and the divine. All leaders in the Harlem Renaissance, these authors used religion in their poetry to link the North and South, the urban and rural, and the old-time religion with new-time social problems. At the end of McKay's "The Lynching" (1922), he presented the victim not as an evil brute, but as a wronged child of God who was being called back to heaven.

> His father, by the cruelest way of pain,
> Had bidden him to his bosom once again.[37]

With perhaps less biblical savvy, but more gritty toughness and shock value, Langston Hughes minced few words in his "Christ in Alabama" (1931) when he declared Christ to be the bastard son of a black woman and a white man in the United States:

> Christ is a nigger,
> Beaten and black –
> *O, bare your back.*

Mary is His Mother
Mammy of the South,
Silence your Mouth

God's His Father –
White Master above
Grant us your love.

Most holy bastard
Of the bleeding mouth:
Nigger Christ
On the cross of the South.[38]

Du Bois's son-in-law, Countee Cullen, provided one of the most interesting narrative links of Jesus and African Americans in "The Black Christ" (1929). As literary critic Qiana Whitted has shown, Cullen demonstrated a keen and perceptive reading of the Bible in his poem. He drew on the Old Testament Book of Job as much as the New Testament in this tale of a black man executed by a lynch mob, but miraculously still alive after the events. Cullen began by declaring Christ to be the first lynch victim:

How Calvary in Palestine,
Extending down to me and mine,
Was but the first leaf in a line
Of trees on which a Man should swing
World without end, in suffering
For all men's healing, let me sing.

Cullen then depicted the South as an evil and cruel land where even the black poet's tongue would have trouble voicing the horror:

This is a cruel land, this South,
And bitter words to twist my mouth,
Burning my tongue down to its root,
Were easily found; but I am mute

As the poem-tale proceeded, the lynching of a young black man led his father to profound religious questions, wondering if God actually cared for black folk at all:

["]Would not a child's weak heart rebel?
But Christ who conquered Death and Hell
What has He done for you who spent
A bleeding life for His content?
Or is the white Christ, too, distraught
By these dark skins His Father wrought?"

But the black Christ—resurrected somehow at the end of the tale—led this
father to cast away all of his doubts and to feel a sense of kinship with Christ.

["]Surrendered, tortured, crucified!
Now have we seen beyond degree
That love which has no boundary;
Our eyes have looked on Calvary."
...
There is no hood of pain I wear
That has not rested on His hair[39]

From Cullen's and Hughes's poems to the artwork of Tanner and Aaron
Douglass, from the questions of Mary Church Terrell to the spiritual angst in
the sorrow songs, from the new religious teachings of W. D. Fard to the Afrocentric faith of Garvey, African Americans responded with a variety of religious teachings and sentiments to the problems of racism and violence in the
United States. By the early twentieth century, black authors and artists were
busily revising the entire sacred canon of white American religion whether by
blackening Christ or ditching him. W. E. B. Du Bois approached these issues
with an innovativeness unappreciated by modern scholars.

The Gospel According to W. E. B. Du Bois

With a host of creative works, including poems, *Crisis* editorials, short stories, and full-length novels, Du Bois joined the chorus of African American
voices seeking to make sense of racial violence in America. Du Bois acknowledged in his fictive work that American brutality led women and men of
color to have serious doubts about the presence and person of God. Yet Du
Bois then used biblical stories to rethink twentieth-century problems of race
and economics, often centering on the Christ figure as a friend of embattled black women and men. Especially drawn to the Sermon on the Mount,

Du Bois vaulted Christ and his teachings into the early twentieth century to determine what Christ's message had to say to racial violence in the United States. Encounters with messianic black figures brought joy and redemption for many fictive African Americans in Du Bois's tales.

Populating his creative writings with prophetic, mystic, and spiritual characters, Du Bois tried to speak with a variety of religious voices. Whether with apocalyptic visions of hell on earth or divine dreams of global peace, Du Bois infused his fictional writings with sacred meaning. All in all, his creative works reveal Du Bois's spiritual pathos and his courage. Through fiction, he tried to redeem white and black Americans from the sins of racial brutality. In his renderings, African Americans became more than mere innocent scapegoats in American culture; they were God's chosen ones with divine messages for the world.

Du Bois routinely associated African Americans with the biblical Christ because of their poverty and the violence committed against them. Du Bois asserted that African Americans actually carried Christ's spirit in an evil and wicked nation. While whites privileged commodities over compassion, celebrated sensuality over spirituality, and committed murder in the name of their crucified messiah, African Americans "exalt the Lynched above the Lyncher, and the Worker above the Owner, and the Crucified above Imperial Rome."[40] People of color, Du Bois added, "brought to America a sense of meekness and humility which America never has recognized and perhaps never will." He also contended, "If there is anybody in this land who thoroughly believes that the meek shall inherit the earth they have not often let their presence be known."[41] Du Bois best connected the status and experiences of African Americans with those of Christ in a 1913 article in *The Crisis,* "Jesus Christ was a laborer and black men are laborers." Christ "was poor and we are poor; He was despised of his fellow men and we are despised; He was persecuted and crucified, and we are mobbed and lynched." If Christ were to visit the United States, Du Bois concluded, "He would associate with Negroes and Italians and working people; He would eat and pray with them, and He would seldom see the interior of the Cathedral of Saint John the Divine."[42] In the American context, Christ's affiliation with the poor meant an unequivocal affiliation with African Americans.

Du Bois despised the bourgeois, white Christ of American culture, and in response he wrote several fictional accounts of black Christs coming to the United States. These tales further aligned African Americans with the divine and challenged the conflation of whiteness and godliness. Du Bois rewrote traditional biblical narratives of Christ's birth, life, and death—usually placing

them in the American South—to dramatize the state of race relations in the country and to sanctify the experiences of embattled African Americans. His black Christ stood in direct opposition to the materialism, racism, and misogyny that dominated American society. The black Christ of Du Bois's works sympathized with oppressed African Americans. He understood their sorrows and their joys. He confronted the evils of white society with love, justice, and compassion. And, in his crucifixion, he demonstrated a divine spirit that should hearten African Americans to stick to the course of racial justice. Du Bois did more than blacken Christ, moreover. On occasion, he rendered God as black. Accounts of a black God and a black Christ served as vehicles for Du Bois to drive his larger social projects—the annihilation of white supremacy and the inspiration of oppressed people of color. In short, Du Bois's narratives of the black Christ served to critique white society and to help people of color maintain faith that someday they would find their Promised Land.

In Du Bois's creative accounts, white society was a wasteland of immorality and evil. In "A Litany at Atlanta," written and published following the Atlanta Riot of 1906, Du Bois ranted against whites as devils. Du Bois invited God to join African Americans in their animosity toward white violence: "When our devils do deviltry, curse Thou the doer and the deed,—curse them as we curse them, do to them all and more than ever they have done to innocence and weakness, womanhood and home." For a moment, Du Bois even wondered whether God was white. "Sit not longer blind, Lord God, deaf to our prayer and dumb to our dumb suffering. Surely Thou, too, are not white, O Lord, a pale, bloodless, heartless thing!" Yet the assertion of God's whiteness was blasphemous. "Forgive the thought!" Du Bois continued, "Forgive these wild, blasphemous words! Thou art still the God of our black fathers and in Thy Soul's Soul sit some soft darkenings of the evening, some shadowings of the velvet night." Du Bois then demanded a sign from God by connecting the historical condition of blacks with that of Christ, "we raise our shackled hands and charge Thee, God, by the bones of our stolen fathers, by the tears of our dead mothers, by the very blood of Thy crucified Christ: What meaneth this? Tell us the plan; give us the sign!" Concluding the prayer-poem, Du Bois announced that he could see and hear a sign. "In yonder East trembles a star, *Vengeance is Mine; I will repay, saith the Lord!*" God—the "god of a godless land"—would bring liberation and revenge.[43]

On several occasions, Du Bois longed for the birth of a black Christ who would right the wrongs of modern civilization. In "The Burden of Black Women," which was first published in 1914, he maintained that the "White World" was polluted by vermin, dirt, scum, and "spoilers of women." Du Bois

fumed with hatred for whites who brought so much evil to society and did so little to aid African Americans. If he were God, Du Bois declared, whites would have much to worry about:

> I hate them, Oh!
> I hate them well,
> I hate them, Christ!
> As I hate Hell,
> If I were God
> I'd sound their knell
> This day!

Only the birth of a black Christ could save the globe. Only a black Christ, Du Bois claimed, could lead all peoples to freedom and to genuine praise of God and humanity:

> And married maiden, Mother of God,
> Bid the Black Christ be born!
> Then shall the burden of manhood,
> Be it yellow or black or white,
> And Poverty, Justice and Sorrow —
> The Humble and Simple and Strong,
> Shall sing with the Sons of Morning
> And Daughters of Evensong.[44]

Du Bois also considered how different groups and individuals would respond to the black Christ's birth. In the short story "The Second Coming," published in *Darkwater*, a mulatto Christ was born in Valdosta, Georgia. Three wise men—a black bishop, a white bishop, and a yellow priest, representing the major races of the world—traveled there to witness the birth. On their arrival, they "heard the faint wail of a child. . . . A white girl crouched before him, down by the very mules' feet, with a baby in her arms." The bishops were dumbfounded by this infant Christ. They expected Christ to return to the earth in apocalyptic glory as foretold in the Book of Revelation. But even more shocking, at least to the white bishop, was the color of the baby: "*It was black!*" The white bishop refused to worship such a creature. He refused to kneel and offer his gift. As Du Bois narrated, this bishop "stepped back with a gesture of disgust." The Japanese priest proceeded to bow his head and to offer incense and gold to the young messiah, and the black bishop did likewise. The

tale ended with the white bishop storming out of the stable, and the Governor of Georgia, a modern-day Herod, trembling that this black Christ might undermine his authority.[45]

Several of Du Bois's stories detailed the black Christ's teachings and experiences in the United States. What would God in the flesh have to say to this "godless land"? Most of the Christs of Du Bois's renderings, but not all, were black. In one story, "Jesus Christ in Georgia," which was also published with slight modification as "Jesus Christ in Texas" following lynchings in each state respectively, Christ's race was ambiguous. Although local whites believed that the Christ-figure of the story was the product of mixed parentage—a "mulatto"—Du Bois described Jesus' dress and facial features to point toward a Middle Eastern or Mediterranean ethnic background. As Du Bois portrayed this Christ, "he did not own the Negro blood. . . . He was tall and straight and the coat looked like a Jewish gabardine. His hair hung in close curls far down the sides of his face and his face was olive, even yellow."[46] Du Bois suggested that southern whites' racial phobias and their ignorance of human diversity led them not only to confuse African Americans and Middle Easterners but also to overlook the son of God. Du Bois believed that white Americans would consider a messiah of Middle Eastern descent as unthinkable as one of black heritage.

In tales of Christ in America, along with Du Bois's prayers and some of his other writings, he expressed special adoration for Christ's emphasis on peace and for the Sermon on the Mount. Leading his students at Atlanta University in prayer shortly before Christmas in 1909 or 1910, Du Bois begged that God would bring peace and brotherhood out of a world that seemed frenzied with the incessant drive to acquire, to possess, and to dominate. "Out of the depths of selfishness and languour and envy," he prayed, "let spring the spirit of humility and poverty, of gentleness and sacrifice—the eternal dawn of Peace, good-will toward men. Let the birth-bells of God call our vain imaginings back from pomp and glory and wealth—back from the wasteful hardships searching the seas—back to the lowly barn-yard and the homely cradle of a yellow and despised Jew, whom the world has not yet learned to call Wonderful, Counsellor, the Mighty God, the Everlasting Father, and the Prince of Peace. Amen."[47] Christ's designation as the "Prince of Peace" appealed to Du Bois. "Give us this night, O God, Peace in our land and the long silence that comes after strain and upheaval," Du Bois prayed on another occasion.[48] Then, when World War I ended shortly before Christmas in 1918, he wrote in *The Crisis*, "And now suddenly we awake. It is done. . . . Behold the Heavens and its stars; and this blood—this warm and dripping blood from our mad

self-laceration. . . . Hail, then, Holy Christmas time, Nineteen Hundred and Eighteen Years after the Birth, and five since the last Crucifixion. / *On Earth, Peace, Good Will Toward Men*."[49]

To Du Bois, Christ's Sermon on the Mount encapsulated the core ethic and spirit of Christianity. In one of his poems written in the early twentieth century, Du Bois praised the sermon and its author by associating Jesus with the disadvantaged:

> There comes a priest of the meek and lowly
> Jesus—a Servant of the Servant who said:
> Blessed are the Meek,
> Blessed are the Poor,
> Blessed are the Merciful,
> Blessed are the Peace-makers,
> Blessed are the Persecuted.[50]

By rewriting Christ's words, especially the Sermon on the Mount, into the American context, Du Bois underscored his conviction that Christianity was a religion of brotherhood and of liberation for the oppressed. "Blessed are the poor," maintained the black Christ in "The Gospel According to Mary Brown": "Blessed are they that mourn; blessed are the meek; blessed are the merciful; blessed are they which are persecuted. All men are brothers and God is the Father of all."[51]

On numerous other occasions, Du Bois invoked the concepts and language of the Sermon on the Mount. Discussing "true" Christianity, Du Bois maintained in one of his prayers at Atlanta University, "we are not Christians because we profess Thy name and celebrate the ceremonies and idly reiterate the prayers of the church, but only in so far as we really comprehend and follow the Christ spirit—we must be poor and not rich, meek and not proud, merciful and not oppressors, peaceful and not warlike or quarrelsome. . . . This is Christianity. God help us all to be Christians."[52] The Sermon on the Mount provided Du Bois with evidence that genuine Christianity and the real spirit of Christ supported the poor, the weak, and the marginalized. The world's wealthy, proud, and belligerent would never find themselves blessed by Christ.

Whites in Du Bois's narratives either rejected the messiah or found themselves rejected by him. In these tales, Du Bois vented his rage at the immorality of whites. They were unmasked as neo-Pharisees and murderers of the divine. In "Jesus Christ in Texas," most of the white characters listened to

Christ's lessons to "love your neighbors as yourself," but when confronted with his non-whiteness, they snubbed him. Concern for material goods or racial etiquette blinded the white characters to the true identity of Christ. Echoing the biblical claim of Jesus of Nazareth that many who professed to believe in him will not enter the kingdom of heaven, the supposedly black Christ in Texas responded to a white minister, "I never knew you."[53] In other narratives, Du Bois described whites as openly hostile to the black Christ. In "The Gospel According to Mary Brown," published in *The Crisis* in 1919, the whites "resented" that the black Christ "carried himself like a man."[54] Likewise, in "Pontius Pilate," published one year later in *The Crisis*, a crowd of whites denounced Christ for wanting "equality for Everybody—everybody, mind you. . . . Turks, Jews, Niggers, Dagoes, Chinks, Japs, . . . everybody."[55]

Unlike pharisaical whites, African Americans in these stories recognized the black Christ as the son of God and tried to follow his commands. The black Christ in the United States had a special bond with poor people of color. He offered them spirit and solace amid their violent circumstances. Whenever black characters witnessed Christ, they identified him as their distinct savior. They found emotional sustenance in being close to him. In "The Gospel According to Mary Brown," Mary recognized that her son felt a special compassion for the downtrodden. He suffered "not simply in himself, but with every other sufferer. That he was wounded by every sin and bruised by every injustice. He was oppressed and he was afflicted."[56] The black Christ's sympathy for exploited people led African Americans to worship him as their messiah. When Christ blessed a black servant in "Jesus Christ in Texas," the elderly man "paused in bewilderment, tottered, and then with sudden gladness in his eyes dropped to his knees." A black nurse-maid then grabbed onto Christ's cloak in this story. As Du Bois wrote, she "trembled, hesitated, and then kneeled in the dust." This Christ touched her hand gently and encouraged her to "sin no more." Hope immediately filled the maid as never before. She let out a "glad cry" and left the plantation house. Christ subsequently ventured into the wilderness and encountered an African American convict who had escaped from prison. The black Christ instructed the convict not to steal and to obey the Lord's commands. The convict agreed, and the two men exchanged clothing. By having this Christ and the convict swap garments, Du Bois alluded to the instructions of Saint Paul in his biblical letter to the church at Ephesus—that each believer must "put on the new man, which after God is created in righteousness and true holiness."[57]

Unlike Countee Cullen's "The Black Christ," Du Bois's modern-day Jesus characters rarely returned from the dead. At the conclusion of Du Bois's tales,

he generally had white mobs lynch the neo-Christ, but he included no resurrection scene. In "Jesus Christ in Texas," a group of whites hanged the messiah from a tree. Du Bois, however, transformed the scene of torture into one of sacred significance. As he described it, "There, heaven-tall, earth-wide, hung the stranger on the crimson cross, riven and bloodstained with thorn-crowned head and pierced hands."[58] Du Bois typically refused to offer readers the solace of a resurrected black Christ. "Jesus Christ in Texas" concluded with Christ crying out to the black convict, "This day thou shalt be with me in Paradise!"[59] The story "Pontius Pilate" ended with the black Jesus shouting, "My God, my God! Why has Thou forsaken me!"[60] In "The Son of God," Christ's mother continued to have faith in him after his death, but her only "Sign of Salvation" was a noosed rope. In the confines of this story, her son did not return.[61] Only in one of Du Bois's stories, "The Gospel According to Mary Brown," did the crucified Christ return from the dead.[62]

Du Bois's neglect of the resurrection fit with his general erasure of supernatural biblical events in his tales of Jesus in America. The black Christ of Du Bois's creative renderings performed no deeds of superhuman ability. He turned no water into wine. He healed no hemorrhaging women. He exorcised no demons. He raised no people from the dead. The ethics of the Sermon on the Mount and the self-sacrifice of the crucifixion were the central elements of Christ's spirit, according to Du Bois. By minimizing the supernatural aspects of the biblical stories, Du Bois drew attention to his view of Christianity as an ethical system and to his insistence that African Americans rely on themselves, not on divine intervention, for their liberation. Hope in the miraculous was not a lesson Du Bois gleaned from biblical texts or sought to inculcate in his readers. Minimizing the supernatural elements of the Bible did not necessarily position Du Bois in the agnostic or secularist camp. Rather, it showed that he was a religious modernist.[63]

While Du Bois portrayed the black Christ as one who joined with oppressed African Americans in opposition to wealthy whites, he also offered black women places of honor in the narratives. African American women in these stories spoke to God with singular openness. They shared their anger and their frustration with the Lord not only about society but also about God's apparent unwillingness to help. Victims of intense brutalization from white and black men, black women looked to God and found a compassionate and inspiring friend who shared their agony. This imagined God emboldened black women to speak as they had never spoken before and to fight as they had never fought before. By suggesting that God maintained remarkable relationships with African American women, Du Bois demonstrated an

appreciation for the plight of African American women who were trapped in a complex web of oppression based on their race, gender, and economic status.[64]

In one short story in particular, published in *The Crisis* in 1931, Du Bois imagined a conversation between a present-day Madonna, "Mary Black," and an angel of the Lord. When this angel appeared to inform her that she would bear a blessed child, Mary was deeply frightened. She responded by questioning the angel and God. Openness and rage marked her conversation with the sacred. "Who? Me? Blessed?" she retorted. "Another baby coming and none of us with a job?" Mary continued. "I can't understand you and God I don't see no call for this soul of mine to magnify nothing!" Mary challenged the Lord to provide tangible relief. "You're mighty, all right, God—I know that you've done great things and your name's holy and all that. But how about me?" And if God was unsure of what kind of help Mary could use, she continued, "Why don't you get busy when you see us hungry and cold with no money and no job? What do you do about it?"[65]

God did not remain silent when confronted by women such as Mary Black. The God of Du Bois's renderings offered reassurance to these women, sometimes unveiling his own blackness in an effort to commune with them. In the case of Mary Black, the angel responded with words directly from the gospel narratives: "For with God nothing shall be impossible."[66] In another one of Du Bois's stories, "The Call," God summoned all of his followers from across the globe to his throne. None, however, heeded his invitation except for one black woman—God's "servant of thy servants." The Lord commanded her to smite his enemies. She resisted, however. How could she, the lowliest of all people, prevail against the world? God continued to make his demand and, after the third time he instructed her, she declared: "Dear God, I am black!" The holy King uttered no words in return, but "swept the veiling of his face aside and lifted up the light of his countenance upon her and lo! it was black." God's blackness inspired the woman. She "went forth on the hills of God to do battle for the King." In the kingdom of God as pictured by Du Bois, black women were not marginal figures but holy warriors.[67]

On one occasion, Du Bois even presented God as a black woman. In "The Crucifixion of God," a short story that was never published, Du Bois told the tale of a priest walking in a wooded area. The Jesus he encountered there was racially ambiguous with "a face white with pain and dark with passion, scarred with the fury of life and yet luminous, strangely and wonderfully luminous with the vision of some Unseen Thing." The priest hoped that this Christ would lead to "Almighty God" but was shocked to learn that God was

not a he. "I am weak but there is One stronger than I," the Christ told the priest, who retorted, "Him then I seek . . . Where is He?" Christ responded, "Her too I seek." Stunned, the priest followed the Christ toward "a crimson glow in the Heaven." There, they found the one stronger than Christ: "Death." "The form was the form of a maiden—a black maiden whose body was like the light of a soft summer midnight and whose hair was as smoke curling and swaying about her head in the crimson halo." Although the priest associated death with sin and the devil, Christ explained that death must happen for new life. Christ's task on earth, he furthered, was the "uprooting of these black trees of Hate. Once they go and from this soil will spring all the flowers of Love and God will wed with Death." As the story progressed, this Christ was crucified on a golden cross and begged the priest to "Help for God's sake!" When Christ died, the priest finally understood the lesson. It was now his turn to uproot the black trees of hate and to sow love and peace. Death, a black woman—as metaphor and example—gave birth to live.[68]

Creating a black female divine and paying particular attention to God's bonds with African American women, Du Bois foreshadowed the extension of black liberation theology into "womanist theology." In the late 1970s and 1980s, African American female theologians were distressed by the lack of concern for issues of gender among black theologians and by the lack of concern for racial and class issues among white feminists. In response, they crafted their own theology—a womanist perspective. They focused on Christ's and God's relationships with women of color. Womanist theologians, such as Jacquelyn Grant, Kelly Brown Douglas, and Diana Hayes, attacked not only the whiteness of Christ but also his maleness. They rejected patriarchal and racist readings of biblical texts and instead focused on God's and Christ's deep appreciation for marginalized women. Christ must not only be black to align with the truly disadvantaged, they insisted. Christ must also be a woman in some sense.[69] Although Du Bois never called into question the gender of Christ, he did liken southern black women to Christ in *The Gift of Black Folk*. "Above all looms the figure of the Black Mammy, one of the most pitiful of the world's Christs," he wrote. "She was an embodied Sorrow, an anomaly crucified on the cross of her own neglected children for the sake of the children of masters who bought and sold her as they bought and sold cattle."[70] By associating black female servants with Christ and by including tales of embattled black women directly encountering God, Du Bois was most assuredly ahead of his time in theological and cultural matters. Amid a culture of violent physical and sexual attacks on black women, Du Bois tried to align these women with an omnipotent, loving deity.

As Du Bois demonstrated in "The Call," he depicted not only Christ as black, but God as well. He refused to accept a God who had anything in common with oppressive whites. Therefore, God could not be white. Du Bois directly associated God with blackness in "Children of the Moon," published in *Darkwater*. He described a black God hidden from the world:

> Heaven and earth are wings;
> ...
> Wings veiling some vast
> And veiled face,
> In blazing blackness,
> Behind the folding and unfolding,
> The rolling and unrolling of
> Almighty wings![71]

With these poems and short stories, Du Bois completely reworked the image of the sacred, of God, and of Christ in the American context. Neither God nor Jesus was white in Du Bois's artistic renderings. Rather, a black God and a black messiah were the ultimate reminders of the hypocrisy of white culture and the limitless potential of African Americans.

By exposing white violence as unholy and then by elevating African Americans to divine status, Du Bois assaulted the persecution narratives floating in American culture. If lynchings were rituals to deify whiteness and demonize blackness for white Americans, they became in the hands of Du Bois and other black authors signs of black sanctity and white blasphemy. If Christ was a white, middle-class businessman in the imaginations of dominant society, then he was transformed into a fellow of the downtrodden and a blackened messiah for those like Du Bois.

Faith in Novel Form

Just as in his short stories and poems, Du Bois saturated his full-length novels with religious images, characters, and ideas. All five of his novels—*The Quest of the Silver Fleece* (1911), *Dark Princess: A Romance* (1928), *The Ordeal of Mansart* (1957), *Mansart Builds a School* (1959), and *Worlds of Color* (1961)—were historical novels that integrated real and fictive events in the United States and the world. In them, Du Bois offered readers a plethora of messianic characters, apocalyptic nightmares, and heavenly dreams. Con-

nections between racial violence and religious questioning abounded, and, often, women of color brought spiritual wisdom and insight to the tale. His novels were replete with white and black prophets critiquing white supremacy for its physical and spiritual brutality, and they envisioned God destroying the world for its sins. On some occasions, these prophets took matters into their own hands and sought to respond to violence with violence, hoping to purify the nation and world. Taken as a whole, Du Bois's novels furthered the elements of his shorter prose and poetry: the dissociation of whiteness and godliness and the linking of blackness with the divine.

The Quest of the Silver Fleece was published in 1911, only a year after Du Bois had left Atlanta University for New York to edit *The Crisis*. Set in the late nineteenth century, it offered a picture of post-slavery black life where two African Americans—Bles and Zora—searched for personal, community, and religious meaning. In a "Note" to the reader that preceded the novel, Du Bois presented his audience with a way to read the book. Unlike *The Souls of Black Folk* or *Darkwater*, where Du Bois instructed his audience to read in a religious register, he began *Quest* by claiming that "there is little, I ween, divine or ingenious" in the book, "but, at least, I have been honest." Interestingly, though, in a postscript at the end of the novel, Du Bois had changed his tune. He asserted that his tale had religious significance, especially hoping that white readers would understand the book in the light of the mass violence of American society. "Lend me thine ears, O God the Reader," Du Bois penned, "whose Fathers aforetime sent mine down into the land of Egypt, into the House of Bondage. Lay not these words aside for a moment's phantasy, but lift up thine eyes upon the Horror of this land; —the maiming and mocking and murdering of my people, and the imprisonment of their souls. Let my people go, O Infinite One, lest the world shudder at . . . The End." Using biblical references and a veiled threat, Du Bois implored his readers to reflect upon the moral meaning of racial brutality and his presentation of black life.[72]

The Quest of the Silver Fleece centered on the lives of three main characters: Bles, a bright young African American man trying to navigate the post—Civil War South and uplift his race; Zora, a young African American girl from the swamps whose childhood was filled with rape and violence from white masters; and Sarah Smith, a white New England woman who had traveled South to teach African Americans after the Civil War. Throughout the novel, Du Bois drew special attention to how each of these characters approached issues of religion, race, violence, and social change. Zora had a deep sense of the spiritual and emotional life and became the leading spokesperson for a new morality for African Americans and whites.

Sarah Smith envisioned her mission as a sacred enterprise and approached African Americans as God's people. She was one of the "saintly souls," as Du Bois referred to the postwar missionaries in *The Souls of Black Folk*. "In her imagination," Du Bois wrote, "the significance of these half dozen gleaming buildings perched aloft seemed portentous—big with the destiny not simply of a country and a State, but of a race—a nation—a world. It was God's own cause" (13). Then, responding to another white woman who asked "what sort of folks" was Smith educating, Smith stated, "God's sort." When the other white woman expressed discomfort at the thought of African Americans as "God's sort" of people, Smith burst out, "I don't want us to be the only ones that count. I want to live in a world where every soul counts—white, black, and yellow—all. *That's* what I'm teaching these children here" (14–15). For Smith, it was her commitment to Christian and missionary principles that led her to embrace the uplift of African Americans.

Smith's student Zora stood as a fascinating black female character. Overcoming a history of physical and sexual abuse (and disdain from black and white communities because of it), Zora was transformed into a moral priestess with a renewed sense of Christian ethics. She came from the swamp, the land of "Dreams!" as she called it (10). She had never been to school, had little training in social refinement, and was rumored to have had a baby by a white man. At Smith's school, Zora learned to read and took up advanced studies. On several occasions, Zora engaged her white teachers in debates about morals and ethics—and, oftentimes, Zora offered a more sophisticated and mature understanding of right and wrong. In a debate on telling lies, Zora concluded that God knows that small lies to make people feel better "are heaps better than blabbing the truth right out." Then, when considering property ownership, Zora declared, "Folks ain't got no right to things they don't need. . . . You don't own what you don't need and can't use. God owns it" (58–59, 65).

Perhaps one of the most remarkable discussions in *The Quest of the Silver Fleece* occurred after Bles and Zora built a house in the swamp and Bles placed a picture of the Madonna on the wall. As Du Bois described, it was "a little picture in blue and gold of Bouguereau's Madonna." A French painter of the nineteenth century, Adolphe-William Bouguereau was known for his tender images of young children and women. Bouguereau painted numerous images of the Madonna, including "The Madonna of the Roses" and "Madonna and Child with St. John the Baptist." The image entranced Zora. She "was staring silently at the Madonna," and asked of Bles, "Who's it?" Bles responded reverently, "The mother of God." Zora expressed confusion over the picture, especially the lily and the baby held by the Madonna. Bles explained

that the lily "stands for purity—she was a good woman" and the baby "is the Christ Child—God's baby." Zora retorted, "God is the father of all the little babies, ain't He, Bles?" When Bles responded, "Why, yes—yes, of course; only this little baby didn't have any other father." Christ's lack of an earthly father resonated with Zora, for either she knew no human father or she had been raped by a white man and her baby had never known its father. "Yes, I know one like that," Zora said softly, "Poor little Christ-baby" (81).

Zora's interpretation of the painting, however, was not finished by her empathy and sense of familiarity with the Christ baby. Referring to the Madonna, Zora exclaimed, "How white she is; she's as white as the lily, Bles; but— I'm sorry she's white—Bles, what's purity—just whiteness?" Unsure of how to answer, Bles claimed that purity was about "being good," not about color. And Zora responded with "a strange breaking voice" and a "sob." "I'm—pure." More of a question than a declarative statement, Zora sought to make meaning of her own soul in terms of her rape and of western culture's fixation on whiteness as godliness (81–82).

In her own unsophisticated way, Zora offered a beautiful analysis of color symbolism; notions of purity, race, and violence; and one soul's hopes to find redemption. To her, purity and whiteness were not the same. They could not be. The conflation, moreover, must be questioned, if not lamented, for it had disastrous consequences on women like herself. She viewed the portrait of the Madonna and the Christ through the eyes of an impoverished and violated black woman. While she related with Christ's seeming lack of a father, she failed to feel that Mary was her sister because of her whiteness and hence supposed purity. Much of Zora's tale in *The Quest of the Silver Fleece* was creating her own sense of purity, one based not on her culture or circumstances but on her moral reserves and ethical actions.

Zora's personal spiritual journey comprised a central feature of the novel, as a renewed faith in the Christian God saved her from the terrors of her past and the disadvantage of her present. Returning South after working and studying in the North, she found herself at a small, rural black church. "It looked warm, and she was cold. It was full of her people, and she was very, very lonely. She sat in a back seat, and saw with unseeing eyes." The church and the minister spoke to her soul (254–255). When Zora entered this church, she felt an intense sense of loss, grief, and self doubt. "She, the outcast child of the swamp, what was there for her to do in the great world—her, the burden of whose sin—." But then "came the voice of the preacher: '*Behold the Lamb of God, that taketh away the sin of the world.*'" The preacher's words caught Zora. She "found herself all at once intently listening. She had been to

church many times before, but under the sermons and ceremonies she had always sat coldly inert." Religion in the South and in the North had failed to comfort her. "In the South the cries, contortions, and religious frenzy left her mind untouched; she did not laugh or mock, she simply sat and watched and wondered," Du Bois narrated. "At the North, in the white churches, she enjoyed the beauty of wall, windows, hymn, liked the voice and surplice of the preacher; but his words had no reference to anything in which she was interested." But here in this swamp church, "suddenly came an earnest voice addressed, by singular change, to her of all the world." Zora could not help but hear. "She listened, bending forward, her eyes glued to the speaker's lips and letting no word drop. He had the build and look of the fanatic: thin to emaciation; brown; brilliant-eyed; his words snapped in nervous energy and rang in awful earnestness" (255).

The minister preached a powerful sermon about the love and sacrifice of Christ. As he implored his congregation to "Come to Jesus," Zora leapt. "Zora rose and walked up the aisle; she knelt before the altar and answered the call: 'Here am I—send me.'" For Zora, this constituted her conversion experience. It was the moment when her worries about purity and worth were dispelled and she accepted a calling as God's emissary in the world. She left the meeting, walked under the stars, and beheld a new world. "Within her soul sang some new song of peace. . . . The Way was opened." Just as Du Bois described his own work as a sacred calling in his autobiographical works, Zora now had heard the "Voice." This was her personal resurrection, "from the grave of youth and love, amid the soft, low singing of dark and bowed worshippers, the Angel of the Resurrection rolled away the stone." "I have found the Way," Zora cried with joy. She now knew that her call was to return to the South for good and "work for my people" (255–258).

Zora's newfound spiritual passion led her to join Sarah Smith at the school. There Zora hoped to protect the black female students from the abuse, torment, and spiritual angst she had encountered as a young woman. "She would protect *all* black girls," Du Bois maintained of Zora, "the innocent girlhood of this daughter of shame must be rescued from the devil. . . . She must offer this unsullied soul up unto God in mighty atonement" (312–313). In short, Zora viewed herself as a savior and divine protector for these black girls; she would shield them from rape and soul desecration.

Established black religious leaders stood in Zora's way, however, just as Du Bois imagined they stood in his way and in the way of the fictive John Jones in *The Souls of Black Folk*. When Zora attempted to share her message of black protection and uplift and when she implored black churchgoers to

"rescue your own flesh and blood—free yourselves—free yourselves" she was rebuffed. The local black minister led the denunciations. He accused Zora of being a tool of the devil, pointing toward her and shouting "beware the ebil one! . . . Beware of dem dat calls ebil good. Beware of dem dat worships debbils; the debbils dat crawl; de debbils what forgets God" (322–325).

Amid the battle between this minister and Zora, a prophet arrived from the swamp to address the crowd. If Zora stood as a messianic figure, this prophet fit the role of a neo-John the Baptist character sent to make straight the paths of the Lord. The prophet challenged all who opposed Zora. "God is sent me," this old man declared, "to preach His acceptable time." The prophet's message was precisely what Zora had been saying. "Faith without works is dead; who is you that dares to set and wait for the Lord to do your work?" Then, the prophet assailed the congregants for their sins—for stealing, for lying, and for raping young women. He then turned his gaze and rage on the minister. "You—you—ornery hound of Hell!" the prophet shouted, "God never knowed you and the devil owns your soul!" The preacher cowered in the corner and then bowed in humble submission to the prophet. Having demanded the attention and respect of the congregation, the prophet announced the plan of the Lord. "God is done sent me to offer you all salvation. . . . not in praying, but in works. Follow me!" (325–326).

The prophet leapt from the church and the congregation followed. They rushed to a cabin and acquired axes, saws, hammers, and several teams of mules. With prayers, songs, and hard work, this congregation transformed the forest swamp into a full twenty acres of good farmland. In the process, Zora's childhood home—the place of her rape and defilement—was destroyed. "Amid a silence she saw in the little grove that still stood the cabin . . . tremble, sigh, and disappear, and with it flew some spirit of evil" (327). Faith in action had not only restored the community economically but also exorcised the demons of Zora's past.

Never one to shy away from a good romance, Du Bois concluded *The Quest of the Silver Fleece* with Zora and Bles reuniting. Even their relationship was spiritualized. Believing that Bles was in love with another woman, Zora declared, "This was Sacrifice! This was the Atonement for the unforgiven sin. Emma's was the pure soul which she must offer up to God; for it was God, a cold and mighty God, who had given it to Bles—her Bles. It was well; God willed it. But could *she* live? Must she live? Did God ask that, too?" Zora never had to answer these questions for herself, though. Bles revealed that he did not love Emma; he loved Zora so the two pledged to marry. And the novel closed with Bles declaring of Zora: "She is more than pure" (378).

By the end of the novel, Zora's redemption and apotheosis was complete. She not only became the mouthpiece for Du Bois's critique of modern religion and for a new faith to come to African Americans, but she also had risen above the Madonna. If the Madonna was pure, Zora was "more than pure." Du Bois blasted away at the association of whiteness and godliness by presenting a black female character who transcended racial and sexual violence to a spot beyond the mother of Christ herself.

Almost two decades after *The Quest of the Silver Fleece*, Du Bois offered readers another messianic figure in the form of another woman of color. In fact, in *Dark Princess: A Romance*, Du Bois presented his readers with not one but two messianic figures. Set in the 1910s and 1920s, the novel revolved around the romance of these two neo-messiahs—Matthew Townes, an African American, and Princess Kautilya of India. The tale followed Matthew from his college expulsion to his travels to Germany, from his return to the United States to his political rise and fall in Chicago. In the background of the novel, a secret alliance of the "dark peoples" of the world labor to undo white global dominance. Notions of the spiritual and sacred dominated the text, and much of the novel involved Matthew's reluctance (and eventual acceptance) to see human drama in a spiritual light. If *The Quest of the Silver Fleece* was the tale of Zora's spiritual redemption and ascension, then *Dark Princess* was the sacred journey of Matthew from a common African American to a god of world rebirth.[73]

Throughout *Dark Princess*, Princess Kautilya invoked a variety of religious traditions, including Buddhism and Christianity, in her efforts to convince Matthew of his central role in the salvation of the world. When they first met in Berlin, Germany, for example, she shared with him a vision about the current state of black life in America: "one picture there intensified and stirred my thoughts—a weird massing of black shepherds and a star" (17). In case any reader might have missed the allusion to biblical events before Christ's birth, Kautilya further maintained, "It seemed almost that the Powers of Heaven had bent to give me the knowledge which I was groping for." By the novel's end, Kautilya's vision of a messianic birth would be realized in the form of a baby born to her and Matthew (17).

Although resistant to many of Kautilya's teachings and to religion in general until the end of the novel, Matthew sensed holy powers throughout his travels. Early in the novel, as Matthew traveled to Germany, he barked at a missionary, "I don't believe in God—never did—do you?" (6). Yet as *Dark Princess* moved forward, much of the storyline involved Matthew's growing appreciation for faith and the spiritual. When he first met Kautilya and the

other leaders of the dark alliance in Germany, he proclaimed that race was not just about physical appearance or community. Race was, at least for African Americans, about the soul. "My grandfather was [black], and my soul is," he declared. "Black blood with us in America is a matter of spirit and not simply of flesh" (19). When asked to demonstrate his blackness—to share an aspect of African American life and spirit—Matthew even turned to one of the "sorrow songs." In *Dark Princess*, as in much of Du Bois's writings, black spirituals seemed to have a power all their own to entrance and inspire. Matthew "threw back his head and closed his eyes, and with the movement he heard again the Great Song." He envisioned himself as part of a long tradition of black soul life. "He saw his father in that old log church by the river, leading the moaning singers in the Great Song of Emancipation. He then "swung his arm and beat the table; the silver tinkled. Silence dropped on all, and suddenly Matthew found himself singing." Matthew's voice was "full, untrained but mellow," and it "quivered down the first plaintive bar: / 'When Israel was in Egypt's land—.'" Matthew continued to sing and felt himself transported metaphysically across the Atlantic ocean " 'Let my people go!' / He forgot his audience and saw only the shining river and the bowed and shouting throng: / 'Oppressed so hard, they could not stand, Let my people go'" (25–26).

Later in the novel, after Matthew traveled back to the United States, spent some time in prison for his activities organizing Pullman Porters, and became a political leader (and hustler) in Chicago, Princess Kautilya returned to save him. She went to great lengths to explain her task as a sacred one. "See, I came to save you!" she commented upon meeting Matthew in Chicago. "I came to save your soul from hell" (209). The princess continued, "I have sought you, man of God, in the depths of hell, to bring your dead faith back to the stars; and now you are mine." Suddenly, "there was light." Matthew was finally able to see his destiny and Kautilya's sacred status, and he responded with a common Christian liturgical phrase "Kyrie Eleison" (Lord Have Mercy).

Du Bois made certain to darken his descriptions of messianic historical and fictive characters and to tie them to the poor of the world. At one point, for example, Princess Kautilya referred to Buddha as "our black and curly-haired Lord Buddha" (19). Later, when an African American minister discussed God and Christ, he acknowledged, "I am not sure that God has any truth. . . . And as to property, I'm sure He has none. Every time He has come to us, He has been disgustingly poor" (148). And, of course, both Matthew and the Princess were members of "darker races."

After Kautilya located and saved Matthew in Chicago, the novel became inundated with religious rhetoric and symbolism. Kautilya declared to Mat-

thew that his poor black mother "is Kali, the Black One; wife of Siva, Mother of the World!" Representative of the destructive and creative power of the divine, Kali was an important goddess for many Hindus. Folklore had it that although black and emaciated, Kali had the power to swallow demons. For Kautilya, Matthew's mother became her salvation, the one who could swallow Kautilya's emotional demons. She described to Matthew the spiritual power of his mother, and in the process offered him her own religious testimony:

> And then came what I shall always know to have been the greatest thing in my life. I saw your mother. No faith nor religion, Matthew, ever dies. I am of the clan and land that gave Gotama, the Buddha, to the world. I know that out of the soul of Brahma come little separations of his perfect and higher manifestations, as eternal life flows on. And when I saw that old mother of yours standing in the blue shadows of twilight with flowers, cotton, and corn about her, I knew that I was looking upon one of the ancient prophets of India and that she was to lead me out of the depths in which I found myself and up to the atonement for which I yearned.

Kautilya apprenticed herself to Matthew's mother. "So I started with her upon the path of seven years which I calculated would be, in all likelihood, the measure of your possible imprisonment. We talked it all out together. We prayed to God, hers and mine, and out of her ancient lore she did the sacrifice of flame and blood which was the ceremony of my own great fathers and which came down to her from Shango of Western Africa" (221). In this scenario, Matthew's mother took on a variety of religious personas. She was the Hindu Kali, "the Black One" and an ancient prophet of India. She was also a carrier of historic African faiths, particularly the "Shango." Kautilya, in this scenario, became a neo-Buddha or a neo-Saint Francis who gave up her royal privilege to learn through poverty, toil, and service.

Reunited and now seeing the world through a cluster of religious prisms, Matthew and Kautilya agreed to work together to bring salvation to the world. They centered their mission on social welfare and justice. The goal, Kautilya proclaimed, was to create a world of joy and peace "here on earth, now and not in your silly Christian parlor heaven, the tiny spark that is God thrills through, thrills through to triumph in a billion years; so vast, and vaster, is the Plan" (290). "We are parts of God," Kautilya continued, "God lives forever—Brahma, Buddha, Mohammad, Christ—all His infinite incarnations. From God we came, to God we shall return. We are eternal because we are God" (295). And finally, Kautilya once again declared Matthew to be

of royal and sacred blood, calling him to the "Immortal Mission of the Son of Man" (308).

The novel ended with a "spectacular messianic finale," as literary theorist Claudia Tate has put it (xxiii). It was a saturnalia of religious symbolism. Now married to Matthew, Kautilya birthed a son. This boy was a new messiah who would follow in the footsteps of Christ, Mohammed, Buddha, and Brahma. At the birth, a black preacher read from the seventh chapter of Revelations to declare the holy second coming of Christ: "After these things I saw four Angels standing on the four corners of the earth'—stumbling over the mighty words with strange accent and pronunciation—'and God shall wipe away all tears from their eyes!'" (309). Then, Matthew's mother joined the minister to bless the baby. Biblical recitations mixed with her prayers to create a sacred atmosphere: "the ancient woman stiffened, closed her eyes, and chanted to her God: 'Jesus, take dis child. Make him a man! Make him a man, Lord Jesus—a leader of his people and a lover of his God! Gin him a high heart, God, a strong arm and an understandin' mind. Breathe the holy sperrit on his lips and fill his soul with lovin' kindness. Set his feet on the beautiful mountings of Good Tidings and let my heart sing Hallelujah to the Lamb when he brings my lost and stolen people home to heaven; home to you, my little Jesus and my God.'"

Then the grandmother and minister joined together to call the babe to a sacred militancy against discrimination and oppression. "She paused abruptly, stiffened, and with rapt face whispered the first words of the old slave song of world revolution: / 'I am seekin' for a City—for a City into de Kingdom!' / Then with closed and streaming eyes, she danced with slow and stately step before the Lord. Her voice lifted higher and higher, outstriving her upstretched arms, shrilled the strophe, while the antistrophe rolled in the thick throat of the preacher: / The Woman: 'Lord, I don't feel no ways *tired*—' / The Man: '*Children!* Fight Christ's fury, Halleluiah!' / The Woman: '*I'm*—a gonta shout glory when this world's on *fire!*' / The Man: '*Children!* Shout God's glory, Hallelu!'" (309–310).

Then, in a chorus, the characters of the novel offered the child a host of sacred names. They drew equally from Buddhism, Hinduism, and Christianity. The son would be "King of the Snows of Gaurisankar!" "Protector of Ganga the Holy!" "Incarnate Son of the Buddha!" "Grand Mughal of Utter India!" "Messenger and Messiah to all the Darker Worlds!" (311). Once again invoking Christian, Buddhist, and Hindu religious symbolism, Du Bois presented his readers with the birth of a black messiah who would fight and bleed for universal social redemption.

What began with Matthew proclaiming to a missionary, "I don't believe in God—never did," ended with the declaration of a new deity on earth. This dark son, born of the twin messianic characters of Matthew and Kautilya and blessed by his sacred grandmother and a black minister, was a new heavenly incarnation. *Dark Princess* stood as a spiritual narrative of redemption and renewal for Matthew, where Kautilya's enduring faith carried him into a new realm of social and world transformation.

It would be more than thirty years after *Dark Princess* before Du Bois once again attempted a historical novel. He published his final set of novels—his Black Flame trilogy—during the late 1950s and early 1960s, the years that he embraced Communism and allegedly atheism with it. Yet the narrative of the Black Flame trilogy showed that Du Bois was still interested in religious reflection, spiritual conversion, and the problem of maintaining belief amid a culture of violence. He filled the Black Flame trilogy with as much religious reflection and apocalyptic vision as he did earlier in *Dark Princess* and *The Quest of the Silver Fleece*.[74]

The trilogy, which included *The Ordeal of Mansart* (1957), *Mansart Builds a School* (1959), and *Worlds of Color* (1961), followed several generations of the Mansart family. From the end of the Civil War to the end of World War II, from the South to the North to Europe to Africa and back again, members of the Mansart clan experienced nearly every facet of national and international change. Born a slave in the antebellum South, Tom Mansart served as the patriarch of the family. He joined the Union army during the Civil War and then became an outspoken advocate of black rights in the Reconstruction South. Yet in the mid 1870s, on the same day that his son was to be born, the Ku Klux Klan dragged Tom by "from his buggy and threw him against his own door. He fell against it with out-stretched arms and blood-shot, staring eyes. A hundred guns thundered and lightened as a wind of lead shattered the house where his body leaned, and left it a jelly of mangled flesh, blood and bone." The howl of death, however, was only one of three great cries that night. The other two were "the scream of birthpain, and the wail of a new-born babe." Although Tom had been lynched by the Klan, his son would carry his spirit (*Ordeal of Mansart*, 71).

As Du Bois did in his other fictive writings, he offered a spiritual interpretation of Tom's death and the birth of his son. "The world began weeping and its tears blinded the stars," Du Bois penned of Tom's mob murder. At the same moment, after Tom's wife gave birth to a boy, the child's grandmother immediately brought the new babe to the black church. As Du Bois wrote,

"In her vast hand lay a blood-stained child. Slowly she swayed and danced through the church. The Bishop, standing behind the altar, saw a thousand years of the African Dance of Death gliding out of the past. Snake-wise, the throng followed the dancer, moaning to her cries." During the dance, the crowd cried and shrieked "with tossing hands and spitting mouths." Then, the grandmother whispered, "His name is Manuel" for "He is Called!" The ritual and the naming of the child were important markers for the rest of the trilogy. This child was not just any child. His name, "Manuel," was a shortened version of "Emmanuel," one of the names given to Christ meaning "God is with us." On this horrid night, the blood of death and the blood of life mixed in the Mansart family. A new black messianic figure had been born, and now in the flesh, cried the "Black Flame." This newborn child carried with him not only the hope of his family but also the redemption of the entire race, if not the world (*Ordeal of Mansart*, 72).

Manuel's childhood stood as an object lesson of the pain and sorrow of America's racialized society. Through his acculturation into the violence of white supremacy, Manuel and those around him sought to make religious sense of their lives. When traveling to school in his early teens, for instance, Manuel experienced white supremacy for the first time. A white conductor callously threw Manuel's pet dog off the train and the dog died. The event shocked, confused, and saddened Manuel.[75] Subsequent fights with white boys led him to a feeling of deep anger. Manuel sought advice from the school's young new minister "Dr. Carter" and his Sunday school classes. Manuel asked Dr. Carter some of the most perplexing questions from black Americans: "Just where did white folk fit into this world? Were they all essentially evil? Or were some fairly good?" (*Ordeal of Mansart*, 116–119).

Dr. Carter's answers indicated that racial violence in the United States forced African Americans to interpret, read, and live the Bible in a distinct manner. When discussing the biblical passage that a Christian should love "one's neighbors as oneself," Manuel asked Dr. Carter if this applied to whites. Carter responded with a fascinating remark on race, violence, and religion in American society, and he brought the passage to bear on Manuel's own experiences. "Well, Manuel, them lynchers weren't no neighbors of mine nor yourn," Dr. Carter explained, "An' tell you the truth, I loves my neighbors as well as may be, considering who they is. But if some white folks is going to heaven, I'd druther go some place else." For Carter, the experience of racial brutality played a central role in how he taught the Bible. Lynchings led him to conclude that whites had no ethical business making it to heaven (*Ordeal of Mansart*, 119–121).

As Manuel came of age, the white South held fast to its racial brutality and religious hypocrisy. For the racial holocaust in the name of Christ, Du Bois blasted the South. Of lynchings, he wrote, "This horror spread in the part of the nation noted for its vociferous religion. The South proclaimed a personal acquaintanceship with God and His Purpose which seemed almost blasphemous to Europeans. The cities swarmed with churches and the countryside was liberally dotted; and no man sought public office unless he was an Evangelical Christian, and preferably a Methodist or Baptist." When it came to brutal mob murders, "the Southern church was strangely silent on lynching of Negroes." Du Bois could only conclude, the South was still enslaved to proslavery teachings. "Of course, the long defense of slavery formed a solid background of thought; . . . The ignorant simply preached that Negroes were not human and not the 'children of God'" (*Ordeal of Mansart*, 224–225).

Even Reverend Carter's faith fell at the hands of racial violence. Following the Atlanta race riot of 1906, a pivotal moment in Du Bois's own life, Dr. Carter "sat in his darkened study. The Atlanta riot had terribly discouraged him, for his belief in God and Ultimate Right was profound." Dr. Carter kept on preaching, but he was never the same. "He had preached this Sunday after the riot and ended with that low monotone of the Negro folk song. The audience joined in the solemn voice of the Negro dirge: 'God's gonna shake this wicked world.'" In the weeks and months following the riot, Dr. Carter taught a new doctrine and experienced a profound crisis of faith. This leading pastor who had long held "God as a personal friend as real as the people to whom he preached; who went to him daily in prayer and praise, now wondered how he had ever believed in anyone or anything who could permit or ignore this Atlanta horror." "He spoke for a God of vengeance" from the pulpit, but then in his home, in his mind, and in his private life he wondered, "Did He ever exist? Did anything good exist? Why, what, where?" (*Ordeal of Mansart*, 245, 249–250).

While *The Ordeal of Mansart* concluded with Carter questioning his religious faith, the second installment of the trilogy, *Mansart Builds a School*, began with an apocalyptic vision of epic proportions. Eight years following the Atlanta riot, and as World War I began to ravage Europe, a new prophet emerged in Atlanta. Huge crowds came to hear this "incredibly old" man with "long, snow-white hair, clothed from neck to instep in a long and not too clean black gown." Each time the prophet appeared, he offered a piece of his message. He attacked materialism, violence, and theft. "Greed nailed the world together into one snarling, scratching, fighting ball of human hatreds," he declared. This aged man prophesied a bitter and everlasting war that would pit race against race, creed against creed, and nation against nation (*Mansart Builds a School*, 28–29).

The prophet had a special indictment for the sullying of Christ in western culture. "They kicked the Prince of Peace in the teeth and crowned him with bayonets," the prophet shouted. "Great nations, too poor to build schools, libraries and hospitals, were rich enough to build magnificent warships at ten million dollars apiece, to prowl the seas and prey or scare the weak into slavery. They could not cure Cancer, but they could spread Syphilis." In the place of this prince of peace, whites created a white Christ to brutalize people of color: "The lowly white Jesus of the West will turn the other cheek and kick his black brother in the jaw so hard that all his bloody broken teeth will seed the earth and popup as well-oiled machine guns, spraying death on vermin called Men" (*Mansart Builds a School*, 29–30).

As the prophet ranted against the violence of the modern world, against its religious hypocrisy and its "Ends fighting Ends; War ending War; Good to stop Evil; Evil to birth God," the crowds swelled. Both white and black felt drawn to his apocalyptic visions. And when the prophet inveighed against racism and slavery, the white crowd and police became enraged. "This is nigger equality!" the whites shouted. "Hustle him away! Drive him home! Stop his mouth! Call the police!" The crowd did not have to shout loudly. The police had been monitoring the prophet almost constantly and set to arrest him (*Mansart Builds a School*, 31).

When the prophet had finished his battery of sermons, it was time for him to act. Secretly, he had harbored in his cottage a black man who planned to burn Atlanta as "a sort of sacrifice to Fire to redeem Manhood." One night, when the prophet had been in Atlanta, a lynch mob attacked the black man. It is unclear in the novel whether he survived the lynching or whether only his spirit returned. But back at the cabin, the now-mutilated black man and the elderly white prophet took to the city. As Du Bois described it, "The black giant . . . with face and body scratched, torn, and blood-stained. He was a ghastly, repulsive ruin of what was once a magnificent human being. His nose had been broken and one eye was gone. Scars crossed his face from chin to forehead. His skull was dented. . . . He had lost his fingers and toes." Yet he was unconquered: "unsubdued above it all, and his voice roared up like a deep growl of unforgetting and vindictive hate" (*Mansart Builds a School*, 38).

Together, the "black giant" and the "old white prophet" took their holy revenge on Atlanta. As they set the city ablaze, the two died amid the fire. Later, some residents of the city remembered seeing a strange vision, one that conflated lynching with crucifixion, and the citywide inferno with hell. "Some men say (others stoutly deny)," Du Bois wrote, "that in this red dance of fire,

there floated at the front, a black and awful shape of One lynched and crucified, a black giant, blood-covered, in swirling smoke." The white prophet and the black man had brought the atoning fire, and even in death, the black man trumpeted his opposition to the white Christ. "As he crossed to the elegant homes of Peachtree Street he raised his terrible arm, looked back and beckoned an Old Man in White. The Old Man followed. The wind tossed him about, his white gown billowed in flame and blood dripped from his crown of ashes. With outstretched arms he rose toward heaven, while the black man disappeared, twirled in a cloud of smoke. He threw his great dark arms athwart the sky as he staggered north and shrieked: / 'I go to haunt the earth—hail little white Jesus—meet you in Hell!'" (*Mansart Builds a School*, 41).

Along with apocalyptic visions and veiled threats, Du Bois also used the Black Flame trilogy to reiterate many of his critiques of organized Christianity. Church segregation continued to rankle him. Of the evangelist Billy Sunday who came to Atlanta after the fictive burning, Du Bois penned, "He was then at the height of his career; a vulgar, loud-mouthed preacher, who yelled at God and scared the people with pictures of Hell and Death." Du Bois blasted Sunday for segregating his revivals. "But they were all white," at the meetings, "No Negroes were admitted" (*Mansart Builds a School*, 42). Then in the third novel, *Worlds of Color*, Manuel's son and daughter-in-law who live in Springfield, Illinois (Abraham Lincoln's hometown), experienced segregation in church far more than any other place. "On the street, in the parks, at the movies," Du Bois explained, "there was no visible color line; in the schools and colleges and politics and elections there were evidences of more or less color prejudice and in business and industry distinct color discrimination. But in church the separation was complete" (*Worlds of Color*, 117–118).

Du Bois denounced faith that never translated into moral behavior. "Everybody 'believed' in religion; most were by profession 'Christians,'" Du Bois continued, "But none of this professed belief had any real practical effect. Nobody or certainly very few believed that a request to God would have any effect on what would occur; few believed really in God as a powerful person who was conducting the world benevolently." Regarding the biblical Christ, Du Bois followed, Americans viewed him as irrelevant. "Most people of Springfield regarded Jesus as a good man long dead, who left a moral program which nobody, least of all an American, could really live up to" (*Worlds of Color*, 118–119).

"And yet," Du Bois intoned, "this professed belief and practical rejection of its implications had a subtle but disastrous effect on honesty and character,

telling the truth, and ability to reason clearly." In fact, according to Du Bois, the continual process of claiming to believe in the high ethics of Christianity and yet behaving as immoral Americans destroyed the power of religion in society. "People got so used to saying one thing and doing another, asserting honestly what they knew was untrue, and calling logic what was patently illogical, that religion as a real moral force was a low ebb in the city." Biblical teachings made no sense in the American context. "How could you love your neighbor and turn the other cheek and fight for your country, right or wrong? How could you lie and tell the truth for the sake of the same God?" And, perhaps most egregious, "It was such a situation that brought anger and frustration when a concrete question demanded answer, as in the matter of letting a family with dark faces join a group of professed followers of God, whose faces were whiter in color" (*Worlds of Color*, 118–119).

At the end of *Worlds of Color*—as the now elderly Manuel lay dying in New York—his death scene provided another moment for Du Bois to offer prophetic visions for the future. Having lived through two world wars, having lost sons and grandsons to white supremacy, and having endured scorn and animosity, Manuel foresaw another terrible global conflict. He prophesied a nuclear catastrophe. "I have come from Hell," he said in a distant voice, "I saw bombs filling the skies—I heard the scream of Death. Moscow was a flame, London was ashes, Paris was a clot of blood, New York sank into the sea." He looked to his children and their children to save the world from this catastrophe. "The world was sorrow, hate and fear—no hope, no song, no laughter. Save me, my children. Save the world!" (*Worlds of Color*, 348). Yet, all in his prophetic gaze was not hell and bombs and blood. When he peered into the future, he also gazed at the rising of darker peoples and of communist governments. "I saw China's millions lifting the soil of the nation in their hands to dam the rivers which long had eaten their land. I saw the golden domes of Moscow shining on Russia's millions, yesterday unlettered, now reading the wisdom of the world. I saw birds singing in Korea, Viet-Nam, Indonesia and Malaya. I saw India and Pakistan united, free; in Paris, Ho Chi Minh celebrated peace on earth; while in New York . . ." (*Worlds of Color*, 349).

Before Manuel could announce his vision for New York, he breathed no more. The black bishop at his bedside read Psalm 23, and Manuel—who with so many black folk had literally and figuratively passed through the valley of the shadow of death in America—died. This black "God with us," this black patriarch who had been baptized on the night of his father's lynching, would no longer be able in person to guide and steer his family. He would found no more

schools and make no more prophetic utterances for those who would hear. But his legacy—his soul—lived on in his family and those he had touched.

Du Bois's historical novels served as testimonials to the power of religion in his creative imagination. He offered readers tales of spiritual journeys, of cosmic rises and falls, and of dark women and men seeking to reform their worlds. From the apocalyptic utterances of the Black Flame trilogy to the spiritual journey of Zora in *The Quest of the Silver Fleece*, from the perseverance of Princess Kautilya to the hopes of Sarah Smith, religion challenged, sustained, and redeemed the main characters. In their social pursuits, moreover, they crafted new approaches to the sacred that provided new visions of heaven and hell, of angels and demons, and of evil and good.

~

Amid his penetrating theoretical discussion of religion and violence, cultural theorist René Girard commented almost offhandedly, "Each person must ask what his relationship is to the scapegoat." Richard Wright's Bigger Thomas wouldn't do it. He couldn't do it. Confused by whites' and blacks' discordant views of the cross, Bigger could only cast it to the ground. But W. E. B. Du Bois and other African American authors took another path. Confronted by their own persecution and the persecution narratives of a white society dedicated to attaching whiteness to godliness, these African American artists and writers performed a theological and social intervention. They aligned the scapegoated Christ with themselves in an effort to overturn the sacred legitimacy assumed and guarded in white supremacy. In so doing, they offered a vision of the sacred and of the nation that found redemption from the physical bloodshed and the spiritual turmoil of America's racist past and present.

In fact, Du Bois inquired not only into his relationship to the scapegoat but also into that of all marginalized peoples. For him, Countee Cullen, and other African American writers, the crucifixion and the narrative of Jesus Christ could be redeemed from the diabolical philosophies and teachings of white supremacists and Klan members. Evil and violence were real—and epidemic. The problem of racial evil was a problem, but it was not a problem to debate. It was one to attack, subvert, and transform. By characterizing lynchings as crucifixions and by linking the lives of embattled blacks with that of the biblical Christ, African American writers reversed the religious and theological universe of whites. In these narratives, blacks were not soulless or subhuman evildoers. Rather, they were the very flesh, figuratively and literally, of God— and, in some cases, God incarnate.

Ultimately, neither the intellectual history of black liberation theology nor the story of how African Americans made sense of violence, can be fully understood without reference to Du Bois. And Du Bois cannot be fully understood without reference to his religious imagination. His writings on God, Christ, and Christianity demonstrate that religious idioms and themes were not ancillary to his overarching attack on white supremacy and economic exploitation. Clearly, religious figures and gospel narratives were important aspects in his assault. Beyond the supposedly agnostic Du Bois stood a religious and spiritual thinker of amazing magnitude. Constructing a black Christ who acted on behalf of impoverished African Americans and crafting novels of female and male messiahs, he foreshadowed the works of black liberation theologians. Imagining unique relationships between God and black women, Du Bois connected race, gender, and religion in creative ways well before womanist theologians radically re-interpreted the Christian scriptures.

Du Bois's God was a God of the oppressed. His Christ was a black man who befriended the marginalized. His heaven was a place with no rich people. Hidden in the American landscape of lynching and horror, of rape and neglect, Du Bois found dramas of redemption. Looking into eyes of the sorrowful, the mourning, and the enraged, Du Bois found a way to conceive of songs of grace. This was the gospel according to W. E. B. Du Bois. By the end of his life, Du Bois would find a new gospel in Communism and citizenship in Ghana, yet all was not as it seemed. Within "atheistic" Communism, Du Bois would conceive of a new Christianity and through residence in Africa, Du Bois would once again follow the divine call.

CHAPTER FIVE

~

Christ Was a Communist

Religion for an Aging Leftist

Horace Bumstead believed that he knew the truth about religion in Du Bois's life. According to the longtime president of Atlanta University, when Du Bois applied for a professorship there in 1895, a number of university leaders wondered "about his religion." "He's studied in Germany," they reasoned, "perhaps if you scratch him you'll find an agnostic." Bumstead considered Du Bois "one of those persons who, when asked their religion, reply that they 'have none to speak of.'" Yet the president and friend of Du Bois knew this was not the case. As Bumstead later remembered of Du Bois's years in Atlanta, Du Bois was a religious force. "Though reluctant to speak of his religion or to say what he would do at Atlanta," Bumstead reminisced, "I observed that at the time of my interview with him he was living with his newly wedded bride in the center of the Negro slums of Philadelphia, doing the beneficent work to which Provost Harrison had called him, and I thought there were some indications of genuine religion in that fact." Then at Atlanta University, Du Bois did not disappoint. In Bumstead's words, "some of the deepest and most vital expressions of religious life came from his lips as he conducted evening devotions at the University."[1]

Bumstead's reflections on religion in Du Bois's life were profound, for the president suggested that the supposedly agnostic Du Bois turned out to be quite spiritual. But just as telling as the content of Bumstead's words were their location. Du Bois himself published these reflections in his final autobiography, written during the late 1950s and early 1960s. In *The Autobiography*

of W. E. B. Du Bois (1968), Bumstead's statement authenticated Du Bois's self-posturing as a religious individual. His was a faith demonstrated in deeds not words and honest prayers not pious speech. Using Bumstead's claim, Du Bois raised the specter of his irreligiosity only then to vanquish it.

By highlighting Bumstead's assessment, Du Bois drew attention to a part of himself during his final decades that historians have brushed aside. Many scholars have not treated Du Bois's last years with much sympathy. His embrace of Communism and his rejection of the United States have led some historians to consider him either a deluded elderly man or the pawn of Soviet forces. For historians interested in Du Bois's religion, his acceptance of Communism appeared the ultimate expression of his agnosticism or atheism. According to Susan Jacoby, for instance, Du Bois's membership in the Communist Party was merely the final proof of "his antireligious views." Literary theorist Arnold Rampersad has asserted that late in life, Du Bois "abandon[ed] the central metaphor of religious experience in his verse in favor of purely secular imagery." Even sociologist Phil Zuckerman, who has expressed deep interest in religion in Du Bois's life, has conceded that the final years of Du Bois's life were marked by a "steady withdrawal and final cleavage from religion."[2]

Why then would Du Bois draw attention to Bumstead's assessment? One of the reasons that Du Bois sounded irreligious or antireligious during the 1940s and 1950s was that the Cold War and the Nuclear Age wrought a religious transformation in American culture. As Communism replaced fascism as America's most pronounced opponent and as the nightmare of global destruction became a real possibility, a conservative, frightened religion became more prominent in the country. Evangelist Billy Graham aroused millions with scare tactics that individuals better "get right with God" before the apocalypse, while religious and political leaders mobilized to demonize everything associated with Communism. Militarism to combat "atheistic" Communism became a holy imperative. "America must move forward with the atomic bomb in one hand and the cross in the other," asserted one senator. In this milieu, capitalism and American nationalism became tied even more directly to Christianity. In 1954, Congress added the phrase "under God" to the Pledge of Allegiance, and, in 1956, made "In God We Trust" the national motto. President Dwight D. Eisenhower boasted in 1954 that "our government makes no sense unless it is founded on a deeply religious faith—and I don't care what it is."[3]

What makes no sense, however, is that an America of bombs and threats and red-scare witch hunts has been painted religious, while Du Bois's en-

dorsements of peace, disarmament, economic uplift, and human brotherhood have been declared antireligious. If we refuse to buy into the rhetoric of
the Cold War that American capitalism was ordained by God and that Russian Communism was inspired by the devil, then our perception of Du Bois
becomes quite different. In Du Bois's mind, he never gave up his religious
battles. During these decades, he routinely wrote and spoke about faith. From
the end of World War II to the early 1960s, he called for religion and science
to work together to fashion a new world; he attended church services in New
York City and found emotional nourishment there. He forged strong bonds
with several ministers and sought out churches for public podiums. His turn
to Communism, finally, was not a rejection of all religion. He pictured Communism as the social realization of Christianity and upheld a belief in the
mystical power of Africa to save the modern world.

Du Bois's final two decades heralded neither the end of his religious influence nor the unveiling of a lifelong antagonism to faith; rather, these
were years when Du Bois continued to stand against the dominant trends
in American religion and culture that upheld structures of oppression. He
extended his vision of social reform as a religious imperative, crying out with
the prophet's voice for an end to war. There may be no greater evidence of
Du Bois's lifelong interest in religion than his consistent focus on it in the
middle of the twentieth century. Whether in *Color and Democracy* (1945); in
his speeches, sermons, and short articles; or, most prominently, in his final
autobiography, these were years that Du Bois, as he put it himself, "loved living, physically as well as spiritually."[4]

"Thank God for Such a Man!"

As World War II gave way to the Cold War, and as anti-Communism took
a stranglehold in the United States, Du Bois found himself increasingly an
outsider in both American and African American society. He was forced to
retire from Atlanta University in 1944, and when he returned to the NAACP
it was only for a brief stint. His increasingly leftist leanings, especially his
public criticisms of the United States and his accolades for Communist Russia and China, made him persona non grata at the NAACP. He befriended
Paul Robeson and author Shirley Graham, whom Du Bois married in 1951,
both of whom were intimately connected to Communists. The U.S. government also monitored Du Bois's actions at every turn, making it increasingly
difficult for him to travel abroad.[5]

Even with surveillance, marginalization, and old age, Du Bois had produc-
tive years. During the 1950s and 1960s, he completed the Black Flame trilogy,
ran for the U.S. Senate on the American Labor Party ticket in 1950, battled
the federal government in 1951, lectured throughout the country, joined the
Communist Party in 1961, and emigrated to Ghana later in that same year.
Ghana became a refuge for him, the place where he hoped to finish his life's
work with a massive *Encyclopedia Africana*. Before he could really even start
it, however, death caught up with him in August 1963.

In 1945, Du Bois set the tone for many of his post–World War II feelings
toward society and religion in *Color and Democracy: Colonies and Peace*.
Researched and written while he was the director of special research for the
NAACP, *Color and Democracy* was a brief in favor of decolonization. Du Bois
insisted that if the world wanted to avoid another world war, then people
shackled by colonial chains must be released, uplifted, and allowed democracy. Specifically, Du Bois railed against missionaries and religious traditions
as furthering conquest and colonization. As he had maintained in many of his
historical and sociological works, Du Bois claimed that organized religion, at
least in the western world, had failed miserably because it had been co-opted
by big business and land-grabbing nations. The world of finance corrupted
the world of faith, Du Bois proclaimed, and this created a world where demons disguised themselves as angels, bullies paraded as benefactors, and the
blind claimed that those with eyes could not see. After applauding missions
to Africa and Asia for bringing modern education, Du Bois then announced,
"The great criticism of this work is that from the beginning it co-operated,
perhaps unconsciously, with industrial exploitation." "The missionaries," he
grieved, "knew little or nothing about modern economics, anthropology, and
the social sciences, and were guided in this growing realm of thought and
action by culture patterns belonging to a different era and differing groups.
In the expert hands of an industrial world, organized for precise aims and
capable of hiring the best brains of the day, the missionaries easily became in
many cases the tools of exploitation." "Government used missionaries," Du
Bois concluded, "as smoke screens to hide the truth from the people of the
possessing country."[6]

According to Du Bois, churches were on the side of oppression abroad and
at home, now and in the past. "Both Catholic and Protestant churches became
in the United States ardent defenders of Negro slavery," he asserted, and not
much had changed since the early nineteenth century. "The Christian Church
in America today is almost completely separated along the color line," Du
Bois lamented, "just as are the army, the navy, the nursing service, and even

the blood banks." Churches had failed to live up to their mission for social good: "In many cases where moral opposition is needed, the Church became strangely silent and complacent, and gave the world a right to say with Lenin, 'Religion is the opium of the people.'" The state of modern Christianity, Du Bois concluded, was one that Christ would find reprehensible:

The Church as organized in modern civilized countries has become the special representative of the employing and exploiting classes. It has become mainly a center of wealth and social exclusiveness, and by this very fact, wherever you find a city of large and prosperous churches . . . you find cities where the so-called best people, the educated, intelligent, and well-to-do, are critical of democracy, suspicious of the labor movement, bitter against Soviet Russia, and indifferent to the Negro problem, because their economic interests have put them in opposition to forward movements and the teachers and preachers whom they hire have fed them on that kind of prejudice, or maintained significant silence.[7]

After excoriating "the missionary effort" for exploiting and subduing peoples "in the name of Jesus Christ," Du Bois then offered a candid appraisal of his own stance on religion. Of "organized religion," he announced himself "distinctly critical." "I cannot believe," he declared, "that any chosen body of people or special organization of mankind has received a direct revelation of ultimate truth which is denied to earnest scientific effort." He furthered, "It may well be that God has revealed ultimate knowledge to babes and sucklings, but that is no reason why I, one who does not believe this miracle, should surrender to infants the guidance of my mind and effort. No light of faith, no matter how kindly and beneficent, can in a world of reason guide human beliefs to truth unless it is continually tested by pragmatic fact."[8]

Yet Du Bois made it clear that neither his personal criticism of organized religion, nor his contempt for its complicity in social exploitation, meant that faith should be abandoned. He was convinced that religious belief was necessary to transform the world. The problem, as Du Bois saw it, was not that there was too much religion but that it was not guided by science and scholarship. "There is a dichotomy between religion and social uplift, the Church and sociology," Du Bois complained. This "leads to deplorable loss of effort and division of thinking." Spiritual traditions needed to speak to social dilemmas. "Religion has been an emotional release and escape method for pessimism and despair, coupled with utter doubt, so far as this world is concerned," Du Bois acknowledged. Science could not abandon faith, though.

"While science, as social reform, has been the optimistic belief in human up-lift, without any compelling reason for accomplishing this for any particular persons, or at any particular time. It is as so often happens, religion without science, science without guiding ideals." In short, science needed religion to give it direction and heart; and religion needed scholarship to give it practi-cality and applicability.[9]

Science and religion must locate common ground for the world to survive. "Is there not, then, a chance to find common ground for a program of human betterment which seeks by means of known and tested knowledge the ideal ends of faith?" Du Bois asked. For this to occur, both science and religion would have to give. "This would involve on the part of the Church a sur-render of dogma to the extent of being willing to work for human salvation this side of eternity, and to admit the possibility of vast betterment here and now—a path the Church has often followed." Du Bois had a clear plan for the churches in the postwar world: "The Church should in colonies adopt a self-denying ordinance: not to stress doctrine or dogma until social uplift in education, health, and economic organization have progressed far enough to enable colonial peoples intelligently and independently to compare the reli-gion offered with their inherited cultures." Science would have to allow faith some privileges as well. "This would involve on the part of science the admis-sion that what we know is greatly exceeded by what we do not know, and that there may be realms in time and space of infinitely more importance than the problems of this small world." At the end of the day, science and religion must join forces for "a realistic program of making this world better now."[10]

Du Bois dreamed of a redeemed world, one that could rise above the ashes of white supremacy, economic exploitation, colonialism, genocide, and world war. He had not lost hope. The world, he declared, "with all its contradictions, can be saved, can yet be born again; but not out of capital, interest, property, and gold, rather out of dreams and loiterings, out of simple goodness and friendship and love, out of science and missions." This new world must be born, Du Bois implored. "The day has dawned when above a wounded, tired earth unselfish sacrifice, without sin and hell, may join thorough technique, shorn of ruthless greed, and make a new religion, one with new knowledge, to shout from old hills of heaven: Go Down Moses." A new religion—one that resonated with the sacred songs of the past and one that was informed by sci-entific scholarship of the present—was the prescription that Du Bois had for an ailing world in *Color and Democracy*.[11]

In the years following *Color and Democracy*, Du Bois expressed these con-victions again and again, and lived them out in his personal life. He interacted

with people and organizations of faith in a variety of ways. Churches—as social communities, as forces for national and international reform, as locales in the public sphere, and as symbolic places of transcendent truth—played a vital role in Du Bois's final decades. Rather than abandon religious congregations, Du Bois found them more vital than ever.

For those church leaders and congregations that advocated global peace, embraced all types of women and men, and hoped for dialogues with Communist nations, Du Bois had nothing but praise and encouragement. In 1948, for a book to commemorate the founding of Community Church in New York, Du Bois praised the white pastor John Haynes Holmes as a true man of God. Graduate of Harvard Divinity School, peace activist, socialist, supporter of decolonization, advocate of religious universalism, social gospel hymn writer, and a founder of both the NAACP and the American Civil Liberties Union, Holmes was in many ways a kindred spirit of Du Bois's and they had a long relationship of mutual affection and correspondence.[12]

The social and international ethics of Community Church revitalized Du Bois's interest in church life during the early twentieth century. Holmes, he declared, "drew my attention to his church. I was not at the time very much interested in churches. I had been brought up in formal religion among Episcopalians and Congregationalists. I had heard all kinds of sermons. I had come to expect from churches and ministers well-bred evasion of all real human problems."[13] But Community Church was different; it was a church that refused to bow to the color line or genuflect to greed. "The Community Church welcomed Negroes," Du Bois cheered. It "discussed the Negro Problem, and evidently did not believe that the white race was the only race on earth worth saving." Du Bois lauded Holmes and his congregation for their willingness to tackle difficult issues. "The Community Church did discuss race problems," Du Bois furthered, "It took special interests in India and I remember when Dr. Holmes began to praise and support Gandhi." "The interest of the Community Church and its minister in human races was not merely sentimental, or a matter of personal charity," Du Bois boasted.[14]

In the end, Community Church was a congregation that Du Bois felt comfortable embracing as his own and Reverend Holmes as a man after his own heart. Holmes was a preacher who regarded Gandhi as a Christ-like leader, who endorsed government control of the economy, and who believed that the house of God was a place where all people were welcomed. "The final triumph of his long-deferred dream of a Community Church in New York 'knowing not sect, class, nation, or race' is not merely local nor purely personal," Du Bois concluded, "but a great step towards making a disillusioned

world regard religion as honest, true, and capable of courage and daring."¹⁵
Holmes felt similarly toward Du Bois. After reading the tribute, Holmes was
deeply moved. "I feel humble as well as proud," he wrote to Du Bois, "for it
seems to me that you stated an ideal of service from which I fall all too short.
But as a testimony to your friendship, enduring now for nearly forty years, I
clutch it to my heart."¹⁶

Reverend Holmes and Community Church were not the only minister and
congregation that Du Bois felt drawn to during these years. He also found
solace at Holy Trinity Episcopal Church in the 1950s. When he and Shirley
Graham Du Bois moved to Brooklyn in 1951, John Howard Melish, the rector, and his son, William Howard Melish, the associate rector, greeted them
warmly. John Howard Melish wrote to give them "a most cordial welcome to
Brooklyn Heights." Melish expressed profound regard for Du Bois: "I hope
to be able to pay my respects in person. My admiration of you began with
the reading of the 'Soul's of Black Folk.'"¹⁷ Graham Du Bois recalled that "a
membership committee gave a reception for us in the parlors of the church;
a famous actor, Howard da Silva, read a number of Du Bois's poems. When
Negro History Week was approaching in February, the Reverend Mr. Melish
asked Du Bois if he would give a lecture on Africa." Graham Du Bois claimed
that she and her husband appreciated the church's enthusiastic reception of
them, and they loved the openness of the church; it defied segregation as
much as Community Church did. "Everybody was welcomed at Holy Trinity," Graham Du Bois recalled, "and this welcome included Negroes, Puerto
Ricans, the foreign-born and poor. Holy Trinity thus became a community
church in the truest sense of the word." Du Bois and his wife were especially
close to William Howard Melish. Graham Du Bois spoke for herself and her
husband when she described the church as "our church" and the white priest,
William Howard Melish, as "our rector."¹⁸

But the Melishes upset the Episcopal hierarchy with their defiance of class
and race separation and their push for improved relations between the United
States and the Soviet Union. The Bishop of the Diocese of Long Island moved
to oust both Melishes from the church, inaugurating a long and divisive battle
with the diocese that divided the congregation and threatened to close the
church. When the Du Bois family heard the news, they rushed to Holy Trinity. On the Sunday when the congregation was to hear the decision of the
Episcopal leadership, they made sure they were present and reveled in the
interracial worship where "Christians, white and black, Jews, dark-skinned
Puerto Ricans, saints and sinners, old and young, sang together." Sadly, after
a legal struggle that went all the way to the U.S. Supreme Court, the Bishop

was successful in removing John Howard Melish and William Howard Melish from their positions at the church, and it eventually closed. This was a severe blow to Du Bois's emotional life, as his wife wrote later. "Nothing that happened during the past five years," she claimed of the mid-1950s, "had more deeply saddened and discouraged Du Bois than the closing of the beautiful 110-year-old Protestant Episcopal Church of the Holy Trinity."[19]

The closure of Holy Trinity did not end the friendship between William Howard Melish and Du Bois. To Melish, Du Bois was a spiritual father, a new Elijah called by God to speak divine words to a deaf America. On reading one of Du Bois's essays, Melish remarked, "I thought of the text: 'Then did Elijah the Prophet burst forth like a fire; his words appearing like flaming torches.' Truly, America needs the flaming torch you are lifting." Melish, however, was not naïve. He recognized that the nation was not turning toward peace or against materialism as Du Bois had long hoped, and Melish lamented to Du Bois, "But you, like Elijah, must keep in mind there are here also hundreds of thousands who have not bended the knee to Baal!" Melish became so important to Du Bois, in fact, that when Du Bois created a funeral scenario for himself in 1957, he maintained, "I want the ceremony short and simple. I would prefer it not in a church, unless Howard Melish is still at Trinity." Six years later, Du Bois got his wish, although not in Holy Trinity but in Ghana, when Melish was flown into Accra to preach a funeral sermon for Du Bois.[20]

Melish, Holmes, Holy Trinity, and Community Church held symbolic and personal meaning for Du Bois. Melish and Holmes stood as men of God to Du Bois whom he could cherish and to whom he could relate. Their passions were his passions; their visions were his visions; and their hopes to use religious teachings and institutions to advance a world of justice, compassion, and universal brotherhood were his hopes as well.

Churches and church leaders, moreover, became indispensable to Du Bois as emotional and political refuges. Forced from Atlanta University and then the NAACP, Du Bois's options for the public advancement of his ideas became more limited. Black and white churches became prized locations for Du Bois to convey his positions and to fundraise. This was nowhere more evident than after Du Bois's federal indictment in 1951. Tried under the McCarran Act, Du Bois and the rest of the Peace Information Society were accused of serving the Soviet Union. In reality, the Peace Information Society was merely a clearinghouse for information on nuclear disarmament. But because it challenged the United States to disarm and refused to paint the Soviet Union as an unmitigated evil, some in the federal government saw the society as a threat. After the indictment, scores of congregations rose to assist Du Bois. The Method-

ist Federation for Social Action condemned the government's actions, and the Inter-Faith Committee for Peace in New York City granted Du Bois time and space to defend himself in the court of public opinion. To raise funds for the court battle, Du Bois toured the nation and often churches were the only doors open to him. In St. Paul, Minnesota, crowds of whites and blacks filled the largest black church of the city, while the same occurred in Los Angeles when Du Bois lectured on behalf of the Southern California Peace Crusade. Support from churches, especially black congregations and denominations, heartened Du Bois in the fight. In his chronicle of the indictment and acquittal, *In Battle for Peace*, Du Bois noted the help he received from churches and made sure to thank "the Baptists of Philadelphia" for "strongly" supporting him.[21]

Through the federal indictment, the ousting from the NAACP, and the church struggles, Du Bois relied on religious images, metaphors, and tropes just as he had in the first seven decades of his life. In his speeches during the 1940s and 1950s, many as part of his run for the Senate in 1950 and in his defense of the Peace Information Society, Du Bois invoked biblical concepts and cultivated the image of himself as a modern prophet. In 1944, for instance, Du Bois characterized himself as a New Testament figure in his "farewell message" at Atlanta University. He turned to the words of John the Baptist and the prophet Isaiah to articulate his relationship to the young women and men. Based on his "long association with the families which you represent," Du Bois asserted, "you are in a sense the children of my efforts to make straight the Way of the Lord."[22] Then in 1949 in a petition to the United Nations to investigate violations of human rights against black Americans, Du Bois centered on the "crucifixion" of one black woman in Georgia, Rosa Lee Ingram, as a moral symbol. "It may seem a very little thing for 59 nations of the world to take note of the injustice done a poor colored woman in Georgia, when such vast problems confront them," Du Bois first admitted. But considered in the light of biblical teachings, especially the prophetic utterances of Micah, it was not unreasonable: "After all, is it in the end so small a thing to 'do justly, to love mercy and walk humbly' in setting this mad world aright?" Concluding the petition, Du Bois implored the United Nations Human Rights Commission to follow the words of the prophet Zechariah: "'Not by might, nor by power, but by my spirit' saith the Lord!"[23]

No issue was more important to Du Bois in the late 1940s and 1950s than peace. He staunchly opposed nuclear weapons and called for disarmament. Appeals for "peace" filled his speeches and lectures, particularly his opposition to the American war in Korea. It was "an absurd idea," Du Bois an-

nounced, to think as one American military general claimed, that the United States could "lick the world." Du Bois looked to the words of Christ to call for an end to this approach. Two thousand years ago, he asserted in a speech titled "Peace and the Church," "a Jewish carpenter tried to teach the world anew the ancient doctrine of humility and love as a way of life. You know this history: 'He was wounded for our transgressions; he was bruised for our iniquities, the chastisement of our peace was upon him.' He died as a criminal." American Christians in 1950, however, seemed anything but true followers. "Americans have long regarded themselves as followers of Jesus Christ. Often in the past it has been difficult to reconcile that claim with the facts, but never more than today when we have become a boastful, arrogant, hating people, worshiping force." Du Bois portrayed the militancy of American religion and culture as part of a long tradition of the church—from its defenses of slavery to its justifications for segregation. Yet Du Bois never accepted that the church's social failings meant that God was dead. "Be not deceived," he concluded, "God is not mocked." Americans could boast all they want of being Christians and of their military power, but they could not decide what was holy and what was not. "No camouflage of prayer or vigil, no rite of bell, book and candle can or will replace that one supreme word: Peace on Earth, Good will Toward Men; and recognition of the vast truth that among men are 200 million Russians and 300 million Chinese and 100 million Communists and socialists all over the world, whom no atom bomb nor hydrogen horror can drive out of the kingdoms of the Almighty God."[24]

With prophetic words and passion, Du Bois inveighed against big business, war mongering, and cowardly religious leaders. He wondered how American Christians could stand for the control of American politics by big business. Referring to the "huge profits of industry" in the United States and the lack of truly progressive tax systems, Du Bois declared: "What church of the lowly Jesus, who railed against the rich, would for a moment admit or preach such doctrine?"[25] On another occasion, when addressing the College of Medicine of the University of Illinois in 1950, Du Bois bemoaned that biblical pleas for peace were passé in the United States. "With 'Peace on Earth, Good Will to Men,' so unpopular and in such disrepute," he declared, "we are prepared and eager to spend three-fourths of every dollar of our immense treasure to murder human beings, and not simply kill soldiers, but women, children, cripples and the old."[26] Du Bois held up his own federal indictment as a moral object lesson. Merely because the government disagreed with the Peace Information Society, it had been targeted for destruction. Perhaps most frightening, according to Du Bois, was the "absence of moral courage" in the United States

to defy the government. "It is clear still today," he argued, "that freedom of speech and of thinking can be attacked in the United States without the intellectual and moral leaders of this land raising a hand or saying a word in protest or defense."[27]

The elderly Du Bois considered religious ideals imperative to inspire the next generation of civil rights activists. This was clear in his speech before the Southern Negro Youth Congress in 1946, "Behold the Land." Addressing more than eight hundred black and white young delegates in the Antisdel Chapel of Benedict College in Columbia, South Carolina, Du Bois declared that the new "battleground" for civil and economic rights was the American South. There, he intoned, "a great crusade" necessitated the energies of "the thinker, the worker, and the dreamer." To the white youth in the audience, Du Bois warned them against avoidance. The more white Americans tried to escape racial issues, "the more they land into hypocrisy, lying, and double-dealing." Salvation could only be found in divine vision. "Behold the beautiful land which the Lord thy God hath given thee," Du Bois boomed with the words of the biblical Moses, "Behold the land, the rich and resourceful land, from which for a hundred years its best elements have been running away, its youth and hope, black and white, scurrying North because they are afraid of each other, and dare not face a future of equal, independent, upstanding human beings, in real and not a sham democracy."[28]

To achieve genuine democracy and real equality, the divine voice "calls for the *Great Sacrifice*." Closing his speech, Du Bois encouraged his audience to take sacred action into their own hands. No longer should they rely on an ancient savior to whisk them away to a heaven in the sky. Rather, they must follow Christ's example on earth and become saviors of the nation and the world. Du Bois called them to sing with Harlem Renaissance poet Arna Bontemps his "Nocturne at Bethesda." This poem, Du Bois declared, was "the quiet, determined philosophy of undefeatable men":

> I thought I saw an angel flying low,
> I thought I saw the flicker of a wing
> Above the mulberry trees; but not again,
> Bethesda sleeps. This ancient pool that healed
> A Host of bearded Jews does not awake.
> This pool that once the angels troubled does not move.
> No angel stirs it now, no Saviour comes
> With healing in His hands to raise the sick
> And bid the lame man leap upon the ground.

The golden days are gone. Why do we wait
So long upon the marble steps, blood
Falling from our open wounds? and why
Do our black faces search the empty sky?
Is there something we have forgotten? Some precious thing
We have lost, wandering in strange lands?

There was a day, I remember now,
I beat my breast and cried, "Wash me God,"
Wash me with a wave of wind upon
The barley; O quiet one, draw, draw near!
Walk upon the hills with lovely feet
And in the waterfall stand and speak![29]

Through Bontemps's words, Du Bois implored the college students to reinvent faith. The new trinity of dreamer, thinker, and worker could bring heaven to earth. The dreamer must cast a vision for a moral society; the thinker must plan for this new world; and the worker must build it.

During the 1940s and 1950s, moreover, Du Bois showed greater interest in and sensitivity toward Jews in the United States and the world. He lobbied for the creation of Israel, lectured on several occasions before the American Jewish Congress, and, in the Jubilee Edition of *The Souls of Black Folk,* removed eight negative statements toward Jews. The Holocaust had a marked effect on how Du Bois viewed the relationship between blacks and Jews. Du Bois now believed that their experiences were similar and drew attention to "the way in which African and Jewish history have been entwined for 3,000 years." Du Bois used the image of Nazism to warn against race supremacists in the United States. In 1950, for instance, speaking before the Jewish People's Fraternal Order, he declared, "It has been said more than once that if and when fascism comes to America . . . it will be the Negro people followed by the Jewish people who will feel the fury of barbaric sadism." For this reason, "The Negro people have an obligation to support the fight for a free Israel as the Jewish people have an obligation to support the fight for a free Africa."[30]

As Du Bois turned to the political left, he routinely drew connections between Communism and Christianity. At no point did he consider Communism a replacement for the teachings of Christ. In his request to join the Communist Party in 1961, Du Bois heralded Communism for teaching "no dogmatic religion," but he never praised it for abandoning all faith.[31] Instead,

to Du Bois, Communism was the political and economic manifestation of the teachings of the biblical Jesus. Using New Testament rhetoric, Du Bois encouraged an audience in 1951 to "Seek the Truth About Communism."[32] Then later, he linked Communism and Christianity by once again invoking Christ's Sermon on the Mount as a moral and intellectual model. "Blessed are the Peacemakers," intoned Du Bois, "for they shall be called Communists. Is this shame for the Peacemakers or praise for the Communists? Accursed are the Communists, for they claim to be Peacemakers. Is this shame for the Communists or praise for the Peacemakers?"[33] Also, in *Color and Democracy*, he declared, "it is to the glory of God and the exaltation of man that the Soviet Union, first of modern nations, has dared to face front-forward the problems of poverty, and to place on the uncurbed power of concentrated wealth the blame of widespread and piteous penury."[34]

In his historical mind, the physical embodiment of the link between Communism and Christianity became John Brown. In the late 1950s, revising his biography of this abolitionist martyr, where Du Bois heralded Brown as a powerful religious figure, Du Bois now presented Brown as both a Christian zealot and a proto-Communist. Still using biblical passages to precede each chapter, Du Bois ended the revision wishing that John Brown could have seen the Russian Revolution and "the resurrection of China." As Du Bois repainted Brown, the abolitionist would have been drawn to the writings of Marx and the social structure of Communism. Even though Brown had never read the *Communist Manifesto*, knew little of socialism and even less of modern science, he had within him the spirit of Marxism: "the right of the enslaved to repel oppression. . . . a new attitude toward human beings and a belief in the abilities and character of the great mass of mankind."[35]

Du Bois's attempt to square the teachings of Christ with those of Communism may sound hollow to historians, but it was a common theme for many leftists in the middle of the twentieth century.[36] As historian Robin D. G. Kelley has shown, black Communists routinely used the image of Christ as a "wanted man" and a "radical activist" much like themselves. In the mid-1930s, for instance, the *Southern Worker* printed a mock "wanted poster" of Christ from leftist cartoonist Arthur Young. According to the piece, Jesus was wanted for "Sedition, Criminal Anarchy, Vagrancy, and Conspiring to Overthrow the Government." At Communist meetings in the South, moreover, Christian hymns were important organizing tools. Some had their lyrics transformed to be more overtly Marxist, such as "Stand Up! Ye Workers" replacing "Stand Up For Jesus." But other hymns were unchanged and sung in original form.

Du Bois's close friend and the executor of Du Bois's literary estate, Herbert Aptheker, was renowned for his Marxist-Christian dialogues and, at one time, wrote that Marxist vision "is a vision that has much in common with the hopes contained in the great religious traditions of the world." For these leftists and for Du Bois, Christian symbols and ideals were not incompatible with Communist revolution or government.[37]

Enthusiasm for Communism among African Americans, however, dwindled markedly in the 1940s. In part, this stemmed from a widespread turn in American culture against Communism with the onset of the Cold War. Perhaps more influential, however, were the twin factors that white Communists in the United States seemed inauthentic in their concerns for racial justice and that reports of Soviet torture, ethnic purges, and mass murders filtered into the United States. Although no one in the United States knew the extent of genocide in Russia in the 1930s and 1940s, white and black Americans did receive word of Nikita Khrushchev's "secret speech" in February 1956 that exposed and denounced the "grave abuse of power" by Stalin and his comrades during the 1930s and 1940s within the Soviet Union. Decades later, when archives from the Stalin era were opened to modern historians, evidence of an ethnic cleansing that rivaled (if not outdid) the Holocaust validated Khrushchev's reports. For radical African Americans in the 1940s, including authors Richard Wright and Ralph Ellison, Communism became a "god that failed," an ideology that promised human brotherhood but refused to practice it.[38]

Yet Du Bois did not pull away when news of human atrocities in Soviet Russia surfaced. This seems a moral conundrum. How could Du Bois, who spent decades attacking social immorality the world over, have turned a blind eye to such despicable acts? How could he characterize Communism as the social realization of Christianity if it was built on murder and dictatorship? In part, Du Bois did not believe the reports of Khrushchev's speech. The CIA obtained a Polish translation of an edited copy of Khrushchev's address and the *New York Times* published it in early June 1956. Yet no one in the United States could verify the information.[39] And, for Du Bois, having lived through almost a century of media misrepresentations of African Americans, he was prone to question the veracity of American news. Du Bois was always suspicious of anti-Soviet reports in the United States. After returning from a trip to Russia in the 1920s, for instance, he wrote, "What I saw convinced me of certain things: that Russia is in earnest; that Russia is a victim of a determined propaganda of lies."[40]

When news of Khrushchev's denunciation of Stalin reached the United States, Du Bois held firm to his adoration for Stalin and the Soviet Union

he built. "I still regard Stalin as one of the great men of the twentieth century," Du Bois wrote to Anna Melissa Graves in July 1956. "He was not perfect; he was probably too cruel; but he did three things: he established the
first socialist state in the modern world; he broke the power of the kulaks;
and he conquered Hitler." As Du Bois saw it, even if some of the news of
Stalin's wrongdoings were true, this would not turn Du Bois away from the
Soviet experiment. "If in his later years he became an irresponsible tyrant,
that was very bad and I am sorry for it," Du Bois continued. "But he was not
the first tyrant in the world and will not be the last." Throughout his letter,
Du Bois expressed tentativeness about what had actually occurred within the
Soviet Union and about what Americans could actually know. He challenged
Khrushchev's allegations. "Moreover, I am not satisfied with Khrushchev's
testimony," Du Bois explained to Graves. "It seems to me irresponsible and
muddled. He lumps together Stalin's fight against Trotsky and the various victims of the purge. From the testimony which I read at the time, I believe that
justice was done to these men on the whole."[41]

Little could Du Bois have known that the depth of brutality in the Soviet
Union was far greater than Americans imagined at the time. Yet his insistent
admiration for Russia was not necessarily naïve or myopic. During the 1940s
and 1950s, Du Bois had no reason to believe the American media any more
than the Russian one. McCarthyism and the Red Scare were running rough-
shod through the nation, while Du Bois himself was the object of a federal
smear campaign. He knew firsthand the power of the government and the
media to twist, to lie, and to spin information for its own purposes. Who
could Du Bois trust for accurate news? Why should he have believed Khrushchev or reports of what Khrushchev said? Du Bois's failure to distinguish between the "propaganda of lies" within the United States and the realities of
Soviet terror was less a moral failing of his own than it represented the confusion of the time. This was an era, as George Orwell so brilliantly satirized in
1984: A Novel (1949), where ministries of peace waged war, where ministries
of truth told lies, where ministries of love tortured civilians, and where ministries of plenty enforced starvation. No moral ground was without its weeds;
no moral road was without its pitfalls.[42]

Even though in Du Bois's embrace of the Soviet Union he overlooked its
moral failings, and it seems a shame that Du Bois had neither the energy
nor the language skills to investigate the atrocities at local levels, he nonetheless saw in Communism a new spirit for a world that teetered on the edge
of obliteration. Then, near the end of his life, Du Bois joined his spiritual-

ized approach to Communism to his sacred view of Africa. In "Ghana Calls," published in 1962 (one year after he moved to Ghana and one year before his death), Du Bois preserved his moral indictments of western society, his characterizations of his life as a divine unfolding of events, and the apotheosis of Africa. In it, a "Seer" directed him to travel throughout the world. After venturing through the Soviet Union and China, Du Bois landed in Africa. There, he would discover the "endless Riddle of the Sphinx." In Africa, Du Bois experienced a bath of radiant and sacred sunshine. It was the location of his personal emancipation and his prophecy of social liberation.

> Here at last, I looked back on my Dream;
>   I heard the Voice that loosed
>   The Long-locked dungeons of my soul
>   I sensed that Africa had come
>   Not up from Hell, but from the sun of Heaven's glory.

Beholding the West, Du Bois believed that it was dying for its many sins, especially its racism, exploitation, and defilement of Christianity.

> From reeking West whose day is done,
>   Who stink and stagger in their dung
>   …
> Enslaved the Black and killed the Red
>   And armed the Rich to loot the Dead;
>   Worshipped the whores of Hollywood
>   Where once the Virgin Mary stood
>   and lynched the Christ.

In Du Bois's cosmic vision, Ghana became the sacred center of the worldly and heavenly axis. It replaced the Christian cross as the symbolic location of divine redemption and history's great divider.

> I lifted up mine eyes to Ghana
>   And swept the hills with high Hosanna
>   Above the sun my sight took flight
>   'Till from the pinnacle of light
>   I saw dropped down this earth of crimson, green and gold
>   Roaring with color, drums and song.

Transported to this new heavenly realm, Du Bois reveled in its sacred glory.

> The lilies hallelujah rang
> Where robed with rule on Golden Stool
> The gold-crowned Priests with duty done
> Pour high libations to the sun
> And danced to the gods.[43]

The Du Bois of the middle of the twentieth century had certainly not abandoned religion as a central metaphor or an organizing set of symbolic principles. And his contemporaries knew it. Du Bois's almost incessant deployments of religion, his consistent use of biblical language, his ostensible preaching in black churches, and his interactions with ministers did not fall on deaf ears. Just as his admirers had done throughout his life, they still characterized him as a prophetic and spiritual leader. Du Bois and his followers united to present him as a messianic character wrongly oppressed by an imperialistic, greedy, and racist society. Actor-activist Paul Robeson claimed in 1951 that the U.S. government must set Du Bois free so that the world would not be cheated of "the artistic gift of this deep-feeling prophet."[44] For poet extraordinaire and neighbor of Du Bois in New York, William Stanley Braithwaite, Du Bois carried the words of God and Jesus into the twentieth century. Braithwaite contended in 1949 that when Du Bois wrote and spoke, he channeled "the authority of Truth that was first transmitted in thunder on Sinai and later reinterpreted with divine melodies on the slopes of Olivet." Again invoking biblical rhetoric, Braithwaite deemed Du Bois "a meditative and dreaming David" who had the wit and will to defeat the "modern Goliath, in the shape of an oppressive and merciless industrialism."[45]

Langston Hughes ripped into the federal government for indicting Du Bois. With a short essay, "The Accusers' Names Nobody Will Remember, But History Records Du Bois," Hughes connected Du Bois to Christ and Du Bois's oppressors to the murderers of God. "Somebody in Washington wants to put Dr. Du Bois in jail," Hughes concluded, just as "Somebody at Golgotha erected a cross and somebody drove the nails into the hands of Christ. Somebody spat upon His garments. No one remembers their names."[46] Then, following the release of Du Bois and his compatriots, conservative black columnist Gordon Hancock claimed that Du Bois was the symbol of black America, carrying a cross for his people. Du Bois was their "symbol of manhood and integrity. . . . It was a shame that Dr. Du Bois, the Negro champion, almost had to bear his cross alone."[47]

Especially following Du Bois's eighty-third birthday in 1951, he received a host of letters praising his moral character and his willingness to fight the federal government. Italian writer Gino Bardi wrote, "When we think of the real America we see this great country in terms of the moral stature of public figures like Dr. Du Bois." Reverend William H. Francis of Woodstock, New York, claimed, "Dr. Du Bois is one of the great pioneers of our new civilization and though for the present day may seem dark—a new day is arising. Thank God for such a man!" Du Bois offered these notes to the public in his *In Battle for Peace*, perhaps to further assert the righteousness of his cause.[48]

Until the very end of his life, Du Bois's many admirers considered him a religious leader. They thanked God for him; they associated him with the biblical Christ; they denounced his oppressors as immoral beasts; and Du Bois never discouraged them. In opposition to an American culture that linked capitalism and the "American way of life" to God, Du Bois stood defiant. During these final decades, he presented himself as a prophetic figure, echoed the Bible by calling for "peace on earth and goodwill to men," coupled Christianity with Communism, envisioned his work as a sacred duty, and looked to churches and synagogues as public platforms for himself. The ultimate expression of his continuing interest in religion and his refusal to be cast off as antireligious or irreligious was in his final autobiography. In this last literary act of self presentation, Du Bois wove together the various strands of his religious thought into one final political, social, and spiritual tapestry.

"I Was Not Without Faith"

Du Bois's most thorough defense of himself and his decisions late in life were contained in his final autobiography: *The Autobiography of W. E. B. Du Bois: A Soliloquy on Viewing My Life from the Last Decade of Its First Century*. This was his last autobiographical narrative to the world. He could be thrown out of the NAACP, pursued by the federal government, and forced from Atlanta University, but with his autobiography he could not be silenced. He worked furiously on it before his death so that individuals across the globe could know where he stood after almost one hundred years of battle. Published in the United States in 1968 (five years after his death and on the centennial of his birth), Du Bois offered his rationale for embracing Communism and let readers into his private life as never before. Similar to his other writings on Communism, Du Bois elided the moral failings of the Soviet Union and Communist China in favor of glowing depictions of regulated economies and religious freedom.[49]

Unlike in his previous autobiographical works, "The Shadow of Years" (1920) and *Dusk of Dawn* (1940), this time Du Bois presented himself neither in the guise of a mythological hero who battled oppressive demons and shared the divine boon with humanity nor in the garb of a biblical prophet directed by a sacred voice to map out a new path for people of color. Rather, Du Bois now constructed himself as an exiled sage who in his globetrotting had finally landed on the key to social salvation: Communism. Du Bois's decision to embrace Communism was completely consistent with his decades-long hatred for materialism and free-market capitalism. Moreover, just as in his other works, Du Bois showed no inclination to dismiss religion in his final autobiography. Communism served as the economic and social fulfillment of Christian morality and, when providing memories from his long life, Du Bois focused more intently on religion than he did in his other autobiographies. It seemed that Du Bois was intent on avoiding being remembered as irreligious or as an atheist. Rather, he appeared intent on protecting the image of himself as a spiritual being.

Just as he had done with his previous autobiographies, Du Bois preceded his final one with a creative literary work that served as a spiritualized key to read the longer endeavor. On February 22, 1959, one day before his ninety-second birthday, Du Bois literally spoke to millions in a radio address broadcast from Peking, China. In "Hail Humankind!" he invited Africa to embrace Communism and to avoid alliances with Europe and the United States. With the address, Du Bois cast himself as a religious teacher in the lineage of Jesus and Buddha. He renounced worldly possessions and positions to obtain his soul. "I speak with no authority; no assumption of age nor rank; I hold no position. I have no wealth," he asserted. "One thing alone I own and that is my own soul. Ownership of that I have even while in my own country for near a century I have been nothing but a 'nigger.'" Du Bois's ability to achieve ownership of his "soul" was all the justification he needed to speak, for it was the one possession that American society did not want a black man to grasp: "On this basis and this alone I dare speak, I dare advise."[50]

Du Bois painted the Cold War as a spiritual struggle that pitted the evil forces of capitalism against the sacred forces of communism. It was not a battle between nation-states or political ideologies but between right and wrong. Du Bois drew on phrases from Julia Ward Howe's "Battle Hymn of the Republic," an American Civil War song in which Union soldiers were transformed into Christ-like figures, when he announced that the goal of Chinese Communism was "to 'make men holy; to make men free.'" He then proceeded to indict western Europeans and white Americans for their falsehoods. "You

have been told," he lectured, "that mankind can rise only by walking on men; by cheating them and killing them; that only a doormat of the despised and dying, the dead and rotten, can a British aristocracy, a French cultural elite or an American millionaire be grown." "This is a lie," Du Bois proclaimed, and he assailed both religious and secular leaders for teaching it. "It is an ancient lie by church and state, spread by priests and historians." Du Bois then warned Africans of the deviousness of Americans, again using religious rhetoric to dramatize his admonition. "Beware Africa," he maintained, "America bargains for your soul."[51]

In Du Bois's estimation, Africa and China had a special kinship, and he used biblical language to unveil it. "China is flesh of your flesh, and blood of your blood," he claimed, invoking the second chapter of the Book of Genesis when the first man, Adam, expressed wonder and joy at the creation of the first woman, Eve. Moreover, Africans must follow the example of their Chinese brethren, because China had not been duped by the false religions of whites. "China does not need American nor British missionaries to teach her religion and scare her with tales of hell," Du Bois maintained. The Chinese knew that if they were to find heaven, it would be in this world and not another. "China has been in hell too long, not to believe in a heaven of her own making. This she is doing." Du Bois expressed specific aggravation with church control over education. To him, it epitomized the sins of western civilization against Africa and China. It hindered true social progress by infusing education with fairy tales and flat falsehoods. "It is wrong for the Catholic Church to direct the education of the black Congolese," he maintained. "It was wrong for Protestant churches supported by British and American wealth to control higher education in China."[52]

In the conclusion of his radio address, Du Bois once more drew on religious imagery to emphasize his call for Chinese-African solidarity. He also linked the teachings of the Bible to those of Communism. "Stand together in this new world and let the old world perish in its greed or be born again in new hope and promise," he announced. Directly invoking the biblical prophet Isaiah, Du Bois declared, "Listen to the Hebrew prophet of communism: / Ho! every one that thirsteth; come yet to the waters; come, buy and eat, without money and price!"[53] Speaking principally to Chinese and African men and women, Du Bois's use of biblical rhetoric said a great deal about him. He certainly did not quote the Bible or draw on biblical phrases for the benefit of his audience, for Du Bois knew that his hearers were just as familiar with other religious traditions and discourses. Rather, as was the case in so many of his writings, biblical language was necessary to convey the spirit of his ideas.[54]

"Hail Humankind!" was an important precursor to Du Bois's final autobiography. In addition to finding its way into *The Autobiography of W. E. B. Du
Bois* as the conclusion to the final chapter and being written during the same
year that he labored on the autobiography, it emphasized many of the points
that were central to the autobiographical narrative. In his autobiography, Du
Bois linked Communism and Christian ethics and described the battle between Communism and capitalism with spiritualized rhetoric. He also went
into much more detail about his own religious development than he had in
his other autobiographical narratives. The personal tale explained how Du
Bois came to possess only, but most importantly, his "soul." Du Bois divided
The Autobiography of W. E. B. Du Bois into three parts: his reflections on his
travels throughout Europe and Asia during the twentieth century, a narrative
of his personal life and development from birth to World War II, and his efforts for peace from the end of World War II to the writing of the autobiography. To present and evaluate himself and his world, each part relied heavily
on religious language, symbolism, and themes.

Du Bois expressed keen awareness that the narrative was a presentation
of "self" and not an objective discussion of his life. "Autobiographies do not
form indisputable authorities," he wrote. "They are always incomplete, and
often unreliable. . . . Memory fails especially in small details" (12). Rather than
an exact compilation of his life's events and thoughts, Du Bois considered this
work "a theory of my life" and one written as much with an eye to self evaluation as to social evaluation. The autobiography was to answer the fundamental question of "Who and what is this I, which in the last year looked on
a torn world and tried to judge it?" Ultimately, Du Bois considered his work
"the Soliloquy of an old man on what he dreams his life has been as he sees it
slowly drifting away; and what he would like others to believe." As an explicit
construction of self for how he wished to be remembered, Du Bois drew on
religious symbols to indicate that his spiritual life was just as important as
other aspects of his life (12–13).

This autobiography's first section deviated from more traditional beginnings that focused on the birth and childhood of the author. Instead, Part
One of Du Bois's narrative centered on his travels throughout Europe and
Asia, especially after World War II, and how he gravitated to Communism as
the harbinger of global justice and equality. At mid-century, Du Bois traveled
to Europe to answer the question, "Was a world of peace and racial equality
about to emerge?" (14). He looked first to Britain, but its citizens still desired
to maintain their status and comfort by exploiting cheap labor and raw ma-

terials. He looked to Holland, but it was unwilling. France was in shambles: "There was death in her eyes, in her speech, in her gestures" (19). All of the western European nations, as well as the United States, Du Bois lamented, were morally unprepared to usher in a new world. They were unwilling to "sacrifice" their own luxuries for the promise of peace and the joy of cooperation. In Eastern Europe and Asia, though, Du Bois encountered a different type of people. Just as he did in his description of China in "Hail Humankind!" Du Bois used biblical rhetoric to wax romantic about the Soviet Union. Discussing World War II and the might of Soviet power, he mused, "to the surprise of mankind, David overpowered Goliath, and the Soviet Union won the war over Germany at Stalingrad" (27). Mapping the David and Goliath story onto World War II in this way, Du Bois associated the Soviet Union with the biblical king and ancestral progenitor of Christ. This was a provocative sleight of hand, for with it Du Bois upset the tendency of Americans to declare themselves God's chosen people and the victors of World War II. In place of the United States, the Soviet Union became God's selected instrument.

When discussing the rise of Communism in Russia and China, Du Bois described it as an amazing movement that for the good of humanity disempowered established religions. He applauded Lenin, Marx, and Engels as visionaries of a new heaven on earth. "Taking inspiration directly out of the mouths and dreams of the world's savants and prophets, who had inveighed against modern industrial progress and poverty," Du Bois maintained, "this new Russia founded by Lenin and inspired by Marx and Engels, proposed to build a socialist state with production of land and capital goods by the state, and with state control of public services, including education and health." Paralleling his discussion of white Christianity in the United States in *Dusk of Dawn*, Du Bois considered the dominant Christianity of Russia in the 1920s a central impediment to social improvement. "A religion led by a largely immoral priesthood," he wrote, "served as a major handicap for the nation." During the 1930s and 1940s, though, the church and its selfishness were being displaced, and consequentially so was poverty. "The golden domes of churches were not so numerous and tall office buildings were taking their place," he reported of his trip to Russia in 1936: "Few priests were visible, and few beggars" (30–32). Then, reflecting on his final visit to the Soviet Union, Du Bois again turned to spiritual rhetoric. "The Soviet Union which I see in 1959 is power and faith and not simply hope" (39).

Du Bois saved his most explicit remarks on religion in the Soviet Union for the end of his chapter on it. He reiterated and further developed the points he had made earlier—that Russia's religious history was one of exploitation

and that Communism was the nation's salvation. Of the early twentieth century, religion "was worse than opium," Du Bois announced. Quoting a Russian
priest, Du Bois condemned the assertion that Tsarist Russia was a Christian
nation: "There is no Christian Tsar and no Christian government. . . . The up-
per classes rule the lower classes. A little group keeps the rest of the population enslaved." According to this priest and to Du Bois, the Tsarist government
and the Orthodox Church had crippled true spirituality. "In the place of religion," they had given the people "gross superstition." "The ruling clergy with
its cold, heartless bony fingers, has stifled the Russian church, killed its creative
spirit, chained the Gospel itself, and 'sold' the church to the government," this
priest concluded (42). In the eyes of Du Bois, the era of state-ruled religion
was marked by immorality. Prostitutes flooded the streets, while poverty and
crime ran rampant.

Russian Communism, however, was creating a new society. Du Bois especially applauded the Soviet government for dissociating religion and education. "Science is free from religious dogma," Du Bois remarked, "and the
Soviet Union does not allow any church of any kind to interfere with education, and religion is not taught in public schools. It seems to me that this is the
greatest gift of the Russian Revolution to the modern world" (36, 42–43).

His observations of the Soviet Union provided Du Bois an opportunity to
assert his own beliefs about God. According to Du Bois, Soviet Communism,
its disestablishment of the Russian Orthodox Church, and its removal of religion from education not only put an end to this social and personal sin but
also made it possible for modern men to be honest—a moral quality that Du
Bois emphasized time and again. He did not articulate a conviction that God
did not exist; rather, Du Bois suggested that traditional Christian approaches
to God were dangerous. "Most educated modern men no longer believe in
religious dogma," Du Bois wrote.

> If questioned they will usually resort to double-talk before admitting
> the fact. But who today actually believes that this world is ruled and
> directed by a benevolent person of great power who, on humble appeal,
> will change the course of events at our request? Who believes in miracles?
> Many folk follow religious ceremonies and services; and allow their
> children to learn fairy tales and so-called religious truth, which in time
> the children come to recognize as conventional lies told by their parents
> and teachers for the children's good. One can hardly exaggerate the moral
> disaster of this custom. We have to thank the Soviet Union for the cour-
> age to stop it. (43)

His assessment of China reinforced the points he made about the Soviet Union—that before its Communist revolution, China was dominated by an otherworldly and exploitative faith that hindered national progress. "I saw a happy people," he reported of his visit in 1961, "people with faith that needs no church or priest, and who laugh gaily when the Monkey King overthrows the angels" (49). Du Bois depicted Chinese women and men as an ethical people, not because of churches but in spite of them: "Their officials are incorruptible, their merchants are honest, their artisans are reliable, their workers who dig and haul and lift do an honest day's work and even work overtime if their state asks it, for they are the state; they are China" (51). As he had in "Hail Humankind!" Du Bois used religious language to conclude his discussion of China. "Fifteen times I have crossed the Atlantic and once the Pacific. I have seen the world. But never so vast and glorious a miracle as China." Du Bois even characterized China with allusions to Christ, suggesting that it had become a neo-Savior for the entire world to behold. "Oh beautiful, patient, self-sacrificing China," he wrote romantically, "despised and unforgettable, victorious and forgiving, crucified and risen from the dead" (53).

If readers had missed Du Bois's religious approach to Communism in the chapters on the Soviet Union and China, they were hit with it once again at the end of the autobiography's first part. In a theoretical "interlude" on Communism, Du Bois defined Communism as "a planned way of life in the production of wealth and work designed for building a state whose object is the highest welfare of its people and not merely the profit of a part." Du Bois painted this system as a new faith that had the power to change human nature. Writing "frankly and clearly" Du Bois declared, "I believe in communism." "It will call for a progressive change in human nature and a better type of manhood than is common today," he concluded, "I believe this possible, or otherwise we will continue to lie, steal and kill as we are doing today." In short, communism was necessary politically and economically for it was the only social system whereby ethical living was possible (57).

The second and third parts of The Autobiography of W. E. B. Du Bois followed a more traditional autobiographical arc, detailing the events of his life from cradle to old age. In them, Du Bois focused on his religious development and demonstrated that religion maintained a special place in his sense of self. He depicted his life as marked by Christian organizations and teachings. By the end of his days, Du Bois still held in high esteem individuals and organizations that embodied the love ethic of Christianity. Ultimately, with his final presentation of self, Du Bois emphasized his own spiritual strivings. His was no simple tale of secularization but one of intense investment in the life and lineage of faith.

Of his family history, Du Bois drew even more attention to the importance of religion than he had in *Dusk of Dawn* or "The Shadow of Years." When he discussed his grandfather Alexander, for instance, Du Bois delved further into Alexander's personal and religious life. Du Bois quoted selections from his grandfather's diary that demonstrated his strong religious faith. "*Thursday, May 9.* Have thoughts of leaving the vessel, but want resolution to do so," Alexander penned and Du Bois reprinted, "If God forsakes me, I am undone forever. 'There is a divinity that shapes our ends, rough hew as we will.'" (69) Du Bois felt such admiration for his grandfather that he hoped to be buried alongside him in New Haven, Connecticut. "Here my grandfather lies buried and here I shall one day lie" (67).

Du Bois expressed significant regard for churches and the Bible when remembering his childhood. In his memory, Great Barrington was not a place of "spiritual isolation," as biographer Elliot Rudwick has claimed, but a land of spiritual delight.[55] "Outside my school," he claimed, "my chief communication with the people of the town was through the church." Du Bois recalled of his Sunday school, "I was always there. I felt absolutely no discrimination, and I do not think there was any, or any thought of it." More than eighty years after this church burned down, moreover, Du Bois still felt the emotional pull of his church: "I was a sensitive mourner and oversaw at every period its pretentious rebuilding. I remember the altar, whose Greek inscription I was proudly able to read: '*He alethia eleutherosi humas.*' (The truth shall make you free.) I heard the dedicatory sermon: 'For thus said the High and Mighty One, who inhabiteth eternity, Whose Name is Holy. I dwell in the high and lofty place. With him also that is of a contrite heart and humble spirit to revive the spirit of the humble, to revive the heart of the contrite ones.'" Du Bois thoroughly enjoyed the new church and new Sunday school building. It "was my chief pride and joy." The aged Du Bois seemed almost able to see and touch the room: "It had climbed out of the basement and had broad and beautiful rooms with sunlit windows looking out on lawn and flowers. The carpet, the chairs, the tables, were all new, and the teachers were inspired to new efforts with their growing classes." Perhaps with a wry smile, Du Bois recalled his own active participation in the church school. "I was quite in my element and led in discussions, with embarrassing questions, and long disquisitions. I learned much of the Hebrew scriptures. I think I must have been both popular and a little dreaded, but I was very happy" (88–90).

As Du Bois related his first experiences as a college student at Fisk, he also sought to disclose much about his religious activities and feelings by reprinting material from a letter he wrote in 1886 to his pastor and Sunday school

in Massachusetts. In it, he noted that he had joined a local congregation, participated in revival services, and anticipated the arrival of the famous white evangelist Dwight Lyman Moody. "In the first place I am glad to tell you that I have united with the Church here and hope that the prayers of my Sunday School may help guide me in the path of Christian duty. During the revival we had nearly forty conversions. The day of prayer for colleges was observed here with two prayer meetings. . . . and tomorrow Mr. Moody will be present in our chapel services" (109–110).

Although Du Bois acknowledged his aggravation with pedantic church rules, specifically those against dancing, he also expressed continuing appreciation for practical Christianity. Including the text from his eulogy of Fisk's president while he was a student, Erastus Cravath, Du Bois lauded Cravath for embracing the "reality of the broader humanity taught by the Christian religion. He did not hold this merely as a theory, as an intellectual belief, but as a thing worth living and fighting for—and for it he lived and fought" (113). Du Bois then commented on his own religious faith when articulating why he was uninterested in attending seminary, as Cravath had hoped Du Bois would after Fisk. "I believed too little in Christian dogma to become a minister," he maintained. Yet, Du Bois stressed that this did not mean he lacked morals or faith. He depicted himself as living the ethical teachings of true religion. "I was not without faith," he explained. "I never stole material nor spiritual things; I not only never lied, but blurted out my conception of the truth on the most untoward occasions; I drank no alcohol and knew nothing of women, physically or psychically, to the incredulous amusement of most of my more experienced fellows" (124).

Of his early career at Wilberforce, the University of Pennsylvania, and Atlanta University, Du Bois once again discussed his battles with the church establishment and used religious rhetoric to describe his feelings. He rehearsed his struggles at Wilberforce over public prayer and quoted from "The Shadow of Years" when he maintained that to remain at Wilberforce would have meant "spiritual death." In his description of Wilberforce, though, Du Bois announced a profound respect for one of the school's leading lights, Bishop Daniel Payne. "He was a man of tremendous character, a Man of God, if such there ever was, " Du Bois asserted. "There he died, but his soul lived on" (190).

In a chapter dedicated to addressing "My Character," Du Bois claimed without reservation, "I loved living, physically as well as spiritually" (284). He described his religious development growing up "in a liberal Congregational Sunday School" and listening "once a week to a sermon on doing good as a

reasonable duty." By the time he left Fisk, Du Bois asserted, "I was still a 'believer' in orthodox religion, but had strong questions which were encouraged at Harvard." In Germany, Du Bois maintained, he "became a freethinker," yet on returning to the United States he found his way back to Christian churches and even taught in a Sunday school.[56] From the age of thirty until the writing of this final autobiography, though, Du Bois had felt disdain for the "church" as an institution. "I have increasingly regarded the church as an institution which defended such evils as slavery, color, caste, exploitation of labor and war" (285).

Although Du Bois opposed the church, his regard for spiritual and religious emotions was another matter. He praised the influence of sacred music in his soul. "I know the old English and German hymns by heart," Du Bois wrote. "I loved their music but ignored their silly words with studied inattention. Great music came at last in the religious oratorios which we learned at Fisk University but it burst on me in Berlin with the Ninth Symphony and its Hymn of Joy." His love for Christian cathedrals and hymns, however, did not stop him from damning American churches for siding with business interests against labor. Denouncing white Christians yet again, Du Bois further characterized Communism as the social realization of Christianity. "I worshipped the Cathedral and ceremony which I saw in Europe but I knew what I was looking at when in New York a Cardinal became a strike-breaker and the Church of Christ fought the Communism of Christianity" (285–286).

The final part of Du Bois's autobiography detailed his work for world peace, the trial of the Peace Information Society, and his focus on bringing socialism to Africa. Du Bois considered each crusade a moral one and expressed heightened animosity for white and black America's failures to assist him. When speaking before more than fifteen thousand in Chicago to earn money for his legal defense, Du Bois invoked God to oppose the ways in which big business pushed the United States to war and silenced leftist opposition. "If sincere dislike of this state of affairs is communism, then by the living God, no force of arms, nor power of wealth, nor smartness of intellect will ever stop it. . . . If this is the American way of life, God save America." Du Bois then assailed the people of the United States for lacking the "moral courage and intellectual integrity" to stand up to the bullying of the federal government and its Communist witch hunt (378, 389).

Finally, in his "Postlude," Du Bois offered a litany of religious reflections on the United States, American churches, the world, and himself. He proclaimed to have "seen miracles" during his lifetime, including human flight, streets lit by electricity, and space exploration. He felt himself an exiled prophet stand-

ing "high on the ramparts of this blistering hell of life, as it must appear to most men, I sit and see the Truth. I look it full in the face, and will not lie about it, neither to myself nor to the world. I see my country . . . as a 'Frightened Giant' afraid of the Truth, afraid of Peace" (415). In addition, Du Bois took one final shot at organized religion in the United States. He depicted the sorry state of Christianity in America by narrating the travails of his friend and priest William Howard Melish, To Du Bois, "the Melish case is perhaps at once the most typical and frightening example illustration of present American religion." Melish was the type of minister that Du Bois could admire, "one of the few Christian clergymen for whom I have the highest respect." Du Bois admitted that he did not hold all of the religious teachings that Melish did, but Du Bois nonetheless depicted Melish as a man after his own heart: "Honest and conscientious, believing sincerely in much of the Christian dogma, which I reject, but working honestly and without hypocrisy, for the guidance of the young, the uplift of the poor and ignorant, and for the betterment of his city and his country." Perhaps saddest of all, in Du Bois's estimation, churches and church people in the United States failed to stand behind Melish, as they had failed to stand behind Du Bois. By using his final pages to denounce white Christianity's hypocrisy and to defend Melish, Du Bois provided his final signal of disdain for the organized church and his respect for believers who upheld a social gospel. (417)

Concluding the narrative, Du Bois returned to his belief in Communism and depicted the world in sacred terms. He ended with a prayer "To the Almighty Dead." Just as in "The Shadow of Years" and *Dusk of Dawn*, Du Bois fused social and spiritual matters to elevate his concerns to the highest heights. "Our dreams seek Heaven," he wrote, "our deeds plumb Hell. Hell lies about us in our Age; blithely we push into its stench and flame. Suffer us not, Eternal Dead to stew in this Evil—the Evil of South Africa, the Evil of Mississippi; the Evil of Evils which is what we hope to hold in Asia and Africa, in the southern Americas and the islands of the Seven Seas. Reveal, Ancient of Days, the Present in the Past and prophesy the End in the Beginning" (422).

Du Bois could now rest in peace for he had battled "Evil" and he had sought "the Present in the Past and prophesy the End in the Beginning" throughout his entire life. With his final presentation of self, Du Bois demonstrated that religion still mattered to him, perhaps more than ever. He embraced Communism not merely as a political and economic system but as a new religion that embodied the biblical teachings of Isaiah and of Christ. He drew on memories of his religious upbringing and love for his Sunday school and in so doing demonstrated his recognition of their lifelong influence on his career.

He again used religious rhetoric to discuss the events of his adult life and his shifting intellectual perspective in ways that revealed his conflation of the sacred and the secular (422).

~

Only if one assumes that Communism and Christianity were mutually exclusive and if one ignores an avalanche of evidence should Du Bois's final decades be cast as evidence of his antireligiosity or irreligiosity. These years were marked by religious expression, just not the types that historians tend to look for. His relationships with white progressive ministers John Haynes Holmes and William Howard Melish sustained his spirit. The pulpits of white and black churches became indispensable public replacements for the NAACP and Atlanta University. Prophetic discourse and biblical passages marked his speeches and writings, while Communism for him stood as the social realization of the spirit of Christ's teachings. Then with his final autobiography, Du Bois presented himself as a spiritual actor. From World War II until the time of his death, Du Bois remained a tireless spiritual warrior. For the women and men who discussed his power, they almost always looked to Christian symbolism. Religious language was the only way they could convey the depth of his power in their minds, hearts, and lives. This became evident at no time more clearly than when Du Bois, at the age of ninety-five and living across the Atlantic Ocean in Ghana, died. In August 1963, the world may have lost a prophet, but his spirit remained in the minds and hearts of so many. And, in some ways, as Du Bois's wife would later remark, true prophets never die.

EPILOGUE

~

The Passing of the Prophet

"GOD IS NO PLAYWRIGHT," reflected the fictive Manuel Mansart of the Black Flame trilogy as he lay on his deathbed in Manhattan. Most "lives end dimly, and without drama; they pile no climax on tragedy nor triumph on defeat. They end quietly and helplessly—they just end." In the case of the real W. E. B. Du Bois, Manuel could not have been more wrong. Du Bois died in Accra, Ghana, at 11:40 P.M. on August 27, 1963, the eve of the March on Washington for Jobs and Freedom. On August 28, Martin Luther King, Jr., electrified the nation with his "I Have a Dream" speech, an address that had much in common with Du Bois's "Credo" of 1904. Du Bois seemed to die as he had lived—with drama and symbolic power. To many, it appeared that God was indeed a playwright. The Deputy General Secretary of Ghana wrote to Shirley Graham Du Bois, "It seems symbolic that this release should come just at the moment when everything he worked for throughout his life is climaxing in the great public expression of racial equality in America and in the sweep to Pan-Africanism, the seed of which he, above all, first planted."[1] Hearing the news while in Mexico, the editor of the *National Guardian*, Cedric Belfrage, claimed, "The pattern of his life is a drama finished by a master playwright's hand. It's a sermon to faint hearts and cynics everywhere on the text that struggle and sacrifice are in vain."[2]

Many in the United States first heard the news of Du Bois's death at the March on Washington. The hundreds of thousands who gathered by the Lincoln Memorial turned to religious idioms to articulate Du Bois's place in their hearts and the world. After Roy Wilkins, the leader of the NAACP, announced Du Bois's passing, "a moment of silent prayer was held." The *National Guard-*

ian reported that amid the gathering, an old woman "wept." She cried out, "It's like Moses . . . God had written that he should not enter the promised land." Educator and peace activist Rachel Davis Du Bois imagined that Du Bois's spirit "in some mysterious way . . . hovered in our midst."[3]

The religious responses to Du Bois's death were fitting. He had lived a life of spiritual insight, craft, and passion. He had raged against the association of whiteness and godliness; he had connected women and men of color with the divine; he had pushed for peace, disarmament, and universal fraternity; he had claimed ownership of nothing but a soul, which for him meant everything; he had approached oppression and resistance as spiritual issues; and he had investigated the tangled relationships among religion, society, culture, literature, economics, and racial categories. Friends, readers, and others had found sacred courage and new cosmic perspectives in his works, his struggle against oppression, and his vision for a redeemed world. Now, with Du Bois's death, they revered him as a spiritual symbol. His ascension to sainthood was more than a typical reaction to the death of a prominent leader; rather, it followed his lifelong cultivation of the prophetic image. The man who had touched souls with *The Souls of Black Folk*, who had inveighed against church segregation, who had seen in Africa a cosmic redemption, who had endeavored to redeem lynch victims with literary tales of black Christs, and who had presented himself as a mythological hero: he was now gone. But his spirit was as alive as ever.

Du Bois had moved to Ghana with Shirley Graham in 1961 at the behest of Ghanaian President Kwame Nkrumah, and there, in the land of the African fathers and mothers, Du Bois died. His funeral on August 29, 1963, brought together a host of sacred rituals. It began at Du Bois's bungalow where Ghanaian artist Kofi Antabaum poured "a traditional libation to the gods in memory of the departed." Then a state linguist "recited a final prayer on [President Kwame] Nkrumah's behalf for the soul of Dr. Du Bois and poured another libation to his memory." At that point, the sky opened and rain "came down in a torrent." This was a sign to many of the locals. As William Branch wrote for the *Amsterdam News* of New York, "Ghanaians considered this sudden rain a genuine libation from Heaven, a sign that the Almighty had accepted with favor [Nkrumah's] prayer asking that the departed by led safely into the next world." Then, the funeral procession began and the crowd sang "I Am the Resurrection and the Light," a hymn that proclaims that all believers in Christ will "never die." Du Bois's body was transported to Castle Osu along the coast.[4]

Hymns and spirituals played an important role in the procession and burial, just as they had in Du Bois's life. During the processional, Ghana's Central

Army Band played "O God, Our Help in Ages Past." Written by Isaac Watts, the slave-trader-turned abolitionist and the author of "Amazing Grace," in 1719, this hymn versed the words of the Old Testament King David. It was a popular funeral hymn; two years after Du Bois's death it serenaded Winston Churchill into the grave. Although the title pointed backward, the thrust of the hymn pushed forward. It envisioned God protecting his people and creation now and in the future.

> O God, our help in ages past
> Our hope for years to come.
> Our shelter from the stormy blast,
> And our eternal home.

Outside of Castle Osu, Ghanaian ambassador Michael Dei Anang read Du Bois's "Last Message to the World." Writing in 1957, Du Bois looked forward to the end. "I am going to take a long deep and endless sleep," he proclaimed. And then his final words invoked life over death. "I charge you to believe," Du Bois spoke from beyond the grave, "to believe in life. The only possible death is to lose belief in this truth." Then President Nkrumah hailed Du Bois as "a phenomenon" and "a real friend and father to me." Following Nkrumah's words, a "final prayer" was read and "Dr. Du Bois reposed in African soil." Now Du Bois was united with the land he had so often approached in mystical terms as the location of human creation, suffering, and eventual redemption.[5]

Almost one month after the state funeral, a special memorial service was held for Du Bois in Accra. Beethoven's "Ode to Joy" began the service and then Nadine Brewer sang Du Bois's "favorite spirituals," as Shirley Graham Du Bois remembered later: "Oh, What a Beautiful City!" and "My Lord, What a Morning!" Both hymns imagined a future where God called all the people of the world to himself. In the "Beautiful City," there were

> Three gates in-a de east
> Three gates in-a de west
> Three gates in-a de north
> Three gates in-a de south
> Making it twelve gates to de city
> Hallelu!

"My Lord What a Morning!" was even more explicit in its appeal to the oppressed of the world.

You'll hear the trumpet sound,
To wake the nations underground,
Looking to my God's right hand,
When the stars begin to fall.
My Lord, what a morning.
My Lord, what a morning;
Oh, my Lord, what a morning,
When the stars begin to fall.[6]

For Du Bois, these spirituals and the other "sorrow songs" of his black ancestors spoke to his lifelong passions. Having first heard them as a student-
teacher in Nashville in the 1880s, Du Bois found meaning within meaning in
the songs. He had found an expression of the "souls of black folk"; he had felt
in them courage and inspiration for the fictional characters of his narratives;
and he invoked them to call the powerful of the world to offer liberation to
the oppressed. These were songs that taught him, that sustained him, and that
carried him to spiritual heights.

Following Brewer's sweet, yet haunting, melodies, Du Bois received one of
his last wishes. His minister at Holy Trinity Church in Brooklyn, Reverend
William Howard Melish, had obtained a special passport, ventured to Accra,
and performed the memorial eulogy. In his address, "One of the Great Companions," Melish invoked a variety of Du Bois's concerns. Melish described
Du Bois's ancestry as racially diverse, yet with no taint of "Anglo-Saxon"
blood, just as Du Bois had boasted in "The Shadow of Years." Melish recalled
Du Bois's revoicing of Queen Esther's words on his twenty-fifth birthday that
"I will go unto the king—which is not according to the law and if I perish—
I PERISH." Of The Souls of Black Folk, Melish heralded it as epic. It "tolled the
death of all such myths and sounded the tocsin of a great new day." Then
Melish drew attention to Du Bois's love for spirituals. They appealed to Du
Bois because of their cosmic and physical meanings. Du Bois "loved" them
so dearly, Melish maintained, because of their "double meanings." Religious
sentiments were crucial to Du Bois's historical mind, Melish furthered. "In
John Brown," Melish recalled of Du Bois's biography of the militant abolitionist, Du Bois "saw a man of Old Testament proportions who had come face to
face with slavery in Kansas."[7]

Painting Du Bois as a godly servant, Melish concluded his eulogy with a series of prayers. "Into thy hands, O most loving Father, we entrust thy servant,
William Edward Burghardt Du Bois, whom we shall ever recall with thank-
fulness, for the faith he held in life." Melish asked God to accept Du Bois into

heaven: "We beseech thee that he may be for ever precious in thy sight, and may go from strength to strength in the life of perfect service; do thou bless him and keep him, do thou make thy face to shine upon him, and be gracious unto him, do thou lift up the light of thy countenance upon him, and give him joy and peace, now and for ever more."

These words typically completed a eulogy or religious service. But not one for Du Bois. His faith and approach to religion were always more about saving the world than himself, and Melish made this point with his final prayer. Invoking Communist and Christian rhetoric, Melish offered the types of words that had so appealed to Du Bois in his final decades. "God, our Father, give to the peoples of the world a new heart of comradeship; the old man of ignorance and cruelty being done away, and the new man put on, renewed in knowledge, to strengthen and to serve the brethren; that every people may bring its tribute of excellence to the common treasury, without fear, and without the lust of domination; and that all the world may go forward in the new and living way which he hath consecrated for us." These were ideals that Du Bois and Melish shared, sacred concepts that bound them as friends.[8]

The service and the state funeral, however, were hardly the only locations for memorials to Du Bois. While the funeral procession and the burial certainly depicted Du Bois as a religious icon, it did not contain all of the religious responses to his passing. The public memorializations were matched by individual testimonies, and as a grand testimony to Du Bois's own religious attitude, women and men throughout the world advanced their own cosmic interpretations of his life and teaching. In Ghana at the time of Du Bois's death, for instance, author and educator Leslie Alexander Lacy was struck to the core by the news. In a biography for children that Lacy published in 1970, he viewed Du Bois as "a prophet" and as a "spiritual and intellectual father." When he and his friends heard that Du Bois was ill in Ghana, Lacy recalled, "we did not want to believe that Du Bois might die. We hoped he would live forever." Lacy was part of a crowd that sang the spiritual "Let Us Cheer the Weary Traveler" when they heard the news of Du Bois's demise. Lacy attended the funeral and was awestruck. "I finally stood before him. I counted the lines in his face and recalled his smile a few days past. I let my tears come freely; I touched him. I closed my eyes and thought of his book *The Souls of Black Folk* and realized that the old man lying before me was the Father of Soul, a brother man." According to Lacy, the presence of a southern white representative from the United States, "a cracker who had come for political reasons," actually "desecrated the meaning of the service."[9]

Yet Lacy found the ceremony disappointing. "I felt strangely detached

from the eulogies of the funeral," he declared. "They were not adequate." Lacy claimed that "the Methodist minister doing most of the Bible reading seemed like a contradiction in terms." The minister, Lacy complained, "spoke about everything except the ideas and values which W. E. B. Du Bois had lived for. He was making ready the Old Man's soul for God; whitewashing a newly acquired Ghanaian spirit." Lacy wanted another pastor to speak, "If only I had shouted: Preacher man, brother man, minister of God! You do not know the man who lies in state beneath you. He comes from another country, another time, another century." Just as Du Bois had looked to dash the association of whiteness with godliness, so now Lacy worried that in their hopes that Du Bois would ascend to heaven they may lose sight of Du Bois's spiritual connection to Africa and that his "heaven" was in Ghanaian soil.[10]

So in his own mind, Lacy constructed what he considered a more fitting funeral for Du Bois. Just as Du Bois had refused to accept blindly teachings about God, faith, religion, Christ, and the rest of the sacred as they were offered to him by religious authorities, Lacy too expressed a vibrant sacred individualism. This fictive funeral would have been a poetic affair, Lacy described, with "all of the great poets (both living and dead) whom Du Bois had either known or respected pass the open coffin and read a few of their lines." In this imaginary funeral, sacred imagery once again was front and center. Poet and longtime Du Bois friend James Weldon Johnson, who had died in 1938, passed and spoke from his book of poetry *God's Trombones*:

> Weep not, weep not,
> He is not dead;
> He's resting in the bosom of Jesus.
> He's borne the burden and heat of the day,
> He's labored long in my vineyard,
> And he's tired —
> He's weary —
> Go down, Death, and bring him to me.

Then Senegal's Leopold Sedar Senghor mourned Du Bois

> And the ears, above all the ears to God
> who with a burst of saxophone
>   laughter created the heavens and the earth in six days.
> And on the seventh day, he slept his great negro sleep.[11]

The poetic words that Lacy drew upon tapped into several elements of Du Bois's religious life and times. The image of Christ as a refuge for tired and embattled individuals in Johnson's poem resonated with Du Bois's literary depictions of Christ, while Senghor's blackening of God and creation was a regular refrain in Du Bois's own verses. Certainly Du Bois would have been pleased by Senghor's and Johnson's poems as much as by Brewer's singing and Melish's preaching.

~

On the other side of the Atlantic Ocean, the news of Du Bois's death elicited similar responses. Time and again, initial reactions expressed the conviction that Du Bois was a modern prophet. Whether as a messianic hero, a wise sage, or an inspired revolutionary, the symbol of Du Bois continued to be one revered in a religious fashion. Proclaiming that Du Bois had lived a life of spiritual importance not only helped women and men grieve but also bore witness to Du Bois's enduring religious power.

Shirley Graham Du Bois held up her deceased husband as a neo-Christ figure. Invoking rhetoric from Easter services when Christians celebrate the resurrection of Jesus, Graham Du Bois wrote, "*He lives* in greater abundance than ever before. *He lives* on both sides of the Atlantic. From the campuses of America's leading universities youth sends his name like a flame across the land." She saw Du Bois alive in children, in the earth itself, and in the minds of so many: "He lives in the face of every black child who laughs with joy; he lives in the orange trees he planted in the garden, in the fragrant blooms that climb up to his window. He lives in our deepest convictions, faith, work, and dreams." Graham Du Bois even associated Christ and Du Bois by turning to lyrics from Julia Ward Howe's "Battle Hymn of the Republic" with the title of her memoir of life with Du Bois: "His Day is Marching On."[12]

For actress Ruby Dee, Du Bois lived on in his "Credo." First published in 1904 and then placed before his autobiographical chapter in *Darkwater*, the "Credo" long served as Du Bois's expression of religious and political faith. It was a professional and spiritual inspiration for Dee. "In searching over the years for special material to do on platforms, street corners, and stages for brotherhoods, sisterhoods, unions, schools, demonstrations, I came upon the *Credo*," Dee recounted. "I read it over and over with joy—I had found an affirmation, a prayer, a poem, a longing for humanity to fulfill its promise of greatness. For a long time, after the discovery, I felt a program was not complete, no matter what went before, without concluding with the *Credo*."

According to Dee, Du Bois was "the prophet" who knew how to present "the soul sweetness, the beauty, and the strength of our people." Dee, however, revised Du Bois's "Credo" when she performed it. She always excluded "the fifth paragraph which begins, 'I believe in the devil and his angels.'" To Dee, the "Credo" was "an affirmation," and she did not want its optimism clouded by the reality or symbolism of the devil.[13]

To express the profound effect Du Bois had, editor and author George B. Murphy mapped a series of biblical typologies onto his memories of their encounters. In Murphy's recollection, Du Bois became a messianic savior and Murphy a devout convert. Murphy remembered first meeting Du Bois in Harlem in the 1930s. In Murphy's narrative, the event became a religious conversion experience where the human sinner (Murphy) approached the divine Christ (Du Bois) in search of forgiveness and direction. When they first met, Murphy recounted, "I asked him to forgive me for being weak before the storm of ignorance, for ever doubting his humanity." Murphy felt that with every admission, his sins were being relieved. "With the strength of those released from a heavy burden, I went further; I asked him for the right to be his friend." Murphy wanted to become Du Bois's disciple. "I asked him for the right to go along with him in the future, even if I had to walk a little behind him until I had proved my friendship." Then, Murphy clearly linked the event to a spiritual conversion by invoking the image of the "Mourner's Bench," the location where would-be converts sit and consider the gravity of their sins and wait for God's healing touch. "I let him know that this confession was painful to me, but I had come, let him know, like the 'Member at the Mourner's Bench,' that I understood him at last." Du Bois accepted Murphy's plea and thanked him for visiting. "I shall be happy to have you as a friend," Du Bois remarked, but "Now, I must leave you; my time is up."[14]

Murphy was ecstatic. "In my joyful confusion I rushed out the door," he wrote, "down the stairs, and out into the street." The entire world had changed. Du Bois had washed him clean. "Forgotten was the lecture I was to attend; forgotten the pain of my confusion, everything," Murphy continued. Meshing together a variety of New Testament stories where Christ transformed a man or woman merely with his words or presence, Murphy was so overjoyed to receive Du Bois's friendship that he rushed out of the building and into the street. Du Bois "had forgiven my weakness, my unkind thoughts," Murphy concluded. "He had said I could be his friend. Nothing else mattered."[15]

Author Elma Stuckey turned to poetry to articulate her feelings on losing Du Bois. She too considered him a Christ figure:

Now the fragrant petals shower downward
That hung suspended in an air of fear
But he is gone and now they fall resplendent
In solemn reverence for that mighty seer.
Our cross like a millstone on his heart
We let him bear the burden all alone
Now we come forward eloquent with praise
Our silence broken after he is gone.[16]

While associations of Du Bois with the biblical Christ were common, depictions of Du Bois as a "prophet" were ubiquitous. White novelist Truman Nelson declared Du Bois "WORLD MAN ONE" and America's premier prophet. "It is the sign of the true prophet," Nelson asserted, "that although he cries out in the wilderness and into the unheeding voice of the whirlwind, he wants to gain the hearts and minds of all men . . . he wants to join the millions; he is not in the least exclusive. . . . Du Bois tried to lead his people into the promised land of equality and fulfillment." To conclude, Nelson announced that Du Bois had risen above Moses and other biblical figures: "But then he had his final triumph . . . greater than Moses, greater than all the prophets." This cosmic event was the call to his homeland: Africa. Just as Du Bois had, Nelson now conceived of African liberation and uplift in sacred terms. "There are few moments in history more moving than when Kwame Nkrumah, in all the erectness and power of a young manhood that had wrested a new nation from a continent thought to be eternally dark and despised, and filled it with effusions of light, came to the old man and said, 'Father, we want you to come home.'"[17]

In the estimates of countless men and women throughout the world, Du Bois was a seer who taught them transcendent truths and revealed to them spiritual vistas. Nnamdi Azikiwe, the president of the Federal Republic of Nigeria, wrote that Du Bois was "a hero and prophet of his age." Educator Horace Mann Bond claimed that Du Bois was "the Great Revelator." Acknowledging that Du Bois tended to keep his inner thoughts and passions to himself, anthropologist Irene Diggs nonetheless claimed that much of Du Bois could be seen "made manifest through his writings" and there "is wisdom, prophecy, sorrow, scorching bitterness, great sensitivity, satire, prayer." Roy Wilkins called Du Bois "a seer" who "prophetically warned at the turn of the century" that the problem of the twentieth century was the color line. Politician Richard Hatcher declared that Du Bois was "our honest black prince

and prophet and we sit yet at his feet to learn, to replenish ourselves and go on in strength."[18]

Five years after Du Bois's death and only two weeks before being cut down in Memphis, another American prophet, Martin Luther King, Jr., paid homage to Du Bois. At a dinner at Carnegie Hall in New York City to honor Du Bois's hundredth birthday, King declared him "one of the most remarkable men of our time." King presented Du Bois as a prophetic and incarnational figure, "an exile only to the land of his birth" and one who "deliberately chose to share [southern blacks'] daily abuse and humiliation." As King recognized, Du Bois was a father of modern sociology, history, and literary studies. But to King, however, Du Bois's most pronounced feature was his spiritual sense. "Dr. Du Bois' greatest virtue," King declared, "was his committed empathy with all the oppressed and his divine dissatisfaction with all forms of injustice." In closing, King joined his rhetoric to that of Du Bois's to call for social justice, "Let us be dissatisfied until this pending cosmic elegy will be transformed into a creative psalm of peace and 'justice will roll down like waters from a mighty stream.'"[19]

By depicting Du Bois, his character, and his words as sacred, King and others traveled a path that Du Bois himself laid. Throughout his ninety-five years, he had often set himself up as a prophetic teacher, a wise sage, a Christian martyr, and a mythological hero. It made sense to consider Du Bois in a religious register, for he had done the same. Whether seeking to unveil the souls of black folk or declaring whiteness a devilish construction, whether evaluating the morality of black ministers or calling the worldwide church to economic and racial reform, and whether elevating the lynch victim to divine status or tying Communism to Christianity, Du Bois lived a life full of religious reflection and insight.

~

"Some day the people in this country will demand that their own records be set straight," wrote Truman Nelson in 1958 for the *Nation*, "and alongside the political accidents, the Presidents and Senators, will go the enduring and usable truths of the American Prophets. Among these Prophets will be W. E. B. Du Bois." Nelson's prophetic claim has been realized, but only in a twisted way. Du Bois has ascended in academic circles, now revered as the leading American intellectual and activist of the twentieth century. Yet Nelson's insistence that Du Bois would be recognized as the quintessential "American Prophet" has yet to take hold.[20] As the years followed Du Bois's passing, the scholarly image of him became secularized. In the hands of professional his-

torians, Du Bois began as "unreligious." Then, by the early 1980s, he became "irreligious." In the 1990s with the works of David Levering Lewis, Du Bois was then transformed into "antireligious." These slight alterations of prefixes created a Du Bois who was secular, then agnostic, and finally atheist, as if somehow secularists are necessarily nonreligious, agnostics are necessarily irreligious, and atheists are necessarily antireligious. Stripping away the religious terrain of Du Bois's life, scholars buried his spiritual side under mountains of political and social commentary.

But the spirit in his works and life could not be contained. If one looks for religion in Du Bois's life and times, it seems ubiquitous. It is there in his childhood at the Sunday school he loved so much. It is there in his first written works as he unveiled black souls in a culture that denied their existence. It is there in the prayers he wrote for his students, in his attacks on church segregation, in his jeremiads against war and unbridled capitalism, and in his literary creations of black Christs and dark princesses. It is there in his friendships with white ministers, in his lectures in churches and synagogues, and in his conception of Communism. Du Bois never hid his assessments and feelings on religion behind codes or riddles or anagrams. They were too vital then. And they are too vital now. Du Bois was, in his self characterizations and in the hearts of thousands, a prophet with sacred insight. He could see past the myths of the present age and reveal worlds beyond what lies on the surface.

Du Bois was an American prophet; he was a moral historian, a visionary sociologist, a literary theologian, and a mythological hero with a black face. In a world marked by white supremacy, capitalistic exploitation, grotesque materialism, and wicked militancy, Du Bois became a rogue saint and a dark monk to preach the good news of racial brotherhood, economic cooperation, and peace on earth. Hopefully in the world to come, he will sit where he belongs, where the fictive Manuel Mansart had hoped, at the table of the "Congregation of the Righteous." This realm of righteousness is one we will have to create before we destroy ourselves. Yet once again, Du Bois pointed the way and offered courage. "Beyond the Veil," he wrote in 1897, "lies an undiscovered country, a land of new things, of change, of experiment, of wild hope and somber realization, of superlatives and italics—of wondrously blended poetry and prose." Du Bois inhabited that realm for much of his lifetime; let us strive to join him there.[21]

NOTES

~

Introduction

1. Hallie E. Queen to Du Bois, February 11, 1907, in Papers of W. E. B. Du Bois (microfilm) (hereafter Du Bois Papers), reel 2, frame 1253–1265; also in Herbert Aptheker, ed., *The Correspondence of W. E. B. Du Bois: Volume I, Selections, 1877–1934* (Amherst: University of Massachusetts Press, 1973), 125–126. W. E. Burghardt Du Bois, *The Souls of Black Folk: Essays and Sketches* (Chicago: A. C. McClurg & Co., 1903).

2. Psalm 137, King James Version. Erich Zenger, *A God of Vengeance? Understanding the Psalms of Divine Wrath*, translated by Linda M. Maloney (Louisville, Ky.: Westminster John Knox Press, 1996), 47–50; R. Kelvin Moore, *The Psalms of Lamentation and the Enigma of Suffering* (Lewiston, N.Y.: Mellen Biblical Press Series, 1996), 24, 27–30, 52, 57–58, 64.

3. Connecting the experiences of African Americans with the biblical Israelites was part of a long tradition in the United States. See Albert J. Raboteau, *Slave Religion: The "Invisible Institution" in the Antebellum South* (Oxford: Oxford University Press, 1978), 311–312; Cain Hope Felder, *Troubling Biblical Waters: Race, Class, and Family* (Maryknoll, N.Y.: Orbis Books, 1989); Eddie Glaude, *Exodus! Religion, Race, and Nation in Early Nineteenth-Century Black America* (Chicago: University of Chicago Press, 2000); Gayraud S. Wilmore, *Black Religion and Black Radicalism: An Interpretation of the Religious History of Afro-American People* (Maryknoll, N.Y.: Orbis Books, 1994).

4. Hallie E. Queen to Du Bois, February 11, 1907, in Du Bois Papers, reel 2, frame 1253–1257.

5. W. P. Thirkield to Du Bois, October 14, 1902, in Du Bois Papers, reel 2, frame 309–310; also in Aptheker, ed., *The Correspondence of W. E. B. Du Bois: Volume I, Selections*, 48.

6. Francis J. Grimké to Du Bois, October 16, 1903, in Du Bois Papers, reel 2, frame 1057.

7. "To W. E. B. DuBois — Scholar" in Georgia Douglas Johnson, *Bronze: A Book of Verse* (Boston: B. J. Brimmer, 1922), 92.

8. John Henrik Clarke, Esther Jackson, Ernest Kaiser, and J. H. O'Dell, eds., *Black Titan: W. E. B. Du Bois, An Anthology by the Editors of* Freedomways (Boston: Beacon Press, 1970), 8.

9. W. E. Burghardt Du Bois, *Dusk of Dawn: An Essay Toward An Autobiography of a Race Concept* (1940; reprint, New York: Schocken Books, 1969), 56; see also *W. E. B. Du Bois: A Recorded Autobiography* (Washington, D.C.: Smithsonian Folkways Records, 1993), side 1, Band 4.

10. W. E. B. Du Bois, *The Autobiography of W. E. B. Du Bois: A Soliloquy on Viewing My Life from the Last Decade of Its First Century* (New York: International, 1968), 210.

11. "William Edward Burghardt Dubois," February 13, 1943, pg. 2. William E. B. Du Bois File, #100-99729; SAC, Los Angeles to FBI Director, "Du Bois, Shirley Graham," July 23, 1951, pg. 5. William E. B. Du Bois FBI File, #100-99729.

12. Du Bois, *The Autobiography of W. E. B. Du Bois*, 43.

13. W. E. Burghardt Du Bois, "Credo," *Independent*, October 6, 1904, 787.

14. E. P. Moreno to Du Bois, October 3, 1948; Du Bois to E. P. Moreno, November 15, 1948, in Du Bois Papers, reel 62, frame 381–385; also in Herbert Aptheker, ed., *The Correspondence of W. E. B. Du Bois: Volume III Selections, 1944–1963* (Amherst: University of Massachusetts Press, 1978), 213, 223.

15. Elliot M. Rudwick, *W. E. B. Du Bois: Propagandist of the Negro Protest* (1960; reprint, New York: Atheneum, 1969), 156. S. P. Fullinwider, *The Mind and Mood of Black America: Twentieth Century Thought* (Homewood, Ill.: Dorsey Press, 1969), 55. See also Francis L. Broderick, *W. E. B. Du Bois: Negro Leader in a Time of Crisis* (Stanford: Stanford University Press, 1959); Keith E. Byerman, *Seizing the Word: History, Art, and Self in the Work of W. E. B. Du Bois* (Athens: University of Georgia Press, 1994).

16. Arnold Rampersad, *The Art and Imagination of W. E. B. Du Bois* (Cambridge, Mass.: Harvard University Press, 1976), 20. David Levering Lewis, *W. E. B. Du Bois: Biography of a Race, 1868–1919* (New York: Henry Holt, 1993), 49–50, 65–66; David Levering Lewis, *W. E. B. Du Bois: The Fight for Equality and the American Century, 1919–1963* (New York: Henry Holt, 2000).

17. Shamoon Zamir, *Dark Voices: W. E. B. Du Bois and American Thought, 1888–1903* (Chicago: University of Chicago Press, 1995), 3; Susan Jacoby, *Freethinkers: A History of American Secularism* (New York: Metropolitan Books, 2004), 191–193.

18. There have been some dissenters from this school of thought. Several scholars have done noteworthy work on religion in Du Bois's life, especially Manning Marable, Wilson Jeremiah Moses, David Howard-Pitney, Phil Zuckerman, and Dwight Hopkins. See Manning Marable, *W. E. B. Du Bois: Black Radical Democrat* (Boston: Twayne, 1986); David Howard-Pitney, *The Afro-American Jeremiad: Appeals for Justice in America* (Philadelphia: Temple University Press, 1990). Phil Zuckerman, ed., *Du Bois on Religion* (New York: Altamira, 2000); Phil Zuckerman, "The Sociology of Religion of W. E. B. Du Bois," *Sociology of Religion* 63, no. 2 (Summer 2002): 239–253; Jonathon Samuel Kahn, "The Religious Imagination of W. E. B. Du Bois," Ph.D. diss., Columbia University, 2003;

Craig A. Forney, "W. E. B. Du Bois: The Spirituality of a Weary Traveler," Ph.D. diss., University of Chicago Divinity School, 2002.

19. See Du Bois, "The Aim and Method of Religious Work in College," in Du Bois Papers, reel 82, frame 1247.

20. W. E. B. Du Bois, *Prayers for Dark People*, edited by Herbert Aptheker (Amherst: University of Massachusetts Press, 1980), viii. See also Herbert Aptheker, "W. E. B. Du Bois and Religion: A Brief Reassessment," *Journal of Religious Thought* 39, no. 1 (Spring–Summer 1982): 5–11. Aptheker also criticized biographies of Du Bois for failing to account for religion. See Herbert Aptheker, review of Gerald Horne, *Black and Red: W. E. B. Du Bois and the Afro-American Response to the Cold War, 1944–1963*, in *Journal of American History* 73, no. 2 (September 1986), 520–521.

21. I have read a plethora of religious biographies in order to write this one, but none has provided what I would consider an adequate framework for studying Du Bois. Edwin S. Gaustad, *Sworn on the Altar of God: A Religious Biography of Thomas Jefferson* (Grand Rapids, Mich.: William B. Eerdmans, 1996); Harry S. Stout, *The Divine Dramatis: George Whitefield and the Rise of Modern Evangelicalism* (Grand Rapids, Mich.: William B. Eerdmans, 1991); Richard Lischer, *The Preacher King: Martin Luther King and the Word that Moved America* (New York: Oxford University Press, 1995); Roger Lundin, *Emily Dickinson and the Art of Belief* (Grand Rapids, Mich.: William B. Eerdmans, 2004); Judith Weisenfeld and Richard Newman, eds., *This Far By Faith: Readings in African-American Women's Religious Biography* (New York: Routledge, 1994); Louis A. DeCaro, Jr., *On the Side of My People: A Religious Life of Malcolm X* (New York: New York University Press, 1997); Patricia A. Schecter, *Ida B. Wells-Barnett and American Reform, 1880–1930* (Chapel Hill: University of North Carolina Press, 2003).

22. Toni Morrison, *Playing in the Dark: Whiteness and the Literary Imagination* (Cambridge, Mass.: Harvard University Press, 1992); David R. Roediger, *The Wages of Whiteness: Race and the Making of the American Working Class* (London: Verso, 1991) and *Working Toward Whiteness: How America's Immigrants Became White, the Strange Journey from Ellis Island to the Suburbs* (New York: Basic Books, 2005); Noel Ignatiev, *How the Irish Became White* (New York: Routledge, 1995); Alexander Saxton, *The Rise and Fall of the White Republic: Class Politics and Mass Culture in Nineteenth-Century America* (London: Verso, 1990); Matthew Frye Jacobson, *Whiteness of a Different Color: European Immigrants and the Alchemy of Race* (Cambridge, Mass.: Harvard University Press, 1998); George Lipsitz, *The Possessive Investment in Whiteness: How White People Profit from Identity Politics* (Philadelphia: Temple University Press, 1998); Grace Elizabeth Hale, *Making Whiteness: The Culture of Segregation in the South, 1890–1940* (New York: Pantheon, 1998); Shelley Fischer Fishkin, "Interrogating 'Whiteness,' Complicating 'Blackness': Remapping American Culture," *American Quarterly* 47, no. 3 (September 1995): 428–466; Abby L. Ferber, *White Man Falling: Race, Gender, and White Supremacy* (Lanham, Md.: Rowman and Littlefield, 1998); AnnLouise Keating, "Interrogating 'Whiteness,' (De)Constructing 'Race,'" *College English* 57, no. 8 (December 1995):

901–918; Robyn Wiegman, "Whiteness Studies and the Paradox of Particularity," *Boundary 2*, 26, no. 3 (Autumn 1999): 115–150. Although not on racial formation, Paul Harvey's *Freedom's Coming: Religious Culture and the Shaping of the South from the Civil War Through the Civil Rights Era* (Chapel Hill: University of North Carolina Press, 2005) is an important work on issues of race and religion in the nineteenth and twentieth centuries. For two works that examine the relationships among race, religion, and American nationalism, see Edward J. Blum, *Reforging the White Republic: Race, Protestantism, and American Nationalism, 1865–1898* (Baton Rouge: Louisiana State University Press, 2005); and Laura Veltman, "Uncle Tom's Nation: Race, Religion, and the American Paradise," Ph.D. diss., University of Wisconsin–Madison, 2005. Michael Barkun, *Religion and the Racist Right: The Origins of the Christian Identity Movement* (Chapel Hill: University of North Carolina Press, 1994).

23. James Cone, *A Black Theology of Liberation* (Philadelphia: J. B. Lippincott, 1970); J. Deotis Roberts, *A Black Political Theology* (Philadelphia: Westminster Press, 1974); William R. Jones, *Is God a White Racist? A Preamble to Black Theology* (Garden City, N.Y.: Anchor Press/ Doubleday, 1973); Albert B. Cleage, Jr., *Black Christian Nationalism: New Directions for the Black Church* (New York: William Morrow, 1972); Albert B. Cleage, Jr., *The Black Messiah* (1968; reprint, Trenton, N.J.: Africa World Press, 1991); William L. Eichelberger, "A Mytho-Historical Approach to the Black Messiah," *Journal of Religious Thought* 33, no. 1 (Spring–Summer 1976): 63–74; Jacquelyn Grant, *White Women's Christ and Black Women's Jesus: Feminist Christology and Womanist Response* (Atlanta: Scholars Press, 1989); Dolores S. Williams, *Sisters in the Wilderness: The Challenge of Womanist God-Talk* (Maryknoll, N.Y.: Orbis Books, 1995); Kelly Brown Douglas, *Sexuality and the Black Church: A Womanist Perspective* (Maryknoll, N.Y.: Orbis Books, 1999); Diana L. Hayes, *Hagar's Daughters: Womanist Ways of Being in the World* (New York: Paulist Press, 1995); Alice Walker, *In Search of Our Mothers' Gardens: Womanist Prose* (San Diego: Harcourt Brace Jovanovich, 1983).

24. Stephen Prothero, *American Jesus: How the Son of God Became a National Icon* (New York: Farrar, Straus and Giroux, 2003), 200–228; Richard Wightman Fox, *Jesus in America: Personal Savior, Cultural Hero, National Obsession* (San Francisco: HarperSanFrancisco, 2004), 293, 358, 359–360, 458 n. 11.

25. "Program for the Celebration of My Twenty-fifth Birthday," in Du Bois Papers, reel 86, frame 468–474; also in W. E. B. Du Bois, *Against Racism: Unpublished Essays, Papers, and Addresses, 1887–1961* (Amherst: University of Massachusetts Press, 1985), 27–29.

26. W. E. B. Du Bois, *Worlds of Color* (1961; reprint, Millwood, N.Y.: Kraus-Thomson, 1976), 342–343.

Chapter 1. The Hero with a Black Face

1. *The Reminiscences of William Edward Burghardt Du Bois* (New York: Columbia University Oral History Research Office, 1963), 13, 56–57.

2. *The Reminiscences of William Edward Burghardt Du Bois*, 12–13. Du Bois maintained almost a lifelong relationship with his Sunday school. See Du Bois to Mr. Van Lannep, December 22, 1908, in Du Bois Papers, reel 1, frame 673–676; Du Bois to Mr. Scudder, February 3, 1886, in Du Bois Papers, reel 3, frame 64–65.

3. *The Reminiscences of William Edward Burghardt Du Bois*, 13–14.

4. *The Reminiscences of William Edward Burghardt Du Bois*, 56.

5. *The Reminiscences of William Edward Burghardt Du Bois*, 56–57.

6. *The Reminiscences of William Edward Burghardt Du Bois*, 58, 129.

7. *The Reminiscences of William Edward Burghardt Du Bois*, 58–59.

8. *The Reminiscences of William Edward Burghardt Du Bois*, 137–138.

9. David Levering Lewis, *W. E. B. Du Bois: Biography of a Race, 1868–1919* (New York: Henry Holt, 1993), 65; David Levering Lewis, *W. E. B. Du Bois: The Fight for Equality and the American Century, 1919–1963* (New York: Henry Holt, 2000), 307.

10. James Olney, *Metaphors of Self: The Meaning of Autobiography* (Princeton, N.J.: Princeton University Press, 1972), 35. See also James Olney, "The Autobiography of America," *American Literary History*, 3, no. 2 (Summer 1991): 376–395; Ellen Peel, "The Self Is Always an Other: Going the Long Way Home to Autobiography," *Twentieth Century Literature*, 35, no. 1 (Spring 1989): 1–16.

11. Joseph Campbell, *The Hero with a Thousand Faces* (New York: Pantheon, 1949).

12. For more on African American autobiographies, see Robert B. Stepto, *From Behind the Veil: A Study of Afro-American Narrative* (Urbana: University of Illinois Press, 1979); William L. Andrews, ed., *African American Autobiography: A Collection of Critical Essays* (Englewood Cliffs, N.J.: Prentice-Hall, 1993); Stephen Butterfield, *Black Autobiography in America* (Amherst: University of Massachusetts Press, 1974); Charles T. Davis and Henry Louis Gates, Jr., eds., *The Slave's Narrative* (New York: Oxford University Press, 1985); Sidonie Smith, *Where I'm Bound: Patterns of Slavery and Freedom in Black American Autobiography* (Westport, Conn.: Greenwood Press, 1974); David L. Dudley, *My Father's Shadow: Intergenerational Conflict in African American Men's Autobiography* (Philadelphia: University of Pennsylvania Press, 1991); V. P. Franklin, *Living Our Stories, Telling Our Truths: Autobiography and the Making of the African-American Intellectual Tradition* (New York: Oxford University Press, 1995); Roland L. Williams Jr., *African American Autobiography and the Quest for Freedom* (Westport, Conn.: Greenwood Press, 2000).

13. "The Negro in America," *Times Literary Supplement* [London] (November 4, 1920); "Books: Darkwater," *Nation* 110 (May 29, 1920), 720–727; "The Negro Speaks," *New Republic* 22 (April 7, 1920), 189–190.

14. W. E. B. Du Bois, *Darkwater: Voices from Within the Veil* (1920; reprint, with an introduction by Manning Marable, Mineola, N.Y.: Dover, 1999). Manning Marable suggests that in *Darkwater*, Du Bois "takes the reader on a spiritual journey." Du Bois, *Darkwater*, vi. Eric Sundquist, *To Wake the Nations: Race in the Making of American Literature* (Cambridge, Mass.: Belknap Press of Harvard University Press, 1993), 544–545. For more on the artistic work of Terry Atkins, see <http://www.sas.upenn.edu/africana/darkwater.html>

15. James Olney, "'I Was Born': Slave Narratives, Their Status as Autobiography and as Literature," in Davis and Gates, eds., *The Slave's Narrative*, 148–175.

16. Du Bois, *Darkwater*, "Postscript."

17. Jaroslav Pelikan, *Credo: Historical and Theological Guide to Creeds and Confessions of Faith in the Christian Tradition* (New Haven: Yale University Press, 2003).

18. Du Bois, *Darkwater*, 1–2; W. E. Burghardt DuBois, "Credo," *The Independent: A Weekly Magazine* (October 6, 1904): 787.

19. Samuel Bishop to Du Bois, April 16, 1907, in Du Bois Papers, reel 1, frame 39–41.

20. Thomas Dixon, *The Clansman: An Historical Romance of the Ku Klux Klan* (New York: Grosset and Dunlap, 1905), 47; Paul Goodman, *Of One Blood: Abolitionism and the Origins of Racial Equality* (Berkeley: University of California Press, 1998).

21. Du Bois, *Darkwater*, 1–2; Du Bois, "Credo," 787.

22. Du Bois, *Darkwater*, 1–2. The "Credo" that precedes "The Shadow of Years" was slightly modified from the original. In a number of instances, Du Bois capitalized several words that had not been previously and removed capitalization from several words that had been capitalized before. Most substantially, he removed his final clause regarding his belief in "patience with God."

23. Du Bois, *Darkwater*, 1–2.

24. Grimké to Du Bois, January 7, 1905, in Du Bois Papers, reel 1, frame 1066.

25. Quoted in Jeffrey Green, *Black Edwardians: Black People in Britain, 1901–1914* (London: Routledge, 1998), 187. For other discussions of the "Credo," see Jonathan M. Hansen, *The Lost Promise of Patriotism: Debating American Identity, 1890–1920* (Chicago: University of Chicago Press, 2003), 104–105; Herbert Shapiro, *White Violence and Black Response: From Reconstruction to Montgomery* (Amherst: University of Massachusetts Press, 1988), 127–128.

26. Herbert Aptheker, ed., *Writings by W. E. B. Du Bois in Periodicals Edited By Others: Volume 1, 1891–1909* (Millwood, N.Y.: Kraus-Thomson, 1982), xi; Manning Marable, *W. E. B. Du Bois: Black Radical Democrat* (Boston: Twayne, 1986), 67.

27. Shirley Graham Du Bois, *His Day Is Marching On: A Memoir of W. E. B. Du Bois* (Philadelphia: J. B. Lippincott, 1971), 45–52.

28. Du Bois, *Darkwater*, 3; on the births and early childhoods of mythical heroes, see Campbell, *The Hero with a Thousand Faces*, 43, 319–329, 334.

29. Du Bois, *Darkwater*, 3–5; W. E. B. Du Bois, *The Souls of Black Folk: Essays and Sketches* (Chicago: A. C. McClurg & Co., 1903), 157.

30. Du Bois, *Darkwater*, 4–5.

31. Rt. Rev. Richard Allen, *The Life Experience and Gospel Labors of the Rt. Rev. Richard Allen, To Which Is Annexed the Rise and Progress of the African Methodist Episcopal Church in the United States of America* (1833, reprint; Nashville: Abingdon Press, 1983).

32. Allen, *The Life Experience and Gospel Labors*, 25; Howard D. Gregg, *History of the African Methodist Episcopal Church* (Nashville: African Methodist Episcopal Church Press, 1980).

33. Allen, *The Life Experience and Gospel Labors*, 26.

34. On the challenge and call motif in mythologies, see Campbell, *The Hero with a Thousand Faces*, 51–60.

35. Du Bois, *Darkwater*, 4–6.

36. Du Bois, *Darkwater*, 6–7.

37. Du Bois, *Darkwater*, 6–7.

38. Du Bois, *Darkwater*, 6–7.

39. Campbell, *The Hero with a Thousand Faces*, 51.

40. Du Bois, *Darkwater*, 6–7.

41. Du Bois, *Darkwater*, 7. On death, see Craig A. Forney, "W. E. B. Du Bois: The Spirituality of a Weary Traveler," Ph.D. diss., University of Chicago Divinity School, 2002, 31–33.

42. Campbell, *The Hero with a Thousand Faces*, 79, 97, 101.

43. Du Bois, *Darkwater*, 7.

44. Du Bois, *Darkwater*, 8.

45. Du Bois, *Darkwater*, 8.

46. Du Bois, *Darkwater*, 8–9; Campbell has noted that the hero becomes in some ways "greater than the gods." In Du Bois's case, it appears that he deems himself greater than the venerated leaders of the United States. Campbell, *The Hero with a Thousand Faces*, 192. For the text of Du Bois's commencement speech, see "Jefferson Davis as a Representative of Civilization," in W. E. B. Du Bois, *Against Racism: Unpublished Essays, Papers, and Addresses, 1887–1961* (Amherst: University of Massachusetts Press, 1985), 14–16.

47. Du Bois, *Darkwater*, 9.

48. Du Bois, *Darkwater*, 9; Campbell, *The Hero with a Thousand Faces*, chapter 3.

49. Du Bois, *Darkwater*, 10.

50. Du Bois, *Darkwater*, 11.

51. Du Bois, *Darkwater*, 11.

52. Du Bois, *Darkwater*, 11–12.

53. Du Bois, *Darkwater*, 11–12.

54. Du Bois, *Darkwater*, 12–13; Emerson in David M. Robinson, ed., *The Spiritual Emerson: Essential Writings* (Boston: Beacon Press, 2003), 246.

55. Lewis, *W. E. B. Du Bois: The Fight for Equality*.

56. Cheryl Lynn Greenberg, *"Or Does It Explode?" Black Harlem in the Great Depression* (New York: Oxford University Press, 1991); Judith Stein, *The World of Marcus Garvey: Race and Class in Modern Society* (Baton Rouge: Louisiana State University Press, 1986); David M. Kennedy, *Freedom from Fear: The American People in Depression and War, 1929–1945* (New York: Oxford University Press, 2001).

57. W. E. Burghardt Du Bois, *Dusk of Dawn: An Essay Toward an Autobiography of a Race Concept* (1940, reprint, New York: Schocken Books, 1969).

58. Lewis, *W. E. B. Du Bois: The Fight for Equality*, 421–494.

59. W. E. Burghardt Du Bois, "The Revelation of Saint Orgne, the Damned," Commencement 1938, Fisk University, n.p., n.d. Reprinted in Philip S. Foner, ed., *W. E. B. Du*

Bois Speaks: Speeches and Addresses, 1920–1963 (New York: Pathfinder, 1970), 100–123. See Wilson Jeremiah Moses, *Black Messiahs and Uncle Toms: Social and Literary Manipulations of a Religious Myth* (1982; revised edition, University Park: Penn State University Press, 1993), 174–175.

60. Du Bois to Thomas E. Jones, April 22, 1938, in Herbert Aptheker, ed., *The Correspondence of W. E. B. Du Bois: Selections, 1934–1944* (Amherst: University of Massachusetts Press, 1976), 165.

61. Ben Witherington III, *Revelation* (Cambridge: Cambridge University Press, 2003).

62. "The Revelation of Saint Orgne, the Damned," in *W. E. B. Du Bois Speaks*, 100.

63. "The Revelation of Saint Orgne, the Damned," in *W. E. B. Du Bois Speaks*, 100–101.

64. Forney, "W. E. B. Du Bois," 126.

65. "The Revelation of Saint Orgne, the Damned," in *W. E. B. Du Bois Speaks*, 101.

66. "The Revelation of Saint Orgne, the Damned," in *W. E. B. Du Bois Speaks*, 102.

67. "The Revelation of Saint Orgne, the Damned," in *W. E. B. Du Bois Speaks*, 104–106.

68. "The Revelation of Saint Orgne, the Damned," in *W. E. B. Du Bois Speaks*, 106–108.

69. "The Revelation of Saint Orgne, the Damned," in *W. E. B. Du Bois Speaks*, 109–110.

70. "The Revelation of Saint Orgne, the Damned," in *W. E. B. Du Bois Speaks*, 110–111.

71. "The Revelation of Saint Orgne, the Damned," in *W. E. B. Du Bois Speaks*, 111–112.

72. "The Revelation of Saint Orgne, the Damned," in *W. E. B. Du Bois Speaks*, 113.

73. "The Revelation of Saint Orgne, the Damned," in *W. E. B. Du Bois Speaks*, 115–123; Isaiah 51:9, 51:17, 52:1.

74. Du Bois may have subtly pointed to his Fisk oration in *Dusk of Dawn* when he wrote that "midway in its writing, it changed its object and pattern, because of the revelation of a seventieth birthday and the unawaited remarks and comments thereon." Du Bois, *Dusk of Dawn*, 1.

75. Martin Luther King, Jr., "Honoring Dr. Du Bois," in W. E. B. Du Bois, *Dusk of Dawn: Autobiography of a Race Concept* (1940; reprint, New York: Schocken Books, 1969), vii–xvii.

76. Du Bois, *Dusk of Dawn*, 2.

77. Du Bois, *Dusk of Dawn*, 3–6.

78. Du Bois, *Dusk of Dawn*, 10, 14, 17, 22.

79. Du Bois, *Dusk of Dawn*, 26–27.

80. Du Bois, *Dusk of Dawn*, 31.

81. Du Bois, *Dusk of Dawn*, 33.

82. Du Bois, *Dusk of Dawn*, 50.

83. Du Bois, *Dusk of Dawn*, 56, 63; W. E. B. Du Bois, *Prayers for Dark People*, edited by Herbert Aptheker (Amherst: University of Massachusetts Press, 1980).

84. Du Bois, *Dusk of Dawn*, 90.

85. Du Bois, *Dusk of Dawn*, 101, 115, 131.

86. Du Bois, *Dusk of Dawn*, 139.

87. Du Bois, *Dusk of Dawn*, 134–172.

88. Du Bois, *Dusk of Dawn*, 140.

89. Du Bois, *Dusk of Dawn*, 141–149.

90. Du Bois, *Dusk of Dawn*, 155.

91. Du Bois, *Dusk of Dawn*, 155–172.

92. Du Bois, *Dusk of Dawn*, 155–172.

93. Du Bois, *Dusk of Dawn*, 170.

94. See Dudley, *My Father's Shadow*; Franklin, *Living Our Stories*, 19, 49, 220, 225–273; Butterfield, *Black Autobiography in America*; Smith, *Where I'm Bound*.

95. Frederick Douglass, *My Bondage and My Freedom* (1855; reprint, New York: Arno Press and New York Times, 1968), 190, 196–197, 203–204. For more on Douglass, see William S. McFeeley, *Frederick Douglass* (New York: Norton, 1991).

96. Douglass, *My Bondage and My Freedom*, 416.

97. *The Narrative of Sojourner Truth* (1878; reprint, New York: Arno Press, 1968), 36, 168, 196. For more on Truth, see Nell Irvin Painter, *Sojourner Truth: A Life, a Symbol* (New York: Norton, 1997).

98. *The Autobiography of Malcolm X* (1964; reprint, New York: Ballantine, 1999), 178, 180, 216, 224, 246. For more on Malcolm X, see Louis A. Decaro, Jr., *On the Side of My People: A Religious Life of Malcolm X* (New York: New York University Press, 1996).

99. Du Bois, *Dusk of Dawn*, 201–202. Du Bois also made this point in a speech in 1936. See "The Negro and Social Reconstruction," in W. E. B. Du Bois, *Against Racism: Unpublished Essays, Papers, and Addresses, 1887–1961* (Amherst: University of Massachusetts Press, 1985), 153.

100. Du Bois, *Dusk of Dawn*, 303, 306, 325–326.

Chapter 2. Race as Cosmic Sight in *The Souls of Black Folk*

1. *Nation* 76, no. 1980 (June 11, 1903): 481–482; Henry James, *The American Scene* (1907; reprint, Bloomington: Indiana University Press, 1968), 418; Max Weber to Du Bois, 1905 in Herbert Aptheker, ed., *The Correspondence of W. E. B. Du Bois: Volume I, Selections, 1877–1934* (Amherst: University of Massachusetts Press, 1973), 106. D. Tabak to Du Bois, in Du Bois Papers, reel 3, frame 279–283; Langston Hughes to Du Bois, May 22, 1956, in Herbert Aptheker, ed., *The Correspondence of W. E. B. Du Bois: Volume III, Selections, 1944–1963* (Amherst: University of Massachusetts Press, 1978), 401.

2. W. H. Johnson, "The Case of the Negro," *Dial* 34, no. 405 (May 1, 1903): 299–302.

3. John Spencer Bassett, "Two Negro Leaders," *South Atlantic Quarterly* 2, no. 3 (July 1903): 267–272. Du Bois also recognized that his work combated Dixon's. See correspondence between Du Bois and Doubleday, Page, and Company Publishers, 1905–1907, in

Du Bois Papers, reel 1, frame 767–774. One Doubleday editor wrote that in contrast with Dixon, Du Bois "represent[s] an entirely different point of view."

4. Larry E. Tise, *Proslavery: A History of the Defense of Slavery in America, 1701–1840* (Athens: University of Georgia Press, 1990). See also Mark A. Noll, *The Civil War as a Theological Crisis* (Chapel Hill: University of North Carolina Press, 2005), 33–50.

5. Stephen R. Haynes, *Noah's Curse: The Biblical Justification of American Slavery* (New York: Oxford University Press, 2002); Genesis 9:25–27.

6. Haynes, *Noah's Curse*; Sylvester A. Johnson, *The Myth of Ham in Nineteenth-Century American Christianity: Race, Heathens, and the People of God* (New York: Palgrave Macmillan, 2004); David M. Goldenberg, *The Curse of Ham: Race and Slavery in Early Judaism, Christianity, and Islam* (Princeton, N.J.: Princeton University Press, 2003); Thomas Virgil Peterson, *Ham and Japheth: The Mythical World of Whites in the Antebellum South* (Metuchen, N.J.: Scarecrow Press, 1978).

7. Quoted in Haynes, *Noah's Curse*, 97.

8. Even following the Civil War, some white supremacist theologians continued to use the Genesis narrative to legitimate racial difference. Southern Presbyterian Robert L. Dabney claimed in his *Defence of Virginia (And Through Her, of the South)* that in the ninth chapter of Genesis, "Noah acts as an inspired prophet." His words "are not a mere prophecy; they are a verdict, a moral sentence pronounced upon conduct, by competent authority; that verdict sanctioned by God." And God's verdict was clear–the descendants of Shem and Japheth would rule over those of Ham. Noah's blessings and curses, furthermore, were associated with God's divine judgment of the moral qualities of Ham, Japheth, and Shem. Ham and his descendants were "wicked" and "depraved," while Shem and Japheth embodied the "true spirit of filial regard, love, honor and obedience." The lessons Dabney gleaned from this story had crucial importance to the postemancipation United States. According to Dabney, the story proved that Africans and those of African heritage were different species from whites and that any children of sexual unions between whites and blacks would be incapable of civilization or of God's glory. Political or social equality, which a host of white authors claimed would necessarily lead to interracial sexuality, stood in opposition to the divine will. "We know that the African has become . . . a different, fixed *species* of the race, separated from the white man's traits bodily, mental and moral, almost as rigid and permanent as those of *genus*," Dabney concluded. "Hence the offspring of an amalgamation must be a hybrid race, stamped with all the feebleness of the hybrid, and incapable of the career of civilization and glory as an independent race." [emphasis in original] Robert L. Dabney, *A Defence of Virginia, (And Through Her, of the South,) in Recent and Pending Contests Against the Sectional Party* (1867; reprint, New York: Negro Universities Press, 1969), 101, 103, 353.

9. James Oliver Horton and Lois E. Horton, *Hard Road to Freedom: The Story of African America* (New Brunswick, N.J.: Rutgers University Press, 2001), 115.

10. George M. Frederickson, *The Black Image in the White Mind: The Debate on Afro-American Character and Destiny, 1817–1914* (New York: Harper and Row, 1971), 85–87; Reginald Horsman, *Race and Manifest Destiny: The Origins of American Racial Anglo-*

Saxonism (Cambridge, Mass.: Harvard University Press, 1981); William Stanton, *The Leopard's Spots: Scientific Attitudes Toward Race in America, 1815–1859* (Chicago: University of Chicago Press, 1969).

11. Josiah Nott and George Robins Gliddon, *Types of Mankind* (Philadelphia: Lippincott, Grambo, 1855), 457, 462–463.

12. Theodore Dwight Weld, *The Bible Against Slavery* (1837; reprint, Pittsburgh: United Presbyterian Board of Publication, 1864), 13–14.

13. "The New Jim Crow Song, About the Darkies and the War," in *American Song Sheets*, series 1, vol. 6 (Washington, D.C.: Library of Congress, 1962).

14. Mia Bay, *The White Image in the Black Mind: African-American Ideas about White People, 1830–1925* (New York: Oxford University Press, 2000).

15. J. R. Oldfield, ed., *Civilization and Black Progress: Selected Writings of Alexander Crummell on the South* (Charlottesville: University Press of Virginia, 1995), 34, 49. See also Alex Crummell, *Africa and America: Addresses and Discourses* (1891; reprint, Miami: Mnemosyne, 1969). For more on Crummell, see Wilson Jeremiah Moses, *Alexander Crummell: A Study of Civilization and Discontent* (New York: Oxford University Press, 1989).

16. Edward W. Blyden, "The Call of Providence to the Descendants of Africa in America" (1862) and "The African Problem and the Method of its Solution" (1890) in Howard Brotz, ed., *Negro Social and Political Thought, 1850–1920: Representative Texts* (New York: Basic Books, 1966), 112–126, 129–139. For more on Blyden, see Hollis Ralph Lynch, *Edward Wilmot Blyden: Pan-Negro Patriot, 1832–1912* (New York: Oxford University Press, 1970).

17. Benjamin Tucker Tanner, "Prayer to Jesu," *African Methodist Episcopal Church Review* 7, no. 4 (April 1891): 392. For another example of African Americans accepting this racialized division of humanity, see Michele Mitchell, *Righteous Propagation: African Americans and the Politics of Racial Destiny After Reconstruction* (Chapel Hill: University of North Carolina Press, 2004), 208.

18. Ariel, *The Negro: What is His Ethnological Status?* 2nd ed. (Cincinnati: Published for the Proprietor, 1867), 10, 12, 21, 26, 31.

19. Rev. G. C. H. Hasskarl, *"The Missing Link"; or The Negro's Ethnological Status. Is he a descendant of Adam and Eve? Is he the progeny of Ham? Has he a Soul? What is his relation to the White Race? Is he a subject of the Church or the State, Which?* (reprinted from "The Eastern Lutheran"; Chambersburg, Pa.: Democratic News, 1898), 19, 127, 148; Mason Boyd Stokes, "Someone's in the Garden with Eve: Race, Religion, and the American Fall," *American Quarterly* 50, no. 4 (December 1998): 718–744.

20. Charles Carroll, *The Tempter of Eve, or The Criminality of Man's Social, Political, and Religious Equality with the Negro, and the Amalgamation to which these Crimes Inevitable Lead* (St. Louis: Adamic Publishing Co., 1902), 219. Charles Carroll, *The Negro, a Beast* (St. Louis: Adamic Publishing Co., 1900). See also William P. Calhoun, *The Caucasian and the Negro in the United States* (Columbia, S.C.: R. L. Bryan, 1902).

21. Bassett, "Two Negro Leaders," 272; H. Paul Douglass, *Christian Reconstruction in*

the South (Boston: Pilgrim Press, 1909), 114. Ray Stannard Baker, *Following the Color Line: American Negro Citizenship in the Progressive Era* (1908; reprint, New York: Harper and Row, 1964), 266–267.

22. E. C. Millard and Lucy E. Guinness, *South America: The Neglected Continent* (New York: Fleming H. Revell Co., 1894), 149, 164.

23. Rudyard Kipling, "The White Man's Burden," *McClure's* 12 (February 1899): 290–291.

24. Rev. Arthur T. Pierson, *The Crisis of Missions: Or, The Voice Out of the Cloud* (New York: Robert Carter and Brothers, 1886), 31–32.

25. Thomas Dixon, Jr., *The Leopard's Spots: A Romance of the White Man's Burden, 1865–1900* (1902; reprint, Ridgewood, N.J.: Gregg Press, 1967).

26. Dixon, *The Leopard's Spots*, 5, 29, 33, 179, 382.

27. Dixon, *The Leopard's Spots*, 128, 152.

28. Dixon, *The Leopard's Spots*, 386, 439.

29. W. E. B. Du Bois, *The Souls of Black Folk: Authoritative Text, Contents, Criticism* (1903; reprint; edited by Henry Louis Gates, Jr., and Terri Hume Oliver, New York: Norton, 1999), 62–63.

30. In addition to biblical allusions and rhetoric, Du Bois also drew on stories from Greek mythology, specifically the story of Atalanta and Jason and the Argonauts. Tellingly, however, when Du Bois invoked Greek mythology, he offered brief synopses of the stories for the reader. Cognizant that most of his readers were more familiar with the Bible, Du Bois felt the need to recount the story of "how swarthy Atalanta, tall and wild, would marry only him who outraced her; and how the wily Hoppomenes laid three apples of gold in the way." Or, when describing the labor and financial troubles of southern blacks who cultivated primarily cotton in the South, Du Bois introduced this analysis by invoking the story of "the winged ram Chrysomallus left that Fleece after which Jason and his Argonauts went vaguely wandering into the shadowy East three thousand years ago." In touch with the power of religious culture in America and its focus upon biblical idioms and metaphors, Du Bois felt no need to explain those references and allusions. Du Bois, *The Souls of Black Folk*, 54–61, 89.

31. "Worlds of Color," *Foreign Affairs* (New York) 20 (April 1925): 423–444.

32. Du Bois, *The Souls of Black Folk*, 5.

33. Du Bois, *The Souls of Black Folk*, 5–6.

34. Edgar C. S. Gibson, *The Thirty-Nine Articles of the Church of England* (London: Methuen, 1896); "Preface," in Du Bois, *The Souls of Black Folk*, xxxiv, 5, 7.

35. Du Bois, *The Souls of Black Folk*, 9–11.

36. Du Bois, *The Souls of Black Folk*, 10–11; Forney, "W. E. B. Du Bois: The Spirituality of a Weary Traveler," Ph.D. diss., University of Chicago Divinity School, 2002, 126.

37. Du Bois, *The Souls of Black Folk*, 14, 48, 60, 74, 131, 163; Warner Sollors, *Beyond Ethnicity: Consent and Descent in American Culture* (New York: Oxford University Press, 1986), 49.

38. "Beyond the Veil in a Virginia Town," in W. E. B. Du Bois, *Against Racism: Unpub-*

lished Essays, Papers, and Addresses, 1887–1961 (Amherst: University of Massachusetts Press, 1985), 50; W. E. B. Du Bois, *Darkwater: Voices from Within the Veil* (1920; reprint, with an introduction by Manning Marable, Mineola, N.Y.: Dover, 1999), 143–144.

39. Du Bois, *The Souls of Black Folk*, 12–13, 15.

40. Du Bois, *The Souls of Black Folk*, 15–16.

41. Du Bois, *The Souls of Black Folk*, 97, 106.

42. Du Bois, *The Souls of Black Folk*, 118, 60.

43. Du Bois, *The Souls of Black Folk*, 24–25, 69.

44. "Note on the Text," Du Bois, *The Souls of Black Folk*, xl–xli.

45. Du Bois, *The Souls of Black Folk*, 50–51, 120–122.

46. Du Bois, *The Souls of Black Folk*, 121–123.

47. Du Bois, *The Souls of Black Folk*, 154–164.

48. Du Bois, *The Souls of Black Folk*, 57–59.

49. Du Bois, *The Souls of Black Folk*, 34, 45.

50. Robert Gooding-Williams, "Du Bois's Counter-Sublime," *Massachusetts Review: A Quarterly of Literature, the Arts and Public Affairs* 35, no. 2 (Summer 1994): 202–224.

51. Du Bois, *The Souls of Black Folk*, 134–135.

52. Du Bois, *The Souls of Black Folk*, 134–142. Gooding-Williams, "Du Bois's Counter-Sublime."

53. Du Bois, *The Souls of Black Folk*, 142–154. See Booker T. Washington, "A Speech Delivered Before the Women's New England Club," in Louis R. Harlan, ed., *The Booker T. Washington Papers: Volume 3, 1889–1895* (Urbana: University of Illinois Press, 1974), 26–27.

54. Du Bois, *The Souls of Black Folk*, 142–154.

55. Du Bois, *The Souls of Black Folk*, 9, 50, 119–120.

56. Du Bois, *The Souls of Black Folk*, 33, 74.

57. Du Bois, *The Souls of Black Folk*, 129, 163.

58. Du Bois, *The Souls of Black Folk*, 134, 142.

59. Bassett, "Two Negro Leaders," 267–272.

60. C. F. G. Masterman, "A Book of the Day: The Soul of a Race," *Daily News* (London), 31 (August 1905), 6.

61. "Two Typical Leaders," *Outlook* 74, no. 4 (May 23, 1903), 214–216.

62. Gladden and Huntingdon quoted in Ralph E. Luker, *Social Gospel in Black and White: American Racial Reform, 1885–1912* (Chapel Hill: University of North Carolina Press), 215–216.

63. John Daniels, *Alexander's* 1 (September 15, 1905): 10–11.

64. Gayle Pemberton, *The Hottest Water in Chicago: Notes of a Native Daughter* (New York: Doubleday, 1993), 74–76; Clarence Wigington, unpublished poem, in his copy of *The Souls of Black Folk*, signed by Du Bois, November 9, 1909, Atlanta, Georgia. In possession of Gayle Pemberton.

65. Kittredge Wheeler to Du Bois, July 20, 1903, in Aptheker, *The Correspondence of W. E. B. Du Bois: Volume I, Selections*, 58–59. See also William D. Hopper to Du Bois,

September 2, 1909, in Du Bois Papers, reel 2, frame 152; Annah May Soule to Du Bois, February 26, 1904, in Du Bois Papers, reel 3, frame 166; J. Douglas Wetmore to Du Bois, October 20, 1903, in Du Bois Papers, reel 3, frame 682; Pauline Schneider to Du Bois, May 23, 1914, in Du Bois Papers, reel 4, frame 933–935; Miner Chipman to Du Bois, December 14, 1915, in Du Bois Papers, reel 4, frame 1198. Du Bois even received a response from a member of his childhood Congregation church. See Frederic Rowland Marvin to Du Bois, June 2, 1903, in Du Bois Papers, reel 2, frame 552–553.

66. William H. Ferris, *The African Abroad; or His Evolution in Western Civilization Tracing His Development under Caucasian Milieu* Volume 1 (New Haven: The Tuttle, Morehouse & Taylor Press, 1913), 273; William H. Ferris, *The African Abroad; or His Evolution in Western Civilization Tracing His Development Under Caucasian Milieu* Volume 2 (New Haven: Tuttle, Morehouse & Taylor Press, 1913), 910–922. For more on Ferris, see Kevin Gaines, *Uplifting the Race: Black Leadership, Politics, and Culture in the Twentieth Century* (Chapel Hill: University of North Carolina Press, 1996), 100–127.

67. Ferris, *The African Abroad, Volume 1,* 276.

68. Thomas Dixon, Jr., *The Flaming Sword* (Atlanta: Monarch Publishing, 1939), 18, 20, 26.

69. "W. E. B. Du Bois as a Prophet," in William J. Schafer, ed., *The Truman Nelson Reader* (Amherst: University of Massachusetts Press, 1989), 217.

70. "Tributes," in John Henrik Clarke, Esther Jackson, Ernest Kaiser, and J. H. O'Dell, eds., *Black Titan: W. E. B. Du Bois, An Anthology by the Editors of* Freedomways (Boston: Beacon Press, 1970), 29.

71. Rhonda Sanders, "Spirituality Beckons All in Bad '90s," *Flint Journal* (Michigan), February 23, 1997: H1. *Souls of Black Folk* was listed among *Christianity Today*'s one hundred best religious books of the twentieth century. *Christianity Today,* April 24, 2000.

72. Rebecca Carroll, *Saving the Race: Conversations about Du Bois from a Collective Memoir of Souls* (New York: Harlem Moon, 2004), 1–9.

73. A'Lelia Bundles, "A Future with Promise," in Carroll, *Saving the Race,* 34–41.

Chapter 3. A Dark Monk Who Wrote History and Sociology

1. "Letter Establishing the Lectureship," in Booker T. Washington and W. E. Burghardt Du Bois, *The Negro in the South: His Economic Progress in Relation to His Moral and Religious Development* (Philadelphia: G. W. Jacobs and Co., 1907); Jacob Riis, *The Peril and Preservation of the Home* (Philadelphia: G. W. Jacobs and Co., 1903); Lyman Abbott, *The Industrial Problem* (Philadelphia: G. W. Jacobs and Co., 1905); Carroll Davidson Wright, *The Battles of Labor* (Philadelphia: G. W. Jacobs and Co., 1906).

2. Washington and Du Bois, *The Negro in the South,* 123–192.

3. Washington and Du Bois, *The Negro in the South,* 188, 187, 168, 171.

4. Washington and Du Bois, *The Negro in the South,* 141–153.

5. Washington and Du Bois, *The Negro in the South*, 155–162. Gayraud S. Wilmore, *Black Religion and Black Radicalism: An Interpretation of the Religious History of Afro-American People* (1973; 2nd ed.; Maryknoll, N.Y.: Orbis Books, 1994); Albert J. Raboteau, *Slave Religion: The "Invisible Institution" in the Antebellum South* (Oxford: Oxford University Press, 1978); Eddie S. Glaude, *Exodus! Religion, Race, and Nation in Early Nineteenth-Century Black America* (Chicago: University of Chicago Press, 2000); Albert J. Raboteau, "African-Americans, Exodus, and the American Israel," in Paul E. Johnson, ed., *African-American Christianity: Essays in History* (Berkeley: University of California Press, 1994). For more on Turner, see Scot French, *The Rebellious Slave: Nat Turner in American Memory* (New York: Houghton Mifflin, 2003).

6. Charles M. Sheldon, *In His Steps* (Chicago: Thompson & Thomas, 1896); William T. Stead, *If Christ Came to Chicago: A Plea for the Union of All Who Love in the Service of All Who Suffer* (Chicago: Laird and Lee, 1894); Washington and Du Bois, *The Negro in the South*, 174, 177.

7. Washington and Du Bois, *The Negro in the South*, 185–191.

8. Shamoon Zamir, *Dark Voices: W. E. B. Du Bois and American Thought, 1888–1903* (Chicago: University of Chicago Press, 1995); Keith E. Byerman, *Seizing the Word: History, Art, and Self in the Work of W. E. B. Du Bois* (Athens: University of Georgia Press, 1994), chaps. 2, 3, 4, and 8; Francis L. Broderick, "The Academic Training of W. E. B. DuBois," *Journal of Negro Education* 27, no. 1 (Winter 1958): 10–16; Judith R. Blau and Eric S. Brown, "Du Bois and Diasporic Identity: The Veil and the Unveiling Project," *Sociological Theory* 19, no. 2 (July 2001): 219–233; John David Smith, *An Old Creed for the New South: Proslavery Ideology and Historiography, 1865–1918* (Westport, Conn.: Greenwood Press, 1985), 209–217; Joseph P. DeMarco, *The Social Thought of W. E. B. Du Bois* (Lanham, Md.: University Press of America, 1983); Phil Zuckerman, "The Sociology of Religion of W. E. B. Du Bois," *Sociology of Religion* 63, no. 2 (Summer 2002); Elliot M. Rudwick, *W. E. B. Du Bois: Propagandist of the Negro Protest* (1960; reprint, New York: Atheneum, 1969); Arnold Rampersad, *The Art and Imagination of W. E. B. Du Bois* (Cambridge, Mass.: Harvard University Press, 1976); Jack B. Moore, *W. E. B. Du Bois* (Boston: Twayne, 1981); Manning Marable, *W. E. B. Du Bois: Black Radical Democrat* (Boston: Twayne, 1986); David Levering Lewis, *W. E. B. Du Bois: Biography of a Race, 1868–1919* (New York: Henry Holt, 1993); Lewis, *W. E. B. Du Bois: The Fight for Equality and the American Century, 1919–1963* (New York: Henry Holt, 2000).

9. W. E. B. Du Bois, "Does Education Pay?" in Herbert Aptheker, ed., *Writings by W. E. B. Du Bois in Periodicals Edited By Others: Volume 1, 1891–1909* (Millwood, N.Y.: Kraus-Thomson, 1982), 14.

10. W. E. B. Du Bois, *Prayers for Dark People* (Amherst: University of Massachusetts Press, 1980), 21. Herbert Aptheker, "W. E. B. Du Bois and Religion: A Brief Reassessment," *Journal of Religious Thought* 39, no. 1 (Spring–Summer 1982): 8–9.

11. Du Bois, "Does Education Pay?" 7.

12. W. E. B. Du Bois, *In Battle for Peace* (Millwood, N.Y.: Kraus-Thomson, 1976), 170–

171. See also "Jacob and Esau," in Phil Zuckerman, ed., *Du Bois on Religion* (New York: Altamira Press, 2000), 194; W. E. B. Du Bois, *The Philadelphia Negro: A Social Study* (1899; reprint, Philadelphia: University of Pennsylvania Press, 1996), 385–386, 396.

13. "The Joy of Living," *Political Affairs* 44 (February 1965): 35–44.

14. "The Enforcement of the Slave Trade Laws," *American Historical Association Annual Report, 1891* (Washington, D.C.: Government Printing Office, 1892), 163–174.

15. Du Bois, *The Philadelphia Negro*, 396.

16. "Violation of Property Rights," in Herbert Aptheker, ed., *Writings by W. E. B. Du Bois in Periodicals Edited by Others, Volume 2* (Millwood, N.Y.: Kraus-Thomson, 1982), 67. See also "The Twelfth Census and the Negro Problems," *Southern Workman* 29 (1900): 305–309; "Caste and Class in the United States," *Boston Post* (February 12, 1904); "The Parting of the Ways," *World Today* 6 (April 1904): 521–523.

17. Du Bois Papers, reel 83, frame 893.

18. W. E. B. Du Bois, "The Color Line and the Church," *Crisis* 36, no. 11 (November 1929): 387–388. See also W. E. Burghardt Du Bois, *The World and Africa: An Inquiry into the Part Which Africa Has Played in World History* (New York: Viking Press, 1946), 26; Du Bois, "The Negro Church," in *Against Racism: Unpublished Essays, Papers, and Addresses, 1887–1961* (Amherst: University of Massachusetts Press, 1985), 83–85. While Du Bois routinely focused on segregation in Protestant churches, he also assailed Catholics in the United States for drawing the color line. See his correspondence with Reverend A. Knecht, 1930, in Du Bois Papers, reel 33, frame 561.

19. Du Bois, *The Philadelphia Negro*, 340.

20. Edward J. Blum, *Reforging the White Republic: Race, Religion, and American Nationalism, 1865–1898* (Baton Rouge: Louisiana State University Press, 2005), 4–5; Edward J. Blum, "'O God of a Godless Land': Northern African American Challenges to White Christian Nationhood, 1865–1906," in Edward J. Blum and W. Scott Poole, eds., *Vale of Tears: New Essays on Religion and Reconstruction* (Mercer, Ga.: Mercer University Press, 2005), 93–111; Robert T. Handy, *A Christian America: Protestant Hopes and Historical Realities* (New York: Oxford University Press, 1971); Sidney E. Mead, *The Nation with a Soul of a Church* (New York: Harper and Row, 1975); Mark A. Noll, Nathan O. Hatch, and George M. Marsden, *The Search for Christian America* (Westchester, Ill.: Crossway Books, 1983).

21. W. E. B. Du Bois, "Caste: That Is the Root of Trouble," *Des Moines Register Leader* (Iowa), October 19, 1904.

22. "The Niagara Movement," in W. E. B. Du Bois, *An ABC of Color: Selections Chosen by the Author from over a Half Century of His Writings* (New York: International Publishers, 1963), 32.

23. See W. E. B. Du Bois, *Mansart Builds a School* (1959; reprint, Millwood, N.Y.: Kraus-Thomson, 1976), 66.

24. Du Bois, "Address of the First Annual Meeting of the Georgia Equal Rights Convention," *Voice of the Negro* 3 (March 1906): 175–177. See also Du Bois, *The Gift of Black Folk: The Negroes in the Making of America* (Boston: Stratford Co., 1924), 173.

25. See also Du Bois, *The Gift of Black Folk*, vi, 295; Zuckerman, ed., *Du Bois on Religion*, 167.

26. W. E. Burghardt Du Bois, *The Suppression of the African Slave-Trade to the United States of America, 1638–1870* (1896; reprint, Baton Rouge: Louisiana State University Press, 1965), 168–169. See also, Du Bois, *The Suppression of the Slave-Trade to the United States*, 37–38, 40, 51, 194–199.

27. Du Bois, *The Suppression of the Slave-Trade to the United States*, 197–199.

28. Du Bois, *The World and Africa*, 24.

29. Toni Morrison, *Playing in the Dark: Whiteness and the Literary Imagination* (Cambridge, Mass.: Harvard University Press, 1992); David R. Roediger, *The Wages of Whiteness: Race and the Making of the American Working Class* (London: Verso, 1991); David R. Roediger, *Working Toward Whiteness: How America's Immigrants Became White, the Strange Journey from Ellis Island to the Suburbs* (New York: Basic Books, 2005); Noel Ignatiev, *How the Irish Became White* (New York: Routledge, 1995); Alexander Saxton, *The Rise and Fall of the White Republic: Class Politics and Mass Culture in Nineteenth-Century America* (London: Verso, 1990); Matthew Frye Jacobson, *Whiteness of a Different Color: European Immigrants and the Alchemy of Race* (Cambridge, Mass.: Harvard University Press, 1998); Grace Elizabeth Hale, *Making Whiteness: The Culture of Segregation in the South, 1890–1940* (New York: Pantheon Books, 1998). Shelley Fischer Fishkin, "Interrogating 'Whiteness,' Complicating 'Blackness': Remapping American Culture," *American Quarterly* 47, no. 3 (September 1995): 428–466; Abby L. Ferber, *White Man Falling: Race, Gender, and White Supremacy* (Lanham, Md.: Rowman and Littlefield, 1998); AnnLouise Keating, "Interrogating 'Whiteness,' (De)Constructing 'Race,'" *College English* 57, no. 8 (December 1995): 901–918; Karen Brodkin, *How Jews Became White Folk and What That Says About Race in America* (New Brunswick, N.J.: Rutgers University Press, 1998).

30. Du Bois, *The World and Africa*, 20.

31. Du Bois, "The Development of a People," *International Journal of Ethics* 14 (April 1904): 292–311.

32. W. E. B. Du Bois, *Darkwater: Voices from Within the Veil* (1920; reprint, with an introduction by Manning Marable, Mineola, N.Y.: Dover, 1999), 17–25. See also Du Bois, "The Souls of White Folk," *The Independent* 69 (August 18, 1910): 339–342.

33. Du Bois, *Darkwater*, 17–25. See also Du Bois, "The Souls of White Folk," 339–342.

34. Du Bois, *Black Reconstruction in America*, 237–324.

35. W. E. B. Du Bois, "The Beginning of Emancipation," *Voice of the Negro* 2 (June 1905): 397–400; W. E. B. Du Bois, "Georgia: Invisible Empire State," in Ernest Gruening, ed., *These United States*, 2 vols. (New York: Boni & Liveright, 1924), 2:322–345.

36. Du Bois, "St. Francis of Assisi," *Voice of the Negro* 3 (October 20, 1906): 419–426.

37. W. E. Burghardt Du Bois, *Dusk of Dawn: An Essay Toward an Autobiography of a Race Concept* (1940, reprint, New York: Schocken Books, 1969), 269.

38. Merrill D. Peterson, *John Brown: The Legend Revisited* (Charlottesville: University Press of Virginia, 2002); David S. Reynolds, *John Brown, Abolitionist: The Man Who Killed Slavery, Sparked the Civil War, and Seeded Civil Rights* (New York: Knopf, 2005);

John Stauffer, *The Black Hearts of Men: Radical Abolitionists and the Transformation of Race* (Cambridge, Mass.: Harvard University Press, 2002). See William E. Dodd, review of *John Brown* in *American Historical Review* 15, no. 3 (April 1910): 633–634.

39. W. E. Burghardt Du Bois, *John Brown* (1909; reprint, New York: International Publishers, 1962), 8, 21, 48, 273. For the lectures, see Jill Watts, *God, Harlem USA: The Father Divine Story* (Berkeley: University of California Press, 1992), 188, n. 15.

40. Du Bois, *John Brown*, 23, 19; see also 21, 24–25, 46, 90, 132, 339.

41. Du Bois, *John Brown*, 374–375. At least one reviewer of Du Bois's biography on Brown recognized the religious approach that Du Bois took. William E. Dodd, a white historian born and raised in North Carolina, noted how Du Bois approached Brown's actions with cosmic meaning. "Harper's Ferry," according to Du Bois, was "the work of God in human hands, as the first battle of the righteous North against the wicked South." See Dodd, review of *John Brown*, 633–634.

42. Wilmore, *Black Religion and Black Radicalism*, 142–143; W. E. B. Du Bois, "Religion and the Problem," *Crisis* 7, no. 3 (January 1914): 129–130.

43. Du Bois, *The Philadelphia Negro*, 115, 206–207.

44. W. E. B. Du Bois, ed., *The Negro Church: Report of a Social Study Made Under the Direction of Atlanta University; Together with the Proceedings of the Eighth Conference for the Study of the Negro Problems, Held at Atlanta University, May 26th, 1903* (1903; reprint, edited by Phil Zuckerman, Sandra L. Barnes, and Daniel Cody (Walnut Creek, Calif.: Altamira, 2003), 154. Many of the works in the Atlanta Studies were filled with commentary on religious ideas and life. See W. E. B. Du Bois, ed., *The Negro in Business: Report of a Social Study Made Under the Direction of Atlanta University; Together with the Proceedings of the Fourth Conference for the Study of the Negro Problems, Held at Atlanta University, May 30–31, 1899* (1899; reprint, New York: AMS Press, 1971), 14–15, 20, 40, 57–60; W. E. Burghardt Du Bois, ed., *The Negro American Family* (1908; reprint, Westport, Conn.: Negro Universities Press, 1969), 68, 72, 75, 130, 131; Du Bois, "The Up-Building of Black Durham: The Success of the Negroes and Their Value to a Tolerant and Helpful Southern City," *World's Work* 23 (January 1912): 334–338.

45. Du Bois, *The Negro Church*, 59, 61, 78. For other examples of Du Bois criticizing the morality of African American ministers and his insistence that ethical black preachers were crucial for racial advancement, see Du Bois, "Does Education Pay?" 17; Du Bois, "The Minister," *Hampton Negro Conference Annual Report* 2 (September 1906): 91–92; *Two Addresses Delivered by Alumni of Fisk University, in Connection with the Anniversary Exercises of Their Alma Mater, June, 1898* (Nashville: Fisk University, 1898), in Aptheker, ed., *Writings by W. E. B. Du Bois in Non-Periodical Literature Edited By Others*, 7–8.

46. Robert A. Wortham, "Introduction to the Sociology of W. E. B. Du Bois," *Sociation Today* 3, no. 1 (Spring 2005); W. E. B. Du Bois, *The Negro Church*; Robert A. Wortham, "Du Bois and the Sociology of Religion: Rediscovering a Founding Figure," *Sociological Inquiry* 75, no. 4 (November 2005): 433–452; Zuckerman, "The Sociology of Religion of W. E. B. Du Bois."

47. Du Bois, *The Negro Church*, 203–204.

48. Du Bois, *The Negro Church*, 189–190. For more of Du Bois on the black church, see W. E. B. Du Bois, *The Souls of Black Folk: Essays and Sketches* (Chicago: A. C. Mc-Clurg & Co., 1903); Du Bois, "Reconstruction and Its Benefits," *American Historical Review* 15 (July 1910): 781–799; Du Bois, "The Negro and Socialism," in Helen Alfred, ed., *Toward a Socialist America* (New York: Peace Publications, 1958), 179–191; Du Bois, "Black America," in Fred J. Ringle, ed., *America as Americans See It* (New York: Harcourt Brace, 1932), 14–155; W. E. B. Du Bois, *The Negro* (1915; reprint, Philadelphia: University of Pennsylvania Press, 2001), 188–189.

Du Bois's contemporaries recognized him as a leading thinker in the realm of childhood morality. As the Moral Education Board completed an "Illustrated Lessons in Morals" for young people, they sent it to Du Bois for advice. See correspondence between Du Bois and Milton Fairchild in Du Bois Papers, Moorland-Spingarn Research Center, Howard University, Washington, D.C.

49. Du Bois, ed., *The Negro Church*, 208.

50. Reverdy Ransom to Du Bois, January 23, 1916, in Du Bois Papers, reel 5, frame 310.

51. Booker T. Washington, *Up from Slavery: An Autobiography* (1901; reprint, New York: Doubleday, 1963), 257. See also Booker T. Washington, "The Colored Ministry and Its Defects and Needs" (1890), in Louis R. Harlan, ed., *Booker T. Washington Papers: Volume 3, 1889–95* (Urbana: University of Illinois Press, 1974), 71–75.

52. Oscar Micheaux (director), *Body and Soul* (film), 1925.

53. See Martin Summers, *Manliness and Its Discontents: The Black Middle Class and the Transformation of Masculinity, 1900–1930* (Chapel Hill: University of North Carolina Press, 2004), 105–106.

54. Quoted in Wilmore, *Black Religion and Black Radicalism*, 138.

55. Carter Woodson to Du Bois, February 18, 1908, in Herbert Aptheker, ed., *The Correspondence of W. E. B. Du Bois: Volume 1, Selections, 1877–1934* (Amherst: University of Massachusetts Press, 1973), 140.

56. E. Franklin Frazier, *The Negro Church in America* (1963; reprint, New York: Schocken Books, 1974); Carter G. Woodson, *The History of the Negro Church* (Washington, D.C.: Associated Publishers, 1921); Benjamin E. Mays and Joseph W. Nicholson, *The Negro's Church* (New York: Institute of Social Research, 1933); Arthur H. Fauset, *Black Gods of the Metropolis: Negro Religious Cults of the Urban North* (1944; reprint, New York: Octagon Books, 1970). For more on Du Bois and the history of the black church, see Barbara Dianne Savage, "Du Bois and the 'Negro Church,'" *Annals of the American Academy of Political and Social Science* 568, no. 1 (March 2000): 235–249.

57. Wilmore, *Black Religion and Black Radicalism*, 45.

58. Anthony B. Pinn, *Why, Lord? Suffering and Evil in Black Theology* (New York: Continuum, 1995); Michael Eric Dyson, *Open Mike: Reflections on Philosophy, Race, Sex, Culture and Religion* (New York: Basic Civitas Books, 2003), 46, 188.

59. Cheryl Townsend Gilkes, *"If It Wasn't for the Women . . .": Black Women's Experience*

and Womanist Culture in Church and Community (Maryknoll, N.Y.: Orbis Books, 2001). Evelyn Brooks Higginbotham, *Righteous Discontent: The Women's Movement in the Black Baptist Church, 1880–1920* (Cambridge, Mass.: Harvard University Press, 1993), 7.

60. Lewis, *W. E. B. Du Bois: The Fight for Equality*, 306; Du Bois, "The Problem of the Twentieth Century Is the Problem of the Color Line," *Pittsburgh Courier*, January 15, 1950; Du Bois, "The Negro and Socialism," in Alfred, *Toward a Socialist America*, 179–191.

61. Du Bois, *Black Reconstruction in America* (1935; reprint, New York: Atheneum, 1992), 123–124.

62. Du Bois, *Black Reconstruction in America*, 124–126.

63. Du Bois, "The Negro as a National Asset," *Homiletic Review* 86 (July 1923): 52–58. For other places where Du Bois suggests that African Americans are the truest Christians in the United States, see W. E. Burghardt Du Bois, *The Gift of Black Folk: The Negroes in the Making of America* (Boston: Stratford, 1924), 53, 76–77, 284–285.

64. Du Bois, *The Gift of Black Folk*, 337.

65. W. E. B. Du Bois, "The Work of Negro Women in Society," *Spelman Messenger* 18 (February 1902), 1–3.

66. W. E. B. Du Bois, "The Problem of Work," *AME Church Review* 20 (October 1903), 176–177. See also Aptheker, *Writings by Du Bois in Non-Periodical Literature*, 10.

67. *Two Addresses Delivered by Alumni of Fisk University*, 4.

68. W. E. B. Du Bois, "On Tolstoy," *Unity* 102 (September 10, 1928): 18.

69. Michele Mitchell, *Righteous Propagation: African Americans and the Politics of Racial Destiny after Reconstruction* (Chapel Hill: University of North Carolina Press, 2004), 16–75; Claude A. Clegg III, *The Price of Liberty: African Americans and the Making of Liberia* (Chapel Hill: University of North Carolina Press, 2004), 201–274; Ibrahim Sundiata, *Brothers and Strangers: Black Zion, Black Slavery, 1914–1940* (Durham, N.C.: Duke University Press, 2003); Sylvia M. Jacobs, *The African Nexus: Black American Perspectives on the Partitioning of Africa, 1880–1920* (Westport, Conn.: Greenwood Press, 1981).

70. Harold R. Isaacs, "Pan-Africanism as 'Romantic Racism,'" in Rayford W. Logan, ed., *W. E. B. Du Bois: A Profile* (New York: Hill and Wang, 1971), 210–248; James L. Conyers, ed., *Afrocentric Traditions: Africana Studies, Volume 1* (New Brunswick, N.J.: Rutgers University Press, 2005); Molefi Kete Asante, *Afrocentricity* (Trenton, N.J.: Africa World Press, 1988); Ibrahim Sundiata, *Brothers and Strangers: Black Zion, Black Slavery, 1914–1940* (Durham, N.C.: Duke University Press, 2003).

71. Du Bois, *The Negro*, 78; Du Bois, *The World and Africa*, 23; Du Bois, *Dusk of Dawn*, 170; W. E. B. Du Bois, "Whites in Africa After Negro Autonomy," in A. A. Roback, ed., *In Albert Scweitzer's Realm: A Symposium*, (Cambridge, Mass.: Sci-Art Publishers, 1962), 243–255.

72. *Report of the Pan-African Conference, held on the 23rd, 24th, and 25th July, 1900, at Westminster Town Hall, Westminster, S.W.* (London, 1900), 10–12.

73. W. E. B. Du Bois, "The African Roots of the War," *Atlantic Monthly* 115 (May 1915): 707–714; reprinted in *Darkwater* as "The Hands of Ethiopia."

74. Du Bois, *The World and Africa*, 42.

75. Du Bois, *The World and Africa*, 28. See also Du Bois, *The World and Africa*, 53, 65, 67, 70, 73; W. E. B. Du Bois, *Color and Democracy: Colonies and Peace* (New York: Harcourt Brace, 1945), 123.

76. Du Bois, *The World and Africa*, 78; "Of Beauty and Death," in Du Bois, *Darkwater*, 131–134; Frantz Fanon, *Black Skin, White Masks: The Experiences of a Black Man in a White World* (1952; translation, New York: Grove Press, 1967).

77. "The Hands of Ethiopia," in Du Bois, *Darkwater*, 36.

78. Du Bois, "The Black Man and Albert Schweitzer," in A. A. Roback, ed., *The Albert Schweitzer Jubilee Book* (Cambridge, Mass.: Sci-Art Publishers, 1945), 121–127. See also Dan S. Green and Edwin D. Driver, eds., *W. E. B. Du Bois on Sociology and the Black Community* (Chicago: University of Chicago Press, 1978), 299; Du Bois, *Color and Democracy*, 23, 41, 134.

79. Du Bois, *Color and Democracy*, 99.

80. Du Bois, *Color and Democracy*, 136.

81. Sundiata, *Brothers and Strangers*, 71–72; see other works on Du Bois's travels. Throughout his life, Du Bois was fascinated by images of the sacred. See his discussion of religion and European art in "The Art and Art Galleries of Modern Europe," in Du Bois, *Against Racism: Unpublished Essays, Papers, and Addresses, 1887–1961* (Amherst: University of Massachusetts Press, 1985), 40–43.

82. Du Bois, *The World and Africa*, 149, 157.

83. Du Bois, *The Negro*, 246. For an earlier example of African Americans asserting the religious creativity and blackness of ancient Africans, see Richard Robert Wright, Sr., quoted in Leon F. Litwack, *Trouble in Mind: Black Southerners in the Age of Jim Crow* (New York: Alfred A. Knopf, 1998), 75–76.

84. Du Bois, *The World and Africa*, 119, 131–137, 147, 177–178, 183, 218–219, 253. Du Bois, *The Negro*, 49, 128–130, 141.

85. Du Bois, *The World and Africa*, 143. Du Bois wrote extensively on African history. See also Du Bois, *The Negro*.

86. Du Bois, *The World and Africa*, 119, 131–137, 147, 177–178, 183, 218–219, 253; Du Bois, *The Negro*, 49, 128–130, 141. Du Bois, "Foreword," in Lorenz Graham, *How God Fix Jonah* (New York: Renyal and Hitchcock, 1946), ix.

87. Du Bois, *Darkwater*, 95–96.

88. Du Bois, *The World and Africa*, 81–93.

89. Du Bois, *The World and Africa*, 67.

90. Du Bois, *Darkwater*, 42.

91. Du Bois, *The World and Africa*, 260.

92. The debate over Afrocentrism and Afrocentricity is ferocious and incorporates numerous texts. For a good start, see Martin Bernal, *Black Athena: The Afroasiatic Roots of Classical Civilization, Volume 1: The Fabrication of Ancient Greece, 1785–1985* (New Brunswick, N.J.: Rutgers University Press, 1987); Mary Lefkowitz, *Not Out of Africa: How "Afrocentrism" Became an Excuse to Teach Myth as History* (New York: Basic Books, 1996).

93. Randall C. Bailey, ed., *Yet With a Steady Beat: Contemporary U.S. Afrocentric Biblical Interpretation* (Atlanta: Society of Biblical Literature, 2003); Frans J. Verstraelen, *History of Christianity in Africa in the Context of African History: A Comparative Assessment of Four Recent Historiographical Contributions* (Gweru, Zimbabwe: Mambo Press, 2002); Michael I. N. Dash, ed., *African Roots: Toward an Afrocentric Christian Witness* (Lithonia, Ga.: SCP/Third World Literature Publishing House, 1994); Ameen Yasir Mohammed, *Afrocentricity, Minus Al-Islam: Exposing the Conspiracy to Rob African Americans of Their Most Precious Heritage* (Los Angeles: Dawahvision, 1994); David M. Goldberg, *The Curse of Ham: Race and Slavery in Early Judaism, Christianity, and Islam* (Princeton: Princeton University Press, 2003); Edwin M. Yamauchi, *Africa and the Bible* (Grand Rapids, Mich.: Baker Academic, 2004).

94. *The Original African Heritage Study Bible: King James Version, with Special Annotations Relative to the African/Edenic Perspective* (Nashville: James C. Winston, 1993); Jeremiah A. Wright, Jr., *Celebrating God's Hand in Black History Kit* (Chicago: Urban Ministries, 1995). Kit includes two books, five posters, one button, and eighteen assorted papers.

95. Walter A. McCray, *The Black Presence in the Bible: Discovering the Black and African Identity of Biblical Persons and Nations* (Chicago: Black Light Fellowship, 1990); Kenneth L. Waters, *Afrocentric Sermons: The Beauty of Blackness in the Bible* (Valley Forge, Pa.: Judson Press, 1993); Cain Hope Felder, *The Presence of the Black in Biblical Antiquity* (VHS, video provided by Eastern Baptist Theological Seminary, Wynnewood, Pa., 1990); Wayne A. Jones, *African Emphasis in the Bible* (VHS, St. Louis Community College at Forest Park, 1995).

96. Marita Golden, *The Edge of Heaven* (New York: Ballantine, 1999), 169, 188.

97. Juan Williams and Quinton Dixie, *This Far By Faith: Stories from the African American Religious Experience* (New York: William Morrow, 2003).

98. Du Bois, *Prayers for Dark People*, 22, 41.

99. Du Bois, *The World and Africa*, 261.

100. Du Bois, *Color and Democracy*, 143.

101. W. M. Brewer, review of *The World and Africa*, in *Journal of Negro History* 32, no. 3 (July 1947): 347–348; Myrtle M. Bowers, "DuBois' Dilemma," *Phylon* 8, no. 4 (Fourth Quarter 1947): 368–369; Eric Williams, review of *The World and Africa* in *Journal of Economic History* 7, no. 2 (November 1947): 241–243.

102. Samuel Usher, taped interview, June 26, 1974; Dorothy Cowser Yancey, "William Edward Burghardt Du Bois' Atlanta Years: The Human Side—A Study Based Upon Oral Sources," *Journal of Negro History* 61, no. 1 (January 1978): 59–67.

Chapter 4. Black Messiahs and Murderous Whites

1. Richard Wright, *Native Son* (1940, reprint: New York: Perennial Classics, 1998), 282–285; 338. For more on religion in Wright's work, see Raman K. Singh, "Christian Heroes and Anti-Heroes in Richard Wright's Fiction," *Negro American Literature Forum*

6, no. 4 (Winter 1972): 99–104, 131; Qiana Whitted, "African-American Literature and the Crisis of Faith," Ph.D. diss., Yale University, 2003.

2. Wright, *Native Son*, 338–340.

3. W. E. B. Du Bois, "The Son of God," *Crisis* 40, no. 12 (December 1933): 276–277.

4. Du Bois, "The Son of God."

5. Du Bois, "The Son of God."

6. Du Bois, "The Son of God."

7. Cheryl Kirk-Duggan, *Refiner's Fire: A Religious Engagement with Violence* (Minneapolis: Fortress Press, 2001); Anthony B. Pinn, *Why, Lord? Suffering and Evil in Black Theology* (New York: Continuum, 1995); Anthony B. Pinn, *Terror and Triumph: The Nature of Black Religion* (Minneapolis: Fortress Press, 2003); Joanne Marie Terrell, *Power in the Blood? The Cross in the African American Experience* (Maryknoll, N.Y.: Orbis Books, 1998). Edward J. Blum, "'O God of a Godless Land': Northern African American Challenges to White Christian Nationhood, 1865–1906," in Edward J. Blum and W. Scott Poole, eds., *Vale of Tears: New Essays on Religion and Reconstruction* (Macon, Ga.: Mercer University Press, 2005); Michelle Kuhl, "Modern Martyrs: African Americans' Responses to Lynching, 1880–1940," Ph.D. diss., State University of New York at Binghamton, 2004.

8. For more on the association of whiteness with godliness and blackness with sinfulness, see Edward J. Blum, *Reforging the White Republic: Race, Religion, and American Nationalism, 1865–1898* (Baton Rouge: Louisiana State University Press, 2005).

9. "The Quest for a Black Christ," *Ebony*, March 1969, 170–178; "Artists Portray a Black Christ," *Ebony*, April 1971, 177–180; Kelly Brown Douglas, *The Black Christ* (Maryknoll, N.Y.: Orbis Books, 1994), 53–77; Gayraud S. Wilmore, *Black Religion and Black Radicalism: An Interpretation of the Religious History of Afro-American People* (1973; revised, Maryknoll, N.Y.: Orbis Books, 1994), 192–242; C. Eric Lincoln, *The Black Church Since Frazier* (New York: Schocken, 1974), 135–152.

10. James Cone, *A Black Theology of Liberation* (Philadelphia: Lippincott, 1970); J. Deotis Roberts, *A Black Political Theology* (Philadelphia: Westminster Press, 1974); William R. Jones, *Is God a White Racist? A Preamble to Black Theology* (Garden City, N.Y.: Anchor Press/Doubleday, 1973); Albert B. Cleage, Jr., *Black Christian Nationalism: New Directions for the Black Church* (New York: William Morrow, 1972); Albert B. Cleage, Jr., *The Black Messiah* (1968; reprint, Trenton, N.J.: Africa World Press, 1991); William L. Eichelberger, "A Mytho-Historical Approach to the Black Messiah," *Journal of Religious Thought* 33 (Spring–Summer 1976): 63–74; Lincoln, *The Black Church*, 135–152.

11. Cone, *A Black Theology of Liberation*, 23.

12. Cleage, *The Black Messiah*, 46–47. Although Cone, Cleage, Roberts, and Jones disagreed whether Christ's blackness was biological, symbolic, or metaphoric, they agreed that the Christian God actively championed the disadvantaged and that his spirit resided with those who fought exploitation. Because African Americans were discriminated against as a group in the United States, then God and Christ must be on their side.

13. For the most part, theologians and scholars have focused on the Holocaust when considering the ways in which peoples and societies make sense of mass bloodshed. Be-

fore Jews and eastern Europeans were targeted by the Nazi regime, however, people of color in the United States had faced widespread and massive terror—and they had done their best to find sacred significance amid the brutality. This is not to suggest that the pain endured by African Americans was greater than or less than that of the Jews during World War II. Of course, the violence that people of color experienced in the Americas was not the same as that faced by Jews in eastern Europe. It differed by place, by context, by degree, and by length. Yet it was devastating, it was debilitating, and it led directly to tough religious and theological questions. For an excellent discussion of theological responses to the Holocaust, see Marc H. Ellis, *Unholy Alliance: Religion and Atrocity in Our Time* (Minneapolis: Fortress Press, 1997).

14. René Girard, *The Scapegoat,* translated by Yvonne Freccero (Baltimore: Johns Hopkins University Press, 1986).

15. Girard, *The Scapegoat.*

16. Pinn, *Terror and Triumph.*

17. Philip Dray, *At the Hands of Persons Unknown: The Lynching of Black America* (New York: Modern Library, 2003); Blum, *Reforging the White Republic,* 199.

18. Grace Elizabeth Hale, *Making Whiteness: The Culture of Segregation in the South, 1890–1940* (New York: Pantheon, 1998); C. Vann Woodward, *Origins of the New South, 1877–1913* (Baton Rouge: Louisiana State University Press, 1951).

19. Blum, *Reforging the White Republic,* 199; Edward L. Ayers, *Promise of the New South: Life after Reconstruction* (New York: Oxford University Press, 1992), 156–159; W. Fitzhugh Brundage, *Lynching in the New South: Georgia and Virginia, 1880–1930* (Urbana: University of Illinois Press, 1993); Dray, *At the Hands of Persons Unknown.*

20. Donald G. Mathews, "The Southern Rite of Human Sacrifice," *Journal of Southern Religion* 3 (2000) (http://jsr.as.wvu.edu/mathews.htm); Orlando Patterson, *Rituals of Blood: Consequences of Slavery in Two American Centuries* (Washington, D.C.: Civitas Counterpoint, 1998), chap. 2. Ralph Ellison, *Shadow and Act* (New York: Vintage, 1972), 37; W. Scott Poole, "Confederate Apocalypse: Theology and Violence in the White Reconstruction South," in Blum and Poole, eds., *Vale of Tears.*

21. Quoted in Eric Tabor Millin, "Defending the Sacred Hearth: Religion, Politics, and Racial Violence in Georgia, 1904–1906," master's thesis, University of Georgia, 2002, 48, 60.

22. Trudier Harris, *Exorcising Blackness: Historical and Literary Lynching and Burning Rituals* (Bloomington: Indiana University Press, 1984); Thomas Dixon, *The Clansman: An Historical Romance of the Ku Klux Klan* (New York: Grosset and Dunlap, 1905), 338; Blum, *Reforging the White Republic,* 2.

23. George S. Schuyler, *Black No More: Being an Account of the Strange and Wonderful Workings of Science in the Land of the Free, A.D. 1933–1940* (1931; reprint, Boston: Northeastern University Press, 1989), 205–213.

24. Stephen R. Prothero, *American Jesus: How the Son of God Became a National Icon* (New York: Farrar, Straus and Giroux, 2003), 65, 87–90; Alan C. Braddock, "Painting the World's Christ: Tanner, Hybridity, and the Blood of the Holy Land," *Nineteenth-Century*

Art Worldwide: A Journal of Nineteenth-Century Visual Culture 3, no. 2 (Autumn 2004); *The Illuminated Bible* (New York: Harper and Brothers, 1846).

25. Anthony B. Pinn, *Moral Evil and Redemptive Suffering: A History of Theodicy in African-American Religious Thought* (Gainesville: University Press of Florida, 2002), 5; Mary Church Terrell, *A Colored Woman in a White World* (1940; reprint, New York: G. K. Hall, 1996), 106.

26. Pinn, *Moral Evil and Redemptive Suffering*.

27. Phyllis R. Klotman, "'Tearing a Hole in History': Lynching as Theme and Motif," *Black American Literature Forum* 19 (Summer 1985): 55–63; Mary Beth Culp, "Religion in the Poetry of Langston Hughes," *Phylon* 48 (Third Quarter 1987): 240–245; Harris, *Exorcising Blackness*; Claude McKay, "The Lynching," in James Weldon Johnson, ed., *The Book of American Negro Poetry* (1922); Qiana Whitted, "In My Flesh Shall I See God: Ritual Violence and Racial Redemption in 'The Black Christ,'" *African American Review* 38, no. 3 (Fall 2004): 379–393.

28. Wilmore, *Black Religion and Black Radicalism*, 36–37; Robert Alexander Young, *The Ethiopian Manifesto: Issued in Defence of the Black Man's Rights in the Scale of Universal Freedom* (New York: Robert Alexander Young, 1829).

29. Peter P. Hinks, ed., *David Walker's Appeal to the Coloured Citizens of the World* (1829; reprint, University Park: Pennsylvania State University Press, 2000).

30. Braddock, "Painting the World's Christ." Some African Americans certainly continued to imagine Christ as white. See Clifton H. Johnson, ed., *God Struck Me Dead: Voices of Ex-Slaves* (1969; reprint, Cleveland: Pilgrim Press, 1993), 59, 74–75, 109, 168.

31. Wilmore, *Black Religion and Black Radicalism*, 124–127; "Christ Jesus Not White," *Cleveland Gazette* (December 16, 1893), 1; W. L. Hunter, *Jesus Christ Had Negro Blood in His Veins* (Brooklyn, N.Y.: W. L. Hunter, 1901).

32. Wilmore, *Black Religion and Black Radicalism*, 153–154.

33. Wilmore, *Black Religion and Black Radicalism*, 157.

34. Frazier, *The Negro Church in America*, 52–69; Randall K. Burkett, *Garveyism as a Religious Movement: The Institutionalization of a Black Civil Religion* (Metuchen, N.J.: Scarecrow Press, 1978); Arthur Huff Fauset, *Black Gods of the Metropolis: Negro Religious Cults of the Urban North* (1944; reprint, New York: Octagon Books, 1970).

35. *The Autobiography of Malcolm X* (1964; reprint, New York: Ballantine Books, 1999), 193–194.

36. Caroline Goeser, "'On the Cross of the South': The Scottsboro Boys as Vernacular Christs in Harlem Renaissance Illustration," *International Review of African American Art* 19, no. 1 (2003): 19–27; Judith L. Stephens, "Racial Violence and Representation: Performance Strategies in Lynching Dramas of the 1920s," *African American Review* 33, no. 4 (Winter 1999): 655–671; Georgia Douglas Johnson, "Sunday Morning in the South" (1925), in Kathy Perkins and Judith Stephens, eds., *Strange Fruit* (Bloomington: Indiana University Press, 1998), 103–109.

37. McKay, "The Lynching."

38. Langston Hughes, "Christ in Alabama," *Contempo* (December 1, 1931); another

version can be found in Langston Hughes, *The Panther & The Lash: Poems of Our Times* (New York: Knopf, 1977), 37.

39. Countee Cullen, *The Black Christ & Other Poems* (New York: Harper & Brothers, 1929).

40. W. E. Burghardt Du Bois, *Dusk of Dawn: An Essay Toward an Autobiography of a Race Concept* (1940, reprint, New York: Schocken Books, 1969), 149.

41. W. E. Burghardt Du Bois, *The Gift of Black Folk: The Negroes in the Making of America* (Boston: Stratford, 1924), 339.

42. W. E. B. Du Bois, "The Church and the Negro," *Crisis* 6, no. 6 (October 1913): 282; also in Phil Zuckerman, ed., *Du Bois on Religion* (New York: Altamira Press, 2000), 99–100.

43. W. E. B. Du Bois, *Darkwater: Voices from Within the Veil* (1920; reprinted Mineola, N.Y.: Dover, 1999), 14–16.

44. W. E. B. Du Bois, "The Burden of Black Women," in Zuckerman, *Du Bois on Religion*, 102–103. Also published as "The Riddle of the Sphinx," in Du Bois, *Darkwater*, 30–31.

45. W. E. B. Du Bois, "The Second Coming," in Du Bois, *Darkwater*, 60–62.

46. W. E. B. Du Bois, "Jesus Christ in Texas," in Du Bois, *Darkwater*, 70–77; "Jesus Christ in Georgia," in *Du Bois on Religion*, 91–98.

47. W. E. B. Du Bois, *Prayers for Dark People*, 15.

48. Du Bois, *Prayers for Dark People* (Amherst: University of Massachusetts Press, 1980), 5. See also W. E. B. Du Bois, *In Battle for Peace* (Millwood, N.Y.: Kraus-Thomson, 1976), 80; W. E. B. Du Bois, *The Autobiography of W. E. B. Du Bois: A Soliloquy on Viewing My Life from the Last Decade of Its First Century* (New York: International, 1968), 378.

49. W. E. B. Du Bois, "Peace," in W. E. B. Du Bois, *An ABC of Color* (1963; reprint, New York: International, 1989), 100.

50. W. E. B. Du Bois, "Satterlee," *Horizon* 1 (June 1907): 4–5.

51. W. E. B. Du Bois, "The Gospel According to Mary Brown," *Crisis* 19 (December 1919): 41–43; also in Zuckerman, *Du Bois on Religion*, 143–146.

52. W. E. B. Du Bois, *Prayers for Dark People*, 63.

53. Du Bois, "Jesus Christ in Texas," 72–73.

54. Du Bois, "The Gospel According to Mary Brown."

55. W. E. B. Du Bois, "Pontius Pilate," *The Crisis* 21, no. 2 (December 1920): 53–54; also in Zuckerman, *Du Bois on Religion*, 157–160.

56. Du Bois, "The Gospel According to Mary Brown."

57. Du Bois, "Jesus Christ in Texas," 70–77; Ephesians 4:24 KJV.

58. Du Bois, "Jesus Christ in Texas," 76–77.

59. Du Bois, "Jesus Christ in Texas," 76–77.

60. Du Bois, "Pontius Pilate," 157–160.

61. Du Bois, "The Son of God."

62. Du Bois, "The Gospel According to Mary Brown."

63. William R. Hutchinson, *The Modernist Impulse in American Protestantism* (Cambridge, Mass.: Harvard University Press, 1976).

64. For more on women in Du Bois's writings, see Nellie McKay, "W. E. B. Du Bois: The Black Women in His Writings – Selected Fictional and Autobiographical Portraits," in William L. Andrews, ed., *Critical Essays on W. E. B. Du Bois* (Boston: G. K. Hall, 1985), 230–252.

65. W. E. B. Du Bois, "Magnificat," in Du Bois, *An ABC of Color*, 167–168.

66. Du Bois, "Magnificat," 167–168. Luke 1:37 KJV.

67. W. E. B. Du Bois, "The Call," in Du Bois, *Darkwater*, 93–94.

68. Du Bois, "The Crucifixion of God," in Du Bois Papers, reel 88, frame 1211–1213.

69. Douglas, *The Black Christ*, 97–117; Jacquelyn Grant, *White Women's Christ and Black Women's Jesus: Feminist Christology and Womanist Response* (Atlanta: American Academy of Religion, 1989); Kelly Brown Douglas, *Sexuality and the Black Church: A Womanist Perspective* (Maryknoll, N.Y.: Orbis Books, 1999); Diana L. Hayes, *Hagar's Daughters: Womanist Ways of Being in the World* (New York: Paulist Press, 1995); Alice Walker, *In Search of Our Mothers' Gardens: Womanist Prose* (San Diego: Harcourt Brace Jovanovich, 1983); Prothero, *American Jesus*, 206–207.

70. Du Bois, *The Gift of Black Folk*, 337–338.

71. W. E. B. Du Bois, "Children of the Moon," in Du Bois, *Darkwater*, 109–13.

72. W. E. B. Du Bois, *The Quest of the Silver Fleece* (1911, reprint; New York: Harlem Moon, 2004), 3. Quotations and references from this novel will be noted parenthetically in the text. For more on *The Quest of the Silver Fleece*, see Maurice Lee, "Du Bois the Novelist: White Influence, Black Spirit, and *The Quest of the Silver Fleece*," *African American Review* 33, no. 3 (1999): 389–400; Arlene A. Elder, "Swamp Versus Plantation: Symbolic Structure in W. E. B. Du Bois' *The Quest of the Silver Fleece*," *Phylon* 34, no. 4 (1973): 358–367; Keith E. Byerman, *Seizing the Word: History, Art, and Self in the Work of W. E. B. Du Bois* (Athens: University of Georgia Press, 1994), 129–141; David Levering Lewis, *W. E. B. Du Bois: Biography of a Race, 1868–1919* (New York: Henry Holt, 1993), 443–451.

73. W. E. B. Du Bois, *Dark Princess: A Romance* (1928; reprint, Jackson: University of Mississippi Press, 1995). Quotations and references will be cited parenthetically. For more on *Dark Princess*, see Dohra Ahmad, "'More than Romance': Genre and Geography in *Dark Princess*," *English Literary History* 69, no. 3 (2002): 775–803; Paul Gilroy, *The Black Atlantic: Modernity and Double Consciousness* (London: Verso, 1993), 140–144; Bill V. Mullen, "W. E. B. Du Bois, *Dark Princess*, and the Afro-Asian International," in Bill V. Mullen and James Smethurst, eds., *Left of the Color Line: Race, Radicalism, and Twentieth-Century Literature* (Chapel Hill: University of North Carolina Press, 2003), 87–106; Arnold Rampersad, *The Art and Imagination of W. E. B. Du Bois* (Cambridge, Mass.: Harvard University Press, 1976); Byerman, *Seizing the Word*, 115–137; Lewis, *Du Bois, The Fight for Equality*, 214–220.

74. W. E. B. Du Bois, *The Ordeal of Mansart* (New York: Mainstream Publishers, 1957); W. E. B. Du Bois, *Mansart Builds a School* (1959; reprint, Millwood, N.Y.: Kraus-

Thomson, 1976); W. E. B. Du Bois, *Worlds of Color* (1961; reprint, Millwood, N.Y.: Kraus-Thomson, 1976). For more on the Black Flame trilogy, see Lily Wiatrowksi Phillips, "W. E. B. Du Bois and Soviet Communism: *The Black Flame* as Socialist Realism," *South Atlantic Quarterly* 94, no. 3 (1995): 837–864; Byerman, *Seizing the Word*, 138–161; Rampersad, *Art and Imagination*, 266–281; M. Keith Booker, *The Post-Utopian Imagination: American Culture in the Long 1950s* (Westport, Conn.: Greenwood Press, 2002), 79–84.

75. As Leon Litwack has shown, incidents of humiliation and violence on public transportation often struck deep for young southern African Americans. See Leon F. Litwack, *Trouble in Mind: Black Southerners in the Age of Jim Crow* (New York: Knopf, 1998), 9–10.

Chapter 5. Christ Was a Communist

1. W. E. B. Du Bois, *The Autobiography of W. E. B. Du Bois: A Soliloquy on Viewing My Life from the Last Decade of Its First Century* (New York: International Publishers, 1968), 210. Bumstead and Du Bois had a long friendship and deep mutual regard. See especially their correspondence in 1914, in Du Bois Papers, reel 4, frame 1023–1025. Bumstead wrote, "You cannot doubt the deep interest I have always taken in you and your work, nor my faith in your call to a marvelously useful service for our country."

Although David Lewis quotes Bumstead that Du Bois seemed to have no religion, Lewis left out the president's remarks on Du Bois's religiosity. The reason is clear: Bumstead's claim belied Lewis's characterizations of Du Bois. David Levering Lewis, *W. E. B. Du Bois: Biography of a Race, 1868–1919* (New York: Henry Holt, 1993), 198.

2. Susan Jacoby, *Freethinkers: A History of American Secularism* (New York: Metropolitan Books, 2004), 192; Arnold Rampersad, *The Art and Imagination of W. E. B. Du Bois* (Cambridge, Mass.: Harvard University Press, 1976), 104; Phil Zuckerman, ed., *Du Bois on Religion* (New York: Altamira Press, 2000), 4–6.

3. Michael S. Sherry, *In the Shadow of the Cold War: The United States Since the 1930s* (New Haven: Yale University Press, 1995), 158–159; Sidney E. Ahlstrom, *A Religious History of the American People* (New Haven: Yale University Press, 1972), 950–955; William L. Vinz, *Pulpit Politics: Faces of American Protestant Nationalism in the Twentieth Century* (Albany: State University of New York Press, 1997); William C. Martin, *With God on Our Side: The Rise of the Religious Right in America* (New York: Broadway Books, 1996), 29–39; William C. Martin, *Prophet with Honor: The Billy Graham Story* (New York: William Morrow, 1991); Joel Carpenter, "Youth for Christ and the New Evangelicals," in D.G. Hart, ed., *Reckoning with the Past: Historical Essays on American Evangelicalism* (Grand Rapids, Mich.: Baker Books, 1995), 354.

4. Du Bois, *The Autobiography of W. E. B. Du Bois*, 13.

5. Gerald Horne, *Black and Red: W. E. B. Du Bois and the Afro-American Response to the Cold War, 1944–1963* (Albany: State University of New York Press, 1986); David Levering Lewis, *W. E. B. Du Bois: The Fight for Equality and the American Century,*

1919–1963 (New York: Henry Holt, 2000), 496–571; Manning Marable, *W. E. B. Du Bois: Black Radical Democrat* (Boston: Twayne, 1986), 166–217; Mike Forrest Green, *Stalking Sociologists: J. Edgar Hoover's FBI Surveillance of American Sociology* (Westport, Conn.: Greenwood Press, 1999), 33–54; William E. Cain, "From Liberalism to Communism: The Political Thought of W. E. B. Du Bois," in Amy Kaplan and Donald E. Pease, eds., *Cultures of United States Imperialism* (Durham, N.C.: Duke University Press), 456–473; Kate A. Baldwin, *Beyond the Color Line and the Iron Curtain: Reading Encounters Between Black and Red, 1922–1963* (Durham, N.C.: Duke University Press, 2002), 149–201.

6. W. E. B. Du Bois, *Color and Democracy: Colonies and Peace* (New York: Harcourt Brace, 1945), 134–135; Horne, *Black and Red*, 38; Lewis, *W. E. B. Du Bois: The Fight for Equality*, 502, 509–510.

7. Du Bois, *Color and Democracy*, 135–136.

8. Du Bois, *Color and Democracy*, 123, 136–137.

9. Du Bois, *Color and Democracy*, 137–138.

10. Du Bois, *Color and Democracy*, 137–138.

11. Du Bois, *Color and Democracy*, 142–143.

12. For more on Haynes, see John Haynes Holmes, *I Speak for Myself: The Autobiography of John Haynes Holmes* (New York: Harper, 1959); Carl Hermann Voss, *Rabbi and Minister: The Friendship of Stephen S. Wise and John Haynes Holmes* (Cleveland: World, 1964); Mark Juergensmeyer, "Saint Gandhi," in John Stratton Hawley, ed., *Saints and Virtues* (Berkeley: University of California Press, 1987), 190–191.

13. Du Bois in *Dedication Book in Celebration of the Dedication of the New Building of the Community Church of New York, October 17, 1948* (New York: Community Church Publications, 1948), 36–37.

14. Du Bois in *Dedication Book*, 36–37. See also W. E. B. Du Bois, "Gandhi and the American Negroes," in David Levering Lewis, ed., *W. E. B. Du Bois: A Reader* (New York: Henry Holt, 1995), 90–92; W. E. B. Du Bois, "In Black," in Eric J. Sundquist, *The Oxford W. E. B. Du Bois Reader* (New York: Oxford University Press, 1996), 59–60.

15. Du Bois in *Dedication Book*, 36–37. See also Du Bois, "Introduction of John Haynes Holmes" (1931), in Du Bois Papers, reel 80, frame 483–484. Holmes was happy to count himself a friend and colleague of Du Bois. See John Haynes Holmes, letter to Du Bois, August 10, 1946. Herbert Aptheker, ed., *The Correspondence of W. E. B. Du Bois: Volume III, Selections, 1944–1963* (Amherst: University of Massachusetts Press, 1978), 152. For correspondence between Du Bois and Holmes, see Du Bois Papers, reel 6, frame 524–530; reel 9, frame 837–840; reel 18, frame 538; reel 31, frame 543–547; reel 51, frame 669–672; reel 53, frame 1003–1110; reel 58, frame 1032–1036; reel 60, frame 110–115; reel 66, frame 835–850.

16. Holmes to Du Bois, October 13, 1948, in Du Bois Papers, reel 62, frame 53.

17. John Howard Melish to Du Bois, July 26, 1951, in Du Bois Papers, reel 66, frame 1155; see also William Howard Melish to Du Bois, June 21, 1951, in Du Bois Papers, reel 66, frame 1155.

18. Shirley Graham Du Bois, *His Day Is Marching On: A Memoir of W. E. B. Du Bois*

(Philadelphia: J. B. Lippincott, 1971), 232–234. For more on Melish and Holy Trinity Church, see Martin Gottfried, *Arthur Miller: His Life and Work* (New York: De Capo Press, 2003), 160–162; William Howard Melish, "Thou Shalt Not Preach," in Bud Schultz and Ruth Schultz, eds., *It Did Happen Here: Recollections of Political Repression in America* (Berkeley: University of California Press, 1989), 35–46; Francis Henry Touchet, "The Social Gospel and the Cold War: The Melish Case," Ph.D. diss., New York University, 1981.

19. Graham Du Bois, *His Day Is Marching On*, 227–235.

20. Horne, *Black and Red*, 355; Graham Du Bois, *His Day Is Marching On*, 227–235.

21. Lewis, *Du Bois: The Fight for Equality*, 546–549; W. E. B. Du Bois, *In Battle for Peace* (Millwood, N.Y.: Kraus-Thomson, 1976), 74, 99, 105, 140, 153; Horne, *Black and Red*, 165–167. Numerous other churches opened their doors to Du Bois; see Du Bois Papers, reel 81, frames 120–149, 290–294, 316–322, 356–362, 403–408, 563–571, 790–791, 1097–1116.

22. "Farewell Message to the Alumni of Atlanta University," in W. E. B. Du Bois, *Against Racism: Unpublished Essays, Papers, and Addresses, 1887–1961* (Amherst: University of Massachusetts Press, 1985), 227.

23. "A Petition to the Human Rights Commission of the Social and Economic Council of the United Nations; and to the General Assembly of the United Nations; and to the Several Delegations of the Member States of the United Nations," in Du Bois, *Against Racism*, 262, 265.

24. Du Bois, "Peace," September 13, 1950, in Du Bois Papers, reel 80, frame 1424–1425; Du Bois, "Peace and the Church," in Du Bois Papers, reel 81, frame 78–80; Du Bois, "The Church and War and Peace," April 24, 1952, reel 81, frame 357–362.

25. Du Bois, *In Battle for Peace*, 170.

26. "Social Medicine" (8 February 1950), in Du Bois, *Against Racism*, 272.

27. Du Bois, *In Battle for Peace*, 153.

28. W. E. B. Du Bois, "Behold the Land," in John Henrik Clarke, Esther Jackson, Ernest Kaiser, and J. H. O'Dell, eds., *Black Titan: W. E. B. Du Bois, An Anthology by the Editors of* Freedomways (Boston: Beacon Press, 1970), 231–237.

29. Du Bois, "Behold the Land," 231–237. For more on Bontemps, see Kirkland C. Jones, *Renaissance Man from Louisiana: A Biography of Arna Wendell Bontemps* (Westport, Conn.: Greenwood Press, 1992).

30. Horne, *Black and Red*, 283–284; Benjamin Sevitch, "W. E. B. Du Bois and the Jews: A Lifetime of Opposing Anti-Semitism," *Journal of African American History* 87, no. 3 (Summer 2002): 323–338. See also "America's Responsibility to Israel" (November 30, 1948) in Du Bois Papers, reel 80, frame 1158–1164; Du Bois, speech before the Jewish Peoples Fraternal Order (1950), in Du Bois Papers, reel 81, frame 60–61; Du Bois, "Negro-Jewish Unity" (1950), in Du Bois Papers, reel 81, frame 60–62; see also reel 81, frame 821–827.

31. Du Bois, "Application to join the Communist Party and Gus Hall's Reply," Perkins Pamphlet Collection, Duke University, Durham, North Carolina.

32. Du Bois, "Seek the Truth About Communism," in Du Bois Papers, reel 81, frame 309–311.

33. Du Bois, *In Battle for Peace*, 160.

34. Du Bois, *Color and Democracy*, 122.

35. W. E. Burghardt Du Bois, *John Brown* (1909; reprint, New York: International, 1962), 395–401.

36. Wilson Jeremiah Moses, *Black Messiahs and Uncle Toms: Social and Literary Manipulations of a Religious Myth* (University Park: Pennsylvania State University Press, 1982), 6; Benjamin B. Page, ed., *Marxism and Spirituality: An International Anthology* (Westport, Conn.: Bergin and Garvey, 1993). For African American encounters with Communism and religion, see Mark Solomon, *The Cry Was Unity: Communists and African Americans, 1917–1936* (Jackson: University Press of Mississippi, 1998), 106, 117, 158. 166. John C. Bennett, *Christianity and Communism* (New York: Association Press, 1948).

37. Robin D. G. Kelley, *Hammer and Hoe*, 135, 151, 196–197. Herbert Aptheker, "The Spiritual in Marxism," in Page, *Marxism and Spirituality*, 65.

38. Richard Wright in Richard Crossman, ed., *The God that Failed* (New York: Harper and Brothers, 1949), 115–162; Richard Wright, *Black Boy (American Hunger): A Record of Childhood and Youth* (1945; expanded edition, New York: Perennial Classics, 1998), 294–384; see also Josh White, "I Was a Sucker for the Communists," *Negro Digest* 9, no. 2 (1950): 26–31; Kate A. Baldwin, *Beyond the Color Line and the Iron Curtain: Reading Encounters Between Black and Red, 1922–1963* (Durham, N.C.: Duke University Press, 2002); Alexander Yakovlev, *A Century of Violence in Soviet Russia* (New Haven: Yale University Press, 2000); William Taubman, *Khrushchev: The Man and His Era* (New York: Norton, 2003), 270–287.

39. Taubman, *Khrushchev*, 284.

40. W. E. B. Du Bois, "On the U.S.S.R." *Labor Defender* (November 1928): 248.

41. Du Bois to Anna Melissa Graves, July 8, 1956, in Aptheker, *The Correspondence of W. E. B. Du Bois, Volume III*, 402. For more on Du Bois's various feelings for the Soviet Union, see Baldwin, *Beyond the Color Line*, 149–201.

42. George Orwell, *1984: A Novel* (London: Secker and Warburg, 1949).

43. Du Bois, "Ghana Calls," in *Black Titan*, 299–302.

44. Paul Robeson, "Set Him Free to Labor On–A Tribute to W. E. B. Du Bois," in Philip S. Foner, ed., *Paul Robeson Speaks: Writings, Speeches, Interviews, 1918–1974* (New York: Brunner/Mazel, 1978), 268.

45. William Stanley Braithwaite, "A Tribute to W. E. Burghardt DuBois," *Phylon* 10, no. 4 (Fourth Quarter 1949): 302–306. For more on Braithwaite, see Lisa Szefel, "Encouraging Verse: William S. Braithwaite and the Poetics of Race," *New England Quarterly* 74, no. 1 (March 2001): 32–61.

46. Langston Hughes, "The Accusers' Names Nobody Will Remember, But History Records Du Bois," *Chicago Defender*, 6 October 1951.

47. Quoted in Du Bois, *In Battle for Peace*, 191.

48. Quoted in Du Bois, *In Battle for Peace*, 189.

49. For more on *The Autobiography of W. E. B. Du Bois*, see Louis Filler, review of W. E. B. Du Bois, *The Autobiography of W. E. B. Du Bois: A Soliloquy on Viewing My Life from the Last Decade of Its First Century, American Historical Review* 74, no. 1 (October 1968): 315–316; Hugh Davis Graham, review of W. E. B. Du Bois, *The Autobiography of W. E. B. Du Bois: A Soliloquy on Viewing My Life from the Last Decade of Its First Century, Journal of Southern History* 34, no. 4 (November 1968): 640–641; William E. Cain, "W. E. B. Du Bois's Autobiography and the Politics of Literature," *Black American Literature Forum* 24, no. 2 (Summer 1990): 299–313; Kenneth Mostem, *Autobiography and Black Identity Politics: Racialization in Twentieth-Century America* (Cambridge: Cambridge University Press, 1999), 57–82.

50. Full text in Du Bois, *The Autobiography of W. E. B. Du Bois: A Soliloquy on Viewing My Life from the Last Decade of Its First Century* (New York: International, 1968), 405–408; also in Philip S. Foner, *W. E. B. Du Bois Speaks: Volume 2, Speeches and Addresses, 1920–1963* (New York: Pathfinder, 1970), 316–321.

51. Du Bois, *The Autobiography of W. E. B. Du Bois*, 405–408; also in Foner, *W. E. B. Du Bois Speaks: Volume 2*, 316–321.

52. Du Bois, *The Autobiography of W. E. B. Du Bois*, 405–408; also in Foner, *W. E. B. Du Bois Speaks: Volume 2*, 316–321.

53. Isaiah 55:1.

54. Du Bois, *The Autobiography of W. E. B. Du Bois*, 405–408; also in Foner, *W. E. B. Du Bois Speaks: Volume 2*, 316–321.

55. Elliot M. Rudwick, *W. E. B. Du Bois: Propagandist of the Negro Protest* (1960; reprint, New York: Atheneum, 1969), 19.

56. For more on Du Bois's Sunday school teaching, see Du Bois, "My Sunday School Class," in Du Bois Papers, reel 82, frame 1251–1252.

Epilogue

1. R. J. Moxon to Shirley Graham Du Bois, August 28, 1963, in Du Bois Papers, reel 76, frame 107.

2. Cedric Belfrage to Shirley Graham Du Bois, August 29, 1963, in Du Bois Papers, reel 76, frame 120.

3. Gerald Horne, *Black and Red: W. E. B. Du Bois and the Afro-American Response to the Cold War, 1944–1963* (Albany: State University of New York, 1986), 356; David Levering Lewis, *W. E. B. Du Bois: Biography of a Race, 1868–1919* (New York: Henry Holt, 1993), 1–3; "W. E. B. Du Bois Is Dead at 95 in Ghana: The Inspiration of the Freedom Movement," *National Guardian* (New York) 15, no. 48 (September 5, 1963), 3.

4. William Branch, "Ghana Gives State Burial to Du Bois," *Amsterdam News* (New York), September 7, 1963, 1, 25; "W. E. B. Du Bois is Dead at 95 in Ghana," *National Guardian*; "W. E. B. Du Bois Dies in Ghana: Negro Leader and Author, 95," *New York Times*, August 28, 1963, 27; "Negroes' Leader a Man of Dignity: Randolph Deeply Influenced in

Youth by Dr. Du Bois," *New York Times*, August 29, 1963, 20; "Marchers Pause to Mourn Dr. Du Bois; Father of Negro Liberation Movement," *Worker*, September 1, 1963, 1, 12.

5. Lewis, *Du Bois: Biography of a Race*, 3-10. "The Last Message of Dr. W. E. B. Du Bois to the World," *Journal of Negro History* 49, no. 2 (April 1964): 145. Herbert Aptheker, "On the Passing of Du Bois," in Du Bois Papers, reel 76, frame 113-116.

6. Graham Du Bois, *His Day Is Marching On*, 368.

7. Graham Du Bois, *His Day Is Marching On*, 368; "Address Delivered by the Rev. William Howard Melish at the Memorial Service of the Late Dr. W. E. B. Du Bois at the Aggrey Memorial Church, Achimota College, Accra, Ghana, on Sunday 29th September, 1963" (Brooklyn, 1963).

8. Graham Du Bois, *His Day Is Marching On*, 368; "Address Delivered by the Rev. William Howard Melish at the Memorial Service of the Late Dr. W. E. B. Du Bois."

9. Leslie Alexander Lacy, *Cheer the Lonesome Traveler: The Life of W. E. B. Du Bois* (New York: Dial Press, 1970), 7-8, 122, 138-139. For more on Lacy, see Leslie Alexander Lacy, *Rise and Fall of a Proper Negro: An Autobiography* (New York: Macmillan, 1970).

10. Lacy, *Cheer the Lonesome Traveler*, 141.

11. Lacy, *Cheer the Lonesome Traveler*, 141-142.

12. Graham Du Bois in John Henrik Clarke et al., eds., *Black Titan* (Boston: Beacon Press, 1970), 5; Graham Du Bois, *His Day Is Marching On*. The *National Guardian* invoked the same ideas as Graham Du Bois, asserting "at his passing, the words echo: 'I still live.' And he does, for the prophet never dies." "W. E. B. Du Bois Is Dead at 95 in Ghana," *National Guardian* (September 5, 1963), 3. For other responses to Du Bois's death, see Du Bois Papers, reel 76, frame 107-401.

13. Dee in *Black Titan*, 9-10.

14. Murphy in *Black Titan*, 28-33.

15. Murphy in *Black Titan*, 28-33.

16. Stuckey in *Black Titan*, 39-39.

17. Truman Nelson, "W. E. B. Du Bois as a Prophet," *Freedomways* 5 (Winter 1965): 47-58. For others who offered religious responses to Du Bois, see Lerone Bennett, Jr., "W. E. B. Du Bois: Prophet of Protest and Pan Africa," *Ebony* (March 1965): 152; Gershon Bumawu Fiawoo, "An Inquiry into the Life and Thought of W. E. B. Du Bois," master's thesis, Southeastern Baptist Theological Seminary, 1965, 105-107. Fiawoo, who had met Du Bois on at least one occasion, thought that Du Bois most assuredly "believed in God." See Fiawoo, "An Inquiry into the Life and Thought of W. E. B. Du Bois," 113.

18. Wilkins in *Black Titan*, 6-7; Hatcher in *Black Titan*, 42.

19. King reprinted in W. E. Burghardt Du Bois, *Dusk of Dawn: An Essay Toward an Autobiography of a Race Concept* (1940, reprint, New York: Schocken Books, 1969), vii-xvii.

20. Truman Nelson, "W. E. B. Du Bois: Prophet in Limbo," *Nation* (January 25, 1958): 76-79; quoted in Graham Du Bois, *His Day Is Marching On*, 229.

21. Du Bois, "Beyond the Veil in a Virginia Town," (1897) in W. E. B. Du Bois, *Against Racism: Unpublished Essays, Papers, and Addresses, 1887-1961* (Amherst: University of Massachusetts Press, 1985), 50.

INDEX

~

ACKNOWLEDGMENTS

~

William Edward Burghardt Du Bois offered words of hope to a world of rage. "It is *never* too late to mend," he prayed with his students at Atlanta University in 1909 or 1910. "Nothing is so bad that good may not be put into it and make it better and save it from utter loss. Strengthen in us this knowledge and faith and hope, O God, in these last days. Amen." This prayer has been my inspiration in trying times, my sun in days of darkness, and my anchor in stormy seas. Throughout the researching and writing of this book, wars and rumors of wars have abounded, while greed and rumors of greed have astounded. Most often, it feels that hate has overcome love, that fear has overpowered faith, and that despair has crushed hope. Through it all, I have clung to the vision Du Bois offered his pupils. Because of him, I still believe that nothing is so bad that we cannot make it better: our communities, our nations, our world, and ourselves. I hope that readers of this book may feel inspired by a similar faith and that we can save each other from utter loss.

The faith and hope of many colleagues have contributed to this work. Kathi Kern and Joanne Pope Melish continue to encourage and correct me. My colleagues at Kean University, Chris Bellito, Frank Freyre, Sue Gronewold, and Mark Lender, were fine mentors. Ann Pfau critiqued the introduction with kindness and insight. Kean's Office of Research and Sponsored Programs provided two excellent student researchers–Katherine Kennedy and Danielle LaPorte. They found a treasure trove of sources and materials. My newest colleagues in the department of history at San Diego State University, especially Sarah Elkind, Joanne Ferraro, John Putnam, and Andrew Wiese, gave me a forum to share my research and the hopeful expectation of a joyful community. Without the editorial staff at the University of Pennsylvania Press, particularly Bob Lockhart, Laura Miller, and Peter Agree, this book never would have been realized. I am deeply honored that this book is in the Politics and

Culture in Modern America series edited by Glenda Gilmore, Michael Kazin, and Thomas Sugrue. Their individual works are changing the historical profession, and I am humbled that they have endorsed this volume.

So many scholars supported this project, and they are a testament to our profession. This book began as a lecture at the Harvard Divinity School, and I am grateful to the faculty and students there for their insights, most crucially Robert Orsi and Diana Eck. Paul Harvey not only critiqued the work in full but also modeled superb scholarship in his own studies. Phil Zuckerman blazed a trail with his edited volumes on Du Bois, and he evaluated an early draft of this book. Dwight Hopkins, David Howard-Pitney, Jonathon Kahn, and Jason R. Young were kind enough to share their research with me, while Michael Emerson was a fantastic conversation partner. I still am encouraged by his pursuit of racial integration in churches. Several other scholars were kind enough to discuss with me their work on Du Bois and religion, especially Craig Forney, Ronda Henry, Terrence Johnson, Michelle Kuhl, Anthony Pinn, Ben Sevitch, and Carole Lynn Stewart. V. P. Franklin and his staff at the *Journal of African American History* also played a profound role in my thinking about Du Bois and religion. Paul Froese let me bounce ideas off him, while he and Jana opened their home when I was in need. I am indebted to each of them.

I also received funding and emotional sustenance from the National Endowment for the Humanities and the W. E. B. Du Bois Institute at Harvard University. Led by Henry Louis Gates, Jr., Waldo Martin, and Patricia Sullivan, our gang of twenty-five intrepid scholars reworked the entire twentieth-century civil rights struggle as we laughed and battled with each other. I am indebted to my new partners, particularly Kevin Boyle, Antoinette Brim, Michaela O'Neill Daniel, Devin Fergus, Jennifer Frost, Lynn Itagaki, Hasan Kwame Jeffries, Randal Jelks, Leon Litwack, Kimberley Phillips, Mark Santow, Chris Strain, Lisa Szefel, and Fanon Che Wilkins. Also, I express appreciation to the University Seminars at Columbia University for its support for this publication. Material in this work was presented to the University Seminar on Religion in America. In addition, I found indirect support from awards for my first book from the George Tyler Moore Center for Study of the Civil War, the Peter Seaborg Award for Civil War Scholarship, the Southern Historical Association, and the C. Vann Woodward Fund. I cannot thank John Boles and Randal Hall enough for their guidance.

I never know where to stop the list of thanks. Daphne Brooks, Jean Pfaelzer, Sonnet Retman, and Lisa Thompson let me into their projects and in the process helped me immeasurably. Russell Harris, Stuart Sanders, and Ken Wil-

liams brought me a lot of laughs in Kentucky. Roger Abrahams, Nick Spitzer, John Szwed, and Robert Farris Thompson had me join them in their Mardi Gras project, and I felt the blues in new ways as they searched for the Creole soul. For reasons uncertain to me, a variety of my friends (all of whom should have been thanked in my first book) continue to care for me. To Chris, Misty, Jack, Kevin, Bryan, Ed, Jennifer, and Matt, thanks for your love.

Although it may sound odd, I also need to express my gratitude and humility to Professor Du Bois himself. He died long before I was born, but his spirit and ideas have changed my soul, mind, and way of life. I wrote this book as an acolyte, imagining myself sitting at Du Bois's feet, reading over his shoulder, and listening to the responses of the many he touched. I wrote this book to learn religion and spirituality from Du Bois. For certain months, I tried to live his day-to-day professional routine: morning walks, regular lunches, and evening conversation. I prayed his prayers to my students and endeavored to feel his moving in their hearts. Certainly, I did not learn of all of his lessons perfectly. My sense is that he would forgive any of my mistakes and point out the path again. My sense is also that he would have smiled wryly at the thought of seeing a "religious biography" of himself. There are many other religious teachings to be gleaned from Du Bois. I hope this book is the start of something new.

The truths of Du Bois's prayer at Atlanta University for good to come from evil have been revealed to me most often in my family life. The good in our Labrador retriever SNCC Blum helped me to endure. He was by my side for every keystroke of this manuscript, although most often snoring. He was there when I treated my keyboard as a piano and stomped my feet to the rhythm of the soul. At the most profound level, the faith and hope of Sarah Hardin Blum has saved me from utter loss. She read every page of this manuscript. She endured yet another labor of love and my emotional storms. Sarah is the most fantastic person I have ever met. My affection for her is pronounced at the beginning of every chapter, and without her all of this would be just words for me.